ALSO BY G. WAYNE MILLER

Thunder Rise

THE WORK OF
HUMAN HANDS

To Martin Schwartzberg
with best wishes

Harold Hirshon

November 1997

THE WORK OF HUMAN HANDS

Hardy Hendren and Surgical Wonder at Children's Hospital

G. WAYNE MILLER

RANDOM HOUSE NEW YORK

Library of Congress Cataloging-in-Publication Data
Miller, G. Wayne.
    The work of human hands : Hardy Hendren and surgical wonder at
Children's Hospital /
    G. Wayne Miller.
        p.   cm.
    Includes bibliographical references and index.
    ISBN 0-679-40264-0
    1. Hendren, W. Hardy. 3. Surgery, Plastic—Case
studies. 3. Surgery, Orificial—Case studies. 4. Children—
Surgery—Case studies. 5. Moore, Lucy. 6. Children's Hospital
(Boston, Mass.)
    [DNLM: 1. Hendren, W. Hardy. 2. Children's Hospital
(Boston, Mass.) 3. Abnormalities—in infancy & childhood.
4. Abnormalities—surgery. Qs675 M648w]
    RD80.62.H46M55   1993
    617.9′8′092—dc20   92-531

Manufactured in the United States of America
9 8 7 6 5 4 3 2
First Edition

To Rachel and Katy,
the two best children in the world,
Love you always!

A Note About Names

Because of the intensely personal nature of their children's abnormalities, some of the parents in this book did not want their full names used. I have respected their wishes. I have also protected the privacy of the main family, at their request, by calling them the Moores. In return for that small concession, they willingly shared everything.

No other names—of patients, doctors, nurses, hospitals, or places—have been changed in any way.

Contents

Foreword

When I set out to visit the outer reaches of medicine, I had to travel no farther than Boston. Home of the Harvard Medical School and Children's Hospital, which gave me unprecedented access during the more than two years it took to complete this book, Boston has become a world leader in medical research, teaching, and healing. Of the handful of places that might rival Boston, most are in the United States.

America's preeminence is a new development in the long history of medicine, occurring only in the years since the Second World War, when Hardy Hendren, the surgeon-scientist profiled in this book, came of age. Americans, of course, were not standing still before the 1940s. Ether, which advanced surgery as few other developments ever have, was introduced at Boston's Massachusetts General Hospital in 1846. Early in this century, Charles H. Best, a native of Maine, participated in the discovery of insulin, in Toronto, Canada. In 1938, heart surgery was revolutionized by one of Hardy Hendren's mentors, Robert E. Gross, a tormented, brilliant surgeon at Boston Children's who throughout his career hid the fact that he had only one good eye. But for the most part, prior to the 1940s the great names in medicine—Pasteur, Lister, Koch, and Fleming, to name a few—were not American. Most of the great medical centers—London, Zurich, Paris, Vienna, Munich—were in Europe.

A measure of just how far the United States has come is the Nobel Prize in physiology or medicine. Before the Second World War, the prize was awarded to Americans in only five years. Since the war's end, Americans have captured or shared it in thirty-five different years, a record that no other nation comes close to matching. Most of the world's leading medical journals are published in English, and the few that aren't are widely available in English translation. American physicians and medical scientists wishing to take the most advanced training no longer feel compelled to study in Europe; visit a distinguished American hospital, and chances are you will find Europeans who have crossed an ocean to learn. The list of great names in medicine that come to mind in the second half of the twentieth century is crowded with Americans—Gajdusek, Lillehei, Harken, Salk, DeBakey, Thomas, Enders, Murray.

Another measure of America's stature, less easily quantified, is popular demand. One of the people I met at Boston Children's was a Jamaican woman whose son had contracted a terrible infection in his right leg. Doctors in their homeland had tried to cure the boy, but they had not had success; as the infection spread and his leg slowly succumbed, amputation seemed the only option. The mother had enough money to get to Miami. Nothing more than that—no referral, no appointment, just two airline tickets, a small amount of cash, and the conviction that in America surely her son could be healed. On the flight over, the mother asked a member of the flight crew what hospital would be best for the boy. "Probably Boston Children's," said the attendant, who happened to be from Boston. With her remaining money, the mother booked passage on a Miami-to-Boston flight, and at Children's her son's leg was saved. Theirs was a story I heard many times in many variations at Children's: the sick and the dying coming to America because they believed their best chance of being healed was here. Some, like the Jamaican woman and her son, had limited economic means. But many were wealthy. Some belonged to royal families. They had the means to go anywhere in the world, and they came to America.

How did it happen? How did America get to the top in medicine? How, at a time when its preeminence in other scientific fields has eroded, has it not only remained there but probably widened its lead?

A major factor has been the emergence of academic medicine—of universities and affiliated hospitals that are philosophically committed not only to healing but to research, whose payoff ordinarily is many years down the line, if at all. Such a philosophy has attracted not only the best talent from the United States and abroad but also the philanthropy and government support needed to underwrite the huge costs of pushing back frontiers. Another factor has been technology—the medicines, machines, and materials that have been applied to increasingly sophisticated and successful healing. America came out of the war victorious, holding a position in the global economy that allowed it to invest lavishly in unproved ideas. In medicine, the payoff is now.

But despite its technology, medicine remains the most personal of the sciences, and ultimately it has been people who have allowed American medicine to flourish. One group has been those patients who have been willing to venture to the outer reaches, offering their diseases and themselves as subjects of experimentation. Another group has been the medical scientists, people whose careers are a paradox. As perfectionists, the men and women of academic medicine despise failure. They are not unlike Robert E. Gross, whose failures in the operating room, however rare, drove him to depression. And yet they have achieved, because their fear of failure has been surpassed by something even more powerful: their obsession with taking risks.

Early in March 1990, I began placing calls to the office of W. Hardy Hendren III, M.D., chief of surgery at Children's Hospital, Boston, and the Robert E. Gross Professor of Surgery at the Harvard Medical School. I knew little about Hendren beyond his titles and the fact that he counted among his specialties the successful separation of Siamese twins. I figured those credentials qualified him to serve as a guide to an outsider who wanted to visit the edge.

After a half-dozen attempts to reach Hendren by phone, I'd pretty much despaired of ever speaking with him. "Dr. Hendren is in the OR," one or another of his secretaries kept saying. To a journalist's ear, it sounded like a brush-off.

One day, my phone rang.

"This is Dr. Hendren," the voice on the other end of the line said. "I understand you've been trying to reach me."

I asked only that I be able to meet with him to discuss the possibility of writing about Children's. Playing a hunch, as he told me much later, Hendren invited me to his oceanfront home. There, he said, we would talk.

When I arrived in Duxbury on a Sunday morning in April about a month later, Hendren was out on the water. Eleanor, his wife, and David, youngest of their four sons, told me to feel at home while I waited. After a bit, a small motorboat pulled up to the Hendrens' pier. A man with coat, rubber boots, and wool cap came across the lawn. He looked like a lobsterman, not a master surgeon.

This is him? I thought.

For two hours, we talked.

Hendren, innately suspicious of the press, was impressed by the amount of time I said I'd need for a book. That day, Hendren invited me to come to Children's for as long as I wished. He had but two preconditions: that I see the entire hospital, not just his department, and that I tell what I saw honestly and without sensationalism.

In the next many months, I did see much of the hospital, although to get through all of it in any journalistically credible fashion would have taken more years than I had. Hendren introduced me to dozens of people on the staff and urged me to spend time with each. I did. But no matter where I went, I kept coming back to him. At the age of sixty-four, Hendren was capable of operating for twenty-four hours straight. His patients were children with deformities the likes of which I had never known existed. Early on, I remember thinking how extraordinary it was that anyone could save these babies' lives, never mind make them normal. As I watched him for hundreds of hours in his operating room, I saw that Hendren could. Here was a man who for four decades had not only stationed himself on the edge, but thrived there.

Before meeting Hendren, I read his curriculum vitae. It contained page after page of professional accomplishments, testimony to the fact that competition is the heart of academic medicine. Those who reach the top have competed virtually all of their lives— for placement in the best high schools, colleges, medical schools, internships, and residencies. They have competed for staff positions at the best hospitals and universities in the best medical towns. Once admitted into this elite company, the competition only intensifies: for professorships, department chairmanships, publication in prestigious professional journals, prizes and awards, the podium at international conferences.

I had expected Hendren's CV to be a summary of professional

success. What surprised me was some of the personal items he'd listed prominently. As a teenager, Hendren had been an Eagle Scout; including it on his CV a half century later struck me as old-fashioned, even hokey, and it wasn't until I'd gotten to know him much better that I discovered its significance. At the age of twenty, Hendren had qualified as a naval aviator by landing on an aircraft carrier. It did not take great insight to see the parallel of that achievement with surgical success. Hendren had been married to Eleanor for more than forty years, and they had five children. Three sons were surgeons, his CV said. The fourth was a lawyer. Next to the name of the Hendrens' only daughter were her degrees, the year of her birth, and the year of her death. When I inquired, I learned that Sandy had died of diabetes, a disease no surgery, not even breathtaking surgery, could cure.

More than a year after meeting Hendren, on one of his rare days of leisure, we sat in the study of his home in Duxbury. He showed me locks of his deceased father's and daughter's hair, his collection of human hearts preserved in wax, his merit badges, and a report card that recorded his failing grade in Latin when he was in the eighth grade, a fourteen-year-old already determined to be a surgeon. He talked about what had motivated him for so long. I knew him well enough by then to know that it wasn't money or some traumatic childhood event or a self-serving desire for medical immortality. "I think that I've been very fortunate," Hendren told me. "I've been put in circumstances where I could work hard and do some things that other people haven't done before. Part of it is because of the talent that I've been given, part of it is by working hard, . . . and part is wanting to accomplish things, wanting to do things that are right. And you know, I don't think those are things you can really take credit for yourself."

There is a flip side. For all its sophistication, American medicine does not place proper emphasis on the other end of the scale: prevention and primary care. Not everyone in America benefits from this science that is capable of such good. Cost and accessibility remain problems of crisis proportion, and until all Americans are guaranteed the opportunity for good health, a black mark will remain on U.S. medicine and the politicians who sooner or later must confront this issue. I leave those worthy topics to others.

This book is not an analysis of America's health-care system, only the story of people who have been touched by extraordinary developments in the science of healing. It is about a little girl born with an enemy for a body and the surgeon who took that enemy on. It is about a family who thought they had everything but found out how wrong they were. It is about wonder in U.S. medicine, which is one of the good stories of the second half of the twentieth century.

October 1992
Pascoag, Rhode Island

Part I

DREAMS

Chapter 1

On the day she mourned the loss of her dream, which is every expectant mother's dream, Beth Moore left the Yale Perinatal Unit in New Haven, Connecticut. She got into her car, an almost-new station wagon, and headed toward home.

She was alone, and she was crying, and by the time she got to Interstate 84, which crosses the border into New York State, everything was a blur in the awful July heat.

"Birth defect," Peter Grannum, the Yale doctor, had said as the probe had traveled across Beth's naked abdomen and flickering images—hieroglyphic to the layperson—had appeared on the ultrasound screen. "See? That's the head. It looks normal. That's the bladder, the stomach, the heart—apparently all normal. Now see this? That's the right kidney. It looks normal, too. But see that shadowy area over there? That's not normal. That's a multicystic left kidney. A birth defect."

I should pull over, Beth thought.

And then what?

Stand sobbing like some crazy lady in the breakdown lane of Interstate 84? Flag down some Good Samaritan and gush about my baby—my poor birth-defective baby? They'd lock me up!

Even on such an afternoon, the afternoon of July 10, 1989, Beth's sense of humor—her saving grace through all that was to come—didn't desert her.

Beth continued on—toward her house, her children, her husband, the life they'd fashioned for themselves in Westchester County, New York. It was a good life, built on the bedrock of a good marriage and enhanced by affluence. Beth loved children, and not just her own. She ran a day-care center, and while technically that made her an administrator, a bureaucrat, she was still very much the teacher—the one who sang the songs and told the stories and took the kids on walks through the Westchester woods, where deer, protected by law from human predators, often were seen. Jack loved children, too. He had a master's degree in education, and he'd worked with troubled kids for a spell before getting into management with Beth's father's wholesale food company. Now Jack was busy with the spirits shop he'd bought and the wine-import business he was getting off the ground.

The family was about to welcome its newest member, a girl, according to an amniocentesis performed last month, another girl, whose name had already been chosen. . . .

"Multicystic kidney," Grannum had explained, "means a kidney that isn't going to work. Your daughter will have only one good kidney. But you know, I don't even know if *I* have two kidneys. You can function perfectly normally with just one."

Grannum's message, intended to soothe, wasn't what had registered with Beth.

Just two words had registered: *Birth. Defect.*

They were devastating words, words she couldn't bring herself to link, not in the context of her pregnancy, which was now roughly halfway to completion. They were words whose impact was so much worse now that she was alone and crying in her car.

Beth drove.

Pregnancy is supposed to produce the perfect child, she thought. *A perfect child, just like our other two.*

Should I have an abortion?

Abortion was all over the news that week. That very day, the paper the Moores read, *The New York Times*, had published yet another piece on the issue. This one was an analysis of electoral politics in the wake of the U.S. Supreme Court's ruling in a celebrated case from Missouri—*Webster* v. *Reproductive Health Services*. The ruling, handed down only the week before, on the Fourth of July, Independence Day, had reignited an issue already among the most explosive of its time. Some people, Beth among them, worried that the Supreme Court someday would eliminate the right to an abortion. But for now, abortion was legal. Beth could drive this very afternoon to a clinic and have her pregnancy terminated if that's what she wanted. Nothing would stand in her way.

But of course I can't, Beth knew, almost as quickly as the thought had come to her. *This is our baby.*

This is Lucy.

Do we want another kid?

That was the question that had bedeviled the Moores ever since their second child, a boy, had been born. There was no quick-and-easy answer. There were only arguments and counterarguments, all with merit and appeal. At times, it was like being involved in some sort of reproduction summit: the positions on both sides thoroughly explored and articulated, with only the outcome left for a final vote.

Another child was not an idle proposition, not one that could be let slide too many more years, the way it might have when the Moore family was forming. On her next birthday, Beth would turn thirty-six. Male physiology might have allowed Jack the luxury of time in matters of reproduction, but his wife's fertility was finite. She was entering a zone where pregnancy becomes a higher risk proposition, where the likelihood of things going wrong begins to increase.

Sometimes Jack would say, "Let's go for it." And Beth would say, "Forget it." And sometimes the roles would switch, and Beth would be in favor, Jack opposed.

"We need a third," Beth would say. "Two parents with two kids around a dinner table doesn't feel like a family."

"It does to me."

"I thought when we got married you said you wanted four."

"I did," Jack would say. "But look at us now. Look at these two great kids!"

Mary, born in 1981, was mischievous, flirtatious, endowed with freckles and red hair and her mother's humor and steel will. James, born in 1986, was also intelligent, also good-looking, and also red-headed. Both children were healthy and normal. In an enterprise where fate can be its cruelest—in procreation—the Moores knew how deeply they'd been blessed.

"See?" the debate would continue. "Two great kids. And finally old enough that we can start taking vacations, stop changing diapers, go out to eat. Why tempt fate?"

"Because we love children" was the obvious answer. "Because God has given us the means to bring children into the world the way they all should arrive, in comfort, security, and love."

But when all was said and done, the answer was no. Two, the Moores finally agreed, was their lucky number.

To lock in their decision, they decided Beth would have a tubal ligation, which would permanently sterilize her. In February 1989, Beth called her obstetrician-gynecologist's office, and the secretary said the doctor would arrange the operation and they would call back with the date.

The Moores were on a visit to Florida when Beth, late with her period, took a home-pregnancy test.

The color stick was confirmatory blue.

That settles that, Beth thought. She was not unhappy, and Jack was not unhappy.

Forget about tying my tubes, Beth said when her doctor's secretary got back in touch. I need a prenatal appointment.

Having been there before, Beth knew the drill. She took vitamins, maintained a balanced diet, got her rest, drank no more than an occasional sip of Jack's hand-selected wine, a staple on the Moore's dinner table. She kept her appointments with her doctor, who estimated a delivery date of November 27, just after Thanksgiving, and outlined what medicine's involvement in her pregnancy would be. It would be substantial. The Moores would not await the stork. They would await the results of tests.

The first was on April 25: a sonogram, which showed only that the embryo, no bigger than a lima bean, was the sole inhabitant of Beth's womb. In the ensuing weeks, Beth was screened twice for Lyme disease; twice she tested positive, although she had no symptoms and could not remember ever experiencing any. Amniocentesis disclosed the fetus's sex and ruled out Down's syndrome and certain other defects. The Moores chose a name, Lucy—for no other reason than that they liked the sound of it. Beth sewed a quilt and bumpers for the crib, a hand-me-down from James. She ordered baby outfits. In June, a sonogram revealed a properly positioned placenta, a normal amount of amniotic fluid, a beating heart, a brain, bladder, and stomach, and fetal movement. Also noted was "a cystic structure" that suggested, but by no means confirmed, some sort of problem with the left kidney. Beth's doctor wasn't overly concerned, but he did recommend follow-up, and Beth decided to have it at Yale Perinatal, whose expertise in diagnosing fetal problems attracts patients from not only Connecticut and New York but also New Jersey, Massachusetts, and Rhode Island.

"There's nothing to worry about," Jack had said after his wife's amniocentesis. Beth, an optimist at heart, had agreed. She was so convinced everything would be fine that she'd told her husband there was no need for him to accompany her to Yale.

Beth pulled into the drive. No one was home. She was calmer, if only marginally.

I have to talk to someone.

She had to talk to Jack—but this afternoon Jack could wait. Beth needed a doctor first, and not some Ivy League stranger, however well-intentioned, but a trusted friend: Martin B. Vita, the Moores' family pediatrician for as long as they'd been a family. Dr. Vita would be able to answer the questions Beth would have asked at Yale had not those two loaded words, *birth defect*, jolted them from her mind.

Dr. Vita's secretary came on the line. Like all doctors' secretaries, she is paid to be protective, to deflect as many calls as possible at the first line of defense: the switchboard. "The doctor is with a patient now; may I ask what this is about? May I take a message, Mrs. Moore?"

But the secretary could see that this time checking the PLEASE CALL box on a pink pad wouldn't suffice.

The secretary put Beth through, and when she heard her doctor's voice, Beth lost it. "They told me my child, my baby, has a multicystic left kidney," she said, crying.

"I'm so sorry for you," Vita said.

"What does it *mean*, Doctor?"

"Let me get my book, and I'll read to you."

Vita read. Whereas the normal kidney is an outwardly smooth and whole organ, a multicystic kidney is a collection of round cysts, resembling, in the pathologist's mind, a cluster of grapes. First described in 1936, the disorder is of unknown cause. But the effect is not mysterious: a multicystic kidney cannot filter blood, maintain

fluid balance, regulate sodium, or perform any of the other functions of the normal organ. In terms of function, a multicystic kidney
is the equivalent of no kidney, a permanent and uncorrectable
deformity. If there is anything good to be said about the disorder,
it's that a multicystic kidney is not life threatening, and it cannot
"spread"—it cannot affect its healthy twin.

"I want you to know I'm sorry," Vita told Beth, "but she can lead
a perfectly normal life with one good kidney. She can do anything."

"Anything?" Beth asked.

"Well, I don't know if I'd let her play football."

"She's a girl anyway!" Beth said, and now she could relax, now
she was no longer crazy, now she could call Jack, and they could
both laugh, envisioning Beth such a blubbering mess all alone out
there on Interstate 84.

This was July 10, 1989.

This was several weeks before another ultrasound would disclose
an unidentifiable mass inside Lucy and long before her parents
would ever hear the word *cloaca*.

Chapter 2

Some 150 miles away, in Operating Room 7 of Children's Hospital in Boston, a man the Moores had never met was opening the belly of a six-year-old boy from Cape Cod.

This was approximately the twenty thousandth operation performed by W. Hardy Hendren III. It would last six and three-quarters hours, putting it at slightly below average length for some of the complex cases referred to Hendren, chief of surgery at Children's Hospital and the Robert E. Gross Professor of Surgery at the Harvard Medical School.

Using a combination of scalpel, scissors, and electric cutting cautery, which produces smoke that smells of red meat over hot coals, Hendren proceeded progressively through skin, fat, and muscle until he could reach inside with his gloved hands. Working steadily, he opened the bladder along a line from bottom to top. He threaded a tiny catheter into the right ureter, which was functioning as nature intended. He could not get a catheter into the left. He wasn't surprised. The left ureter was a megaureter: a grotesque caricature of the right, appearing on X ray not as the spindly tube it should have been but as a bloated, tortuous thing that was dangerously crimped at the point it entered the bladder. It was not doing what nature intended. Instead of freely draining urine from the boy's left kidney, it was creating pressure. Untreated, that pressure eventually would cause infection and fever and pain, perhaps even blood poisoning. Untreated, the kidney would slowly die.

Until 1969, when Hendren published a scientific paper his colleagues would in time recognize as another of his profound contributions to surgery, no one really knew what to do with megaureter, which had the potential to kill.

It was not for lack of trying.

Megaureter was truly devilish, the sort of problem that prompted ordinary physicians to throw up their hands—and challenged those who considered themselves better than ordinary to try something, anything. Some took the so-called conservative approach, prescribing antibiotics and chemicals. Some put their faith in the catheter, that old urologic standby. Others, not grasping the anatomic nature of the problem, advised children to urinate thoroughly and repeatedly—a regimen known as triple voiding. Still others sought solutions in surgery. One idea with early promise was replacing bad ureter with good bowel. A variation of that theme was wrapping the megaureter with a sleeve of bowel, but it was an innovation that worked better in the laboratory dog than in the human patient. Various trimming, tapering, and shortening procedures were prescribed, with mixed results.

Some surgeons abandoned altogether the ideal of correcting megaureter while keeping the urinary system intact—at least for those children in danger of dying. To save them, the ureter was brought out through a hole cut in the abdomen. Urine seeped out of the hole. Bladders were left fallow. Kidneys were spared. And children went home wearing bags that looked like hot-water bottles and were called appliances, a peculiar euphemism that in the minds of laymen conjured images of refrigerators and TVs.

Why should anyone have to wear a bag? These kids have enough trouble just staying alive. Why should they have to be stigmatized on top of everything if there's any way around it?

That was Hardy Hendren's philosophy. Growing up in Kansas City, Missouri, heart of the heartland, Hendren had a good friend who had an incurable urinary disease. Ben Trelease had worn a bag. Ben had spent time, too much time, in hospitals. Like his pal, Ben wanted to be a doctor when he grew up. But Ben did not grow up. When he was thirteen, Ben's urinary system poisoned him, and he died, slowly and painfully.

Hendren was the first chief of pediatric surgery at Boston's Massachusetts General Hospital, one of the great hospitals and medical research centers in America. He had a lab and the freedom to innovate when, in the early sixties, fresh from the top surgical training spot at nearby Children's, he decided megaureter was one he had to tackle. Improving life was the primary appeal, but it was not the only one. Things seemingly out of reach had always fascinated Hendren, who at the age of four had asked Santa for a microscope in order to see germs. Hendren took intractable problems personally, as if megaureter, or any of the other deformities he took on, had been put into existence with the specific purpose of taunting him.

With megaureter, he moved methodically: a case here, a case there, children of parents who came to the General because word was out that a young doctor in a new department there welcomed what others had given up on as impossible.

"He's writing the book on all this," they'd heard. "He fixes kids others can't."

Hendren had hit on the basics of megaureter repair on the first case he'd seen: Buddy, a seven-year-old boy from Tampa, Florida, who was Hendren's patient when Hendren was chief resident at Boston Children's in 1960. As more victims found him, Hendren went deeper into the defect. He studied peristalsis, involuntary muscle contractions that move urine down ureters into the bladder. He took still photographs of megaureters. He made movies of megaureters. He injected dye into kidneys and watched what happened on cine-x-ray, a new technology that married sixteen-millimeter filmmaking to radiology. He would do ten, twelve, fourteen, or more hours' surgery on his other patients, and then, long after most of his colleagues had gone home to dinner, Hendren would go to his office to work. He sketched. He calculated. He examined records and family histories. He read virtually everything ever written on megaureter and hydroureter and megaloureter and all of the other names by which the condition was known. He reviewed notes from conferences where surgeons had expounded on the subject.

He thought and thought, and he took what he'd learned into the OR, where he refined his technique.

And on the twenty-two children he saw through April 1968, Hendren had success. He'd proved he could cure megaureter.

Hendren's description of his operation, accompanied by the illustrations of his artist, Paul Andriesse, filled seventeen pages of the April 1969 edition of *The Journal of Urology*, the preeminent publication in the field. Step-by-step, with the sharpest of detail, Hendren outlined the stitching patterns and the suture materials that were required, what vital blood supplies had to be preserved, where to trim, where to implant, how to precisely place the Hendren megaureter clamps he'd designed for his operation. Even the prose was masterly, Hendren's distinctive blend of scientific precision and literary eloquence.

"It should be emphasized that this is major surgery which, for success, demands precise technique, gentle handling of tissues, lack of tension on anastomoses, etc.," he cautioned. "It must be done with the care used by the plastic surgeon in repairing a cleft lip in a small infant. Gross technique, large suture material and inaccurate refashioning of the ureter will give disappointing results which sometimes cannot be remedied."

Not just any surgeon would be able to copy him, Hendren implied, and perhaps it was this elitism—blunt but not unjustified—that explained the reception his paper received when he read it to an auditorium of urologists at a conference in Miami Beach. Most were indifferent. A few were offended. One skeptic went so far as to publicly accuse Hendren of falsifying his results by fiddling with his pre- and postoperative slides. Clearly, the skeptic told several hundred doctors at a subsequent conference, Hendren must have shown preoperative X rays of one patient and postoperative films of another—and claimed they were the same person! This wasn't elegant ingenuity—this was fraud!

Perhaps it was medical politics, always a clash of egos. Hendren was gifted in urology, but unlike the basic urologist he was also an accomplished surgeon of the heart, the intestines, the stomach, the liver, the gallbladder, the esophagus, the pancreas, the lungs and skin, and the female reproductive organs. Except for nerves and bones, there were few places in the child or adult body he wasn't comfortable. In an era when specialties already were beginning to spawn subspecialties, Hendren was on his way to becoming an anachronism.

Or perhaps Hendren's audience knew his implication was correct. Megaureter repair, indeed, was not for everyone.

"Although Hendren's work is impressive, we have not been able to duplicate it," wrote a urologist at the George Washington University Medical Center in Washington, D.C., in a paper published in 1972. His recommendation was bags, placed early and for life.

But Hendren's results could be duplicated.

If you doubted, you were invited to watch the movie he made or come to the General to see for yourself. Many did, among them a young French physician, Gerard Monfort, destined to become one of Europe's most distinguised pediatric surgeons. Monfort spent a year in Boston in Hendren's OR, and when he returned to the Continent, his student, Philippe Menguy, wrote *L'Opération de Hendren, Techniques-Résultats,* a 1971 doctoral thesis for the Medical School of the Université d'Aix-Marseille. As Monfort, Menguy, and others spread the word, Hendren lectured on both sides of the Atlantic, and he wrote more articles with more and more successes to report; and eventually enough surgeons at enough institutions had successful outcomes that Hendren's surgery became the universally accepted correction of the defect. Today, young doctors studying *Campbell's Urology,* the three-volume authoritative text, do not learn how to fashion bowel sleeves or what cement best holds appliances in place. They learn Hendren's operation. They see Hendren's artist's illustrations, little different from when they were first drawn, a quarter of a century ago.

On that tenth day of July 1989, as the Moores of Westchester County, New York, tried to imagine the changes a birth-defective baby would soon bring, Hardy Hendren was restoring order inside the six-year-old boy from Cape Cod.

Although Hendren is capable of great speed, a characteristic prized by many surgeons because it is a tradition and because it increases income, he worked as he always has: unhesitatingly, self-critically, taking no shortcuts, wasting no movements, keeping no eye on the clock. During periods when peak concentration wasn't a necessity, Hendren told jokes. He lambasted liberals, his favorite target. He made small talk with doctors who'd crossed oceans for the privilege of watching him work. He maintained, as he does almost daily, how the assistance of his personal scrub nurse, Dorothy Enos, is such an important part of his success in his difficult cases. With his blue eyes, made even more intense by magnifying glasses, he scrutinized two young residents after he'd permitted them to tie a few knots.

Hendren closed the Cape Cod boy's belly with three layers of synthetic sutures, then cleaned and bandaged the wound, an unglamorous chore many chief surgeons relegate to their assistants. Like a schoolboy shooting rubber bands across a classroom, he slung his dirty gloves one at a time into a waste bucket. He removed his headlamp and surgical glasses. He put on his regular glasses, which are bifocals, and went to the OR phone to dictate his operative note. The note ended "I think that this should solve the problem." It would.

Between the megaureter repair and an earlier kidney operation, Hendren had spent eleven hours today, a Monday, in his OR.

Tomorrow, he would see thirty-one office patients, attend a two-hour hospital staff Executive Committee meeting and preside over a difficult-case conference. On Wednesday, after attending his department's weekly grand rounds lecture, he would perform four operations, and on Thursday, six. Friday would be another full day in Room 7; between cases, he would duck out to attend a funeral. He would spend all day Saturday in his office. On Sunday, one of his three surgeon sons would visit him at the oceanfront home he and Eleanor, the woman he married in 1947, keep on Duxbury Bay, near Plymouth. Hendren and his son would water-ski.

Satisfied there was nothing more he could do tonight for the Cape Cod boy, Hendren bid good-night and went to the locker room. He changed into a dark suit, knotted his tie, combed his hair, and made his way back to his office. He had a fruit salad and tea. After telephoning Eleanor, he began the second half of his day.

Tonight, he was working on a paper on cloaca, a defect that involves multiple organs and systems and that had moved past megaureter to become his most consuming surgical passion.

Of the many abnormalities Hendren had taken on, cloaca, in all of its twisted variations, was the toughest—in many respects, more difficult even than separating Siamese twins, another of his specialties. Few surgeons anywhere on the planet had ever tackled a cloaca. Fewer had had success, and none Hendren's degree of it. One key was his power of concentration, impressive even by surgeons' standards. Rebuilding cloaca babies frequently took several operations, and often the primary one lasted twelve hours straight. Some took longer.

Lucy Moore, who would not be born for another four months, would be cloaca number 104 in Hardy Hendren's series.

Chapter 3

The news this time was bad. Very bad. It made multicystic kidney seem as threatening as diaper rash.

September 1989, and the Moores had moved to Florida from Westchester County. Their lives were more hectic than ever—a thousand new demands at once. Jack had one wine business to close and another to start up. The children had new schools and a new home. Beth had a new job, as director of a day-care center at a synagogue. There were friends to be made, routes and stores to be learned, child-care arrangements to be concluded. The Moores were having a house custom-built, and every day brought decisions on that.

And there was a baby on the way, a baby whose problems under the smoothest of circumstances would bring change.

For Beth, the most critical task once in Florida had been finding a new doctor. Friends had recommended Donna Goss, whose practice was in Sarasota, across the bay from Longboat Key, where the Moores were renting while their house went up. The recommendation was solid: Goss was experienced and understanding, and on the first visit Beth entrusted her with her care. In light of the findings back North, Goss suggested Beth see someone specializing in high-risk pregnancies. There was a very good practice in Tampa, about an hour up the coast.

On September 13, Jack and Beth Moore rode an elevator to the fourth floor of the Harbour Side Medical Tower on the grounds of

Tampa General Hospital. In the waiting room, Beth filled out a gynecologic-history form. She listed her age, thirty-five. She listed the years her girl and boy had been born and the fact that both deliveries had been cesarean sections. No, she did not own a cat. Her work did not involve chemicals or fumes, nor did it bring her into contact with blood. There was no history in either family of birth defects. She did not smoke or diet or use a hot tub. She did take vitamins, and she was on a medication: penicillin, for a case of Lyme disease that had shown no recognized symptoms but had been picked up on a blood test early in her pregnancy.

"Mr. and Mrs. Moore?"

The door to the inner suite opened. Kathy B. Porter motioned them in.

Porter is businesslike, a doctor whose profession does not allow her emotional extremes, certainly not in the company of patients, many of whom arrive at her door after long, unpleasant rides on emotional roller coasters. Porter trained in Kentucky and Texas and is licensed to practice in three states. She is an assistant professor at the University of South Florida College of Medicine, Department of Obstetrics and Gynecology, Division of Maternal-Fetal Medicine. Porter is a birth defect specialist. One of her responsibilities is chairing the university's Fetal Board, a group of diverse specialists who meet monthly to evaluate high-risk pregnancies and decide how best to handle them.

As Beth and Jack entered an examination room, they passed a wall-mounted display of pamphlets. *Peace of Mind for an Unexpected Problem* was the title of one. *Preparing for Surgery* was another. The worst was a twelve-page brochure whose cover had a charcoal sketch of a wilted orchid: *Grieving: A Way to Heal*, a publication of the American College of Obstetricians and Gynecologists. "If you prefer, the hospital may be able to arrange for disposition of your baby's body" was one piece of advice the pamphlet offered. *Get me out of here!* Beth wanted to shout. She wanted to take Jack's hand and run.

For the fifth time in a pregnancy that still had more than two months left, Beth lay seminaked on a table and let a stranger use sonar to illuminate the contents of her womb.

Porter found the defective kidney quickly enough; like fruit gone bad early in the season, she knew it would never develop into much.

But the kidney was not what preoccupied Porter. She focused on something mysterious: a small patch of brightness near the bladder, what fetal specialists call an echogenic area, or mass. Something dense had formed inside the Moores' unborn baby. Something that didn't belong there.

As useful as it can be as a diagnostic tool, ultrasonography has its limits, sometimes raising more questions than it answers. Porter knew the mass spelled trouble, but what kind? She reached for her copy of the textbook she calls the bible: *Prenatal Diagnosis of Congenital Anomalies*, written by a doctor at Yale, where Beth had been seen on July 10.

The word from the bible was that until the baby was born, it would be impossible to say, with any kind of certainty, what the mass was. But the range of possibilities was uniformly grim—a grouping of disorders so uncommon, so foul, that even Porter, the very model of control, was taken aback. The mass, she told the Moores, could indicate that a virus or bacteria had taken root. It might be suggestive of cystic fibrosis or an ovarian cyst. It could be the result of some sort of bowel obstruction. Or it could be evidence of any number of tumors: *hepatoblastoma*, which involves the liver; *hemangioendothelioma*, which involves the nerves; *teratoma*, which can involve hair, bone, and other parts and tissues of a twin that never fully formed. Whatever it was, the mass was a potential killer. Lucy might die during, or shortly after, birth. She might not make it to birth.

"I will be presenting this case to a urologist as well as to a pediatric surgeon for evaluation at the Fetal Board," Porter said.

Fetal Board? Beth thought. *It sounds like science fiction. "Welcome, earthlings, the regularly scheduled session of the Fetal Board will now come to order."*

While the Fetal Board was a valuable educational tool for University of South Florida students and staff, Porter knew its ability to help Beth's baby would be restricted. In 1989, medicine's miracles with early life were virtually all performed on delivered babies. You could leave the womb early, underweight, ungrowing, in desperate pulmonary or cardiac trouble, and you could be saved—but first you had to arrive. You had to do your part and be born. Only a handful of surgeons, including Michael Harrison of the University of California at San Francisco, who'd trained with Hardy Hendren at the Massachusetts General Hospital, had had any success in helping defective fetuses. And those successes, while spectacular enough to make *People* magazine, were with only a few disorders. As seriously as the Fetal Board would ponder Lucy Moore, as much as they might wish to do, she was like an unlighted, unmarked ship approaching in the dark. You knew it was coming, knew it was in distress, but where it would hit and at what cost, no one could predict. No one could change its course.

The Moores drove home, stunned.

They hadn't been expecting anything like this.

True, during Beth's last ultrasound, in Westchester County, the doctor had found a questionable area in Lucy's lower abdomen. "It could be normal intestine," he'd said, "although the possibility of some sort of mass cannot be excluded." He'd recommended keeping a careful eye on things, especially in light of the kidney situation. The word *possibility* was what the Moores had tried to focus on, and for the most part they'd been successful.

"How bad could it be?" Jack would say to Beth. "Not so bad that we can't deal with it."

Beth adopted what she called her Pollyanna attitude. The way she figured it, she had a good husband, two good children, a good home. Thanks to her father, she would never have to worry about money. *Whatever happens, we'll be able to handle it,* she thought. *We'll love this baby no matter what.*

Besides, in all the commotion of moving to Florida, who had time to be consumed with worry about vague unknowns?

But that was back North.

That was before today, before hearing about the Fetal Board, before confirmation of the abdominal mass, before a word worse than *birth defect—death—*had been introduced into the darkening dialogue about Lucy Moore.

All my positive energy and all my Pollyannaisms aren't going to work anymore, Beth thought as she and Jack drove home from Kathy Porter's.

"I'm scared," she told her husband.

"I'm scared, too," he said.

Like consideration of a third child, getting to Florida had not been easy.

The Moores were native New Yorkers: Beth, the middle child of

Westchester County Jews; Jack, the oldest of seven children of Long Island Irish Catholics. Jack's father was an engineer. Beth's father, in business with his brother, was on his way to making a fortune in the wholesale food business.

Having graduated from Cornell University, Beth was teaching at a day-care center in the Bronx in 1976 when she met Jack, a wisecracking, long-haired jock who wanted to be a teacher, too. Jack was a year older than Beth, and he'd been married briefly but that was history now. Jack was on the rebound.

He's gorgeous, Beth thought. *He's just my type—a hippie jock. And I just know that if I date him, we're going to marry.*

Beth waited for Jack to ask her out. When two weeks had passed and they'd become day-care-center buddies but he still hadn't made a move, Beth invited him over for dinner.

"Well," he said, "I have therapy Tuesday night, but if you don't mind my coming at eight, I'd love to."

And Beth thought, *Great! A man who's in touch with his feelings!*

They went steady from the start. For the first year, they kept separate apartments, but it was a rare night they spent apart. At the beginning of their second year, Beth and Jack moved north of the city, to one of two caretaker's cottages on the grounds of her parents' Westchester County estate. The other cottage became Beth's nursery school. Jack taught for a while, worked on his master's degree, and coached youth basketball, while Beth ran a program for troubled teens. Two years and ten months after meeting, in August of 1979, Beth and Jack married. In 1981, their first child, Mary, was born.

Mary needed thirty-six hours of labor to arrive, but when she did, she was normal and healthy and to Beth's mind, cherubic—a nine-pound, twelve-ounce baby who was smothered in love and attention from the moment of her birth. *I'm lost in love,* Beth thought. *I'm on a cloud.* Jack thought that way, too.

Even before Mary was born, teaching had been wearing thin for Jack. The pay was low, seemingly in inverse proportion to the hassles of the job. Jack took work in a bank, and a short time later, when he had a chance to take a position in one of Beth's father's firms—a cheese company in northern New Jersey—he took it. By 1987, when he left to run the wine shop he'd bought, Jack was vice president of manufacturing. It was a year of change, 1987. *Time to break free*, Beth thought. The Moores had a new baby, James. They wanted a new house, wanted out of Mommy and Daddy's cottage. In another part of Westchester County, they found a four-bedroom neocolonial with a deck that ran the length of the house. There were five acres of land, including a huge front lawn and woods out back that were home to white-tailed deer.

Born-and-bred New Yorkers the Moores were in love with Northeast springs, summers, and autumns. Westchester was sophisticated but rural; you could get lost in the woods there—and barely an hour south was Manhattan. Most of their friends lived no more than an hour away. This was where they would grow old. This was where their grandchildren would visit.

Beth's parents had said that once, too. But Florida has a way of seducing people who tire of snow and high taxes. Not long before Beth's final pregnancy, when a restructuring of her father's business empire gave the family a windfall, two cousins were lured south. So were Beth's parents, who'd vacationed in Florida for years. New York's income tax was killing Beth's folks—but Florida's wouldn't. Florida didn't have an income tax. Florida wanted you to have your money, to invest it in Florida real estate, Florida banks, Florida restaurants. Florida wanted to cut you a nice little piece of the action.

"Are you crazy?" Beth would say to her family after hearing again that relocating to Florida was the best move they'd ever made.

Jack didn't think her family was so crazy. "I want you to know I hate it here," he would say to Beth in the dead of the New York winter. "I hate the cold."

"Stop being a wimp," Beth would reply. "I'll never move."

On a visit to Florida in January 1989, Beth had to listen to her mother and father, who'd taken up permanent residence in Sarasota. "It's not just old people," her father said, "it's young people, too. Your family's here. You'll have a great time. So many opportunities." Beth saw sunsets over the Gulf of Mexico. She saw short-sleeved shirts. She saw the beach where her cousins were building a house. It would have made a picture postcard, the kind tourists send to snowbound friends, pearl-white sand against a backdrop of deep blue sea.

"Let's move!" Beth said to Jack, as impulsively as that.

In February, the Moores selected an architect for their own beachfront house, their dream. They were in Florida for meetings with him when Beth took her pregnancy test.

The Fetal Board agreed with Porter that Beth could have her baby at Sarasota Memorial Hospital, close to the place the Moores were renting.

Sarasota had an excellent staff, an excellent intensive care unit for newborns, an excellent neonatologist; and it was where Donna Goss, Beth's doctor, delivered babies. In the board's judgment, Sarasota would be able to stabilize Lucy, and there would be time to transfer her north to All Children's Hospital in Saint Petersburg, the closest pediatric hospital, if a greater level of care were needed—as in all probability it would be. The plan assumed that Lucy would be born alive. Everyone involved knew what kind of an assumption that was.

On November 20, 1989, Beth and Jack and their two children had dinner at the home of Beth's parents. In years to come, they would not pull out the photo album to reminisce fondly about the evening. Beth's father, an even-tempered man, tried to put a good face on things but his sentiments did not prevail. Beth's mother had come to believe that her daughter's life was on the line. It wasn't—the risk was all the baby's—but in the condemned-prisoner atmosphere of the final hours before Lucy's arrival, the idea had currency.

"If there has to be a choice," Beth's mother said during dinner, and after dinner, and right on up to good-night at the front door, "if they can save only one of you . . . I don't care about this baby. I care about you, Beth, *you!*"

Beth and Jack had their own children to worry about. As the news that fall about the baby had become grimmer, they'd spent more and more time preparing Mary and James. At eight, Mary could manage a tolerable understanding. She understood there was a chance Lucy would die. She knew that if she made it, she would be different from other girls in some unpredictable way. In her mind, Mary had an image of a little sister with a long nose and a funny face. She worried about what she would tell her friends. She knew, because Mom and Dad told her, that you could learn to love anyone.

James was trickier. He was only three, but already he was laying claim to the title of Most Sensitive of the Moores. James worried about ordinary things. Extraordinary things had the potential to really throw him, as Beth knew.

All fall, Beth had been explaining the unexplainable to her son.

"When you're very sick, you have to go to the doctor, but the doctor makes you better, and all is well," Beth would say. "Right?"

"Right," James would agree.

"And sometimes when you're very, very sick, it takes some time, but the doctor makes you better."

James would shake his head in understanding. He'd been very, very sick before, with colds and sore throats and the flu. He'd been to the doctor. He'd always gotten better.

"But when you're very, very, *very* sick, it's possible that the doctor can do nothing to make you better, and you die. And Lucy might be very, very, *very* sick. We just don't know."

James would turn that one over and say, "You mean if you're one sick or two sick you're OK, but if you're three sick, you die?"

"Yes," Beth would say, unable to lie. "Sometimes when you're three sick, you die."

At evening's end, when only Beth's mother had anything left to say, none of it uplifting, the family kissed and hugged, and Jack and Beth drove off into the night. On their way home, they drove past Sarasota Memorial, where they'd be in less than ten hours. As irrational as her mother's words might have been, Beth couldn't get them out of her mind.

"I hope you feel the same way," Beth said to her husband. "I mean, I love this kid, whoever she is, but if it means dying, . . . if it means there has to be a choice . . ."

"Nobody's going to die," Jack said.

"But if someone has to, you're going to save me, not this kid, aren't you?"

"Of course," Jack said.

Cutting through scar from Beth's previous two cesareans, Goss opened her patient's womb and gently pried Lucy from her mom. It was seven thirty-five A.M. on Tuesday, November 21, 1989.

Lucy let out a strong cry—a good sign. She had good color and good reflexes and good muscle tone and bright, alert eyes, and those were promising signs, too. Goss clamped and cut her umbilical cord and handed her to Carmen L. Villaveces, a neonatologist who'd been waiting for Lucy. Villaveces went to work. She listened to Lucy's heart and lungs. She did a quick visual examination. Before she took the baby to the neonatal intensive care unit, before the real work began, she cleaned Lucy and swaddled her in a warm blanket and carried her over for Jack and Beth to see.

"I don't want to be here," Beth had said as she'd been wheeled into the delivery room.

Now, she didn't want to look at her daughter.

I can't love you, Beth thought, *if you're going to die.*

"Look," Villaveces said. "She's a beautiful girl."

And she was—with big eyes, strawberry-blond hair, and an Irish face, impish and round, just like her dad's. Even at the moment of her birth, you could look at Lucy Moore and know that if she made it, her personality was going to be all sparkle and bright colors.

Villaveces carried Lucy to her mother. During her initial examination, the neonatologist had made a discovery.

"See?" Villaveces said, unwrapping the blanket, "if you look right there, you see she doesn't have an anus."

"This is really good news, Beth." Goss said. "That's what we were looking for. That's what the problem was!" Lucy's intestines had no outlet, which had caused meconium to back up, creating the mass.

Beth got the sillies then. It seemed so absurd—all this worry and talk of dying *because the kid can't take a crap!* Beth's humor kicked in then, and she was laughing and crying, crazy with joy. And the nurses were thinking, *What a beaut. Imagine her for a mom.*

"You mean I can't call my daughter an asshole?" Beth said.

"Beth!" Jack exclaimed.

"Kiss her good-bye," Villaveces said. "We're taking her to the intensive care unit."

There, Villaveces placed an intravenous line into Lucy and threaded a tube through her nose into her stomach. She was given oxygen through a hood to help her breathe. She would need monitoring and tube feeding and, soon, surgery.

Over the next two years, Lucy would have hundreds of tests. Her bodily fluids would be centrifuged, subjected to chemical analysis, smeared across glass slides, and examined under microscopes. She would be X-rayed and fluoroscoped and put through CT and MRI and ultrasound. The activity of her heart and brain would be translated into electrical impulses, which would be visualized on screens. Like detectives combing the scene of some heinous crime, surgeons would examine her heart, lungs, liver, bladder, small and large intestines, kidney, ureters, pancreas, gall bladder, spine, and spinal cord. She would be photographed and videotaped, and an accomplished medical artist would draw her in cross section. Pathologists would pick apart pieces of her flesh. Put on paper, the details of what made this round-faced little girl tick would weigh several pounds. Few people would be as well catalogued throughout their lifetime as Lucy Moore would be by the time she reached the age of two. Few would have so many secrets about themselves revealed, discussed, and shared, through papers and lectures, to the international medical community.

The tests started the day Lucy was born, when Villaveces ordered blood analysis and X rays and ultrasound of her abdomen. But Villaveces really didn't need anything but her eyes to make the probable diagnosis. She'd known about Lucy's kidney problem. Now, it could be seen that she had no anus; where nature should have put one was only featureless skin, a blank canvas. Her genitalia were abnormal, too. Her labia minora were fused, except at the very top, where there was a long, narrow opening into Lucy's insides. It didn't look like a urethra or a vagina; it didn't look like anything recognizable at all. "Ambiguous genitalia," Villaveces wrote in her chart.

Together, it seemed to add up to VACTERL association, which Villaveces had seen but once before, while training in Tampa at the University of South Florida College of Medicine, Kathy Porter's school. VACTERL association is a grouping of several defects that occur in differing combinations, depending on the baby. The association, once called VATER but broadened through later study to the more accurate VACTERL, refers to vertebral defects (V); absence, or atresia, of the anus (A); cardiovascular problems (C); an abnormal passage between the trachea and the esophagus (TE); kidney, or renal, anomalies (R); and disfigurement of the limbs (L). Lacking a letter, but frequently seen with the association, are genital abnormalities such as Lucy's.

At eight-thirty on the night of her birth, Lucy was brought to her mother's room. Beth held her and wished the doctors would let her breast-feed her, as she had her other two. She kissed Lucy—the Moores' last child, no question about it this time. Minutes after her cesarean, Beth had a tubal ligation.

At a quarter to nine, Lucy was in an ambulance. She was bound for Saint Petersburg and All Children's Hospital.

Over the next week, the hospital's entire staff, it seemed, converged on Lucy Moore.

Her defects were rare, exceptionally rare; in any good teaching hospital, with its unquenchable thirst for knowledge and newness, there is no bigger attraction. Have you heard about the Moore baby? went the buzz at All Children's. The one from Sarasota? You have to have a look! She's VACTERL association. Major problems. Won't see one like her again for a long, long time.

On Wednesday, November 22, the day before Thanksgiving, the tests and examinations and consultations began in earnest. With so much so wrong already, who knew what other problems might be lurking inside Lucy? Who knew how far into freakishness this otherwise beautiful baby had gone? Whole departments and divisions became involved: Endocrinology, Urology, Cardiology, Nephrology, Pediatrics, Radiology, Genetics, Surgery, Ophthalmology, Otolaryngology.

Beth went home for Thanksgiving, without her daughter. Over turkey dinner, the Moores gave thanks that the fifth and final member of the family was alive.

By Friday, the picture of Lucy—still developing, still full of halftones and muddled grays—was the proverbial good news–bad news. The good news was mostly what she didn't have. She didn't seem to have any mental troubles, although the final verdict on that was still not in. Her limbs were OK. Her esophagus looked normal, and she was eating well. She didn't have two faulty kidneys; only one, the one that was multicystic.

The bad news was her heart, which cardiologists had found was defective. Lucy had a ventricular septal defect, or VSD: a hole in the wall between the right ventricle, which pumps blood to the lungs, and the left ventricle, which moves blood through the rest of the body. VSD is a common congenital heart defect. In more severe cases, and Lucy's was one of those, surgery is needed. But for Lucy, the situation was not immediately life threatening.

What was a threat to life was her anal atresia. Without some outlet, some way for her bodily wastes to get out, Lucy's intestines would back up. She would be poisoned. After a few days or a week, maybe a little longer, she would die.

On the day after Thanksgiving, Lucy went to an OR for the first time. Her surgeon was Richard P. Harmel, Jr., forty-two, a mustachioed, bespectacled father of three who'd arrived in Saint Petersburg with some fanfare. A native of New York City, Harmel was a summa cum laude graduate in chemistry from Harvard College and a magna cum laude graduate of the Harvard Medical School. Harmel was good, and not only in the classroom. In his first year in medical school, he'd visited the Massachusetts General Hospital, where he'd been introduced to the chief of pediatric surgery, Hardy Hendren. Hendren made a profound impression on the twenty-one-year-old Harmel. Here was the surgeon who'd made the first successful separation of Siamese twins in Boston, a man of prodigious talent and energy and self-assurance and a way with a story unlike that of any doctor Harmel had ever met. Hendren took Harmel into his operating room, and it was then he knew the direction in medicine he wanted to take. Later, while serving an internship and residency at the General, Harmel scrubbed in on many of Hendren's tough cases. Harmel finished his training as the chief surgical resident at Children's Hospital, Boston, in 1980–81. Like the Moores, he came to Florida from the North: from the Ohio State University College of Medicine, where he was associate professor of surgery.

Harmel opened Lucy's belly and found her transverse colon, the middle section of the large intestine that runs from side to side across the abdomen. He cut into her colon, anchored it to outlying muscle and tissue, and then closed Lucy up, leaving an opening, or stoma, out of which her bowel could safely empty. Lucy would need a bag after her colostomy. Bags would become Beth's bane, especially in a month, when the colostomy would fail and she would wind up holding her daughter's intestines in her hands. But Lucy would live. There was no longer any doubt about that.

Before sending her to recovery, Harmel gently pushed an endoscope up into the single opening on Lucy's bottom. He put his eye to the scope and went on a visual journey.

What he found was anatomic anarchy—a body so confused, so

perversely unique that it would take more than a year for physicians at two major medical centers to figure out what they were dealing with. On this first exploration of Lucy's insides, Harmel found a bladder, but he could not identify ureters, which drain the kidneys. He could not find a vagina. In that long, single opening, which was called a urogenital sinus—or, more commonly, cloaca—he found stool. That told him Lucy's large intestine had to be connected to the cloaca through a slim, abnormal passage known as a fistula. It was anyone's guess whether Lucy had ovaries or Fallopian tubes.

Chapter 4

As a colleague pays tribute to him—going so far as to call him a hero, and not gratuitously—Hardy Hendren sits in a crowded auditorium at Tufts University School of Medicine in Boston, across town from Harvard and Children's Hospital. In a moment, Hendren will receive a medal. He will deliver a lecture no one else in the world could give. He will get a standing ovation. And when he's done, fellow surgeons will line up to shake his hand.

Hendren is an average-size man. His arms are muscular, his grip strong. His nails are clipped and clean, never anything but clean, but his fingers give no further clues to his profession and the prominence he has in it. His upper body is sturdy and broad—an enduring product of prep school, where he was a varsity wrestler, and Navy flight school, which gave him wings of gold. He is wearing a gray suit. His hair is thinning and graying. His skin is less wrinkled than that of most men his age; for this, he can thank a career spent indoors. Hendren's eyes are grandfatherly today, benevolent, for he is among admirers and friends. When he's angry—and nothing angers him more than lies or stupidity—his eyes sear.

Hendren's nickname is Hardly Human, a name he finds amusing. Some consider it a slur, a reference to his bedside manner, which would not be mistaken for Marcus Welby's. Others wonder if it isn't an allusion to his memory, which allows him to recall names, middle initials, and the most minute details of even run-of-the-mill operations he performed when Eisenhower was president. Not everyone who's encountered Hendren considers that steel-trap memory of his a blessing.

A more probable explanation of Hendren's nickname is his OR stamina. Well into his sixties, Hendren can go twenty-four or more hours on the most complicated reconstructive operation, stopping only once or twice to empty his bladder and eat a hot dog or microwaved popcorn or some other food similarly rich in carbohydrates. Among the few who match him is Dorothy Enos, who has worked with him for thirty years. Hendren is convinced the body undergoes profound metabolic changes during such spells, when the brain does not perceive hunger, does not acknowledge the urge to urinate or take a drink. He thinks there might be an interesting scientific paper in these changes, whatever they are, some valuable insights into human physiology to be gleaned, and he's repeatedly suggested to anesthesiologists at Children's that they monitor urinary output and blood pressure and the activity of the heart of someone during such an odyssey. Hendren has offered himself as a guinea pig, but so far no anesthesiologist has taken him up on the offer. No one knows if he's serious. He is.

"I came because of Hardy Hendren," says Martin W. Abrams, the man introducing him. "There is no man I respect more in the field of pediatric surgery than my friend."

Like Hendren and many of the more than one hundred physicians in the auditorium, Abrams is a pediatric surgeon. His practice, well respected and firmly established, draws on patients from the New York City area and well beyond. Abrams excels in a very difficult field. And yet he, like others here today at Tufts, gladly refers some of his worst cases to Hendren.

Abrams tells the audience about a case on which he was asked to consult. The child in question, genetically a male, had been born with ambiguous genitalia—genitals that were not properly male or female but belonged to some confused zone in between. What the boy had was small and misshapen, closer to a clitoris than a penis, and the doctors who'd sought Abrams's opinion believed it had little or no potential to function like the penis of a normal male. In the worst cases of ambiguous genitalia—and this boy's certainly seemed one of them—conventional wisdom holds that it is better to raise the child as a female, eventually constructing a vagina from a length of freed-up colon and producing breasts by administering female hormones at the age puberty normally begins. But the boy's father didn't want that kind of a child. He wanted a boy with a working penis.

"Fortunately for me, I don't do that kind of work," Abrams says. "But I knew Hardy did, and I called him on the phone, and I said to him, 'Hardy, I'd like to send these people up to you.' And I described the situation to him. I sent him up to Hardy, and Jonathan today is a boy, and he's a hell of a boy! I just fixed one of his undescended testicles—that was the lesser of the many evils that had been inflicted on this child. But he is the happiest little boy I have ever seen."

The introduction complete, Hendren comes forward, smiling while the Orvar Swenson Medal, a bronze medallion, is placed around his neck. The medal honors the surgeon—retired and in his eighties but in attendance today—who pioneered correction of Hirschsprung's disease, a life-threatening bowel disorder that as recently as the late 1940s was believed impossible to fix. Like Hendren, Swenson trained at Children's at almost the same time as Robert E. Gross, who would be surgeon-in-chief at the hospital from 1947 to 1967. When a young Hendren was enrolling at the Harvard Medical School, Swenson left Children's to become surgeon-in-chief at the Boston Floating Hospital.

When the applause subsides, Hendren takes the podium.

"I would like to talk on the subject of cloaca, which, as you know, is a congenital persistence of an early embryologic stage where everything empties into a single chamber," Hendren says. "Cloaca in Latin is the word for sewer."

Academic doctors almost never lecture without a trayful of slides; their reluctance to do so is a bit of an inside joke. Hendren asks for his first: a photograph of the pelvic organs of a cloaca baby who died in 1955, when survival—never mind reconstruction—was fantasy. Hendren dissected the organs during an autopsy he requested to learn more about this bizarre condition no one knew how to fix. For just that reason, Hendren, still a resident, was hooked. Someday, he would solve this problem, this certain death sentence for innocents.

The slide is not something you would want to view over dinner. Without the labels, even an anatomist would need time to identify all of the organs. Vagina, rectum, urinary tract—all are intertwined in a brown-and-yellow jumble suggestive more of an undersea organism than a human being, a baby.

"This is the second cloaca that I had occasion to see, many years ago, in 1955," Hendren begins.

Not so long ago, rectal abnormalities imposed a life sentence as a freak—if the victim somehow managed to survive. Like the two patients Hendren saw at Children's in the 1950s, most did not, not for long. It was a fate earlier generations of doctors construed as evidence of a kind and merciful God.

> Although we have showed that the unfortunate subjects of this affliction are generally in no immediate danger of death, yet the imperfection is one of a peculiarly delicate character and one that, should life be spared and prolonged, would only entail misery upon the unfortunate victim of it. The manner in which such a malformation would operate upon the mind, should the patient thus afflicted arrive at the age of reflection, can well be imagined, when we take into consideration the disgusting and the repulsive nature of the deformity itself.

So wrote the surgeon William Bodenhamer in a text published in 1860, nine years before Children's Hospital opened. Cloaca, the most extreme form of rectal malformation, was considered so hopeless that it barely rated a mention: "With regard to the prognosis of those extremely rare cases in which the rectum, together with the genito-urinary organs terminates in a cloaca in the perinaeum, as observed in the monotremata, in birds, in reptiles and in many fishes, it is useless to conjecture. Such cases would seem, as a matter of course, to be beyond all hope of remedy."

What could cause such horror?

How could nature, normally the very model of symmetry and perfect design, go so wrong?

What in God's name has happened here?

Answers eluded nineteenth-century physicians and scientists, who were laying the groundwork for an emerging field: embryology, the study of human development from conception through about the eighth week of pregnancy, the period when tissue is dividing and growing and fashioning itself into recognizable structures. In explaining how development could go so far off track, scientists a century ago were no more successful than scientists today have been. All they had were theories. Some nineteenth-century physicians made reference to "formative energies" somehow being interrupted early in pregnancy. Others assumed disease had to cause cloaca. Bodenhamer wondered if the expectant mother's attitude might not be responsible. Given the power of the nervous system, wasn't it possible that an overly excitable mother-to-be could transfer her anxiety to her unborn child—with disastrous results?

If cause remained a mystery and cure a dream, empirical observations over the decades at least gave physicians a more detailed picture of what they were dealing with. The most profound lesson was that once having decided to be cruel, Nature could demonstrate almost satanic creativity.

The basic problem, understood more than a century ago, was that instead of having three openings on their bottoms—anus, vagina, and urethra—cloaca babies have only one, the urogenital sinus or cloaca. From there, the variations are stunning for such a rare defect (approximately one in fifty thousand live births). Cloaca babies may have a single vagina or two vaginas or no vagina. The vagina or vaginas may be deep inside the pelvis or just beneath the skin. There may or may not be ovaries and Fallopian tubes, which may or may not connect to a vagina—if there is a vagina. Cloaca babies may have two kidneys or one. Their ureters may be properly connected to the bladder, but frequently they are not. The bladder may be properly formed—or so deformed as to have no functional value whatsoever. The rectum may communicate with the vagina or the bladder by an abnormal passage called a fistula. It may end blindly before reaching the bottom.

In one respect, cloaca was like other formidable surgical problems: it would not be solved by a single brilliant stroke, by revolution. The solution would be evolutionary, one small part of the problem solved at one time, with dozens of surgeons contributing, often at plodding pace, over a period of many years. Surgeons mastered the colostomy, which gave life, at least to babies with less severe cloacal anomalies. They refined the technique of making a functional anus and became progressively better at repairing bladders, urethras, and ureters. But not until the 1960s did the increments add up to a base of knowledge and technique broad enough to support the vision of a young surgeon who'd trained at both Children's Hospital and the Massachusetts General.

Hendren's first significant advances with cloaca came after he'd left Children's for the staff of the Massachusetts General Hospital, in July 1960. As with megaureter, he moved methodically, applying the lessons of one case to the next and the second to the third and so forth until his series numbered in the dozens. As with mega-ureter, word began to get out. It really got out in the 1970s, when Hendren—heeding the words of his old mentor, Gross, who'd advised "pulling a new rabbit out of the hat every two or three years"—began to lecture and publish his results.

On the day Hendren is honored by Tufts, Swenson recalls being at Children's with Gross in the late forties and early fifties. He remembers seeing cases of cloaca and ambiguous genitalia and all of the associated disorders, which not even the legendary Gross, annointed by many as the Father of Modern Pediatric Surgery, had fully figured out.

"I hated to see them come along," Swenson says, "because regardless of what we did, we made them worse, it seemed. I congratulate Dr. Hendren for taking this group of very discouraging patients that most of us just gave up on and diligently working with them and showing real results and giving all of us an understanding that enables us to recognize various groups of patients and differences in treating them.

"I'd like to say that Dr. Hendren has made a very large contribution to the care of children."

Hendren has, by far, the largest series of cloacal patients in the world. By summer 1992, his list had 113 children and adults from twenty-five states and twelve foreign nations.

"I have found certain things that I would like to emphasize to you," he says as his slide tray advances. "One is that they're all different, one from the other. The second is that although they're all different, there are general principles that will guide us in figuring out what to do."

Across the screen flash case histories of babies, toddlers, and teenagers, each an incomplete child whose parents brought her to Hendren with the same hopes and prayers the religious carry to Lourdes. Some are virgin cases, presented shortly after birth with the hope that Hendren could heal them. Those are the lucky ones. The less fortunate have been on long, expensive, and ultimately unsuccessful surgical odysseys to other hospitals, to other so-called experts. These are the veterans, of inexperience and experimentation, children with such severe deformities that with any justice they would have been referred somewhere else at the start. They have come to Hendren wearing diapers and bags, they and their families aware that in the eyes of the world they are freaks.

"I saw one just last week who has seen twelve previous surgeons," Hendren says about a ten-year-old girl from Wisconsin whose mother had taken her to major medical centers in that state, Minnesota, and Texas.

Twelve surgeons—and not a one could explain, let alone cure, the child's persistent infections, bleedings, and mucous discharge that had made her life hell. They couldn't because her pelvic anatomy, confused at birth and complicated by ill-advised surgery, was too Byzantine for them to sort out. What was repeatedly described in her record as vagina was actually a piece of colon—misshapen and quite some distance from where nature ordinarily puts colon, but colon nonetheless. The girl had been born without a vagina, a fact Hendren understood the first time he put an endoscope into her.

"This had been called vagina by a series of people, including several gynecologists," Hendren says. "What the problem is, of course, is the child in fact had a cloaca—with no vagina. That isn't vagina 't all. That's a piece of colon segment connected to the urethra that needs to be removed, and then she needs to have a vagina made from something else and her uterus hooked up to a piece of bowel. So you really sort of have to scratch your head and think about How does this fit into the developmental spectrum? to figure out what you're dealing with."

The standard surgical presentation includes slides of drawings, photographs, X rays, bar graphs, computer-generated statistics, and long names with Latin roots. Hendren's do, too. But he always includes color photographs of his patients taken after their operations, after they're normal—or as close to normal as he can get them. Hendren doesn't have the girl from Wisconsin's photo yet because he hasn't fixed her. But when he does, in several weeks, he'll ask her and her mother if he can add her picture to his gallery for possible use in some later lecture. Honored to be asked, both will say yes.

As he nears the end of his lecture, Hendren shows a slide of a smiling girl in a skirt. She, too, is an OR veteran. One of her previous doctors, thinking he was doing good but really not having any idea what he was dealing with, wound up discarding pieces Hendren could have used in her reconstruction. Somehow, Hendren found enough intact tissue to at least be able to spare her a lifetime of wearing two bags, for urine and feces.

Hendren walks his audience through the operation, expounding on anesthesia, the importance of positioning on the table, the imperative of maintaining good blood supply to organs the reconstructive surgeon must move to places nature never intended them to be. He issues a caution about the use of electric cautery, an efficient and powerful cutting tool—too powerful for separating some of the fine tissues a surgeon encounters when rebuilding. He notes that in the most severe cases, such as this girl's, more than one operation typically is needed. Free of charge, Hendren is providing a wealth of technical detail that might help some exceptionally bright, exceptionally bold surgeon to duplicate his results.

"She's an intact little kid," Hendren says. "She looks like a little girl, she does all the things all the other little girls do, and I think she's a lot better off having not given up and put a couple of bags on her side: a colostomy on one side and a urostomy on the other. And there are lots of them out there who have those double bags. I would urge you all to look for them and get them in and think about what you can do to have them reconstructed."

Today's final slide shows an attractive young woman in a red dress. Like the previous patient, she is a veteran. She walked into Hendren's office wounded and wearing a label: *hopeless*. "She came from a very fine institution and her surgery had been done many, many years ago, before any of us understood much about cloacas," Hendren says. "At age twenty, she wore diapers. She was totally incontinent of urine, and she was totally incontinent of stool."

Hendren walks his audience through the thirteen hours of major surgery that were needed to rebuild the woman. He describes how he removed the bud of raw intestine that protruded from her anus, how he made one good vagina out of the two she'd had at birth, how he used a section of vaginal lining and a flap of buttocks to fashion a urethra, the passageway that drains urine from the bladder to the outside. He explains what he did to stop urine from leaking into her vagina and how he made an anus that finally worked.

"She came back for her first postoperative visit, and she walked in, and she said, 'Guess what? Last Friday night, I went to a dance. And it's the first time I ever felt I could go to a dance. I was wearing real panties just like everybody else! I didn't have on diapers.'

"And that was a profound thing to her socially, to get that fixed. She has subsequently become married and is leading a normal life as a housewife in New York City."

Hendren closes with a call to arms.

"The thing that I'd like to stress," he says, "is that these are all tough cases; they're all different, one from another, but nearly all of them have a pretty good way to get solved if you're willing to roll up your sleeves and do it. We can end with a pretty good group of functional citizens instead of patients coming into our various clinics constantly having their ostomies and so forth tended to.

"Thank you very much."

The audience stands to applaud.

"When he's gone," Abrams says to a friend who's in line to congratulate Hendren, "a lot of kids are going to be screwed up."

Chapter 5

On the morning of August 26, 1938, Mary Ellen Sweeney said a prayer for her seven-year-old daughter, Lorraine—her baby, this pale, underweight, slowly failing child whose heart made a buzzing that could be heard clear across a room.

It was a cloudy day, cool for August in Boston, but the windows in Ward 4 of Children's Hospital were open in order that fresh air, valued for its therapeutic effects, could circulate. Lorraine Sweeney had been awakened early, and she'd been given breakfast, a bowl of clear broth. A nurse had bathed her and combed her black hair. Robert E. Gross, chief surgical resident at Children's, was opening Lorraine's chest today.

At around eight, when the operating room called, Lorraine urinated one last time. A tag identifying her name, age, religion, and date of baptism was tied to her left wrist. As her mother prayed, she was rolled down a hall that connected with the surgical building, a two-story stucco structure of no particular architectural distinction.

Lorraine was anxious, but she was not scared.

Only needles, which hurt, scared her, and there had been but one needle this morning. This other medical stuff—what was the big deal? Lorraine's heart defect, which had a long name, patent ductus arteriosus, often abbreviated to *ductus*, had been diagnosed when she was barely out of toddlerhood. She'd been to doctors, been in and out of hospitals, had every conceivable test, been pawed over by experts who couldn't offer much but a prognosis of steadily failing health that could end in death, perhaps in her third decade and quite possibly before. Except for the needles, hospitals were no big deal. Lorraine Sweeney was a veteran.

"Leave it in God's hands" is how Mrs. Sweeney's parish priest had put it when she'd gone to him for advice. "This Dr. Gross," Mrs. Sweeney had said, "this nice young man thinks he can cure our Lorraine. He thinks he can cut her open and fix her heart. But it's the heart he wants to operate on, Monsignor. *The heart.* His operation has never been tried on a person before, only on some dogs in his laboratory. He's very smart, and he says it will work, but how can he know from working on dogs? Who is he but a surgeon?"

"If God wants your little girl," the priest told Lorraine's mother, "he'll take her—one way or another. Let this doctor do what he thinks best. He may be the answer to our prayers. He may be the miracle we've been beseeching God to work."

Lorraine was wheeled into Operating Room 3 and gently transferred to Gross's table. Her left arm was positioned by her head, and a small sandbag was placed beneath her left shoulder to elevate her chest. Looking up at the gallery, Lorraine saw visiting doctors and medical-school students, drawn by the chance to witness the kind of history a little girl with a buzz in her chest couldn't possibly comprehend. Gross smiled and made small talk with his little patient as Bessie Lank, the nurse-anesthetist, placed a music box next to Lorraine's ear. In getting children to sleep, Lank had few peers. Sometimes she sang hymns she knew from being in her church choir. Sometimes, with babies, she let patients suck on sterile nipples dipped in a mixture of one part brandy, five parts glucose. The older children liked her music box. It reminded them of bedtime, of being home and tucked in safely for the night.

As Brahms's "Lullaby" played, Lank placed a rubber mask over Lorraine's face. Lorraine breathed cyclopropane, a new gas that was replacing ether as an anesthesia.

Gross, thirty-three years old and not yet finished with his surgical training, got ready to attempt what no one had done before.

Bob Gross was a shy child, a reader, a scholar, one of eight children, an outdoorsman and tinkerer who loved to take things apart and put them back together. Bob could break down and rebuild an automobile engine. He could mend clothes. He loved hammers, screwdrivers, motors, pumps, and knives. He was good with his hands, very good.

Bob, a dark-haired, handsome boy, had a bad eye. He was all but blind in that eye, his right.

A bad eye deprived him of normal depth perception, and while he could have taken apart its engine, he probably could not have flown a plane, not with a comfortable margin of safety. His eyesight was a problem when he was a boy, but Bob's father, a Baltimore piano maker of German Lutheran descent, had learned that most problems were not really problems, not with the right attitude. The solution to this one, Bob's father decided, was clocks. Mr. Gross gave his son a large clock and encouraged him, bad eye and all, to figure out how it worked. "Go ahead," the father urged. "Take it apart. Never mind your bad eye; just take that clock apart." Bob did—the gears, the spring, the hands, the pallet and spindles, the whole works. "Now, put it back together," Mr. Gross said. "Forget about your eye; just make that clock tick." Bob did, and when he was done, the clock kept time again, showed no trace of the boy's ever having been there. Mr. Gross gave his son a smaller clock, and another smaller still, until Bob had trained himself in fine work, which would be Lorraine Sweeney's best shot at a long life.

On high school vacations, Gross went to central Minnesota, where he worked on a farm. Being in Minnesota drew him to Carleton College, in Northfield, and he enrolled in the fall of 1923 with the idea that he would be a chemist. A Christmas gift changed that. The gift was a Pulitzer Prize–winning biography of the British physician Sir William Osler, written by Harvey W. Cushing, who elevated the crude science of slicing brains into a bona fide specialty, neurosurgery. Cushing was chief of surgery at Boston's Peter Bent Brigham Hospital and a professor at the Harvard Medical School—an imposing man of great international prominence, a fearless innovator and saver of lives. Gross read Cushing's book over a Christmas holiday that he spent, as he did all of his college vacations and breaks, alone in a Carleton dormitory. Gross did not have the money to return to Baltimore to be with his family, which included five sisters and two brothers. From the first day of his freshman year until his graduation, Gross did not go home once.

"The full development of the mental faculties and the appreciation of the fine and artistic cannot be attained when fettered by a diseased or afflicted body," Gross wrote on his application to the Harvard Medical School, filed after Cushing's book moved him to cancel plans to pursue a doctoral degree in chemistry.

> The first step then in a process of education lies in the producing of bodies which are healthy, strong and active. In work with children, it has touched me deeply to realize the handicaps with which many humans start their lives. These observations fire me with a passion to learn the structures of the body, to know its functions, and to study its diseases that I might be able to allay human suffering and thus free individuals to grasp life in its larger meanings.

Gross was no straight-A student. Latin especially troubled him, and only once, in the four semesters he took it, did he get better than a C-minus. Gross pulled A's in English, calculus, physics, psychology, and biology, but in chemistry, his major, his final grades over four years included only one A. In the more competitive era that came later, Gross's grades would have doomed any chance at admission to Harvard Medical. But this was 1927. Gross was president of his student body. He came highly recommended by Lindsey Blayney, the dean of Carleton College, and his essay conveyed powerful emotion, intelligence, and determination.

Gross excelled at Harvard, and it was there he learned his first lesson about the politics of academic medicine: it isn't always who you are or where you've been or what your promise is—it's what the guy on top thinks of you that counts, and ambition and merit and common courtesy may or may not factor into the equation. Gross wasn't long in Boston when he decided he had to meet Cushing, the great doctor he'd admired from afar, and if not meet him, if not actually shake his hand, then at least watch him work. Unobtrusively, the twenty-two-year-old Gross took a seat one day in the visitors' gallery of Cushing's operating room at the Brigham. Cushing watched Gross settle in, saw that he was a stranger—a very young looking stranger, uninvited by the chief to his table.

"What is your name?" the great surgeon asked.

"Robert Gross" was the timid response.

"And what brings you here?"

"I'm a student," Gross said. "I'm in my first year at the Harvard Medical School."

"I will not have students in my room!" Cushing thundered. "Get out! Go! And don't return until you are a real doctor!"

If Gross had dreamed of studying under Cushing, the dream was dashed that day. After graduation, in 1931, Gross learned pathology from S. Burt Wolbach (whose son, William W. Wolbach, future chairman of Children's board of trustees, would have a building at the hospital named for him) and Sidney Farber, the great cancer scientist and one of the men who conceived chemotherapy. He studied surgery at Children's under its chief surgeon, William E. Ladd. Gross—quiet, serious, confident—had promise. Ladd recognized that promise in naming him chief surgical resident at Children's Hospital in 1938.

By that summer, the summer the world was careening toward another war, the secrets of the human body were yielding to surgeons and scientists at an accelerating pace. The lungs, the liver, the kidneys and intestines, the muscles and bones, the genitourinary system, the spinal cord and the brain—doctors were increasingly confident, not simply in explanation and description, but in correction and repair.

But the heart—the ancient seat of the soul, the very symbol of life itself—the heart had barely yielded anything at all. What limited success surgeons had enjoyed involved the peripheral structures: the pulmonary artery; the pericardium, which encases the heart; the myocardium, the middle layer of the wall of the heart. The living human heart had never been successfully opened and closed; not even Gross would dare attempt anything like that, not in 1938. The heart was formidable, unconquerable, many in and out of medicine believed. Perhaps there was a reason nature had designed the heart to be so impregnable: perhaps it was never intended to be touched by human hands.

To Gross, so well grounded in pathology, there was nothing impregnable about a dead heart inside an infant cadaver splayed open atop an autopsy table. There was only endless fascination, the chance to examine tissue in a lesiurely fashion, to chart a course into territory few surgeons had ever contemplated visiting. There was the opportunity for a brilliant mind to dream about conquering the final surgical frontier. Patent ductus arteriosus was a logical place for Gross to begin his journey. The defect was congenital, and it was life threatening, and it was sufficiently common—about one birth in two hundred—that he would never lack for specimens to autopsy. The similarity of dog to human anatomy made animal experimentation credible, and a research culture that had not yet heard the battle cry of *animal rights* made those animals readily available, in unlimited quantities, to anyone who wanted them. Ductus was a distinctive defect, one easily diagnosed—requiring, in most cases, only a stethoscope and a practiced ear.

"The heart action is extremely forceful and overactive and the rate may be increased," Gross wrote. "There is a loud, rough, continuous murmur with systolic accentuation, heard best in the second or third interspace to the left of the sternum. The quality of this murmur has been described as sounding like 'machinery,' 'train in a tunnel,' 'mill wheel' or 'rumbling thunder.' " In the same article, published in the prestigious *Annals of Surgery* and read in May 1939, at a national medical convention, Gross wrote, "A 'buzz' or 'burr' or 'hum' in the chest is frequently spontaneously noticed by the individual. At times the mother will volunteer the information that she feels a 'buzz' (as she calls the thrill) when dressing, bathing or otherwise attending her child."

Like that of his later pupil, Hardy Hendren, Gross's writing married scientific precision to literary polish. He wrote for a medically educated audience, but the layperson with even the most elementary familiarity with anatomy could understand what ductus was.

During fetal life the incomplete expansion of the lungs produces a high resistance to blood flow in the pulmonary vascular bed. It is necessary, therefore, to have a compensatory mechanism whereby blood can be short-circuited around the lungs. Nature provides this shunt in the form of the ductus arteriosus which diverts blood from the pulmonary artery directly into the aorta. When the fetus is born and the lungs expand, the ductus normally closes and all of the blood passes through the lung bed to be aerated. If this vessel fails to close, a reversal of flow takes place within the ductus because pulmonary artery pressure is reduced and aortic pressure is increased. . . . The child or youth who possesses a patent ductus faces an uncertain future. He may live in relatively good health till old age, or his life might be quickly terminated by some complication arising from his long existing lesion.

Like Damocles, he leads a precarious existence, never knowing when he might be cut down by the danger which menaces him.

Although they didn't know how serious things were, before she was two, the Sweeneys suspected there was something wrong with their second daughter. A bright, active baby, she tired easily and was often short of breath. As she got older, she could not play sports, could not keep pace on the playground, could not do anything strenuous without getting winded. Often, Mrs. Sweeney would find her separated from the crowd, standing, her hand over her heart, a frightened look on her face.

"What is it, my baby?" Mrs. Sweeney would ask.

"There's something wrong inside of here," the little girl would whisper.

The Sweeneys knew it was true. Clear across a room, they could hear the buzzing.

By the middle of 1938, Gross felt ready. For two years, he'd worked on the hearts of dead children and living dogs, perfecting his approach, selecting his materials and instruments, settling on his route in through the chest to the ductus. Two years sequestered in the lab, oftentimes alone, as he'd been every vacation at Carleton College. He'd consulted with Paul Dudley White, eminent cardiologist from another Harvard affiliate, the Massachusetts General Hospital. He'd worked closely with John P. Hubbard, a physician with the congenital cardiac clinic at Children's and a strong supporter of Gross. By the middle of 1938, all Gross needed was a candidate.

All he needed was the permission of Ladd, his chief.

But Gross knew the chief would not give that permission. Gross was brilliant, anyone could see that, but Ladd also considered him—well, *reckless* wasn't quite the word. Reckless implied bad results, and no one had better OR results than Bob Gross, who, at the beginning of his career was more accomplished than most surgeons with a lifetime of experience. No, Gross was . . . overly eager. He was, in some respects, too ambitious. Or so Ladd judged. "I'm sorry, Bob," he told his resident; "I'm sorry, but you mustn't do it. Your dog work is all well and good, but for humans . . . it's just too strange. It won't work, Bob. No one touches the heart! Once touched, the patient would almost certainly die."

Gross listened, but he was not convinced. If anything, Ladd's stubbornness fed his obsession, nurtured by infant cadavers. By the middle of 1938, Gross could wait no longer. He was losing sleep, so fired up was he about this new idea. When Ladd left Boston on vacation that summer, Gross knew that when the right child came along, he would operate. He would not tell Ladd. He would go ahead and deal with his chief later.

On August 17, 1938, patient number 196163 was admitted to Children's Hospital. Along with Lorraine Sweeney that day came two children with hernias, a child with cellulitis, and a child with acute appendicitis. Gross would operate on some of them, expertly if perfunctorily. He would be taken with Lorraine. He would sit her on his lap, hold her hand, smile in a way he rarely smiled at adults and tell her she was going to be all right. He explored her medical history, weighed her, took her blood pressure and pulse, conducted X-ray and fluoroscopic examinations and electrocardiography.

Mostly, he listened to her heart. He listened while she was sitting. He listened while she was lying down. He listened after he'd had her run up and down flights of stairs. To his ear, Lorraine's heart sounded like machinery, like something he'd taken apart as a kid.

Brahms's "Lullaby" played.

"We're going to make you brand-new," Gross whispered to this little girl of whom he was so fond.

Soon, Lorraine was asleep. Lank put away her music box, and Gross got down to business.

Working without speaking, working with that one good eye, he made an incision that followed the lower curve of her left breast and continued down through fat and muscle until he'd reached her third rib, attached by cartilage to her sternum. He cut the cartilage, pulled back the rib, and moved it out of the way with a retractor. His work in the dog lab told him Lorraine's left lung should collapse, and it did, providing good access to the heart. To protect the lung, Gross covered it with moist gauze. Then he cut through the pleura, a membrane that lines the chest wall. Carefully separating vessels and nerves, he found the ductus, a small, stubby tube about a third of an inch wide and less than a quarter of an inch long.

Placing a finger on Lorraine's ductus, he could feel the buzz—strong, continuous, frightfully abnormal. With a sterile stethoscope, he listened. What a sound! What a signal of distress! Not a buzzing now that his ear was almost literally on her soul, not a hum, but a monster of a noise—an explosive, angry roar. *Like a large volume of steam escaping in a closed room*, Gross thought as he got ready to shut it off.

Putting the stethoscope away, Gross dissected the tissue and nerve that cradled the ductus. He was handed a length of heavy braided silk ligature. Threading it with a needle, he looped it around the ductus and tied a tight knot. The ductus was closed. Gross watched, aware that his future depended on what happened next.

What happened was nothing. No buzz. No escape of steam. No cardiac arrest. Glorious nothing! Blood now flowed through Lorraine's body on the proper course.

That night, Lank and Gross and a few others celebrated over dinner. Ladd would explode when he returned. He would explode again the next year when Gross mentioned his operation during a speech at a scientific forum at Children's seventieth anniversary celebration—and newspaper reporters covering the festivities featured the young surgeon prominently in their accounts. NEW HEART OPERATION IS ANNOUNCED, read the headline over a front-page story in the June 10, 1939, *Boston Traveler*. HAS REMEDY was the headline over a picture of Gross in the next day's Boston *Sunday Post;* ". . . a new treatment for a certain type of hitherto hopeless heart ailment in children," read the caption beneath the photograph. A rift between Ladd and Gross would develop that would never heal. But tonight—tonight Gross could toast Lorraine Sweeney and a pack of mongrel dogs from a sympathetic animal shelter. Without those dogs, Lorraine might have died. And thousands like her in decades to come might have gone to early graves as well.

Mrs. Sweeney thanked Gross. Mrs. Sweeney thanked God. "God closes one door and opens another," she said, and what she had in mind was her husband, Daniel. Like so many of Children's patients—all the way back to the first, Ellen McCarthy, who was also seven—Lorraine was the child of Irish immigrants. Daniel and Mary Ellen Sweeney had emigrated from their native Ireland in the early part of the century. Daniel was an elevator repairman, a good husband and father. He was on his way home from shopping when he was struck and killed by a car one evening six months before Lorraine's operation.

The day after her operation, Lorraine was sitting in a chair, smiling for Dr. Gross's camera as she held her doll. By the third day, she was walking. On September 8, almost two weeks after her surgery, she was well enough to be transferred to a convalescent home that Children's operated in Wellesley, a rural community west of Boston. The home had formerly been used for tuberculosis patients, for whom sunlight and air were considered curative. The belief in the healing power of freshness had survived into 1938, and Lorraine spent much of her recuperation lying outside in the sun, attired, on Indian summer days, in nothing but underwear. On September 29, she went home. In time, she would marry and have children and become a grandmother. She would become a spokesperson for the Heart Association. She and Gross would remain in touch until Gross died, in October 1988. No matter how little contact there'd been during the rest of the year, the two would correspond faithfully every Valentine's Day.

"You know, Lorraine," Gross said when she visited him at his retirement home, "if you hadn't made it, I might have ended up here in Vermont as a chicken farmer."

Before he died, Gross would be honored with medals. He would receive honorary degrees and written tributes. He would be the distinguished guest at testimonial dinners. A chair in his name would be established at the Harvard Medical School. And the first person to hold the Robert E. Gross Professorship of Surgery would be Hardy Hendren.

Hendren could not remember a time, not even in the farthest reaches of his midwestern childhood, when he'd seriously wanted to be anything but a surgeon. Surgeons helped people. Surgeons were their own bosses. Surgeons always had work, which meant a great deal to a child of the Great Depression. Surgeons had an extraordinary grasp of anatomy, an endlessly interesting subject. They were intrigued by the harmony of organs and systems that make the creature work. In Kansas City, Missouri, his hometown, Hendren had lived near Loose Park, site of the Battle of Westport, a minor engagement of the Civil War. There was a pond in Loose Park, lily padded and home to frogs. One day when he was in the fourth grade, Hendren caught a tadpole.

I wonder what it looks like inside? he thought as he held it, wriggling, in his hand. *Why not cut it open and see?*

With his pocketknife, Hendren did, there on the banks of a pond on a spring day in 1936. *There's the blood. That part beating there must be the heart. Look at the veins.* Never mind that when he went home for lunch, his mother had cooked macaroni, creating an unfortunate association with tadpole intestines that kept pasta off his plate for decades. Something else that would last had been created, too.

After grammar school, Hendren went one year to Kansas City's Southwest High School, then to Woodberry Forest, a college-preparatory school in Virginia. War postponed his medical education. Hendren wanted to be a fighter pilot, and after a semester at Dartmouth College, the Navy took him. He was seventeen. America's mounting successes slowed pilot training, and war's end gave candidates a free ticket out, but Hendren had set a goal: he wanted his wings. In October 1946, after repeated landings on an aircraft carrier, he got them. He was a naval aviator. From then on, his certificate would hang next to his burgeoning collection of diplomas and awards.

Hendren returned to Dartmouth, graduated with honors, and then completed Dartmouth's medical program, which at the time was only two years. He was accepted as one of eight transfer students from Dartmouth who joined the Harvard Medical School's class of 1952. In the summer of 1950, Hendren, his almost-three-year-old daughter, and his young wife, who was pregnant with their second child, Douglas, left Hanover, New Hampshire, for Boston.

The class of '52 was mostly male and mostly white, and more than a few members had a *Jr.* or a *III* affixed to their names. Affirmative action, consumer rights, Medicaid, medical-malpractice attorneys who hawk their services on TV—all of that belonged to a world that did not exist. In 1950, the physician was still firmly on his pedestal, and the Harvard physician—he was somewhat higher, somewhat closer to God.

The belief in invincibility, if not immortality, suffused Hendren's class. In this respect, these doctors-to-be were not so very different from their countrymen. America had won a war. Its economy was the engine that powered the very world, and its culture was imitated everywhere, the highest compliment a people could be paid. Early in the century, U.S. medicine had pretty much followed Europe's lead, but now, wedded to a technology that rejected the concept of limits, it was setting the pace. London and Berlin and Vienna were no longer the places to be; Philadelphia and Baltimore and New York and Boston, especially Boston, were. Boston had the Harvard Medical School, and on its faculty were many great scientists, including three from Children's: Gross, Farber, and John F. Enders, whose cultivation of the polio virus led to a vaccine and a Nobel Prize in medicine. In July 1918, twenty-eight years before Hendren earned his wings, Enders had become America's eight-hundred-and-ninety-first naval aviator, a fact he recalled with pride throughout his distinguished research career.

In this era, in this environment, you could not be anything but cocksure. You were good, and you knew you were good, and you knew that the greater society, seeing that Harvard diploma on your office wall, hearing that Harvard accent, with its calculated inflection, would know you were good, too. Even in this crowd, Hendren stood out. Never lacking in confidence, he'd left the Navy with more than wings. He'd left with a pluck and poise that enveloped those who came near him. Hendren did not have charisma, not in the movie-screen or political sense, nothing Kennedyesque, but he had a sense of humor and impeccable manners and speech, and he never had any trouble filling whatever space he happened to be in.

In the fall of 1951, his senior year, Hendren took on the medical establishment. What provoked him was the system by which medical-school seniors wound up in the hospitals where they served their internships. To all intents and purposes, there was no system. Students were free to apply wherever they wanted. Hospitals were free to recruit. In a profession priding itself on its order and control, serendipity ruled. "As long as both hospitals and students have to go through the last-minute rush of not knowing whether places will be available or will be filled, there will be instances of pressure and unfairness and consequent disappointment in the selection process," the National Interassociation Committee on Internships, or NICI, a professional group of doctors and administrators, wrote in announcing the creation of a new plan to match students' preferences with hospitals'.

The new plan was to take effect in the 1951–52 academic year. Hendren and the sixty-two hundred other medical-school seniors nationwide would be the first students whose internships would be decided accordingly. On paper, the plan looked equitable enough. Each student would compile a list of hospitals, ranked in descending order of preference. In turn, each hospital would rank the students it sought. The lists would be compared several times, each successive time being called a run, until each student was matched to a hospital.

One of the big supporters of the new plan was the dean of the Harvard Medical School, George Packer Berry, who, perhaps inevitably, had been tagged with the nickname Pecker-Berry. At a meeting of the entire senior class in the fall of 1951, Berry, a bacteriologist by training, outlined the plan. Hendren listened to Berry's explanation, which lasted half an hour. The more he listened, the more he saw flaws. The first run, Hendren concluded, was fair: students' first choices were matched with hospitals' first choices, and everyone went away happy. But the way the second run had been structured, Hendren believed, was weighted against the best students. On the second run, a less highly ranked student would be matched with a highly desirable hospital if that student had placed the hospital at the top of his list. And that hospital, now filled with "alternates," would no longer be available to a highly ranked student who'd placed it second on his list and had not been accepted by his first choice. *Pandemonium would ensue!*

Hendren rose to speak. He hadn't gotten far when the dean cut in on him. Why, the plan as proposed was a brilliant piece of work! Dean Berry didn't know who this Hardy Hendren was, but he didn't like his attitude. Who was he, anyway, questioning the dean of the Harvard Medical School?

"Excuse me, sir," Hendren said. "I don't want to be disrespectful, but you've had thirty minutes to talk here without interruption, and I need five minutes to explain this without being interrupted."

Hendren went to the blackboard and drew a diagram of how he would revise the plan.

Again Berry challenged him.

"Well, excuse me, sir," Hendren said; "let me sample the entire senior class, here in the room. Is there anybody that doesn't agree with what I've just said?"

There wasn't.

The assistant dean, Reginald Fitz, a medical historian, turned to Berry and said, in a whisper loud enough for the whole room to hear, "I think this young man may have something here."

Berry was incensed. "I don't give a good goddamn if any of you get your internships," he said as he stormed out. "I have spent three years working on this concept, and we have spent $100,000 of funds, and it's your responsibility now!"

What a windbag! Hendren thought. *What an arrogant man this Pecker-Berry is!*

He was not alone in his thoughts. After the meeting, Hendren got together with a group of seven other students. Calling themselves the National Student Internship Committee, the eight decided to take on Berry and his plan. On October 17, 1951, the committee presented a three-page letter to Berry. Point by point, the letter detailed the committee's objections and then outlined a better way to organize the match.

Berry was even more incensed. But the students were playing for keeps now. Borrowing three thousand dollars from his father, Hendren hired a secretary to help with correspondence. Polling every medical school in the country, the committee of eight found that the great majority supported the proposed modifications. A meeting of student delegates was held in New York City. NICI was persuaded. On November 9, 1951, the matching plan was changed to reflect the students' wishes.

Berry was not amused, nor was he convinced the modified plan would work. On the night before the first matches were to be made, in March 1952, he told Hendren that his career at the Harvard Medical School was finished if there was any problem, even the slightest little problem, with the maiden run.

There wasn't. For forty years, the system Hendren and his group refined has been used for internships. Recently, it has been expanded to handle most residency programs as well.

In the fall of 1950, Gross lectured to a class of third-year students at the Harvard Medical School. He spoke of an emerging new discipline, pediatric surgery, and his contributions to it: among them, repair of patent ductus arteriosus, the operation that had inaugurated modern heart surgery. Gross was now surgeon-in-chief at Children's, having replaced Ladd, who retired from that post in 1945. Gross also was William E. Ladd Professor of Children's Surgery at the Harvard Medical School, the first such chair in the nation.

What a figure Gross cut, with his red bow tie and starched white lab coat and spit-polished shoes and perfectly slicked hair. How he spoke—eloquent, educated, totally in command of his audience, this bunch of Harvardians. A true giant in their midst. Not only had Gross done the ductus, but he'd also shown the world (together with Clarence Crafoord of Stockholm) how to repair another major heart defect, coarctation of the aorta. Exciting things were happening in Gross's lab. Surgeons from all over the world were coming to watch him work. Patients were traveling thousands of miles to have him operate. He had published nearly one hundred scientific papers on the heart, gallbladder, pancreas, anus, rectum, intestines, lungs, nerves, liver, esophagus, urethra, kidneys, arteries, and veins. By the age of thirty-six, he'd written, with Ladd, a surgical textbook, *Abdominal Surgery of Infancy and Childhood.* Even as he spoke to Hendren's class, he was at work on a text of his own, *Surgery of Infancy and Childhood,* first published in 1953 and every one of its exactly one thousand pages written by him and him alone. If any book established pediatric surgery as a legitimate specialty, this was it. Translated into several languages, the text would sell more than forty thousand copies, remarkable in light of both the topic and the time. It was a monumental work, still occasionally consulted, one of the last single-author texts covering so vast a field. Before long, medicine would become too complex, too technologically sophisticated, too steeped in vital minutiae for any mind, even a mind as brilliant as Gross's, to master so sweeping a subject—and then to elucidate it so articulately. The age of subspecialties was already on the horizon.

Hendren knew, listening to Gross, that he wanted pediatric surgery. He knew that he wanted to study under Gross. He did not know, nor would he for years, how complicated Gross was, how utterly inscrutable and contradictory, how unpredictable. But Hendren would learn, ultimately the hard way, and his lesson would send him into a sort of exile.

When he returned, twenty-two years later, he would be the world's expert at rebuilding children like Lucy Moore.

Chapter 6

Beth kept coming back to the deer.

Everywhere she looked, and she left few stones unturned, she saw deer. They carried the ticks that harbored the bacteria that had caused her Lyme disease, which had been diagnosed in the first trimester of her pregnancy with Lucy. In her search for what had deformed her daughter, Lyme disease would lead Beth's list of suspects.

They were so tame, she thought, *so pretty and tame. Straight from a Walt Disney cartoon.*

White-tailed deer were the unlikely scourge of Westchester County, where the Moores had lived during the first two thirds of Beth's pregnancy. Lacking natural predators, protected from humans during all but a brief hunting season, during which the bow and arrow constituted the only legal weapon, deer had found Westchester County's woods much to their liking. And if they had stayed in the woods, if they had been closer in temperament to Bambi than Godzilla, perhaps they wouldn't have been a problem. But they did not stick to woods. Westchester deer got into gardens and backyards. They went after apple trees and sweet corn and tulips and yew. They darted in front of cars, especially at night. Cornell University, which studied the problem, estimated that it would cost millions to replace just the garden plants alone in northern Westchester County. Damage to autos cost hundreds of thousands of dollars more every year.

The Moores lived on five acres, much of it wetlands, which deer favor. Their house abutted a wooded hill, and stone steps led down the hill into their yard. On misty mornings, when their property was pretty enough to have graced the pages of *Country Living,* the deer would descend those steps and head for the Moores' rhododendrons, a year-round treat. Finished with their meal, the animals would sometimes mosey up to the Moores' deck. Sometimes the Moores would look out a window and see them, tawny and beautiful. Sometimes the family saw their calling cards: droppings on the lawn. Occasionally they spotted something else they left behind—ticks, no bigger than a period on the printed page—crawling across the deck.

Until the 1970s, when reports of this never-before-described disease began to crop up in the medical literature, Lyme disease did not have a name. As more and more cases came to light in the area where it was first reported—the vicinity of Lyme, Connecticut—it got one. Word of the disease spread, and by 1989, the year Beth became pregnant with Lucy, cases had been identified in all regions of the United States as well as in Europe, Asia, Africa, and Australia. Lyme was not a merciless killer, not like AIDS, another epidemiological newcomer of the time. But neither was Lyme benign. Innocuous at first, producing nothing but a rash that resembles a bull's eye, the disease can lead to fever, chills, aching joints, stiff neck, confusion, fatigue, and hallucinations. In its late stages, Lyme can badly damage the heart, the joints, the central nervous system, the liver, and other systems. Its effect on the unborn has not been scientifically established, but Lyme is increasingly implicated as a cause of birth defects.

Like everyone in Westchester in 1989, the Moores knew about Lyme. They knew it was spread by bacteria that lived inside ticks. They knew the ticks were parasites and white-tailed deer were their favorite hosts. Those graceful, wild creatures you'd see out your window—they were probably crawling with ticks. Before going near the woods, Beth and Jack made sure they and their children took the proper precautions: long socks, long pants, and long-sleeved shirts. After any time outside, the parents carefully checked themselves and the children for ticks.

Westchester was plagued. In 1983, the first year the Westchester County Department of Health began keeping track, 48 cases of

Lyme were reported. The next year, the number rose to 175. Five years later, 1989, the year of Beth's pregnancy, 2,745 cases were reported. Universities and governments studied the situation. Support groups formed. Paradise had been invaded.

Beth's prenatal care was mostly handled by a group practice in Mount Kisco, New York. On her first visit, a doctor took the usual history and ordered the usual tests, including a sonogram. The doctor also inquired about Lyme; the causative bacteria, the doctor knew, could cross the placenta. Beth didn't recall having had symptoms. But Lyme doesn't necessarily fire with both barrels. The unbloated tick is tiny, the rash it leaves not always recognized, the symptoms not always severe. Some of them—fatigue, for example—can blend into the discomfort of early pregnancy, when a mother's body is no longer solely her own.

Beth tested positive for Lyme. Penicillin was prescribed. And she never did develop symptoms.

Deer, Beth would think during the 1989 Christmas holidays, when Lucy's survival was no longer in doubt, though her future as a fully functioning human being was. *Those goddamn deer.*

But deer were not the only possibility that ran through her mind and ran through Jack's mind.

Was it something I ate? Beth thought. On an overseas trip early in her pregnancy, Beth had tried steak tartare. Maybe something in the raw meat was to blame.

Something I drank? On the same trip, she'd tasted some of the wines Jack had under consideration for import.

What about the gypsy moths? In New York, there'd been a problem with gypsy-moth caterpillars, which are leaf eaters with appetites capable of turning trees into skeletons overnight. Skeletonized trees not in the spirit of Westchester County, which calls itself the Golden Apple of New York State, many residents hired private contractors to spray their trees. In her mind's eye, Beth could still see the signs tacked to neighbors' property, announcing the presence of pesticides.

Maybe it was the genes. But no one on either side of the family, Beth's or Jack's, had had birth defects.

How could this happen?

Science could not say. No one knows what causes VACTERL association and cloaca, only that these defects arise in the first six to eight weeks of life, when the embryo is smaller than a penny and vulnerable to mutation. Beyond that fact, there are only questions. Maybe the cause of Lucy's problems was a bacterium spread by a tick that had visited their backyard, as Beth suspected. Maybe the cause was a virus or an environmental agent or a haywire gene or some combination of the three—or something else entirely, something with greater, cosmic meaning.

"Sometimes God entrusts us with a special gift from heaven," Sharon K. Light, of Oklahoma, the mother of one of Hardy Hendren's most difficult cloaca patients, wrote in a book she published, *Still a Miracle*. "This gift of life may require more from the one that brings them into this world. This gift will need special love and understanding. I am prone to believe that these special babies that are born with birth defects hold an even greater place in God's heart. Since I am a mother of a child with multiple birth defects, I believe that these babies are special to God in a real and definite way."

Beth's philosophy was shaded more toward the secular. But like Sharon Light's, it acknowledged the existence of some higher power, some greater plan.

I've always been fortunate, Beth had thought during her pregnancy. *So we're getting shit on now—big deal. Whatever this child is she will enrich our lives. This child is going to have it made because she's coming into this family. We can take this. Our marriage can survive this. Our family can survive.*

Jack thought often of his father's words: *God never gives you more than you can handle.* For whatever short period she's here, Jack believed, it will be a positive experience.

By December 1989, cause was academic.

Lucy was here now. Lucy was demanding. Lucy needed constant attention and observation, constant trips to the pediatrician. She wore diapers that collected the urine that seeped out of that solitary hole in her bottom. She had a bag capping her stoma, and the bag was gross but not as gross as what happened four days before Christmas.

Lucy's initial stay at All Children's had been complicated by prolapse of her stoma, one of many possible problems when intestines meet the outside world through a man-made hole. A transverse colostomy, which Lucy had, is particularly susceptible to prolapse. It is not a pretty sight, a prolapse. The intestine, raw looking and red and sometimes bleeding, seems to be growing out of its owner—seems to be trying to unhook itself and squirm free of the belly that's holding it back. As sickening as it looks, a prolapse is rarely life threatening, as long as medical attention is speedily provided.

Lucy's prolapse occurred on December 1, a week after Richard Harmel had performed a colostomy. Lucy had not yet been discharged from All Children's, so it was a simple matter to return her to the operating room, where Harmel put in another set of sutures. "This had the effect of anchoring the prolapse at this point," the surgeon wrote in Lucy's record, "and hopefully should prevent further prolapse."

Once Lucy came home, on December 7, Beth fixated on that possibility. She knew pressure in Lucy's abdomen—the kind of pressure brought on by crying or coughing—could activate the forces that might set that intestine on the march again. In Lucy's first days at home, prolapse served as a lightning rod for Beth's anxieties. *What if she starts crying and her body convulses and that forces it out again? What if I can't get to a doctor fast? Would I be able to push it back in? Would it keep growing longer and longer? What would I do?*

Beth thought she knew the answer: *I wouldn't be able to handle it. I'd freak out.*

On December 21, as Beth was driving on a Florida freeway, Lucy with her in the car, the baby started to cry.

"Shhh," Beth said.

But Lucy could not be quieted. Her crying only got worse.

"Shhh, Momma's baby," Beth said.

Lucy cried. And Beth was thinking *prolapse.* And Beth was thinking, *I have to hold her. I have to calm her down. If I don't, it's going to happen, I just know it is.* Beth looked for a place to pull over safely, but there wasn't one. She was getting nutty now. It was starting to feel like the drive back from Yale, the walls closing in on her again, the world going by in a dangerous blur.

Beth made it home. She changed Lucy's diaper and then gently peeled off her baby's colostomy bag, a plastic device that attaches to the abdomen with special adhesive.

Lucy's stoma had prolapsed.

And not a prolapse like before, not a thumbnail's length of intestine sticking out. Like some alien life form, three or four inches of Lucy's bowel had wriggled free.

"Oh my God, no," Beth said. "No, no, no, no, no!"

She lay her head against Lucy and said, "I can't do it anymore. I just can't take it again."

But she could. She bundled up her baby, and she and Jack brought their daughter back to All Children's.

Given the size of the vessels, it is not always easy to draw blood from an infant. It is not always easy to get a line into an artery or a vein. But certain infants, Lucy among them, are not just difficult to stick; they are a nightmare. Lucy's arms and legs, so chubby and cute, were ideal places for vessels to hide. So much baby fat! And those few vessels that were not concealed—those had been found on Lucy's first hospitalization, and now they were scarred, narrowed to next to nothing. With babies like Lucy, getting a preoperative blood sample can take half an hour or more. It means trying this vessel and that one and this other one here, and now maybe we'll have luck with the other arm or one of her feet, and I think if we just squeeze a bit we'll be all set, . . . *and please, sweet Jesus, just give us blood.* It is a process made even more difficult by the infant's response: one long, convulsing bawl that has a profoundly disturbing effect on parents and many professionals.

As the nurse hunted for blood, Beth held Lucy. Jack was furious. He couldn't believe what he was witnessing.

Lucy's cries quickly became screams, which had the predictable effect on her prolapsed bowel. Inch by inch, scream by scream, it was emerging, oozing and red.

Beth was holding it.

There were four, five, six inches of it.

Beth was trying to get it back in.

"Stop!" she hollered. "She's turning inside out. This is like a sci-fi movie. Get a doctor in here to convince me you need blood before surgery. Look what you're doing!"

A doctor was summoned, and the doctor explained that, indeed, they had to have the blood. Lucy's safety in the OR was at stake.

"All right," Beth said. "Do what you have to do. But please just get it over with. *Please.*"

The nurse continued. Finally she got enough blood.

For the third time, Harmel took Lucy into his OR.

His original operation had been a loop colostomy: a section of colon had been brought to the surface and slit, but not cut clear through, not cut in two, only crimped and opened. Still connected, both sections of her colon—the upper end, which connected to her small intestine, and the lower end, which trailed off to where her anus should have been—exited her belly through a single stoma.

But a loop colostomy had failed twice; it made no sense to give it a third try. In difficult cases like this, the standard strategy is to cut the intestine clean in two and bring each end to the surface through separate holes. Two stomata are a better anchor for an uncooperative colon than one is. And this is what Harmel did: a divided colostomy.

This time when Lucy was discharged from the hospital, on Christmas Eve, she went home with two holes in her belly. One did what the original stoma had done: discharged feces, the by-product of normal digestion, into a bag. The other was connected to that length of intestine that dead-ended inside her. That piece, supposedly dormant now, was described to the Moores as a mucous fistula. It would discharge mucus, the Moores were told. But it wouldn't be a big deal. They probably could handle it with a Band-Aid. The Moores stocked up on Band-Aids and prayed for Lucy to be spared a third prolapse.

Even before Prolapse, Part Two: The Nightmare, the Moores had been looking ahead. Lucy's heart had to be fixed eventually, but they'd come to the conclusion that that was the less immediate of the two major hurdles facing their daughter now. Many surgeons could do open-heart. The biggest challenge, in their view, was lining up someone to fix her cloaca.

The Moores had no quibble with All Children's. It was a fine institution, and Harmel was a board-certified pediatric surgeon, but they wanted to know what else was out there. They wanted the absolute best. They were consumers making their most important investment ever: their daughter's future. They knew it depended almost entirely on a surgeon's skill. They knew that skill would have to be unsurpassed if Lucy were to have a shot, any shot at all, at ever being normal. They would be very careful in their search, very demanding. They knew enough about medicine to suspect that there were those who would grab a case like Lucy's with little but their ego to offer as qualification. What a paper she'd be if the results were good! Imagine how the before and after slides would look, projected before a packed audience at some major meeting. And if the results weren't so hot, if somehow the whole thing wound up in court—*Well, Your Honor, may we remind the jury just how bad things were to start? Without meaning to be insensitive, have you ever seen such a twisted anatomy?*

In the Moores' discussions with friends and relatives and physicians—everyone had an opinion; everyone had advice; everyone went running for the medical texts and journals—the name Boston Children's Hospital kept cropping up. So did the name of a doctor: Hardy Hendren. The literature told of a man who had stationed himself on the edge, where nature's worst mistakes taunt medicine's best minds. Starting with bad tissue, or with misplaced or missing tissue, or with tissue mutilated by someone else, Hendren sifted through grotesque confusion and then set about rebuilding people. Here was a man for whom nothing was too weird or too hopeless. If medicine were law, the Moores decided, Hendren's operating room certainly would be the court of last resort.

Boston is the mecca, Beth concluded. *And this is the guy who has literally written the book.*

The Moores were not the first to discover Hendren on their own. Although he has worked diligently to build a referral system and he now has doctors around the world pleased to recommend him, Hendren, since his days as a resident at Children's, has had his reputation and his writings cast out there like a net. His patients talk about him. His published papers, well over 150 in all, speak for him, as do the more than sixty chapters he contributed to numerous textbooks. The occasional newspaper piece and television appearance have brought him patients, too.

Hendren has never sought publicity—he has made no secret of his distrust of the popular media, which, he believes, lack the kind of attention to detail and power of concentration that is the hallmark of his work—but there have been times when he could not avoid the spotlight. One occasion was in 1990, when he testified for the prosecution against a Christian Scientist couple accused, and ultimately convicted, of manslaughter for relying on prayer when their son was dying as a result of an obstructed bowel. (Hendren agreed to testify only when assured by his friend John A. Kiernan, the special prosecutor, that the goal of the case was not to punish already grieving parents but to establish case law that might motivate Christian Scientists to seek medical attention for a critically ill child. The judge imposed ten years' probation, a sentence that satisfied both Kiernan and Hendren.) Another occasion when Hendren found himself in the spotlight was in 1969, when he separated a set of Siamese twins, both of whom lived. Television and print accounts of the operation, the first such in Boston's rich surgical history, went worldwide.

Some patients show up unannounced at Hendren's door. Some track him down at conferences. Others have had the good fortune of being selected for presentation as difficult cases in the dozens of cities in the United States and abroad where, as visiting professor, Hendren has lectured and then gone into the OR to show his hosts how it's done.

Some, like Scott Cormier, have come to Hendren through chance encounter.

Scott was thirteen and living in Wilkes-Barre, Pennsylvania, on September 22, 1975, the day he decided to take the shortcut home from a friend's house. The shortcut was the tracks. Trains ran pretty regularly through Wilkes-Barre, and Scott didn't have to wait long for a freight that was headed his way. He jumped onto a boxcar and hung off the side. He didn't see the signal lamp coming. It caught him on his right side and knocked him to the tracks, leaving him unconscious. When he came to, he was dazed. His right arm felt strange. He tried to move his hand and fingers but couldn't. He was bleeding at a point about three inches above the elbow, where the bone was broken in two. Vessels, nerves, muscle—all were shorn. All that connected the rest of his arm to him was a thin bridge of skin.

Somehow, Scott got to his feet. Holding the severed limb in his left hand, he managed to walk, managed to find a house. A woman came to the door.

That was Scott's first stroke of luck that day.

The woman was Helen Igo, who happened to be a retired nurse.

Scott was no longer bleeding much; after an amputation like his, the major vessels typically contract and close, the body's defense

against hemorrhaging to death in minutes. Using a towel as a tourniquet, Igo stopped what bleeding was left. She called an ambulance,
which took Scott to Mercy Hospital, where an IV was started, and
life-saving fluids were given, and the wound was cleaned and bandaged, and Scott's arm was packed in ice and encased in a brown
plastic trash bag. Scott would not die, but that mangled arm—the
good folks in Wilkes-Barre did not have the skill to reattach a limb.
Vincent A. Drapiewski, a doctor in Mercy's emergency room,
figured doctors in Boston might. He called the Massachusetts General Hospital, where, in a highly publicized case thirteen years
earlier, surgeons had reattached an arm lost by a boy in a train
accident strikingly similar to Scott's. Yes, Drapiewski was told, the
General would take Scott. But time was critical. The longer the arm
was away from the boy, the less the chance his body would accept
it back. A call was placed to the Wilkes-Barre–Scranton airport.
Were there any scheduled flights for Boston?

That was Scott's second stroke of luck. An Allegheny Airlines
flight was bound for Boston. But it was now six twenty-five P.M. The
flight was already boarded and cleared for departure.

"Hold that plane!" the Wilkes-Barre team said. "We have a
patient who's headed for the Massachusetts General Hospital."

Scott's third stroke of luck was Hardy Hendren.

Hendren was on the plane, a DC-9, returning home from a meeting. He was in the first row on the right, wondering what in heck
the delay was, when the pilot, Captain Clifford R. Barraclough of
Bethel Park, Pennsylvania, asked him if he would mind moving.
They had a badly injured child they had to get on board, and where
Hendren was sitting—facing a reading table installed in the first row
on this particular model of the DC-9—was the best place for the
stretcher to fit.

Of course he wouldn't mind, Hendren told Barraclough.

"In fact," he said, "I'm a doctor. Maybe I can help. What's
wrong with the boy?"

"He lost an arm," the captain said.

"And where are you taking him?"

"To Boston."

"What a coincidence!" Hendren said. "I'm the chief of pediatric
surgery at the Massachusetts General Hospital."

Hendren helped unscrew the table from the floor, and when
Cormier arrived, by helicopter from Mercy Hospital, he helped get

the boy on board. As Barraclough prepared for takeoff, Hendren asked if there was any way to call ahead to the Massachusetts General Hospital. Yes, the pilot said, they could get a message through by radio. Samuel Kim, Hendren's associate, was contacted. Kim would have everything ready. He would contact two surgeons to participate in the operation: the orthopedist Richard J. Smith and Ronald A. Malt, who as a chief surgical resident in May 1962 had been part of the first team at the General to successfully re-attach a severed arm.

Before taking off, Barraclough was busy on the radio, arranging with flight controllers for speedy passage through the Northeast corridor, one of the nation's busiest air-traffic zones. Given a straight route at an unusually low altitude, Barraclough flew at nearly 550 miles per hour, well past the speed limit for a Wilkes-Barre to Boston run. When the DC-9 touched down at Boston's Logan International Airport, an ambulance was waiting. With the assistance of Malt and Smith, Hendren performed a seven-hour operation that ended, at three-thirty A.M. on September 23, 1975, with Scott getting his right arm back. Seventeen years later, Scott would have 90-percent use of it. He would drive tractor trailers for a living.

"You talk about miracles," Scott's mother said. "That was a miracle."

Before calling Boston, the Moores went to Harmel.

Although nothing was firm yet, the Saint Petersburg surgeon had assumed he would be the one to rebuild Lucy, the first cloaca patient he'd seen in Florida. Harmel did not have broad experience with cloacas, but he had some. At Children's Hospital in Columbus, Ohio, his previous post, he'd reconstructed a cloaca patient of his own and assisted with others. He was well-read on the subject. At meetings, he'd heard other surgeons, including Hendren, speak.

"I don't mean to insult you or hurt your feelings," Beth said, "but we've chosen somebody else to do the reconstruction."

"May I ask who?" Harmel said.

"Dr. Hardy Hendren, in Boston," Beth said. "Do you know him?"

"I trained under him," Harmel said. "Without a doubt, he would be the most proficient in the country for Lucy."

Shortly after Christmas, Beth dialed Hendren's office.

What if he's not taking new patients? she wondered. *What if he doesn't accept our insurance? What if he doesn't take patients from so far away? What if . . . ?*

Even before meeting him, Beth had a *feeling*. That was the only way to describe it, just a feeling, strong and instinctive. The feeling told her that if she got to Boston, she would like this surgeon, this chief, whatever his personality—and she suspected that all the personalities at this level of medicine, the very top, were fire and ice. The feeling told Beth that if he agreed to take the case, Hardy Hendren would be able to fix Lucy.

"Dr. Hendren's office," the voice in Boston said.

Beth explained who she was and what she wanted. "Yes," said Barbara Cosgrove, one of Hendren's secretaries, "Dr. Hendren would be glad to see you, just not quite so soon; the best time would be when your daughter's a few months older. Meanwhile, have Dr. Harmel send his records." Before hanging up, Beth asked Cosgrove's help in coordinating scheduling with another doctor at Children's: Aldo R. Castaneda, a heart surgeon. In their search for Hendren, Beth and Jack had looked for someone to fix Lucy's heart, too. They'd learned they don't come any better than Castaneda, who inherited Robert E. Gross's job at Children's when Gross retired in 1972.

Barbara put the Moores down for an August 1, 1990, visit with Hendren. Open-heart surgery was scheduled for May 17.

Chapter 7

On May 15, 1869, readers of *The Christian Register,* a Boston newspaper, were treated to a passage by Charles Dickens. In his wanderings through London, Dickens had stumbled onto something.

"I found the Children's Hospital established in an old sail loft or storehouse, of the roughest nature, and on the simplest means," the novelist wrote.

> In its seven-and-thirty beds I saw but little beauty, for starvation in the second or third generation takes a pinched look; but I saw the sufferings both of infancy and childhood tenderly assuaged; I heard the little patients answering to pet, playful names, the light touch of a delicate lady laid bare the wasted sticks of arms for me to pity; and the claw-like little hands, as she did so, twined themselves lovingly around her wedding ring.
>
> One baby mite there was as pretty as any of Raphael's angels. The tiny head was bandaged for water on the brain, and it was suffering with acute bronchitis, too, and made from time to time a plaintive, though not impatient or complaining, little sound. The smooth curve of the cheeks and of the chin was faultless in its condensation of infantine beauty, and the large bright eyes were most lovely. It happened, as I stopped at the foot of the bed, that these eyes rested upon mine with that wistful expression of wondering thoughtfulness which we all know sometimes in very little children. They remained fixed on mine, and never turned from me while I stood there. When the utterance of that

plaintive sound shook the little form, the gaze still remained un-changed. I felt as though the child implored me to tell the story of the little hospital in which it was sheltered to any gentle heart I could address.

Reprinted from his London magazine, *All the Year Round*, Dickens's essay was but one of many voices enlisted in a campaign being waged in Boston for the establishment of a free hospital for poor sick children. The campaign played out in newspapers, in State House speeches, in the drawing rooms of certain society ladies who embraced the idea as a noble and worthy crusade, one that would heal bodies—and minister to souls as well. "You can each do a part towards making these poor little ones happy," one lady of standing wrote to *The Register* after visiting a New York hospital, where she'd visited a children's ward that boasted of a chapel, a caged canary, and red balloons tied to the beds. "Playthings, no matter how small; a few flowers, even a kind word, can be taken, and will do much to cheer the heart of a child suffering and longing for sympathy. And you all know how Jesus Christ loved little children and called them his lambs; and how, for his sake, we should do all in our power to help them bear their trials and sufferings; and in so doing we shall bring ourselves much nearer to him."

Boston was a city in explosive transition in 1869. From forty-three thousand residents in 1820, in five decades the population had soared to more than two hundred thousand. New waves of immi-grants were calling Boston home, among them Germans, Scan-dinavians, Italians, English, Scottish, and French. Most plentiful were the Irish, who'd crossed an ocean, penniless and trusting in fate, to escape a blight that had destroyed the mainstay of their diet, potatoes, turning the Emerald Isle into a graveyard. Like other foreigners who would follow them to the Promised Land, the Irish in the mid-nineteenth century were reviled. In the upper-crust view, they were filthy, uneducable, and lazy, except in regard to brawling and drinking. Worse, their allegiance was to Rome. The Catholic menace was to be despised. Xenophobia was the sentiment of the day.

But the power of numbers could not be checked, not forever. More than 125,000 Irish came to Boston during the 1846–56 period alone; by 1869, having achieved some respectability by their service in the Civil War, many were emerging from poverty. Some were making headway in politics, an endeavor that eventually would transform one Irish family, the Kennedys, into an American dynasty. Bigotry remained strong at the time a children's hospital was being contemplated, but like most bigotry, it was succumbing to the truth. By 1869, some proper Bostonians were beginning to think kindly of the Irish. Some went beyond thought. They believed it proper to turn sympathy into action, especially for the children.

As in Dickens's London, children's health care in Boston in the mid-nineteenth century was primitive, particularly among the poor, whose standing on the economic ladder precluded access to medical care and confined them to neighborhoods lacking even rudimentary sanitation. In such circumstances, germs proliferated. Smallpox claimed hundreds. Tuberculosis took its toll, as did typhoid fever, spread by fecal contamination of food and water. Diphtheria, measles, scarlet fever, pneumonia, and whooping cough all contributed to an infant mortality rate that was significantly higher than that fifty years earlier. Medicine may not have been able to save everyone, but the visionaries were convinced it could do better.

"If these diseases do not entirely exhaust nature and cause death," Children's founders, four Harvard-educated physicians and Civil War veterans, wrote in a pamphlet they distributed in early 1869,

> they very frequently leave the patients with enfeebled frames, and many a little ache and ail which future years only serve to strengthen, not efface. Many, very many children sink into early graves, and greatly swell the bills of mortality of those who die before reaching adult life. We not only desire to treat these cases, and such as these, successfully, but we also wish to give a tone to the general health of our patients, which may have an influence on their future life.

Who could resist such heartfelt appeals? Who could cast aspersion on such a noble cause, the salvation of poor, deserving innocents? Who could say no to the children?

Some senior people at Boston's most prominent medical institution, the Massachusetts General Hospital, could.

Their institution had been chartered for more than a half century—and sensing special destiny since the first, much-heralded public demonstration of ether as surgical anesthesia in 1846—many at the General were offended by the notion that there could be an area where they'd come up short. The General was, after all, a Harvard hospital.

"As there seems to be a general impression that no adequate provision exists in the city of Boston for the medical and surgical treatment of the diseases of children, some statement to the contrary is called for," the physician Benjamin S. Shaw, the hospital's chief administrative officer, wrote to *The Boston Daily Advertiser* in April 1869. After citing statistics that constituted a flimsy defense of his position—190 children had been seen at the hospital the year before, but no mention was made of the needy who remained unseen—Shaw concluded, "Our existing institutions, public and private, provide adequately for the hospital treatment of children."

Shaw's attitude infuriated the friends of Children's, who suspected, not without reason, that the General's outlook was colored by concern for its purse; like its fledgling competitor, the General depended on giving for its financial health. Even in 1869, Massachusetts medicine was part excellence and part gamesmanship, played on the field of philanthropy.

"Whatever excuse may exist for the jealousies of medical men in their private relations to each other, there can be no condoning attempts to thwart public charities," an unsigned editorial in the August 1869 issue of the upstart *Journal of the Gynaecological Society of Boston* proclaimed. The editorial spoke fondly of the founding of the General and Harvard. It spoke admiringly of the high regard in which the institutions were currently held and the contributions each had made to the advancement of medical knowledge. Then it took up a lancet. Perhaps, the unnamed editorialist mused, Harvard feared a new hospital would give birth to a new medical school. Perhaps a competing hospital would compete for philanthropy. The editorialist reminded readers of the scandalous sarcasm of a New York journalist who'd recently taken a shot at Brahmin Boston. Ebenezer R. Hoar, a Massachusetts judge, had had fun of his own recounting that sarcasm at a Harvard function.

"It would be unworthy to refer to a third reason that has been suggested as possible," the editorialist wrote,

namely, a desire to retain in the old channel any streams of beneficence that may flow from charitable coffers, save to express our disbelief in such a slander. It was very wrong of Judge Hoar to quote at the recent commencement dinner at Cambridge that malicious fling of the New York journalist who stated as "an astonishing occurrence that two rich men had died last month in Boston, neither of whom left anything to Harvard College, and neither did either of them leave anything to the Massachusetts General Hospital, another sponge," says the vile satirist, "that has sucked up its hundreds of thousands from the community." May a gracious Providence send it hundreds of thousands more, provided only that a little broader professional charity on its part be the result.

In the end, the ladies and their physician friends prevailed. The Massachusetts legislature passed a bill incorporating the Children's Hospital. Money was raised. Seven pages of bylaws were written. Officers were named. Physicians and surgeons were appointed, and a "lady superintendent" was brought on board: Adeline Blanchard Tyler, an Episcopal deaconess and experienced nurse. Under her were "lady nurses" and "nurse pupils," who, the bylaws stated, "shall have board and lodging within the hospital, but no wages." A brick house on Rutland Street in the city's fashionable South End—"a healthy locality," one newspaper said—was purchased for $12,150 in cash.

The building at 9 Rutland was not ideal for its new use, but neither was it as ill suited for the care of the sick as was the warehouse of Charles Dickens's East London. There were three stories in the first home of the Children's Hospital. The ground floor had a dining room, business office, bath, and dispensary, where medicines were kept in a custom-built walnut cabinet. The second floor became a ward for children with general disorders, including the many fractured limbs the hospital soon was treating. The third was for isolation cases. Twenty iron beds with casters and hair mattresses, the best the age could offer, outfitted the wards. A skylight let in sun and air, central to the nineteenth-century concept of healing.

On August 3, 1869, two weeks after the first admissions, the Children's Hospital was dedicated.

It was an occasion well attended and extensively covered by the press, a blending of celebration, speech making, and touring that set the pattern for official hospital functions for the next century and a quarter. Flowers decorated the wards. Each patient was presented a bouquet. A prayer was recited, and Scripture was read. The keynote speaker was cofounder William Ingalls, a Harvard Medical School classmate of Oliver Wendell Holmes, the great physician and poet.

The oldest Massachusetts doctor to serve in the Civil War, Ingalls at the age of fifty had operated on wounded soldiers for five consecutive days and nights, taking only six hours' sleep during the interval and subsisting on a glass of milk and nibbles of bacon and hardtack. "I was not tired at the end of it," he later said. Ingalls would remain a surgical consultant at Children's until the age of ninety, one year before he died. He would help inaugurate the academic tradition at Children's by publishing papers, among them, "Report of a Number of Cases of Wounds from the Use of Toy Pistols; Tetanus and Death." For more than a century he would serve as the model for Children's surgeons.

In 1990, nearly 16,000 admissions were recorded at Children's, and there were an additional 250,000 outpatient visits. More than 3,000 of the admissions came from outside Massachusetts, including 184 from foreign countries. Saudi sheikhs and Massachusetts Kennedys were counted among the hospital's benefactors. Five livers were transplanted, 900 hearts opened and repaired, 108 AIDS patients treated. A half-dozen cloaca babies had their insides rebuilt by Hardy Hendren. A Nobel Prize in medicine, the second for someone at Children's, was awarded to Joseph E. Murray, the surgeon who opened up the field of organ transplantation in 1954 when he successfully transplanted a kidney from a healthy identical twin to his dying brother. (Murray was on the staff of neighboring Peter Bent Brigham Hospital, later called Brigham and Women's, when he performed the operation.)

No honors came the way of Children's Hospital the year it opened. Only sick children, thirty in all from July 19 to December 28, 1869, the period described in the first annual report.

The first was Ellen McCarthy, seven, of 66 Cove Street, located near Boston's busy waterfront. Miss McCarthy, who had a broken arm, was "kindly cared for," according to Superintendent Tyler, the Episcopal deaconess. The second patient was also of Irish descent: Bartley Carr, son of Mr. Andrew Carr, of 45 Second Street in South Boston, who was pushed off a sidewalk by a young friend the evening of July 20. Sustaining a broken leg, he was carried to his home, where at midnight he was visited by Ingalls and Francis Henry Brown, another of the physician-founders of Children's. The doctors took him to their new hospital, where he was etherized and his leg was lanced, drained, and splinted. After his surgery, he was placed in traction. Nearly two months later, on September 12, he was "discharged well."

The remaining twenty-eight patients had a range of ills that reflected both the times and the timeless nature of childhood. A broken shoulder was treated, along with an injured ankle and a sprained leg. Children with dysentery, diarrhea, and Saint Vitus's dance, a neurological affliction associated with rheumatic fever, were seen. There were cases of eczema and inflammation of the eye. A girl with paralysis of one side of her body was admitted, as were two children with heart disease. "We really have such a pretty lot of children & so many of them motherless that our work seems such a Godsend to the poor helpless ones," Superintendent Tyler wrote on August 18. Remarkably, in light of the era, none of Children's first thirty patients died.

Although no procedure done at Children's in its initial years advanced the state of the medical art, the groundwork was laid for a rich research tradition. To this end, a policy of open admission was not charity—it was Yankee foresight. With more and more patients came more opportunities to learn. "Another object which we have in our view is to supply a want in our community which has long been felt in the medical schools," the hospital's chairman wrote in late 1869. "Namely, an opportunity to study infantile diseases. These, as every mother and every nurse knows, are so sudden, so fluctuating, and so mysterious in their nature, and often so fearfully rapid in their fatality, that they furnish a distinct branch of medical science, the importance of which can hardly be sufficiently recognized."

Nothing was more important than money.

It came, more than twenty-five thousand dollars through the end of 1869, in increments of one hundred dollars and one thousand dollars. Several Browns gave, as did an Endicott, a Greenleaf, a Winthrop, and a Weld. Two hundred dollars came from a fair, forerunner of the twentieth-century telethon, put on by Misses Carrie Blanchard and Lizzie Gould and seven of their lady friends.

"Four little girls of Longwood," who wished to remain anonymous, raised twenty-two dollars. Three thousand dollars came, as would so many subsequent bequests, from the dead: the estate of Miss Abigail Loring, whose will provided for many other charities, among them the Penitent Female Refuge and the Industrial Aid Society for the Prevention of Pauperism.

The largest donation, ten thousand dollars, came from a surprising source: Nathaniel Thayer, vice president of Massachusetts General from 1869 to 1883. The General's official policy may have been opposition, but there were dissenters in the ranks.

Although cash would become the preferred gift to Children's, any donation was welcome in the early days. To the Ladies Aid Association and a handful of merchants and doctors fell the job of outfitting the hospital and meeting its operating needs. Children's received nightgowns, bibs, aprons, bandages, socks, flannel underwear, calico skirts, slippers, stockings, linen, an ax, knives, dolls, gingerbread, jelly, subscriptions to children's magazines, strawberries, apples, pears, and baby carriages. Thanksgiving dinner consisted of two turkeys, a ham, a gallon of oysters, sponge cake, and a gallon of ice cream. For Christmas, there was a similar dinner and barley candy, cakes, toys, and a tree.

"On entering the general ward," the chairman wrote shortly after Christmas 1869, "one almost forgets that he is in the midst of the sick and suffering, as he sees on all sides smiling faces, and little hands playing with toys, or turning over the pages of illustrated books, and hears cheerful voices prattling merrily, or singing alone or together pleasant songs." It could have been Dickens writing. And it set a tone in official hospital publications that would endure until Lucy Moore's time.

Soon after opening, Children's Hospital had outgrown its house on Rutland Street, and the next year it made the first of many moves, to a five-story mansion around the corner.

As the years passed, the census climbed. The staff grew correspondingly. The clinical accomplishments became more sophisticated, research flourished, and Harvard was sufficiently impressed to enter into lasting affiliation with the hospital it once had eyed so suspiciously. Advances in several fields, notably orthopedics, fostered a national reputation. The hospital's spiritual mission began to recede, although it would never disappear. Grants and gifts in the millions were made. Talented physicians were drawn to Children's, among them William E. Ladd, surgeon-in-chief from 1927 to 1945. A tall, white-haired man, Ladd was interested in birth defects—and what surgery could do to fix them. He was a pioneer in the correction of harelip, but his successes with that deformity did not leave him content. Like his successors, Ladd turned to new, more difficult problems once old ones were solved. Congenitally malformed bile ducts, esophaguses, bladders, and ureters caught his attention. His greatest contribution to an emerging field, pediatric surgery, was his insistence that children were not simply miniature versions of adults whose only special surgical requirement was smaller instruments. Children, Ladd insisted, were physiologically different. Their surgery had to be, too.

Ladd's successor was Robert E. Gross. Among Gross's most promising students was a former Eagle Scout and Episcopal choirboy, Hardy Hendren.

Chapter 8

Lucy Moore's chest has been opened, her sternum split, her heart exposed. A patent ductus arteriosus—the defect that made Robert E. Gross a giant—has been discovered and tied, almost as an afterthought. Two cannulas have been connected to Lucy's heart; they, in turn, have been connected to the bypass machine, a pump that will do the work of her heart and lungs during the start and end of her open-heart surgery.

May 17, 1990. Children's Hospital, Boston.

"OK," says Aldo R. Castaneda, chief of cardiovascular surgery, "let's go."

Castaneda's assistant on the pump—the perfusionist—adjusts the controls so that Lucy's blood, which has been kept at normal temperature, will be cooled as it cycles through the machine. An anesthesiologist packs sterile ice around Lucy's head. Lucy is lying on a heating pad, but with the turn of a dial, the temperature of the water circulating beneath her begins to drop.

Thirty-seven degrees centigrade, normal body temperature.

Thirty-two.

Twenty-eight.

In the pioneering days of this kind of surgery, the fifties and sixties, patients were placed in claw-foot bathtubs and buried in ice to get them to the point where Castaneda is bringing his six-month-old patient from Florida.

Twenty-three degrees.

Twenty.

Nineteen.

On the ceiling-mounted monitor, an extraordinary development is taking place.

The lines of Lucy's EKG, which normally would be a moving pattern of cones and jagged curves, are going flat. Lucy's heart is starting to fail, as Castaneda intends. Looking at it, you see aimless quivering. You see surprising fragility. You see tissue—not bright red, as the artist commonly depicts it, but pale, more the color of uncooked veal than crimson. You do not think of the seat of the soul. You think of something washed up on the ocean shore, not dead, but not really alive.

Eighteen degrees, the temperature of a New England root cellar.

Castaneda injects a chemical, and Lucy's heart stops completely. Her EKG lines are flat. She is not breathing.

By those measures, Lucy is clinically dead.

"OK," says Castaneda, "turn off the pump, please."

His assistant does. There is still blood in Lucy Moore's body but it is stagnant. Her lungs are at rest. Their metabolism slowed by the cold, her cells are demanding less oxygen. There is no noise now in Castaneda's room, no electronic pulse, no reassuring hiss-whoosh, hiss-whoosh, hiss-whoosh of the ventilator bellows, no numbers on the blood pressure monitor, nothing. Lucy is in deep hypothermic arrest. Like a bear in the dead of winter, she is hibernating. She would have bled incredibly if they'd cut into her beating heart, and the sheer volume would have made it impossible for Castaneda to see or sew, and Lucy would have died. Now, Castaneda can safely fix her.

"We have suspended animation, as they say," Castaneda says.

While waiting for Lucy to chill, Castaneda has been busy. He's been cutting a small patch from a sheet of Dacron, a synthetic material—polyester—that can also be fashioned into carpets and clothing and sails.

Until the 1950s, when Castaneda was a medical student, there was no way to mend a ventricular septal defect and end up with a live patient. Like ductus in the years before Gross, life with a VSD as large as Lucy's was a life without guarantees. You might make it to ripe old age. You might be walking down the street at age twenty-five and drop dead. Most likely, you would not survive childhood.

Castaneda puts the patch aside momentarily and surveys the operative field.

All is still. All is clear.

With a small scalpel, he cuts into the heart. It opens like any other muscle tissue, cleanly and easily, no match for the surgeon's blade. It does not bleed.

This is what the heart-lung machine has helped achieve, what deep hypothermic arrest is all about—a heart that does not move, does not bleed, does not compromise the surgeon's vision or ability to sew. Although open-heart can be performed on bypass alone, doing so involves a more cluttered arrangement of cannulas and lines. With bypass, there is some bleeding. These are not huge problems with adult-size hearts. But with the tiniest hearts, such as Lucy's, hypothermic arrest—comparatively simple, completely bloodless—is preferred.

"That's a pretty big hole down there," Castaneda says.

Aware of the clock—aware of the fact that you have at most an hour before the wonder of hypothermic arrest becomes a brain-damaging catastrophe—Castaneda starts stitching. If he can get done in thirty minutes, all the better.

The Moores were at wits' end when they arrived at Children's this first time.

There had been no more prolapses of Lucy's stoma, but something else was going on, something they hadn't been expecting, something frustrating and embarrassing. A clear liquid was leaking out of the mucous fistula, that length of colon that ended blindly near where Lucy's anus should have been. And not the dribble of mucus they'd been led to expect. This was a continual discharge bubbling out onto her belly through the second of her two stomata.

The Band-Aids the Moores had been advised to put over the hole didn't stop the discharge, couldn't absorb it. Beth would change Lucy, and it wasn't an hour before the new outfit was soaked through; and if she was sitting in her stroller or lying in her crib, they would be sopping, too. Beth turned to gauze pads, two by two inches square. She tried single pads first, but that proved futile. So she doubled them up, but that didn't help. Neither did four pads. The Moores were buying two-by-twos by the gross, and still it was like shoveling against the tide. On to four-by-fours, and Lucy's clothes were soaking through almost as soon as they were changed. Lucy was uncomfortable, the skin around her stoma irritated and sore. The supposed mucus would drip down her belly, reaching her other stoma, the one with the bag for feces, weaken the adhesive, causing the bag to fall off.

By the time they got to Children's, Beth had abandoned gauze pads for sanitary napkins—maxipads—which she kept in place by wrapping bandages around Lucy's body. And her daughter was a soggy mess. *Still,* Beth was constantly excusing herself, asking to be shown the bathroom, changing clothes and maxipads and colostomy bags and diapers. It wasn't only the mucous fistula that was leaking. Urine was escaping from that single hole in Lucy's bottom, too.

Like many surgeons, the man who would fix Lucy's heart was profoundly influenced by war.

Born in Italy in 1930, Aldo Castaneda was with his family in Munich when Hitler started his march across Europe. The family tried to leave, through Switzerland, but the Nazis would not let them go: the Castanedas were Guatemalans, and Guatemala, following the lead of the United States, had declared war on Germany. The only Castaneda to escape was Aldo's father, a physician, who happened to be out of the country in December 1941.

During the war, Aldo, the family's only child, continued his schooling, becoming fluent in five languages, including English. But the comfort to which the family had been accustomed was gone. Their food was rationed, and some nights Aldo went to bed hungry. On the night of his fourteenth birthday, July 17, 1944, the apartment house where he lived with his mother and grandmother was hit by British bombers. The Castanedas, huddled in a section of the basement, survived. Others did not. That's how it was in Germany toward war's end. When one of your classmates didn't show up for school, you didn't think cold or flu. You thought about last night's air raid and corpses in the rubble.

As the war wound down and German casualties mounted, Aldo learned about the human body. He learned, as many before him had, by observing war injuries and war deaths. The young boy helped pull the dead and dying from bombed-out buildings, and he hung around first aid stations and makeshift hospitals while Germany's medical corps, what was left of it, did what it could. The young boy saw amputated limbs and eviscerated abdomens and chests, and he saw hearts—beating, bleeding, dying hearts. When liberation finally came and the air raids stopped, he rode with Allied soldiers to Dachau, the concentration camp on Munich's outskirts. He saw cadavers piled in pits, and it was during this period of his life that he decided he wanted to help; he wanted to be a surgeon.

Castaneda was in medical school in Guatemala when he started to read, in their original English, medical texts and journals from America. Minnesota was quickly on his mind. Such unbelievable things were happening in that state, half a continent away from Central America. Building on the work of many others—including a Boston legend, Robert E. Gross—surgeons were zeroing in on the ability to open a human heart, repair a severe defect, close up the organ, and have the patient live. What an incredible goal! What amazing experiments they were conducting with pumps and dogs and cow hearts and refrigeration! What an especially brilliant idea a surgeon at the University of Minnesota had! To bypass the heart, making it bloodless and thus ready for surgery, C. Walton Lillehei proposed using cross circulation. Both the patient and a relative would be anesthetized, their blood supplies linked by an arrangement of tubes, and when the operation was under way, the relative's heart and lungs would do the work for two. In the laboratory, Lillehei had succeeded with dogs. On March 26, 1954, he tried his first human—a one-year-old boy with Lucy Moore's defect, a severe VSD. The boy's father was the donor. The VSD was repaired. Father and son survived.

A medical-school student could do nothing so bold, but Castaneda could buy a pump from America, and he could find dogs, plenty of stray dogs, roaming the streets of Guatemala City. Thursday afternoons in 1957, when he was a senior, Aldo and his student colleagues would grab three strays and take them into the lab, where the pump was ready. The dogs were put to sleep. One was arranged on the operating table. The other two were drained of their blood, which was used to prime the pump. It was time to begin. The subject dog was opened and connected to the pump. The pump was started. The heart was bypassed. The heart was stopped with an injection and then opened. It was not tinkered with—Castaneda did not yet have the skills for such work—it was only opened and explored. And when the exploration was done, when Castaneda's curiosity was quenched for the moment, the dog's heart was closed. Castaneda's first dog, which he named Columbus, did not live. But subsequent ones did.

This is fantastic, Castaneda thought. *I've got to get myself to Minnesota.*

He did, in part because of a little trick. He played it the same year he was doing his dogs, 1957, a year in which he was asked to translate English into Spanish at a pediatrics conference held in Guatemala. Castaneda had no trouble handling most of the sessions. But then came a different sort of speaker, a psychiatrist from the University of Minnesota. Castaneda was worried. What did he, an aspiring surgeon, know about psychiatry?

He was doing all right until the Minnesota doctor started telling a joke. Castaneda didn't have a clue to what the joke was about. All he could gather was that maybe it had something to do with Minnesota culture, which is heavily influenced by the Scandinavian roots of many of its settlers.

"Listen," Castaneda told his Spanish-speaking listeners through his microphone, "this guy is telling a joke that I don't understand. But when he finishes, I'll tell you to laugh. I mean, that's all we can do."

The joke ended.

"OK," Castaneda said. "Laugh. Laugh hard."

The audience howled.

"You know," the Minnesota doctor later said to Castaneda, "I've told that joke in many places, but I've never had anyone translate it so well." When he returned to Minnesota, the psychiatrist mentioned Castaneda to Owen H. Wangensteen, chairman of the university's Department of Surgery, the man who created the climate in which Lillehei had flourished. Such a promising student, this handsome young Latino. He's put dogs on bypass—successfully! In Central America, no less. And so gifted with translation. Such impeccable English. When Castaneda applied to Wangensteen to study in his department, he was invited to Minnesota.

Castaneda would stay fifteen years, and his research and his surgical skills would save children who had never made it before. He would begin a career that would produce more than 325 scientific articles and a dozen chapters in books. Like Hardy Hendren, he would lecture and operate around the world. Broken hearts by the thousands would come to his table. And when he left Minnesota, it would be to replace the retiring Gross, chief heart surgeon at Children's Hospital.

Castaneda has fallen silent. He is aware of the clock. More than twenty minutes have elapsed. Past about thirty minutes, some studies have shown, is when the chance of brain damage slowly begins to climb.

Castaneda is putting eight sutures, each as fine as one of Lucy's hairs, along the circumference of the hole in her heart. When they are in place, he does the final tailoring of his Dacron patch. Satisfied, he positions the patch above the hole and brings the eight sutures through. He seats the patch. It fits snugly over Lucy's VSD. One by one, he ties knots. This is not an area of the body where you can afford to have your sewing fail, and so Castaneda puts six strong ties into each knot. When the patch is anchored, when not even perpetual pumping will be able to disturb what he's done, Castaneda fills Lucy's heart with saline. You do not want to leave air in the heart, for air circulating in the blood can cause a stroke, damage a kidney, do many bad things that would make a VSD repair so much wasted effort. Castaneda closes the heart, injecting smaller and smaller amounts of saline as he stitches the atrium shut.

"OK," Castaneda says. "Back on bypass, please."

"You want to start warming?" his perfusionist on the heart-lung machine asks.

"Sure. Please."

"Pump is back on."

As it cycles through the machine, Lucy's blood is warmed. The ice packs around her head are removed. The heating pad heats again. Castaneda places onto the heart tiny wires that will be brought out through Lucy's chest for connection to an outside pacemaker should her heart falter postoperatively. He adjusts clamps and tubes, bleeding off tiny pockets of air still trapped in the heart. On the overhead monitor, glimpses of resumed activity appear. Probes in Lucy's esophagus and ear register a reassuring rise in temperature. With warmth comes resurrection. The heart sputters, quivers like before, but only briefly. Soon it is beating—strongly, normally, completely on its own. Lucy has been in hypothermic arrest for one half hour, still within the margin of safety.

"OK," Castaneda says. "Time to come off."

"Coming off," says the assistant on the machine. "We're off."

"Very good," says Castaneda. "We're off bypass. Everything is fine."

Part II

BUILDING

Chapter 9

Two and a half months after the heart surgery, Beth, Jack, and Lucy have returned from Florida to Children's.

They settle into the waiting room on Fegan Three, the floor occupied by Hardy Hendren and several of his surgeons and staff. It is a Tuesday, the only day of the work week on which the chief ordinarily does not operate. What he does is see patients, an average of four per hour, every hour—including the lunch hour—starting at eight A.M. and ending, with luck, by five P.M., when he presides over his department's difficult-case conference: the Morbidity and Mortality meeting, or M&M, as he and his residents call it. Hendren started M&M when he was Robert E. Gross's chief resident, in the 1959–60 academic year. Along with Wednesday's grand rounds, which are a year-round lecture series, M&M is one of the rare events that survives on the hospital's surgical calendar on any regularly scheduled basis. Being any more rigid would be impractical in a hospital that never sees an end to emergency cases—the children with appendicitis or life-threatening birth defects, the transplant candidates for whom an organ finally has been found, the victims of accident and trauma.

Hendren, as usual, is running behind schedule, and his waiting room is jammed. Kids play with dolls. Kids pick apart magazines. Kids climb over chairs and toddle across the floor. Phones ring at the desk. Elevator doors open, and more people get off than get on. A TV is on, but no one pays more than fleeting attention to it.

Everyone's more concerned with the clock, an unusual presence in a doctor's waiting room. *Yes, time drags here*, it seems to say. *But what can you do? You're not in control in this place. You gave that up when you came through the door.*

Few complain about their wait for Hendren, just as few seek a second opinion after he's rendered his. One who did object but wished he hadn't was the father of a boy whose badly deformed urinary system Hendren was going to rebuild. Hendren had asked to see the boy the day before his surgery, scheduled for a Wednesday. On Tuesday, Dad and son waited, patiently at first. Two hours passed and still no sign of the chief. Dad went down the hall to Hendren's office and asked to speak with him. Hendren gave Dad his due. "What's going on? Is there a problem?" When Dad was done, the chief fixed him with those steely blue eyes and told him, in no uncertain terms, how deeply he appreciated reprimands from irate strangers. Hendren then explained, in a voice equally chilling, that when he is with a patient, that patient has his entire attention for as long as it's needed. No one else but that patient matters then. That, the chief explained, would be the dad's privilege as well once it was his turn. That was how Hendren worked, and if Dad didn't approve—well, Hendren would be happy to refer him to another doctor whose terms were more agreeable. Dad mumbled a few things, one of them being, "No, I'll wait." The terms of the relationship having been clarified, Dad and doctor went on to become amicable acquaintances, if not lifelong friends.

The Moores wait.

Lucy, eight and a half months old now, is beginning to fuss. It threatens to develop into a full-blown cry.

Beth is thinking about her nightmare, prolapse.

A boy of about three ambles over. "Dr. Hendren is going to fix my penis," he informs the Moores.

Beth laughs. When you think about it, what kind of comment would you expect to hear here, anyway?

Lucy is really beginning to fuss.

Around the Moores, many conversations are taking place. Some are in foreign languages. Some are in accented English. Men in suits are sitting alongside women in sweatshirts and jeans. There are single mothers, married couples, adults who started with Hendren when they were babies and never left, not even when they passed the age of twenty-one. Hendren has more than one patient whose mother or father was his patient, too.

Like his hospital, which has turned no child away since it was founded in 1869, Hendren is democratic. His thousands of patients include royalty, the son of a leading Democrat in the U.S. House of Representatives, the grandchildren of men whose names every year appear near the top of *Forbes* magazine's list of America's four hundred wealthiest people. Hendren sees children from Iceland, China, Australia, and Peru. He sees many children of the American inner city, of Boston and Chicago and Los Angeles and Houston and Miami, children whose families do not own property or hold jobs, do not even have the bare minimum that God has given most: an intact body. Hendren has patients and families who could write out a check for his services, whatever the cost, and he has many who can offer only Medicaid. For those with nothing—no public assistance or insurance of any kind—Hendren operates for free. For some, he has gone so far as to pay their way to and from Boston. Some he has even put up at his house for their posthospital recovery.

Almost an hour has passed.

Lucy is fussing. Lucy is wet. Since Christmas Eve, the day she came home with two stomata, she's never been dry.

"Excuse me," Beth says to a secretary, speaking softly, still unable to escape embarrassment at this recurring moment, "do you have someplace I could change my baby?"

The secretary shows mother and daughter to an empty examining room. Beth strips Lucy, changes her diaper and maxipad, and slips on a new outfit. The ritual is no more enjoyable than it's ever been, but at least Beth has a better understanding of the forces at work. During Lucy's recovery from open-heart surgery, the staff at Children's made a discovery. That wasn't mucus leaking out of Lucy's mucous fistula, urologists who took a peek at her found. That was urine. Somehow her bladder connected not only to the single opening in her bottom—her cloaca—but also to her lower colon. Along a course as yet uncharted, urine was seeping into that colon. The colon was filling, and when it was full, urine was taking the path of least resistance: up the colon and out that second hole in the belly. It was a startling revelation, a reminder of just how deformed Lucy was. Beth and Jack could only wonder what other mysteries of their daughter's anatomy remain unplumbed.

"Mr. and Mrs. Moore?"

"Yes?"

"Dr. Hendren will see you now."

The secretary leads the Moores down a hall. More than an hour has passed.

Hendren's office is a suite of six rooms. One is for examining patients. Another is for the production and copying of documents. Others are for Hendren's five secretaries and assistants. Positioned like a spine down the middle of the suite is a hall. Along one wall are stacked reprints of dozens of Hendren's most popular papers, which he gives, free of charge, to anyone who requests them. On the facing wall is a gallery of framed photographs of every one of Children's Hospital's chief surgical residents over the years. Gross's picture is there. Also Harmel's and Hendren's. Also photos of the ten surgeons whom Hendren has trained at Children's. Among them is Craig W. Lillehei, a specialist in lung and kidney transplants whose father is C. Walton Lillehei.

The people surrounding Hendren, and not only his surgeons, are tremendously loyal. The six members of his personal staff together have accumulated over a century of service to him. Dorothy Enos joined him in 1962, when he was at Massachusetts General. Paula Zafferes has been with him since 1963, first as a typist, then as head secretary, and finally as department manager, with major responsibilities for hiring and budgeting. His secretary-typist, Linda Lapham, began in 1970. Constance Bova has been Hendren's billing secretary since 1980. Four years later, he hired Barbara Cosgrove, who handles admissions and insurance. The newcomer on his staff, Pam Spinney, came aboard this year. Among her duties is assisting Hendren with a book on reconstructive surgery that he is coauthoring with Seattle's Michael E. Mitchell, a surgical innovator who trained with Hendren many years ago.

Hendren's inner office, the sixth room, is toward the rear of the suite. It is not the neatest space at Children's Hospital. It does not feature the regimental tidiness of his OR, which is overseen by Enos. An absorbed mind occupies Hendren's office, a mind with too much spinning through it to be concerned with whether the paper clips are in their proper place.

Hendren has a desk, cumbersome and wooden and befitting of a

CEO, but he doesn't much care for it. His work station is a round table with telephone and dictating machine and a brass lamp, onto which his secretaries tape notes requiring his immediate attention when he emerges from the OR, usually after they've gone home for the day. Hendren has several chairs in his office, some of which he keeps clear for visitors and staff. He has a couch, but its primary purpose is not for sitting. It's to hold X rays and videotapes and briefcases and a suitcase in which he lugs around papers in process and operative notes and journals and articles by others submitted for his prepublication review. Books fit where they can—on shelves and stacked on the floor. Hendren has a copy of *The Litigation Explosion*. He has several copies of *Jury of My Peers*, a surgeon's account of being sued. Hendren gives them to people whose opinions he'd like to be in line with his own.

The walls of the inner sanctum are as crowded as those of the outer hall. Hendren has the requisite certificates and diplomas, confirming graduation from Harvard programs and memberships in professional groups. There are pictures of Eleanor and their children and grandchildren. There is a picture of their boat, *NOMO*, which they bought when David, their last child, had finished his schooling and the Hendrens finally had no more tuition to pay. There is a picture of one of Hendren's two mentors, Edward D. Churchill, a chief of surgery at Massachusetts General Hospital. Below Churchill is Gross, Hendren's other, less gentle, mentor. There is a painting of a fighter plane circling an aircraft carrier and a certificate proclaiming Hendren's status as a naval aviator. He earned his wings on October 4, 1946, after making six deck-top landings on the carrier *Saipan*, cruising off the north Florida coast.

On the door is a letter from a patient. Hendren is always receiving thank-yous. They come typewritten, decorated with hand-colored flowers, scrawled in childish script across sheets of ragged-edge paper, accompanied by an occasional bottle of Chivas Regal, his favorite whisky. Hendren personally answers his letters, and over four decades he's never thrown one out. Every so often, he posts a new favorite on his door. "How does one go about thanking you?" reads one from the mother of a boy whose defective urinary tract Hendren repaired. "I can only tell you how grateful I am for your care of Trevor. Thanks to you, he will be able to 'shoot the pee' with the best of them. Our entire family was touched by your incredible skill and caring. . . ." And this, from a young California woman whose bags Hendren got rid of in an operation when she was twelve, and who recently returned for a final repair: "I feel as if my kidneys have been given room to breathe and that many years have been added to my life, because of you. Now that I am older, I am more aware of the intensity of my previous condition and regret that I did not express my thanks thirteen years ago. My adolescence was a happy and fulfilled one, as I am confident that my adulthood will be. . . ."

What is not displayed is Hendren's curriculum vitae, the most scrutinized credential in the world of academic medicine—and not just for content but for length. Hendren's CV is twenty-four single-spaced pages. Some entries seem inconsequential—his honorary membership in the Brazilian Society of Surgery, for example, or the fact that in 1972 he received Second Prize from the Biological Photographers Association or that he once delivered the William P. Burpeau Memorial Lecture in Newark, New Jersey. But most entries describe his position in the realm of medicine. He has lectured and operated throughout the world. He is visiting surgeon at the Massachusetts General and senior surgeon at Brigham and Women's Hospital, another Harvard affiliate. Page after page of credentials—all the titles, the academic appointments, his military record for both active duty and the reserves, the awards and honors, his Eagle Scout standing.

Hendren has his priorities. The first page of his CV is personal, not professional. Like many men of his generation, he built his career on the foundation of family—even though his moments with his wife and children have been scarcer than a younger generation would deem acceptable. Below Hendren's date of birth, February 7, 1926, is the name of his "Momma": Eleanor McKenna of Wilmington, Delaware, whom he married in early 1947, four months after they met. Next are the names of their living children, all sons: three surgeons and a corporate lawyer, each with an Ivy League education. Hardy and Eleanor's first child and only daughter, Sandy, was a nurse. Born in late 1947, when Hendren was at Dartmouth College, she died in 1984 and was buried in a pine grove behind an Episcopal church near the Hendrens' home. Should you ask, Hendren will tell you how his girl died: after a lifelong battle with juvenile diabetes, a disease Hendren personally diagnosed but no surgery, not his or anyone else's, could cure.

. . .

"I see we have a problem here."

Hendren smiles and welcomes the Moores into his examining room. He's reviewed the records sent from Florida. He knows the broad parameters of what's facing him with Lucy.

Cloaca baby. Number 104, if I recall correctly. Cute little girl. Parents seem nice—should be a pleasure working with them. So Aldo did her VSD. Colostomy by Rick Harmel. I remember Rick well. He's a fine surgeon.

"OK," Hendren says, "why don't you get her up on the table and get her undressed."

Beth does.

Hendren spreads Lucy's legs, investigates as deeply into her cloaca as he can without instrumentation, feels her featureless bottom, checks her stomata.

Already, he is developing a strategy.

Single opening, no evidence of a vagina . . . I wonder if she has one, tucked up in there somewhere? Divided colostomy . . . someday, we'll have to take that down. Multicystic kidney . . . that'll have to come out. And we'll have to have Mike Scott check on her spinal cord. It's going to be a tough one.

"All right," Hendren says. "You may get her dressed."

Sometimes on first meeting, Hendren will start to dress a baby himself. He'll get the zipper halfway up or complete a few of the buttons, and then, pretending to have trouble, he'll ask the parent to finish. "You'll have to excuse me," he'll say dead seriously, "I'm not very good with my hands." Hendren loves this prank, loves the reaction it inevitably elicits. He's pulled it at the start of lectures before hundreds of his colleagues, fumbling with the slide projector's remote control as the audience begins to get antsy. "I'm sorry," he's said, "I'm not very good with my hands." But Hendren does not spring his little joke today. A joke gets tired done too many times. As Beth dresses Lucy, the chief talks through his plan. He does not speak in what-ifs, does not outline alternatives or choices the Moores must make. This is how he intends to reconstruct Lucy Moore, cloaca number 104. *This is how it shall be.*

Tomorrow, he says, he will take Lucy into his operating room and get a good look with his scope. He will videotape his endoscopy, letting the Moores see the tape later if they so desire. He will send Lucy to Robert L. Lebowitz, head of uroradiology, who will employ a number of tests to further define her anatomy. He will contact R. Michael Scott, clinical director of neurosurgery at Children's, for an opinion on her spinal cord, often defective in cloaca babies.

And in about six months, Hendren will set aside an entire day and night to rebuild her.

The Moores say their thanks. Hendren goes to his collection of reprints and selects two on cloaca. To have a better understanding of what lies ahead, the Moores really should read them, Hendren says.

OK. Are there any questions? "I'll be glad to answer anything," the chief says.

Beth hesitates. Should she speak—should she tell Hendren her latest big fear, that something awful will happen to him between now and early next year, when he tackles Lucy's reconstruction? Should she ask what they'll do if, God forbid, he should drop dead? Hendren looks healthy enough, but he *is* in his sixties. He *does* have a career in an extremely high-stress field. What has *that* done to a heart, even a strong heart, over so many decades?

"I'm not leaving this office," Beth says, "until you answer one question."

"Yes?"

"What happens if . . . what happens if you are hit by a car before her surgery? Who else could do the surgery?"

Good, Hendren thinks. *That's a good one!*

The chief puts his arm around Beth. There is strength and warmth in his embrace, that good feeling Beth knew she would have. Hendren tells her that earlier in his life he flew military aircraft—safely, because he was careful. He tells her that he has a motorcycle, and he sometimes rides it, but he is always careful and safe with that, too.

"Nothing's going to happen to me," he says, smiling. "All right? All right."

On the next day, Hendren brings Lucy to his table. She is anesthetized and put up in stirrups. Her body is draped with a sheet, all but the area around her cloaca. Hendren scrubs and gowns and comes into the operating room. Dorothy Enos slides him a stool, and he sits.

His eye is level with Lucy's bottom.

"Scope, please."

A resident hands him an endoscope, an optical instrument that illuminates the interiors of organs while delivering a steady flow of water or saline to ease passage and improve visibility. An endoscope can be configured to perform minor surgical procedures, such as electric cutting of unwanted tissue, which Hendren often encounters. A camera can be attached to the eyepiece for videotaping and group viewing. At a teaching hospital, a setup like Hendren's is indispensable.

As carefully as he might handle a Ming vase, Hendren inserts the scope into Lucy's single hole.

"Dorothy, may I have the camera, please?" he says.

Enos often ribs Hendren about his obsession with filming. And there are times when she would enjoy wrapping the cable around his neck.

The chief wants just about everything on film. Bladders, tumors, vaginas, intestines, penises, anuses, chests, normal parts, deformed parts, and extra parts. Certainly every one of his cloacas. In the old days, it was sixteen-millimeter technology he brought into the OR, and a Nikon thirty-five-millimeter camera, which, held together with tape, he still uses. From the perspective of the support personnel, the Nikon is but a minor annoyance. Hendren sometimes needs new batteries or film, but those are easy problems. That video, on the other hand—that damn twenty-thousand-dollar video and endoscope setup of his—is a major pain in the ass. Tapes must be labeled and cued. The VCR must be started and stopped, stopped and started, the instant Hendren wants. Depending on the size of the scope or the region of anatomy, the brightness must be adjusted. The camera must be focused. Enos is a most proper and mannered woman, a gardener and fancier of theater and ballet, but she can have a sharp bite to her wit. She does not attempt to disguise her feelings toward the video. It was she who helped popularize the term Hendren cooked up: *fideo*, which combines video and the *f* word, a word Enos would never use. Hendren finds *fideo* highly amusing and rarely misses an opportunity to explain its etymology to a newcomer.

Enos attaches the camera, no bigger than two size-C batteries, to the endoscope's eyepiece. A bright circle appears on the monitor, perched on a shelf of the video cabinet, which is on casters. Much to everyone's dismay, the fideo can follow the chief if he goes to another operating room.

"All right, Dorothy," Hendren says, "shoot it."

Lucy's insides appear on the screen. As nurses and residents gather around the monitor, Hendren travels slowly in.

Flooded with saline, her cloaca looks like something that belongs deep undersea, not inside a little girl. It resembles a coral bed, perhaps, the pink and white folds of tissue slowly undulating as the current eddies and flows. Seeing his first Hendren endoscopy, Lawrence Rangecroft, a pediatric surgeon visiting from Newcastle upon Tyne, England, thought it resembled a Jacques Cousteau production, and it does.

Hendren travels farther in, straight in, on through a narrow fistula into the rectum, which is the end section of the large intestine. In a normal child, of course, he would not be able to get to the rectum by any path but through the anus, but Lucy has no anus. The rectum is enlarged. The urine that has been escaping her stoma has first been collecting there.

Hendren is pleased that Harmel did not attempt anything with the rectum. Many children have come to him after surgeons have mucked around with rectums, which to the inexperienced seem the part of the cloacal puzzle that is easiest to solve. In fact, whereas the surgeon may manage to get the rectum pulled through to the bottom, Hendren often has found that damage has been done to surrounding tissues vital for the definitive reconstruction. Even if adjacent structures remain intact, rectal repair is deceptively difficult. The best intentions without experience, as Hendren has often seen, can lead to bad trouble. "In general," wrote Willis J. Potts, a surgeon influenced by Gross, "atresia of the rectum is more poorly handled than any other congenital anomaly of the newborn. A properly functioning rectum is an unappreciated gift of greatest price. The child who is so unfortunate as to be born with an imperforate anus may be saved a lifetime of misery and social seclusion by the surgeon who with skill, diligence and judgement performs the first operation on the malformed rectum." Hendren remembers the passage well.

Retracting the scope a bit and then angling up, Hendren finds the bladder neck. It doesn't look too bad, a promising sign, since urinary continence depends on a functioning bladder neck. The bladder itself is abnormally small, but in some measure that's due to Lucy's urine-filled rectum compressing it. Most likely, he will not have to enlarge her bladder with intestine or a wedge of stomach, a situation that would further complicate the already complicated. Hendren finds the point where a ureter, the one that drains her normal kidney, enters into the bladder. He does not find a second ureter. She probably doesn't have one; but in any event, it wouldn't do her much good. It probably would connect only to her multicystic kidney.

Hendren does find four small pits marring the otherwise smooth lining of Lucy's bladder. One by one, he tries getting a catheter into them. No go. Hendren has no idea what these pits are, not a clue to what nature intended when they were made.

Like Harmel, Hendren fails to discover a vagina. Until he opens her up, he will not know for sure whether she has one. Or two. "I just reconstructed such a case from Oklahoma where there were two small vaginas that communicated with the bladder neck that we simply could not see," Hendren writes in a letter to Harmel, whom he will periodically update. "Also, I recently operated on a youngster in Cologne, Germany, where the same thing was true, where at the operating room table we found a well-formed vagina on each side, one pointing off to the left and the other pointing off to the right, so that they were really not between the rectal segment and the bladder at all.

"Thus, anything is possible up in there."

No question, Hendren thinks, *it's going to be a tough one.*

When next he saw Lucy in January 1991, Hendren would have several missions in addition to the fundamental mission of any surgery—which is getting the patient through alive, uninfected, and headed home in an improved condition.

First, he would have to discover, through dissection, exactly what he had to work with. He would have to find or fashion a vagina so that someday Lucy could have sexual relations. He would hope to find an ovary or two, one or two Fallopian tubes, and a uterus. He would hope to find a way to connect them to whatever he came up with for a vagina, so that someday Lucy would have a chance at having a baby of her own.

He would have to make an anus and hook up her rectum so that, in time, she could be continent of stool. He would have to make a urethra and, possibly, tailor the bladder neck so that she could be continent of urine. At some later operation, he would have to get rid of her stomata. *I will do whatever I can so she doesn't have to go through life leaking or with a bag.*

He would have to make Lucy's genitalia appear outwardly normal so that when she was old enough to know, about the time she was three or four, she would not consider herself different from other little girls.

He would have to take Lucy apart in order to put her together again.

Chapter 10

The qualities Hardy Hendren would need to excel as a surgeon were not spontaneous with him. They were family characteristics, rooted in Southern gentility, refined by one generation before being passed to the next. They can be seen at least as far back as Hendren's great-great-grandfather Jeremiah, a Baptist preacher and merchant in Norfolk, Virginia. His memorial stated:

> Brother Hendren had extraordinary powers of exhortation. His candor and honesty in all his dealings were such as never failed favorably to impress his customers; he never sold an article, the strict morality of which he had any doubt; he never took advantage of his neighbor in either buying or selling; and his promises to pay were always redeemed at the time specified. His word was literally as good as his bond. . . .
>
> He was not an educated man in the scientific sense, though his father was a schoolteacher, but he possessed a powerful, clear and well balanced mind, read much and carefully, especially in the Bible and other approved books, and his knowledge of Christian doctrine and principles was minute, correct and thorough. His habits of study, the topics of his conversation with friends and his general information made the arrangement of his discourses in his own mind rapid and easy. He was therefore always ready for his congregation.

The author of Reverend Hendren's memorial, a certain R.B.C. Howell of Nashville, Tennessee, told of the Hendrens' arrival in

America. William and John Hendren were brothers, twenty-one and twenty-three years of age, respectively, when they left their native northern Ireland for Virginia in about the year 1733. They were weavers—hardworking, prosperous, but not wealthy. William married Annorah Howell, daughter of the woman who had arranged for his passage to America. Their son, Downing, would become a schoolteacher, but first, at the age of eighteen, he would be a warrior—a cavalryman and lieutenant—in the service of George Washington's revolutionary army. Over the generations, war would not simply touch the Hendrens. It would shape how they viewed the world, in ways both good and bad.

Jeremiah, born in 1793, was Downing's son. He, too, fought for his country: in the army during the War of 1812, when he was nineteen. A tall, heavily bearded man with intense but not unkind eyes, just like his great-great-grandson's, Jeremiah started out as a clerk in a lumber business. He soon had his own grocery business, soon was a man of means, someone whose opinion was sought and valued. In 1819, he married Sarah Griffin, also of Norfolk. Like her husband, Sarah believed children should have a strong religious upbringing and that parents owed their offspring a good education in science, literature, and the arts. She believed a woman should not only nurture her children but also support her husband in his professional pursuits. "Such a wife," R.B.C Howell wrote, "is an incalculable blessing."

Sarah Griffin Hendren died in 1859, and it was Howell's belief that her death left Jeremiah a broken man. Or perhaps it was the Union army's occupation of Norfolk during the Civil War that put him in the grave in 1864, the year he turned seventy-one. Hendren, like other leading citizens, was placed under house arrest.

"The day before his death," Howell wrote, quoting from an account by one of Jeremiah and Sarah's daughters,

he arose in the morning, dressed with his usual neatness, and sat up most of the day. This was the Lord's day, and after the morning service, several of the deacons, and other members, called to see him. He was perfectly calm and collected; talked of death as a quiet sleep; repeated many scriptures to that view of the subject; and spoke of heaven as a place where no oppression or cruelty would ever come. . . . The day following, he was much worse, and kept his bed. About an hour before he died, he arose, but lay down again, and sent for his lawyer, with whom, in a deliberate manner, he transacted his final business, his mind being as clear as when in health. Just before he expired, he called the name of my mother. He then calmly composed his limbs and ceased to breathe.

Jeremiah Hardy Hendren, born in 1825, was one of the seven children of Sarah and her preacher husband. Young Jeremiah, a Confederate major, was taken prisoner by the Union army. Like his father, he lived in Norfolk, married, and had seven children. One son, William Hardy, left Norfolk in 1900 for New Orleans, where he was general manager of Texas Transport and Terminal Company, a steamship firm. During his time, William Hardy Hendren was vice president of the New Orleans Board of Trade, a charter member of the New Orleans Country Club, and junior warden of Saint Paul's, an Episcopal church in New Orleans. When he married and had children, a girl and a boy, William Hardy Hendren passed on his name.

W. Hardy Hendren, Jr., was born in Virginia. He was a pretty baby—so pretty his baby picture wound up on the Mennen talcum powder can. Raised in comfort in New Orleans, he graduated from the Woodberry Forest School in Virginia and flew Army airplanes during the First World War, although the war ended before his training was complete. Hendren, Jr., attended the University of Virginia, where he took his degree in mechanical engineering, a discipline requiring an analytic mind and an ability to visualize. Dr. Hendren's father was ambitious, but he was not cutthroat or greedy. He was easygoing and warm, a golfer, frequent tourist, and spinner of yarns. He was devoted to his religion, which by his father's generation had become Episcopalianism.

Hendren, Jr., was good with his hands. He could fix cars and take down and rebuild his son's motor scooter. He also knew how to handle money, how to save and invest while providing his family with a standard of living that included new automobiles on a regular basis and summer camp for the children and live-in help. He was well dressed, always well dressed, down to the folded white handkerchief in his suit pocket. He smoked cigarettes with a long-stemmed holder, a touch of class that would give him lung cancer,

from which he would die at the age of eighty-one. In family por-
traits, usually posed by the hearth, with his wife, son, and two
daughters facing him, the patriarch's resemblance to Franklin D.
Roosevelt was striking.

Margaret Inglis McLeod, the woman he married, also grew up in
New Orleans. Margaret's mother's people were Fentresses, and
they'd come to America from Protestant England at about the time
two Hendren brothers had left Protestant Ireland. James Fentress,
Margaret's great-great-grandfather, was a captain in the revolutionary war, then a lawyer, state representative, and for ten years
Speaker of the Tennessee House of Representatives. James was the
first of many Fentresses who went into law, making a respectable
living from it. Margaret's father's people were McLeods—Island of
Skye, Scotland, McLeods. The American progenitor, David
McLeod, was twenty-one when in 1828 he crossed the ocean and
landed in Nova Scotia, the shortest and presumably cheapest passage he could find to the new world. David was a mason, and he
passed through Philadelphia and Florida before winding up in
Louisiana, where he bought a plantation that was worked with
slaves. His son was Margaret's father, William Charles McLeod, a
lawyer and elder in the Presbyterian church.

Margaret was refined and attractive, and she took her education
at Sophie Newcomb, the women's college at Tulane University. She
was a gifted pianist, strong willed and smart as any man, and like
her surgeon son she had an eye for detail and a memory that was
photographic. She was, and is, vigorous—ninety-four years old and
still living independently. Margaret had known W. Hardy Hendren,
Jr., since they were kids, and she considered him quite fine, but she
worried he wouldn't amount to much. Hadn't he been raised in the
lap of luxury? Didn't old money stifle the ambition of successive
generations?

But W. Hardy Hendren, Jr., was already amounting to something
when he proposed marriage. He had a job in Detroit with a new
motorcar company, Packard, and starting from the ground up—
from the assembly line and foundry—he was learning auto manufacturing and engineering. It was only a matter of time before he
would be in management. Not long after Margaret accepted his
hand, he decided punching someone else's clock wasn't for him. He
wanted to be his own man. With his new wife, W. Hardy Hendren,

Jr., moved back to New Orleans, where he opened a dealership for another line of car, the ones Walter Chrysler was building. He might have made a fortune selling cars if he hadn't had a wise-cracking customer by the name of William Johnson.

Johnson was in the film-advertising business. He made commercials for soft drinks, department stores, and the like, and he showed them at movie theaters. It was good work, satisfying and lucrative work, combining creativity with financial reward. Motion pictures in the 1920s were making lots of people lots of money. Everyone was going to the movies.

Hendren sold Johnson a Chrysler. One day, Hendren went out to his own car. Johnson had parked next to it and left a note on Hendren's windshield.

"Why don't you get yourself a good job!—W. Johnson," the note said.

"What have you got to offer?—W.H. Hendren" is the note Hendren left on Johnson's windshield.

What Johnson had to offer was a job. Hendren took it.

William Hardy Hendren III, the second of Margaret and Hardy's three children, was born at the Touro Infirmary in New Orleans on February 7, 1926. His sisters were Peggy and Carol.

Hendren was a bright though not precocious child; a precocious child never would have flunked eighth-grade Latin, which Hendren did, to his parents' distress. He was instinctively curious—a boy fascinated with things that lived under logs and in streams and at the bottom of ponds.

I wonder what makes them work? he thought.

Knowledge was a treasured commodity in the Hendren household, and investing in it was more important for a child's future than any bank account, although financial security had its place. At the age of four, when Hendren asked for a microscope—"I want to see germs," he explained to his mom—Santa brought him one. Santa was always bringing gifts like that, chemistry kits and A. C. Gilbert Erector Sets and Lincoln Logs, toys that challenged the mind and occupied mischievous hands. Santa took special note of the way the young Hendren approached his pile under the tree on Christmas mornings. He did not, like his sisters, tear through everything in thirty seconds flat. He did not make a mess of the wrappings. He was methodical and precise, one present untied, opened, and examined at a time. If he unwrapped American Flyer trains first, he didn't move on to his next gift until the railroad was running. An Erector Set, and he was lost for the morning.

In 1933, when Hendren was seven, his father decided to take a chance. Dad for several years had been vice president and general sales manager of William Johnson's film company, Motion Picture Advertising, or MPA, which had acquired an interest in a similar company in Kansas City, Missouri: United Film Service. United Film was bankrupt, another victim of the Great Depression. Dad was offered United Film's presidency and part ownership in the firm. If he managed to turn it around, it might pay off handsomely. Dad accepted the offer.

On August 16, 1933, he packed his family into a Packard sedan and headed north toward Kansas City. It was a two-day journey, much of it on gravel roads, dusty and dry in the southern summer. Shortly before leaving New Orleans, the young Hendren had come down with pneumonia, and he'd been treated by the family pediatrician, Ludo R. von Meysenbug, a 1917 graduate of the Harvard Medical School who'd trained at a Yankee hospital: Boston's Children's. Hendren was recovering when his family set off on the trip north, but he was not yet well. As his father drove and his sisters played, the Packard kicked up dust, irritating his weakened lungs. Mrs. Hendren put a moistened linen handkerchief to her son's mouth. Periodically, she freshened it with chilled water from a thermos bottle she'd filled before leaving New Orleans.

For her son's first day at his new school in his new city, Mrs. Hendren dressed Hardy in knickers, the uniform of the day for second-grade boys. She walked him to the Bryant School, a redbrick building built in 1915 and named for William Cullen Bryant, editor and poet best remembered for his poems about the outdoors. At Bryant, the American flag flew, and the days began with the Pledge of Allegiance.

Hardy took his seat in Miss Wally's class. It was a big room with towering windows, high ceilings, and desks with inkwells. Miss Wally's class had forty second-graders. Hardy had attended first grade at Miss Aiken's Primary School, a small private school in the Garden district of New Orleans, the neighborhood on the banks of the Mississippi River where he'd lived his whole life, and he just couldn't get a grasp on Bryant. It wasn't what he'd expected, driving north in his daddy's Packard.

Look at all the kids, he thought. *I don't know anyone!*

And the first thing that happened was that George Kerdolff, the boy sitting behind Hardy, picked his nose and wiped his finger on Hardy's hair. And the next thing that happened was Miss Wally saw this boy with the III after his name looking around the room, trying to get a handle on things. Miss Wally decided that the first hour of the first day was none too soon to set a new pupil straight. In Miss Wally's class, students kept their eyes on their teacher.

"Young man," she said, "is this the way you're accustomed to behaving where you came from?"

"Oh, yes, ma'am, and much worse," Hardy said. Hardy thought that was what Miss Wally, this overweight, bosomy schoolmarm, was hoping to hear.

But it wasn't. Miss Wally thought that Master William Hardy Hendren III, late of New Orleans, Louisiana, was fresh. And so she outlined in detail to the young man what fate awaited those who stepped out of line in Miss Wally's class. Miscreants would be brought to the front of Miss Wally's room, and they would be ordered to extend their open palms, and then Miss Wally would administer several good whacks with a twelve-inch ruler. In extreme instances, Miss Wally would not use a twelve-inch ruler, and the palm of the hand would not be the object of attention. Miss Wally had a yardstick, and if she were forced to—if a very bad pupil *made her do it*—Miss Wally would have no choice but to use it, on the back of the leg. Miss Wally did not tolerate whispering or clowning around or pulling girls' pigtails—all of which, at one time or another, constituted Hardy Hendren's behavior. More than once in the months ahead, he found himself at the front of the class, closing his eyes and extending his open palms.

But Bryant turned out to be all right. Bryant was a melting pot, and among those who would attend over the years would be a congressman, golfer Tom Watson, Hallmark Cards head Donald Hall, and Dick Bloch of H & R Block, the tax-preparing firm. Hardy's contemporaries included children of lawyers and bankers. There were children from the wrong side of the tracks—children who came to school in the same clothes day after day because that's the best their families could do. There were the two brothers, whose father was rumored to be a gunman for T. J. ("Big Tom") Pendergast, the Kansas City political boss and tax dodger who launched Harry S Truman on the road to the presidency. The two brothers could take apart a .45-caliber automatic pistol and put it together again, or so they bragged on the Bryant playground. Hardy Hendren didn't know if it was true or not, but it hardly mattered. Just thinking it might be it was awesome.

Virginia Major was Hardy's girlfriend, a position she accepted not because he was a boy who always had to have his way—which he did—and not because he could be a smarty-pants—which he could—but because he was funny, liked ice-skating, and came from a good family. Virginia was slender and tall, fully a head taller than Hardy, who didn't have his growth spurt until his late teens. She was the uncontested brain of Bryant's class of 1939, a sweet, studious girl whose father was one of the leading men of American medicine—a girl who became a nurse but probably would have been a physician if she'd been born a generation later.

If anyone in Kansas City could serve as a role model for a boy with the idea that he wanted to be a doctor, it was Ralph H. Major, Virginia's dad, a professor at the University of Kansas School of Medicine. Major was an accomplished linguist, scientist, and author who'd graduated college at the age of seventeen, a man fascinated by the impact war and disease have had on the human race—a soft-spoken, firm internist who was convinced many years before the scientific evidence was in that cigarettes caused cancer. His library had floor-to-ceiling bookshelves and a glass case in which he kept the choicest volumes from his collection of rare books. This was where Dr. Major wrote—in longhand on lined tablets, with a precision and surety that made the editing of his work little more than rubber-stamping. Of an afternoon when her beau had come calling, Virginia would go with Hardy to the library, where they would lose themselves, poring through all those marvelous books. Years later, when he was at Dartmouth College pursuing his dream of becoming a surgeon, Hardy Hendren would find one of those books, Dr. Major's own *Classic Description of Disease*, on the curriculum.

Slowly, Hardy's father's gamble paid off. United Film, which before his tenure had employed an ambitious but unknown cartoon-

ist named Walt Disney, began to prosper. Mr. Hendren made more
and more film commercials, and in several—one for Coca-Cola,
another for a Kansas City ice-cream company, and a third for Crown
Drug Company—he used his son as an actor, paying him a dollar
a commercial. Eventually, he was able to open offices in Chicago,
Cleveland, and New York. As his fortunes improved, Mr. Hendren
took his place in Kansas City society. He was invited to join the
Kansas City Country Club, the University Club and the Mercury
Club. He was a member of the Friends of Art and the Society of
Fellows at the Nelson Gallery of Art. He was a director of St. Luke's
Hospital. He was senior warden of Saint Paul's Episcopal Church,
where a bronze plaque would be erected on his death—as one would
be on the death of his friend Ralph Major. Mr. Hendren was generous with his money, always tithing 10 percent to his church and
helping family, friends, and employees without fanfare or expecta-
tion of earthly reward. He believed that quiet philanthropy is an
absolute obligation of personal good fortune, a philosophy that his
son, so successful in surgery, would also embrace.

The rector of Saint Paul's was the Reverend Richard M. Trelease,
an Englishman who, like Mr. Hendren, had trained as an engineer.
Trelease and his wife had four children. Ben, one of their three sons,
was a friend of the young Hardy Hendren.

Ben was a thin boy, small for his age, with twinkling green eyes
and blond hair. Ben loved to build. With his father's help, he
constructed boats. He put together a crystal radio and assembled his
own motor scooter from a kit. Using lumber and coat hangers, Ben
built toy guns. They were realistically carved, with a compartment
in the handle to store rubber bands, the ammunition. Ben sold his
guns: the snub-nosed model for a dime, the six-shooter for a quarter. Ben had the devil in him. He loved to tease his sister and play
practical jokes on his teachers. He loved spitballs, and there were
times at Sunday services when he'd let one go during his father's
sermons. Ben's friend Hardy had his shenanigans, too, and he had
his stories, like the one about Elsie, the Hendrens' maid and cook.
Hardy didn't like Elsie, and it was Hardy's prank with a wooden
snake that drove her to quit.

But in the mischief department, Ben was operating on a higher
level than Hardy Hendren. Ben was two and a half years older than
Hardy, three grades ahead of him at Bryant. A big kid. Big kids
pulled big-kid pranks, like the Halloween Ben scooped some dog

doo off the street, packaged it in a brown paper bag, placed the bag on an older lady's doorstep, set the bag afire, rang the doorbell, and watched from darkness as the old bird stomped the fire out. It may have been the oldest Halloween trick in the book, but Hardy had never seen it before, and he was suitably impressed. This rector's son was A-OK.

Ben made mischief with his guns. He brought them to choir practice, and there in the chancel of his father's church he entertained his friends by shooting rubber bands. At St. Luke's Hospital, where Ben Trelease was a frequent patient, he shot his nurses.

Ben was dying.

He'd been born with a defective urinary tract (probably urethral valves, a condition that would be of great professional interest to Hardy Hendren in years to come). Fevers and sweats caused frequent absences from school; Ben's anatomy was slowly killing him, but no one had a cure.

In his final months, when the Treleases could see they were losing Ben—when they knew that all the years of tests and second opinions and medicines would be for naught—they brought him to California, where a big name in surgery opened him up and sent him home with a tube draining his bladder through his abdominal wall. The tube emptied into a bag, which Ben tied to his leg. And for a few months, but only a few, Ben was spared. In 1939, the state of the art was not enough advanced to save children with rare urologic defects like his.

On the day Ben died, March 12, 1939, Hardy Hendren asked Murray L. Trelease, Ben's younger brother, if he wanted to go for a ride on his motor scooter. They rode through the Country Club district of Kansas City, at one point swinging through Loose Park, where Hardy had caught and dissected a tadpole and known beyond all doubt he wanted to be a surgeon when he grew up.

Like Hardy, Ben dreamed of being a doctor.

That fall, Hardy Hendren started as a freshman at Southwest High School. In Europe, tanks were on the move. In America, an aircraft manufacturer was designing a single-engine fighter plane, the XP-47, prototype of one of the deadliest aircraft the Allies would put into the air in the war against the Axis.

Chapter 11

On January 15, 1991, the deadline George Bush has given Iraq to leave Kuwait or face war, Beth, Jack, and Lucy Moore fly into Boston's Logan International Airport. A cab delivers them to Longwood Avenue, where people walking the streets in lab coats and surgical scrub suits don't rate a second look.

Several North American centers could claim the title of medical mecca of the world. Philadelphia legitimately could. Baltimore. Pittsburgh. Toronto. New York. Houston. Chicago would be in the running, as would Seattle and San Francisco. The state of Minnesota could stake a claim. But many consider Boston, with its concentration of hospitals and schools and research centers, the top contender.

There is nothing in Boston like the Longwood complex. Here in this roughly twenty-block neighborhood is the Brigham and Women's Hospital, where the world's first organ transplants took place. Here is the Dana-Farber Cancer Institute, beneficiary of Boston's most famous charity, the Jimmy Fund, which the Red Sox, among others, have generously supported for decades. Here are the Harvard School of Public Health, Beth Israel Hospital, Massachusetts College of Pharmacy and Allied Health Sciences, Harvard School of Dental Medicine, New England Deaconess Hospital, Simmons College, Joslin Diabetes Center, Countway Library of Medicine, and Children's Hospital, which can claim many firsts. And like some father figure influencing all, the Harvard Medical School, affiliated with all of Longwood's hospitals. Twenty-two Harvard Medical School graduates and faculty members have won or shared Nobel Prizes. Most were in chemistry or medicine, but the 1985 Peace Prize went to the International Physicians for the Prevention of Nuclear War, founded by a group that included four with Harvard ties.

Like any entity bearing the Harvard name, Children's has a robust ego. For decades, it called itself not Boston Children's Hospital, or the Children's Hospital, Boston, but The Children's Hospital, with *The* an official part of its title. Only recently has The Children's Hospital become Children's Hospital, out of some new-found fear the old name was perceived as elitist. But no one was heard to disagree when physicians surveyed by *U.S.News & World Report* rated it America's best pediatric hospital in 1990, 1991, and 1992, the three years the magazine has published a listing of the nation's top hospitals by specialty. (In the 1992 survey, Brigham and Women's topped the list for gynecology. And that year, the Massachusetts General Hospital, located across town and also affiliated with Harvard, was rated by physicians as one of the best hospitals in eleven specialties: treatment of AIDS, cardiology, endocrinology, gastroenterology, geriatrics, gynecology, neurology, orthopedics, psychiatry, rheumatology, and urology. Only two hospitals, the Mayo Clinic and Johns Hopkins Hospital, were rated among the best in a greater number of specialties, twelve and thirteen, respectively.) Elitism runs deep in the Harvard soul. It has ever been thus. You would not prosper in Boston if you were not good. You would not get your share of philanthropy without inferring that you are not only good but *very* good—and quite possibly the best—at what you do. This is not boasting. This is just Boston.

In the 1985–90 Children's fund-raising campaign, $71.5 million was collected, a figure the hospital proudly announced but did not trumpet. Banks gave, as did a razor-blade company, the Boston Celtics, Polaroid, IBM, the New England Car Wash Association, the South Shore Corvette Club, the New Engand Patriots Women's Association, and the consul general of Greece. Children put on a raffle. The Children's Hospital League, successor to the Ladies Aid Association, which donated ice cream and bandages in 1869, contributed $2 million. Bill Blass hosted a fashion show. There were matching gifts and bequests and anonymous donations of cash.

Former patients and people who have never set foot in Children's gave. Take it all away, all the giving, and operating revenues would be Children's main source of income. In an era in which consumers and their insurers fiercely guard every cent, it would not be enough to keep a hospital on the leading edge of medicine.

Medical fund-raising is a peculiar business when sick children are involved. You cannot always tell the whole story because sometimes the story is death, which has no appeal to the philanthropist, except when charity can help avert it. But neither can you mislead. You must be very, very careful with your image. It's no accident that at Children's, development and public affairs functions are run by the same person: Anne Malone, who has a doctorate in English. Nor is it a coincidence that her office is in the hospital's administration building, or that she reports only to the president, David S. Weiner, who reports only to the board, which has always taken its steward-ship very seriously.

Since before Children's opened, since Charles Dickens was solic-ited for the cause, since the General flung its first aspersions, public relations has been imperative to the well-being and survival of the hospital. The dawning of modern communications has only made it more so. Instant information, investigative reporting, TV news—it can be a minefield out there. Reporters and photographers are welcome at Children's, but there are rules. All requests for inter-views must be handled through Anne Malone's department; direct calls to patients or staff are discouraged. When a member of the media arrives at the hospital, he must be met at the door by a member of Public Affairs. His escort will accompany him through-out his hospital stay, including, ordinarily, during interviews—and always during photo shoots. Pictures of smiling children are en-couraged. Positive stories are appreciated. If you plan on coming back, you should remember that.

In Children's own media—monthly bulletin and quarterly news-letter and annual report and Christmas telethon—the message is of expertise, compassion, and the forward momentum of science. The message is miracles, although in Boston that word is judiciously used. You must read between the lines to find the downside of pediatrics, the pain and suffering of families walloped by impossibly cruel disease. Pick up a Children's Hospital publication, and almost without exception you will see smiling kids. They may have lost their hair to chemotherapy, but they are smiling. They are resilient and brave and deserving of help. They are proof that at Children's miracles happen. Babies with bad hearts go home with good hearts. Leukemia is cured. Cystic fibrosis patients live longer and better lives. Diseases that have stumped the local pediatrician are identified and cured. And smaller miracles are performed—miracles only in the context of a family—the tonsils removed without complication, the appendicitis caught in time, the fever arrested, the infection cleared up, the child sent home, the hospital stay soon only a memory.

On the day the Moores arrived at Children's, Max Warburg had just gone home. He'd been a patient for more than a month.

Max was eleven—intelligent, handsome, kind, the son every parent hopes to have. He lived with Mom and Dad and his younger brother, Fred, in Boston's Back Bay, where fireplaces and chandeliers are pedestrian decor. Their home was sprawling and elegantly decorated, but amid the antique furniture and heirlooms, priority had been given to Lego toys, Nintendo, a CD player, and GI Joe. Stephanie's paintings hung on the drawing room wall. Her husband, Jonathan, an architect, designed hospitals, a cruel irony in what was to come. The Warburgs were prominent bankers, and they'd increased their wealth, generation after generation. But they were not miserly, these Warburgs. They were good people, committed to community, dedicated to civic duty. For decades, they'd stood with Rockefellers in the front ranks of America's most generous philanthropists.

Stephanie, Jonathan, Max, and Fred were a family in love with the sea. They loved swimming, beachcombing, skipping stones, and sailing *Halcyon*, their thirty-eight-foot sloop. They loved the salt breeze as it came off the ocean in Marion, a community spared the indiscriminate development of much of the Massachusetts coast. When it was July and *Halcyon* was in the water and the water was warm enough to bathe in, Max's dream was never having to leave his summer home.

His illness arrived without warning. No lingering colds, no inexplicable exhaustion, no swollen glands.

Max was just a boy on vacation in Marion that morning in July 1990 when Stephanie found bugs on the front porch.

"Centipedes," she said. "We need some spray."

"Can I get it?" Max said. "Can I, please? I could take my bike. I promise I'll go and come right back!"

The hardware store was ten blocks away. Max had never ridden that far without supervision, but Stephanie figured it was time. In September, her first child, her baby, would be entering the sixth grade at Park School, a private academy in Brookline.

"Go," she said. "Just come right back."

Coming back, Max skidded on a patch of sand. He was tossed over his handlebars, but when he got home, Stephanie couldn't find any scratches or bruises. All Max complained about was pain in the vicinity of his spleen, which plays a pivotal role in the body's immune system. When Max couldn't get comfortable, Stephanie drove him to a hospital in neighboring Wareham, the gateway to Cape Cod. Blood was drawn. Tests, including a CT scan, were administered.

"I've called an ambulance," the emergency-room doctor said when the tests were completed. "We're sending him to Children's Hospital."

"What do you mean?" Stephanie asked. "What's going on?"

The doctor led Stephanie out of Max's earshot and said, "Mrs. Warburg, your son has leukemia."

More tests were run, and Max was bedridden at Children's, and suddenly Marion was far, far away. "Mommy, I don't like having leukemia," he said. "It's like having little monsters running around inside of me, eating up the good stuff."

The specific diagnosis was made: chronic myelogenous leukemia, or CML, unusually resistant to treatment. There were no options. If Max were to have any hope at all, his defective immune system had to be destroyed, down to the last bad blood cell, and a new one created in its place. For that, he'd need someone else's marrow. A transplant. Although successful for other types of leukemia, in late 1990 bone-marrow transplants for CML came without a guarantee.

Marrow makes blood cells. It is a wondrous material with great responsibility for a person's survival in a world awash in germs. Marrow is also finicky. Not just any marrow would do for Max: he needed a perfect match of antigens, or his body would not accept its potentially life-saving gift. Siblings are the best chance for a perfect match. Fred was tested. But Fred did not match. Neither did other relatives. That left only strangers, all with their own genetic imprints, their own finicky marrow. The odds were put at one in twenty thousand of finding someone compatible with Max.

Stephanie is a great believer in the power of faith. She believes in positive outcomes, in marshaling positive energies and focusing them on a worthy cause. She and Jonathan are blessed with friends, many of them made in their travels throughout the world. Stephanie called on those friends. Before long, priests, nuns, Buddhists, Jews, Muslims, congregations of Protestants and Catholics, healers and mere well-wishers were pushing for Max, who'd gone home to wait for a donor. The Warburgs did not idly wait. Jonathan and Stephanie had established a project that was sponsoring public drives for prospective donors, who had their antigens catalogued and entered into the national registry. The Warburgs hoped, of course, to find a match for Max. But they also hoped to help some of the approximately six thousand other American children who were waiting, too. KIDS WITH CANCER AREN'T CONTAGIOUS, THEY'RE COURAGEOUS, the buttons of the Max + 6000 campaign proclaimed. Max was in the *Boston Herald, The Boston Globe*, the national news syndicates. He went on radio and TV, and he liked it, thought when he grew up he might like a career on TV. Almost three thousand people turned out for five donor drives in the metropolitan Boston area, and nearly $175,000 was raised for antigen typing and the National Marrow Donor Program, which connects donors with recipients. No one used the word *miracle*—it was much too early for that—but shortly before Thanksgiving, a match for Max was found through the national program. The donor was anonymous, although word leaked out that she was a physician living on the West Coast. Many months later, Stephanie and Jonathan would learn that her family, too, had come from Germany, and that the name of one of her ancestors had been Warburg.

One day after Thanksgiving, Max visited Marion. He granted interviews for newspapers and television stations, and when they were gone, when he'd discharged his duties as spokesman, he and his dad skipped stones from a breakwater. He selected Christmas ornaments he planned to hang on the tree. He imagined what his boat—the very first boat of his own!—would look like. For Stephanie and Jonathan had made Max a promise: next year, when he was recovered, when the ocean was warm again and it was summer, they were going to get him a sailboat of his own.

"The wind is my friend," Max always said.

Five nights before he was admitted to Children's, Max had a dream. It was a stormy, gray day, and he and his father were on a sailboat. The water was crowded with sailboats, all of them small, but for one. The large sailboat had a skipper who wore a hat, and on his hat was a bright star. The skipper's boat was stuck—on a shoal, perhaps. Suddenly, the clouds parted, and a beam of light shone down. Max set sail for the big boat. He reached it and released it to safety. The skipper with the hat with the star waved and sailed happily away.

On November 29, Stephanie and Jonathan packed T-shirts, underwear, track shoes, computer, toys, and books. Max played a game of Nintendo before his parents drove him across town to Children's. He was admitted to Six West, the bone-marrow transplant unit, run by Joanne K. Geake, a registered nurse who for two decades has helped save children and has watched helplessly as children have been lost. Max went into a laminar flow room, where the air is continuously replaced and germs are filtered out, a process that sounds like the inside of a jet. Max's defective immune system had to be destroyed before he could receive the new bone marrow, the seed of its rebirth. Chemicals and radiation, both cell killers, both poisons, would be asked to do the job.

Max made an adventure out of his leukemia. An adventure, as taking the rudder of his own boat would be an adventure.

Max kept a diary. He took pictures of his room, his parents, and the staff. He made plans with one of his doctors to write a book. Over the phone, he gave his friends detailed accounts of his chemotherapy and radiation and the crazy hand washing and dressing in yellow johnnies his family had to go through before visiting him. When he felt up to it, he colored or read or watched TV or played computer games. He set up a toy net and shot hoops with a foam rubber ball. He constructed a doll, using a urine bottle for the abdomen, a mask for the hair, a plastic pill cup for the nose, and IV-line caps for the eyes. He tape-recorded his trips to Brigham and Women's Hospital, which has a radiation machine.

On days he was to receive radiation, a nurse would transfer him from his bed to a stretcher. A plastic bubble would be closed around him. A tank of oxygen would be turned on, creating positive pressure to help keep the germs away. Stephanie went first, clearing elevators and halls and the bridge that joins Children's to Brigham. "Don't breathe," Stephanie said to passersby. "All clear!"

Max spoke into his tape: "It feels kind of cool. . . . It's like a huge air bubble. . . . We're bulldozing through the hall. . . . They're hauling me up this ramp . . . big bump . . . here we are in the radiation room. . . . Look at my chest, all the markings. . . . What will that stuff do to my skin? . . . Why is this so red? . . . My teeth feel weird."

Max's body was no longer his. At times, he was groggy. He itched. He lost his appetite and threw up. He lost weight. His skin turned the color of cork and began to slough. Because the fastest-growing cells were the most vulnerable to the bombardment his body was taking, he got mouth sores, and his hair—that thick, beautiful, dark hair—fell out in clumps. When it did—all of it eventually but at first only that at the edges—he looked in the mirror and saw the tuft on top, and he said, "Look at my hair. A Mohawk!" And when his little brother saw it, Fred said, "Hey, Max, I like your hair a lot better like this. Do you think you could keep it?"

Only occasionally did Max say, "Why me?" Only late at night, unable to sleep and in pain. Only when it really got to him, prisoner of a room that sounded like a 747 but went nowhere.

No one else was with Max more than Stephanie. She went home nights, but only for a few hours, only to give Fred some time with his mom. Jonathan went to his job by day, that was his way of coping, but he was with Max every morning and every evening, when he played guitar and sang his boy to sleep. One night when Jonathan was despondent, Max said, "That's all right, Dad, we're going to get through this."

As Stephanie was tucking him in that same night, he told her, "Mom, this is all going to turn out OK."

"Of course, darling," she said. "There was never any doubt about that."

What they did not grasp, not then, was that Max's treatment was a relatively new approach to fighting this stubborn form of leukemia. What they could not accept was that any approach, old or new, carried no guarantees. "This is his disease," Stephanie said. "We're his lieutenants, generals, admirals. We're all working for him, but this is his disease. Max wants to be in control. We're always encouraging him: don't give up control."

But when he was out of earshot, when she could show emotions she kept hidden from him, she said, "Every inch of the way is . . . I can't even think of the word. Excruciating? Everyone feels the same. I've talked to the mothers on the floor. Every second of every day . . . *excruciating.*"

In concert with Max's primary physicians, Howard J. Weinstein and Susan K. Parsons, Joanne Geake and her staff steered Max and his parents along.

Geake has an easy laugh and a dry sense of humor. She has been at Children's longer than most of her staff, very few of whom, if history is any guide, will be able to last as long as she has on a transplant ward. Daughter of a machinist and a housewife, Geake grew up in Hopedale, outside of Boston. In high school, she knew that medicine would be her career. Her first job, in 1969, was at Children's, where she worked in the cardiac intensive care unit and knew Robert E. Gross, who was closing out his career. She subsequently left to travel and work in an orphanage in Connecticut, but by early 1973 she wanted Children's again. She wanted to grow intellectually and to be excited by her work, and she wanted a chance to be in on something new and promising and hopeful. Her assignment was Division 20, one of only a handful of wards anywhere in the world where children with leukemia, aplastic anemia, and other blood disorders were receiving bone-marrow transplants and, with encouraging frequency, surviving. Only the worst cases came to Division 20, where two of the hospital's most promising young scientists, David G. Nathan and Fred S. Rosen, were making names for themselves. Only those children for whom all else had failed. Only the dying.

Geake has seen them all—every emotion unleashed when diseases are slowly sucking the life out of a child, emotions only magnified by captivity in a place with nowhere to hide. She has seen the pure exhilaration of a child finally going home, disease in remission. She has seen the quiet satisfaction of children who have returned to visit years later, cured, happily forgetful, their lives profound in their ordinariness. She has seen anger and frustration and rage and denial and the deepest fear. *I don't need to do this*, she has told herself time after time; *I don't need to be here. I could do many other things.*

In education, experience and responsibilities, Geake is the quintessential modern nurse. Since graduating in 1969 from the New England Baptist Hospital School of Nursing, she has earned a bachelor of science degree from Northeastern University and a master's in public health from Boston University. In 1984, she was a consultant for the bone-marrow transplant program at the King Faisal Specialist and Research Hospital in Riyadh, Saudi Arabia. In her spare time, such as it is, she is learning Arabic. She travels on her vacations, always to some far-off land. At home, she reads the want ads regularly, and her CV is always up-to-date. Sometimes, she wonders why she doesn't put it in the mail. She has no children, no pressing financial obligations. Her skills are highly marketable; she could easily go. She does not. "Maybe it's because the hard ones years ago are now simple cases for us," she says. "We're on the next step. Now we're doing kids we wouldn't have done two years ago and giving them a chance at life. We're taking the next step, and next year we'll take the next step, and we just keep on going." She believes in God, that the children she has lost are in heaven now. But she cannot explain the route that took them there, the suffering, the families ripped apart. "I don't think we're smart enough to know," she says. She does not dwell on it.

"If I had a wish," she says instead, "it wouldn't be money. I'd wish to be able to cure people. *Everyone.* Like with a magic wand or just touch somebody. When you see families suffering in there and you know that all they want in the world, maybe forever and ever, would be to cure this child, . . . to be able to go in there and do it would be amazing."

Packaged and protected, the marrow crossed a continent by midnight plane. It went by car to the Dana-Farber Cancer Institute, next door to Children's. At Dana-Farber, the marrow was purified to remove bone chips dislodged during donation, which involves repeatedly plunging needles into the hips.

Early in the morning of December 7, Jonathan and Stephanie came into Max's room. A tagged plastic bag filled with reddish liquid was on the counter; from a distance, it looked like Hawaiian Punch. A pint of a stranger's marrow. Jonathan touched the bag. It was warm. It had come three thousand miles, and it had been kept warm. He got a shiver.

"The emotional side is profound thanks," Jonathan said. "This person didn't have to do it. I can't think of anything more voluntary. That person has a faith that this world is going to be better with families intact, not having to live with the death of an offspring—which is not how it's supposed to work."

Stephanie said, "They say it's a great harvest. They say the count is very high."

At seven thirty-five A.M., Colleen Nixon, one of Max's nurses, hung the bag from an IV pole at the foot of his bed. The marrow started slowly into a vein. Science could not say how it would reach its destination, the insides of Max's bones, only that somehow it would. Max watched cartoons, and when he tired of that, he colored.

"Mom was guarding the bone marrow with her life," he wrote in his diary, "and Dad was taking lots of pictures, but the day seemed quite ordinary to me. Not that I wasn't grateful for the new life I was receiving, but the bone marrow went in without causing any problems, and everyone was happy."

In transplant parlance, December 7 was zero day.

During the next two weeks, everyone watched for signs that the marrow was beginning to engraft, that it was beginning to produce healthy blood cells that would restore Max's immune system and return him to health. A chart of his blood cell counts was posted to his door and updated daily. Jonathan made a graph of the progress. Never before had the Warburgs watched a document more closely.

Visitors were not encouraged, but there were exceptions. Fred came by, along with a few close friends and relatives. Stephanie's friend Joan Kennedy and Joan's son Teddy Kennedy, Jr., who'd lost a leg to cancer and had been cured more than a decade earlier at Children's, visited. So did Cam Neely, Boston Bruins star, and André Tippett, a New England Patriot. On December 13, Max's day six, two Boston Celtics visited. Quietly and insisting on no publicity, the Celtics come every year, breaking up into small groups so that every child can be seen, have a Polaroid picture taken with a star, and receive an autographed team photo.

Celtics Joe Kleine and Kevin Gamble toured a surgical floor, where one of the patients was George, a young boy whose urinary system, unsuccessfully operated on several times by surgeons at a hospital out West, had been reconstructed by Hardy Hendren. Hendren needed twenty-three hours for the operation, which had taken place on December 7, Max's zero day.

From the surgical ward, Kleine and Gamble went to Six West. Joanne Geake greeted them and advised them on washing hands and slipping on a johnny. "Go in," she said. "Just don't sit on anything."

"How you doin', buddy?" Kleine said, standing at the foot of Max's bed. "Just hangin' out? I'm Joe Kleine from the Celtics. This is Kevin Gamble. You like basketball?"

Max said that he did. "How'd you guys get started on your careers?" he wanted to know.

"We just started playin' ball," Kleine said.

"Max was wondering what you guys do in the summer," Stephanie said.

"A lot of fishing," said Gamble.

"I have a little guy," Kleine said. "I'm chasing him around a lot. He's hard to guard! He's two. The terrible twos."

Jonathan took a picture of the Celtics. "Hey, Max!" he said, "let him try your basketball hoop."

Kleine tried and failed.

"I hope that's not a sign of things to come," he joked. "Well, we got to get going. Hope you're feeling better. Merry Christmas. Take care."

"Merry Christmas, guys," Jonathan said. "Thanks for dropping by."

A few days later, Max wrote in his diary, "I've learned that Christmas isn't what I thought it was. You can have Christmas anywhere. You don't need a Christmas tree and all the old familiar things. All you need is the spirit of Christmas—and a lot of presents. Just kidding!"

No one could believe it. Not really. Not even the Warburgs, who'd been so astonishingly upbeat during the torment of their son.

According to the most optimistic scenario, Max's transplant would work, the blood counts would begin to climb, a healthy immune system would rise from the ashes of chemotherapy and total-body irradiation, and Max would go home a week or two into January. A more likely script was discharge somewhat later. After a long recuperation at home and, come good weather, in Marion, Max could expect to return to school in September.

But here it was January 2, 1991, not even a month since zero day, and Max was in his room, buttoning up his parka. He had his ski cap and mittens on, and he was ready with his mask, which he would wear in the elevator and while crossing Children's lobby, places frequented by strangers and their germs.

"Knock on wood," Stephanie said. "I know we're not out of the woods yet, . . . but in my mind I know we are. The longer I'm on this floor, the more I know this is a miracle."

"What's taking you so long?" Max asked. Stephanie was getting last-minute guidance from a nutritionist, Andria Mitchell. At Max's request, the first order of business when he got home would be having a pizza delivered from Domino's.

"Mushrooms are OK," Mitchell told Stephanie. "Hamburger is OK on top of pizza because it's cooked."

"With Chinese takeout, anything's OK?" Stephanie asked.

"Yup."

"Candy bars?"

"Yup. Apples and everything make sure you wash real well."

"I'm definitely going to eat some candy bars," Max said. "Definitely ice cream, popcorn."

In preparation for his return, the Warburgs had had their house rigorously cleaned. The curtains and comforters had been to the dry cleaner, the sheets laundered in detergent and bleach. Air purifiers had been set up. Max's guinea pigs and bird were on open-ended loan to a friend. Afraid of infection from a scratch, the doctors had warned the Warburgs that the only way they could keep the cat was to have it declawed. Max thought that sounded cruel. At his suggestion, the pet was taken to an animal shelter to be put up for adoption.

Jonathan was smiling this morning, the second day of the new year. Stephanie was, too. During the dark period, the period of paranoia, she'd kept her hair in a net, for there are many germs on a human head. She'd looked tired as only people desperately needing sleep look tired. She did not linger by the mirror. But on December 29, when it was apparent Max was coming home, Stephanie got rid of the net. She made up her face. It was her forty-ninth birthday, "the best one of my life."

A crowd of the doctors and nurses who had cared for Max came into his room. He was getting fidgety. He wanted that pizza.

"Max, I think you set a record," one resident said. "A bone-marrow record. You only whined twice."

"Go home," said Susan Parsons. "See me next Tuesday. Take a week off. Go on. Get out of here."

"Thank you very much, everybody," Stephanie said.

"See you later," said Colleen Nixon. "Come back and visit."

Before leaving Six West, Jonathan took one last look around. "It's fun to see an empty room," he said. "I almost want to take a picture of it."

Max was home nine days when he spiked a fever. Concerned but not alarmed, Children's wanted him back in. He stayed three days. The fever disappeared.

"Hopefully this is a viral syndrome which will resolve," a doctor wrote in his record.

Max went home for another nine days. Again, he developed a fever—and a renewed complication, nausea. Again, a hospital admission, this time for more than a week. No cause of the fevers could be found. On February 1, when he went home again, his newly reconstituted immune system seemed well.

Five days later, Max was back at Children's.

"I know you," joked Maureen Rohan, Max's favorite nurse. "You missed us too much and wanted to come back."

Max's weight was down. His belly hurt and he was vomiting. What was wrong? Was it merely another bump on the rocky road to recovery? Or could it be the first sign that things were starting to fall apart? Joanne Geake had a bad feeling. The doctors ordered tests, prescribed drugs, but still they couldn't find the cause. By mid-February, they began to suspect Max was infected with the Epstein-Barr virus, responsible for mononucleosis, which does not kill a healthy child.

On February 25, Max went on oxygen for the first time. The next day, the staff met with Jonathan and Stephanie.

The transplant, the Warburgs were told, had failed.

"We will be sure to keep Max comfortable," one doctor said.

Said David Nathan, Children's physician-in-chief and a friend of the Warburgs, "When we met together in July and confronted the diagnosis of leukemia together, my advice to you was to take the energy of all your terror and anguish and direct it toward the survival of Max. . . . Now I ask you to focus the energy of your terror and anguish more toward the preservation of Max's dignity rather than his life."

Out of sight of their son, the Warburgs cried.

When they had composed themselves, they called a boat builder in Rhode Island, not far from Marion.

In the gathering darkness of a cold Friday afternoon, March 1, Max's family assembled in his room. They were joined by friends.

"Go to the window," someone said to Max.

"Why?"

"Just go. Go and look down."

A friend with a video camera started filming. A cousin took some stills.

Max looked down six stories and saw a brand-new sailboat. On the hull was the name he'd chosen, *Take It to the Max.*

Down in the alley, Jonathan waved. Max waved back. Stephanie kissed her son. He breathed deeply, inhaling the humidified oxygen, and smiled. Even so sick, so weak and so sick, he had a child's capacity for joy.

A few minutes later, Jonathan came into the room with the boat's rudder and tiller. A bottle of champagne was opened. David Nathan handed it to Max.

"I christen thee *Take It to the Max!*" the eleven-year-old declared as he poured champagne over the rudder. Paper cups were filled and passed around. Nathan hoisted his. Everyone followed suit.

"Hip, hip, hooray!" Nathan said.

Max raised his cup and joined in, too. In an hour or so, he would be told that his condition, already serious, had become "life threatening."

"I don't like what they said to me," Max said to Stephanie.

"I told you, darling child, they just like to talk like that. Don't pay any attention," she said. Even so late, she had faith.

The next day, March 2, Joe Kleine revisited. He brought an autographed basketball, a shirt, jacket, and pennants.

On March 3, Max got morphine.

The next evening, Fred visited. Stephanie took pictures of them until the film was all used up. Max began building a launchpad and spaceship, complete with tiny astronaut, from his Legos. He finished around eleven. Then he said a prayer, "Dear God, thank you for all the people helping me and my donor. Please make me well. I deserve to get well and go home and lead a normal life with Mom and Dad and Fred."

Max asked when his prayer was said: "Mommy, were you with us when we went to the top of the Statue of Liberty?"

"Yes."

"Remember when Fred cried when we got to the top?" It was so high up there for a little kid.

Max drifted off.

Two hours after midnight, an alarm went off. The oxygen level in Max's blood was dropping. Jonathan played his guitar. Stephanie, who'd been holding Max's hand, whispering how much they loved him, crawled into his bed.

Max stirred.

"Hey, what's going on here?" he asked.

"I love you, and I want to snuggle you," Stephanie said.

Max's breathing grew more difficult and stopped.

"There's no pulse anymore," Jonathan sobbed.

"What do you mean, no pulse?" Even so late, Stephanie could not give up.

"Put your hand on his heart."

At six fifty-five A.M. on March 5, 1991, Max Warburg quietly died.

Chapter 12

The Moores get out of a cab on Longwood Avenue.

They check into a hotel next to Children's, have an early dinner, and get into bed early, and on the next day, Wednesday, January 16, 1991, Lucy is an outpatient. Radiologists examine her spinal cord, which Hardy Hendren suspects is not normal. If she has the condition known as tethered cord, so frequently associated with cloaca that Hendren automatically screens all of his patients for it, she will need neurosurgery. But that operation, which could last four hours or more, can wait. The first order of business is rebuilding her lower anatomy.

The next day, the Moores rush up Longwood. In fair weather, street vendors hawk pretzels and soft drinks and stuffed animals along the avenue, whose most formidable presence is the Harvard Medical School, undergoing yet another expansion this winter. In fair weather, Longwood is crowded with students and families and secretaries on break. But today, only Sami's takeout, a restaurant in a building shaped like a trolley car, is open for business—as it is twenty-four hours a day 365 days a year, conditions stipulated in its lease with Children's.

The Moores leave Longwood for the hospital's driveway. Like any thriving enterprise in the urban environment, where land is more valuable than gold, Children's has grown however it could: by bulldozing outdated structures, buying up neighbors, spreading out and reaching toward the sky. After almost eighty years on Longwood, Children's is more than a dozen buildings scattered over five blocks—physical testimony to enduring financial vigor and medical achievement. The hospital's heart, the complex at 300 Longwood, is a mix of brick and granite, concrete and steel, copper and glass. The parts fit together because they have been forced to, not because they have obeyed any laws of architectural harmony or balance. Inside, Children's is an agglomeration of corridors, bridges, tunnels, stairways, elevators, and doors. Even longtime employees sometimes have difficulty finding their way to its distant corners.

Past taxicabs the Moores go, past vans for the handicapped, past shivering smokers, whose habit is banned inside the building. Into the Children's lobby and past a life-size wooden giraffe and pay phones that are always in use and sofas and chairs, where somebody is almost always sitting, day or night. Hospitals are the most public of private places, sheltered, but not isolated from the world outside their walls. Bullets were sprayed one time inside Children's by a gunman who wanted cash. The hospital has problems with people stealing Pampers and food. As a matter of routine, its legal staff is trained to handle restraining orders brought by one parent against another in a domestic dispute. You cannot move for long through Children's without encountering a uniformed security guard.

The Moores pass the wishing pool, its tile bottom glittering with coins. Up on the glass elevator to the patient entertainment area, which is next to the admission desk. The entertainment area has a TV, tuned to Boston's Channel 4, WBZ-TV, which has raised millions over the years for Children's in an annual telethon and other events. All day today, only news has been broadcast. Now, NBC's Pentagon correspondent, Fred Francis, is telling America about strikes against Iraq's nuclear-research facilities. Parents and children watch. As absorbed as they are in their own dramas, they cannot resist this larger one. For the first time in a generation, America is at war.

After getting an update, the Moores check in at Admitting, but there is little paperwork; they've been here before. They are beckoned into a back room, where a phlebotomist will draw blood, which will be analyzed to help determine if Lucy is suitable for surgery. Beth settles her baby onto her lap. Jack stands close by. Lucy won't let Daddy out of her sight these days. Last fall, Beth went back to work at her day-care center, but Jack put his plans for his new wine business on hold. He's become Lucy's primary caretaker, Mr. Mom, as Beth calls him.

"OK, Lucy," Jack says, "this is the fun part."

"She knows it already," Beth says.

She does.

Lucy is fourteen months old now, as cute as any baby on the cover of a magazine. Although her development has been slower than normal, she is not disturbingly behind. Only a few days before leaving Florida, she took her first unassisted steps. She is not producing recognizable words yet, but the sounds she makes won't need much refinement before they are there. Of her personality, much is already known. Lucy smiles easily, laughs readily, plays contentedly with her dolls and stuffed animals. She's smart. She's been around enough hospitals and health professionals to make the connection between gloves and white uniforms and the deepest, most terrible pain. She knows that people with gloves come after you with needles. She knows those needles can go in almost anywhere: an arm, a foot, the neck. She knows there is no escape. Not even Mommy and Daddy save you from needles.

"OK," says the phlebotomist, Lawrence Brott. "Can I see this arm?"

Lucy whimpers. She's seen the gloves. Brott takes her right arm, tightens his rubber tourniquet, and probes for a good vein. He doesn't find one.

She's so hard to stick, Beth thinks. She remembers that scene at All Children's, holding her daughter's prolapsing intestines while the hunt was on for blood.

"It only hurts a minute," Beth says, "and then it stops. It's OK."

Brott concludes that his prospects with Lucy's right arm aren't good. It will have to be her left. His instincts are sound. He is skilled at a job, professional vampirism, that is highly prized at a children's hospital, where only the fear of being abandoned overshadows the fear of being hurt.

"It's going to be real quick," Jack says.

"Just an ouch, and then it stops," says Beth.

"Then it's going to be all over. This is the worst part."

Lucy is bawling now.

Please, Beth thinks, *not another prolapse.*

Brott connects on his first shot. He fills the first of three vials that the order sheet says he must get.

"See the red coming out?" says Beth, who before her third child was born would faint at the sight of blood.

"Good girl!" says Jack.

"We'll stop right there," says Brott.

"That's all honey," Beth says.

"Did you get enough?" Jack asks.

"Yup."

"You can stop crying now," Beth says as she cuddles Lucy. "This isn't so bad now. You know what's going to be fun? When they start giving you enemas."

Nine West is a general surgical ward, and in the years that Hardy Hendren has been chief at Children's, hundreds of his patients have benefited from its care. An arcane art, cloaca recovery, is regularly practiced here.

Carole C. Arenge runs Nine West. Her title is nurse manager, a title that reflects the tremendous political strides nursing has made in the modern hospital, where *shared governance* and *participative management* are everyday terms. Arenge has a sharp sense of humor, but like her colleagues on other floors, like Joanne Geake, she can be tough. Under her control are hiring, firing, scheduling, training, budgeting—the myriad details someone must oversee if nursing is to be blended with doctoring so that children are made well. Arenge also runs Eight North, the organ-transplant floor. No matter which way she turns, it seems, there's Hendren—Hendren or one of the surgeons on his staff. Arenge has tremendous admiration for the chief. She knows how extraordinary his surgical skills are. She knows how exacting he can be, how demanding, and she knows what he thinks of the evolution her profession has made during his forty-year career—an evolution that has taken nurses from handmaidens to managers. But Arenge has also seen a gentle, almost childlike side to Hendren. She's seen kids who came to him utterly desperate and went home normal.

On Nine West, the Moores are directed to their room. Beth wants a private, but there are none. Only semiprivates in Nine West: two kids to a room, separated by a curtain.

"She sleeps in a crib, by the way," Beth says when she sees a bed.

Marilyn Moonan, the nurse who will provide much of Lucy's care pre- and postoperatively, goes to find a crib, while Maria Mullin, the surgical resident, does a routine check of vital signs: pulse, blood pressure, breathing.

Let loose on the floor, Lucy crawls immediately for her roommate's bed. The girl is a patient of John B. Mulliken, a surgeon in the Division of Plastic Surgery, which is in Hendren's department. Mulliken's specialty is craniofacial repair: rebuilding deformed or damaged faces and heads. Mulliken is an heir to the legacy of William E. Ladd, the chief who brought Robert E. Gross on board. His patient is asleep, a bandage swaddled around her head.

Lucy spots the balloon at the foot of her bed.

"Buh!" Lucy says "Buh! Buh! Buh!"

"Daddy's going to go downstairs and buy you a balloon," Beth says.

By the time Jack's back with it, a steel-barred crib has been rolled into the room. Beth is with Lucy in Nine West's playroom, whose official title is Activity Room. The playroom overlooks the Dana-Farber Cancer Institute, which is not as pleasant a panorama as the view from Nine East's playroom; from there, you can see Fenway Park. No patient will ever get a shot in the playroom, which is decorated in bright colors and is equipped with kid-size furniture and a TV, not tuned to the war. The playroom boss, activities therapist Beth M. Donegan never wears rubber gloves or an all-white uniform. PLAY, A SPECIAL KIND OF MEDICINE, reads the banner she has hung in her refuge.

Marilyn Moonan, the nurse, needs information. As Lucy busies herself with Fisher-Price toys, Moonan finds out about the newest family on the ward. Beth tells Moonan about Lucy's brother and sister, who are staying with relatives back home in Florida. She says that both she and Jack will be with Lucy through her surgery and during the immediate postoperative period, but then they'll be taking shifts, with one parent staying with Lucy while the other returns home. This is the best the Moores can work out for Mary and James. With a child as demanding as Lucy, family parity has been an unachievable goal.

"Does she use any security object?" Moonan asks.

"No," Beth says.

"No hearing aids? No glasses?"

"No."

Moonan describes life on the floor—the taking of blood pressure and pulse, the unavoidable interruptions of sleep. Beth understands, but that doesn't mean she'll accept everything she's told. She's enough of a hospital veteran by now to know that with persistence, it's sometimes possible to bend the rules. Those nightly interruptions, for example—can't Lucy do without *those?* "I'll make a note here you'd like her to sleep at night, not to be interrupted," says Moonan, even more the hospital veteran. Note or no note, Lucy will be awakened for one thing or another every night until she leaves.

Moonan outlines the drill in the hours before Lucy goes under Hendren's knife. Later this afternoon, she will visit Philip J. Spevak, the cardiologist who has handled her cardiac care in concert with Aldo Castaneda. A magna cum laude graduate of Williams College, Spevak earned a master's degree in economics before going into medicine. He trained at Children's and the Massachusetts General Hospital, where in 1980, as a pediatric intern, he served a rotation under Hendren, chief of the General's pediatric surgical service at that time. Spevak will give his former teacher a reading on whether Lucy's heart can handle so many hours of surgery. Back on Nine West, Lucy will have her bowels cleaned out. The process will involve a flushing with Golytely, a purgative whose name must be something of an inside company joke since its action is anything but light. Her Golytely will be administered through a nasogastric tube, and before long, Jack and Beth and Nine West nurses will be emptying bag after bag after bag of increasingly clear liquid. "You'll smell like New Jersey, Lucy!" Beth will say. Lucy will indeed smell bad, but no one on the staff will complain. Most Nine West nurses will go to lengths to avoid upsetting Hardy Hendren. And they know that one situation that really riles him is having a patient like Lucy arrive in his operating room with dirty intestines.

Before Lucy is taken off to Spevak, who will perform an echocardiogram, anesthesiologist Mary Rabb drops by Nine West to discuss tomorrow's anesthesia. Someone has mentioned something to her about a possible eighteen or more hours of surgery, but she hasn't given that much heed. *Eighteen hours or more?* Who the heck operates for that long in one stretch? Instead, she gives the Moores the standard preoperative talk about anesthesia's many risks, which include infection, paralysis, and death. She gives a broad outline of postoperative care, the early stages of which involve anesthesiologists' assistance in bringing back children from the land of sleep.

"I want her to sleep for the next month," Beth says. She signs the permission forms.

Rabb started at Children's only two weeks ago. A graduate of Louisiana State University School of Medicine in New Orleans, she is spending her fourth year of training in anesthesiology as a fellow at Children's. Rabb is not yet up to speed on the ways of the chief, but sometime in the half hour after leaving the Moores, she runs across someone who is. At three-twenty P.M., just as Moonan and the Moores are about to set off for Cardiology, Rabb is back on Nine West. She apologizes to Jack and Beth; Lucy's postoperative care could be considerably more involved than she earlier represented, she says. That's because Hendren's surgery actually could go an entire day and half the night.

"It's really going to be eighteen." Rabb says. "I thought that was a little joke."

Lucy is whimpering. She's been given chloral hydrate, which is supposed to make her nap—an unmoving, unprotesting patient being desirable for echocardiogram—but the medication isn't having its intended effect. Beth cuddles her baby and, with Jack, walks with her up and down the Nine West hall.

"You know what?" Beth says. "We have a sleepover tonight! You and I—we're going to stay up all night. We're going to kick this guy out and have some girl talk."

At six the next morning, as Nine West begins to stir, Beth opens her eyes. She has spent the night at Lucy's bedside, sleeping—or engaging in what passes for sleep—on a chair that converts into something that conceivably could be called a bed.

For decades, parental visits to Children's were restricted to two hours on Sunday afternoons; the idea of Mom or Dad spending the night would have been considered ridiculous. *Sick children need their rest. They do not need distractions. They must not be spoiled. Sick children are here to get well, not to socialize.* Today, parents are welcome anytime, and others may call during liberal visiting hours seven days a week. If only the convertible beds matched this benevolent new policy.

Lucky Jack—last night was his turn to sleep at the hotel. At six-thirty A.M., he arrives on Nine West with a cup of coffee for his wife. Lucy, who finally went off about the time the eleven-o'clock news came on, stirs. She is hungry, but there can be no breakfast this morning. The Moores change her, hug her, give her kisses. At seven, anesthesiologists appear. With Beth and Jack each holding a hand, Lucy is wheeled to an elevator and taken down six stories to pre-op holding, where patients await the call to the operating suite. Beth nestles her daughter while a short-lasting sedative, midazolam, a cousin of the more familiar drug Valium, is given through her IV. Soon, her body is limp, and she is struggling to keep her eyes open. Just when she was almost awake, she is headed back toward sleep.

"Take care, my baby," Beth says.

"I love you," says Jack.

The Moores kiss their daughter one last time and hand her over to Veronica Miler, today's anesthesiologist-in-charge. Miler has administrative responsibilities for the operating suite today, and she will personally supervise several operations in the next twelve hours. But she will supervise none as closely as Hendren's.

"She's going to be fine," Miler says.

I'm just not going to think about it, Beth thinks. *That's how I'm going to deal with it.*

Jack's thoughts are darker. For weeks, he's had a sense of foreboding. He can close his eyes and see Lucy in a coffin.

The Moores leave pre-op holding, where bed after bed of children wait for the call, and they and their parents try, rarely with success, not to dwell on what lies just through those automatic doors. Jack and Beth find chairs in the waiting room, which is full. Thirteen cases, including Lucy's, are scheduled for seven-thirty starts. Another four are on for eight.

I'm just not going to think about it, Beth thinks. But it's all she can think about.

What will Dr. Hendren be able to do? How normal can Lucy be made? Will she be able to have sex? Will she have to wear diapers for life? Will he find any ovaries? Will she need hormones to look like a woman?

How is she ever going to deal with it if there's not much he can do? She'll be spending her life on an analyst's couch.

As preoccupied as the Moores are, they can't ignore the TV. No one can. The Pentagon has just released videos taken by U.S.

warplanes on the first nighttime raids on Baghdad. It is astonishing footage, even for such a technologically sophisticated people as Americans. A camera, mounted aboard an F-117 Stealth fighter plane, shows gritty urban landscape. Ahead is a high-rise building, headquarters of the Iraqi Air Force. The Stealth fighter zeroes in. The cross hairs lock onto the center of the building. A smart bomb is loosed. It drops precisely onto its target, what is presumed to be an elevator shaft. All four walls of the high-rise blow out. The headquarters of the Iraqi Air Force is destroyed.

Almost eight o'clock, and still no sign of Hendren.

Where is he? Beth wonders. *He said he'd talk to us before he started.*

Chapter 13

The P-47s were coming.

Hardy Hendren could hear their propellers, could feel their two-thousand-horsepower engines, faint but getting louder, getting closer, until the windows were rattling, and he could concentrate on his studies no more.

Out of their dorm and into the autumn sunshine they poured—Hendren and his classmates, teenagers all, not a girl among them, spreading out onto the lawns and playing fields of Woodberry Forest, this private boarding school in Virginia.

Suddenly, they exploded into view: fighter planes, so low you could almost touch their wings.

"Here they come, guys!"

"Thunderbolts!"

"Coming in low!"

The cockpits were open.

You could see the pilots—boys who fancied themselves men, with their goggles and helmet and their right hand on the stick. You could see their grins, as wide as a tarmac. You could just about smell the exhaust and oil and gasoline. A shiver ran down your spine, and soon you couldn't help yourself—you were shouting and waving, and these fighter pilots, hotdogging for the boys below, were shouting and waving back.

Fighter planes: P-47 Thunderbolts, capable of 429 miles an hour, armed with eight .50-caliber machine guns.

Fighter pilots: from the 328th Fighter Squadron, based in Richmond, where they were staging for European duty. Some of the pilots were Woodberry grads.

I want to do that! Hendren thought.

War was everywhere that fall of 1942. It consumed the newspapers, the Saturday-afternoon newsreels, the radio broadcasts. Inevitably, it had found Woodberry Forest School, opened in 1889 to give southerners of standing the foundation they would need for success later in life.

Less than a year before, on a cloudy and cool December day a generation would never forget, Hendren and his friends had listened to a radio in the room of their dormitory master, English teacher Arthur S. Latham. President Roosevelt was addressing the nation, and fifteen-year-old boys should hear what he had to say. If history took the course the president predicted, they would soon be needed in the cause.

Hendren had not come to Woodberry on a wave of glory. He'd come with an academic problem. A big-time problem, if surgery were to be in the cards.

At Bryant, his grammar school, Hendren had been a good student—a bright, eager pupil who would shoot up his hand when the teacher asked a question. He was not at the top of his class—his girlfriend, Virginia Major, held that honor—but his grades in reading, spelling, penmanship, geography, English, and math were respectable. A solid A and B student. His parents, who already figured their son was going places, had reason to be proud.

Hendren graduated from Bryant School in June 1939. That fall, he entered eighth grade at Southwest High School, a public school in Kansas City. Few of his close friends had gone to Southwest; they'd been lucky enough, most of them, to attend private schools. Not since his first days with Miss Wally, his second-grade teacher, had Hendren felt so alone.

I don't want to be here, he thought. *I want to be at Woodberry Forest, where Dad went to school.*

But this was 1939; apples were still being sold on street corners, and soup kitchens still had lines. And while W. Hardy Hendren, Jr., was making a go of it in film advertising and laying the foundation for solid profit later, money wasn't rolling into the Hendren household by the barrel. Woodberry's tuition, room, and board was one thousand dollars a year. With books, stationery, laboratory fees, travel expenses, pocket change, and the mandatory contribution to the General Athletic Association, which awarded the varsity letters, the total bill for a boy from Kansas City would certainly top fifteen hundred dollars.

There he was, unhappy at Southwest and struggling. Hardy had algebra, and he wasn't doing well in it. Hardy had Latin—the subject that had so bedeviled Robert E. Gross—and in that ancient discipline, which he knew was necessary in the training of a doctor, he *really* wasn't doing well. He was flunking. Hendren's teacher, Katharine M. Morgan, didn't think Master Hendren was trying very hard, and she was right.

I hate Latin, Hendren thought. *And I don't like Miss Morgan. I want to go to Woodberry.*

Mrs. Hendren told her husband that he should consider sending their son to Woodberry. Mr. Hendren called the school. They would love to have the boy, headmaster J. Carter Walker said. In light of the family's financial situation, they would even extend him a $250 scholarship—with one condition. To keep his scholarship, W. Hardy Hendren III had to remain in the top of his class, the class of 1943.

I'm going! Next year, it's off to Woodberry!

But first, Hendren had to get through the year at Southwest. He did, but not without flunking Latin, just as Miss Morgan had predicted. That summer, as he waited for Woodberry, he repeated Latin in summer school. This time, he passed.

Woodberry Forest School is in Virginia's Piedmont Region, where corn grows tall in red-clay soil. Woodberry's main buildings, clustered on a knoll, afford a magnificent vista of the Blue Ridge Mountains. They were the backdrop against which P-47 fighter planes buzzed the school that autumn of '42.

Woodberry was a conservative school with a curriculum grounded in the classics and an athletic program that required participation. "To give moral and religious guidance," Robert Stringfellow Walker had set as one of his goals when founding the school in 1889, "to help young pupils in forming correct habits of study, and to direct such physical exercises as are needful for healthy development." Woodberry's sons were to be pillars, as sturdy and tall as the pillars that supported the Walker Building's grand portico. In keeping with the philosophy of the founding father, a man whose word was his bond, Woodberry's system of discipline did not rely on the ruler, as Miss Wally's had. "All possible trust is reposed in the boys," Hendren's first catalogue said. "Their word is accepted in all matters of discipline without question, and in every respect they are treated as upright and honourable."

This, Hardy Hendren could relate to. This had echoes of his Kansas City upbringing, his Boy Scout oath. *"On my honor, I will do my best: to do my duty to God and my country, and to obey the scout law; to help other people at all times; to keep myself physically strong, mentally awake, and morally straight."*

Hendren arrived at Woodberry a seemingly reserved, meek boy who was a long way from home. It didn't help that he was not yet one hundred pounds, too light for football, Woodberry's major sport. It didn't help that he was too short for basketball, which ran a close second in the prestige department. It didn't help that his first roommate was from old southern money, which was vastly different from being the son of an entrepreneur, even one with deep Virginia roots. Nor did it help that on the very first day of classes, there was his old enemy, staring him in the face.

Latin.

You can't be a doctor unless you're good in Latin. I can't flunk it.

On his first monthly test, Hendren got a 54.

I'm going to lose my scholarship, he thought. *I'll never be a surgeon.*

But Woodberry's Latin teacher, Hubert S. Covington—he wasn't any Miss Morgan. Everybody liked Mr. Covington. A Woodberry fixture for a decade, he was a man who believed heart and soul in Robert Stringfellow Walker's values. Covington was the baseball coach. He coached football and wrestling. And as Hendren found out, he was a patient, supportive man who wanted nothing better than to see his students succeed.

Covington called the new boy into his office. "There's nothing wrong with your brain," he said. "You just aren't doing the work. I want you to come in and study with me every afternoon. And if you work, and work hard, you'll ace Latin."

On the next test, Hendren scored an 86.

"Nice going!" Mr. Covington wrote in red pencil. When the year was done, Hendren would receive a B in Latin and move in class rank from forty-first of forty-nine students to fourth.

But Covington wasn't done. He'd set Hendren down an academic track that would lead him to a cum laude degree and acceptance into the only college to which he'd apply, Dartmouth, but there was still the matter of athletics to resolve. Hendren wanted membership in the "W" Club, for students who'd earned a varsity letter in a major sport. But no way was this short, skinny kid cut out for football or basketball. And baseball just wasn't his sport.

"Wrestling," Covington said.

"I'm too small," Hendren said. "There isn't any weight class below 121 pounds."

Not necessarily a problem, the coach told his pupil. Covington said he would call the coach of Woodberry's opponent for the next match, the Severn School, which prepared students for the U.S. Naval Academy, and see if they had somebody who weighed in at 100, 105 pounds. If they had such a boy, Covington would put in a special class for him and Hendren.

"They have a man," Covington said when he'd made the call. "Now we have to go to work."

Hendren did. His first match was a victory.

At first glance, it seemed nothing had changed when Hendren returned from Kansas City for his senior year. The Tigers headed toward Woodberry's second straight state football championship. Risking six blows of an oak paddle, boys too young for smoking privileges still sneaked down to the river for their cigarettes. Sunday chapel services were held as usual; the choir, of which Hendren was a member, still sang. *The Woodberry Oracle,* whose reporting staff included Hendren, was still published every second week. The yearbook was still being produced, and Hendren made that staff, too.

But in the fall of '42, Woodberry was being fundamentally transformed. A replica of the West Point obstacle course had been erected on a school field. A scrap drive was being organized. The vacation schedule was changed so that railroads could better accommodate an overload of soldiers and sailors home on leave. One of the widely read additions to the school library was a book entitled

Victory Through Air Power. An aeronautics course, endorsed by the Army and the Navy, was added to the curriculum. *The Oracle* editorialized on democracy and war. Woodberry, like thousands of other high schools across America, was doing its part. By the time the last bullet had been fired, thirty-nine Woodberry alumni would have died in the Second World War.

When warplanes buzzed Woodberry that fall, Hendren wrote letters. One was to Dartmouth College, which he had never visited but had heard described in glowing terms. Mr. Hendren had wanted his son to go to the University of Virginia, his alma mater, but after three years at Woodberry it was time to get out of Dad's footsteps. The other letters were to the Army and the Navy. Hendren wanted information on enlisting. He particularly wanted information on military aviation.

Christmas 1942 came and went. Sixty girls attended the Midwinter Dances. It snowed at Woodberry, enough for a Rat Run, the traditional winter rumble pitting lowerclassmen against upper. Hendren and his roommate, Fletcher Rieman, also planning to be a doctor, made varsity wrestling. In the 121-pound class, a class for which he was still light by several pounds, Hendren posted two victories against a single loss in a season abbreviated by gas rationing, which restricted extracurricular travel. The only opponent to beat him was Thomas Massey III, undefeated captain of Pennsylvania's Mercersburg Academy team, a boy from Wilmington, Delaware, whose muscled physique and dark hair had earned him the nickname Moose. Massey, Lehigh interscholastic champion in the 121-pound class, took the match by decision. But he could not pin Hendren, who'd spent the week before in Woodberry's infirmary being treated for a case of strep throat.

As graduation approached, Hendren was faced with a decision. Not whether to serve—since Pearl Harbor, few teenage boys in America saw any option. And not how—since those P-47s, Hendren knew he had to be in the air. The only issue was Army or Navy. What swayed him was thinking about being trapped on some airfield under attack, waiting for the bombs to fall. Being a sitting duck didn't strike Hendren as the most valorous way to serve your country. At least on a carrier, you had a fighting chance of getting out of harm's way. And landing on carriers made flying that much more of a challenge, that much more reason to be proud.

Hendren was barely home from graduation when in June 1943 he went to an office in downtown Kansas City and introduced himself to the Naval Aviation Cadet Selection Board. He was not interested in V-12, which combined college with officer training. To Hendren, V-12 seemed like a draft dodge. *By the time those guys are done, the war could be over.* Hendren wanted V-5, the naval aviation cadet training program. That was the honorable thing to do. That was the quickest way to get into the air—less than a year, according to the Navy, which badly needed pilots at that stage of the campaign.

An excellent candidate, Hendren was told he was. At seventeen, he just met the minimum age. His grades were outstanding, his eyesight perfect. He was well coordinated, and his varsity letter in wrestling spoke volumes . . . and if only he weighed three pounds more, the yeoman told him. I'm sorry, young man, but the minimum weight is 120. If you're serious about this, you'd better eat some bananas. Drink some water. Come back, and we'll weigh you again.

"I'll be back in an hour," Hendren said.

He left, ate all the bananas he could, drank all the water he could. When he was weighed again, he was up to 119.

"OK," the yeoman said. "I'll cheat a pound for you."

He got his V-5 card. All he needed now was the call.

That summer, Hendren headed off to Hanover, New Hampshire. On the long train ride north, he and his roommate-to-be, John Crowe of Kansas City, toasted their futures with a bottle of Bushmills Irish whisky. They got bombed.

During his first semester at Dartmouth, Hendren took English, German, economics, chemistry, physics, and History of the United States, 1783–1865. He met a friend he'd have throughout his life, Alan W. Zeller, who would be the godfather of his first child, Sandy. But by early fall, Hendren was getting antsy.

I want to fly. Why haven't I been called?

Back in Kansas City on vacation, he returned to the Cadet Selection Board to see what the delay was about. The yeoman pulled Hendren's card.

"You're listed as being in college," he said. "There's an automatic deferment until you finish the first year."

"How did that business about my being in college get in there?" Hendren asked.

"Mr. Washburn made that notation."

Edward Washburn was chairman of the Cadet Selection Board. He had worked for Hardy's father. He was Mr. Hendren's friend. And Mr. Hendren had misgivings about his only son being put in the line of fire over some godforsaken ocean halfway across the world. His boy, his future doctor son, was only seventeen.

"I want to be called," Hendren told the yeoman.

In a week, in November of 1943, he was.

"Who is this William Hardy Hendren the Third? That sounds like Little Lord Fauntleroy."

That was Hendren's welcome to the Navy as he traveled with a trainload of seventeen- and eighteen-year-old recruits from Kansas City to a naval air station in Hutchinson, Kansas. It came from a fellow recruit, a bantam rooster of a boy, and it came as a challenge. Dick Hooper was going to show the guys who was who on this train. Dick Hooper knew how to deal with prep school types who spoke the King's English and wore tweed suits. But when Hooper came at Hendren, he didn't reckon that the preppie with the slicked-back hair had been a wrestler, that he might not wait to be pasted to the wall and would strike first. But that's what Hendren did. That's how he got Hooper to the floor. That's when he and Hooper started becoming good friends.

In Hutchinson, this latest bunch of recruits had drilling and riflery and gassing of planes and hand cranking of engines. Up before dawn, they spent cold days on the tarmac, getting the feel of aviation, watching the older boys climb into their cockpits and roar off into the sky, where you wanted so desperately to be. Hendren got his first ride in a plane, a Douglas Dauntless SBD dive-bomber, and when the pilot put it into a dive, Hendren threw up, and the wind plastered the vomit all over his face, but that only made him want to become a pilot all the more. There was Navy pomp and Navy circumstance and the beckoning glory of dogfights. There were men who would be fine officers and upstanding, productive citizens when the war was won. Hendren planned to be one of them. To invest in his future, he spent half of his fifty-four-dollars-a-month pay on war bonds, a practice he continued throughout his service.

But the Navy was not all God and country and honor and duty, which is what Hendren had been led to expect. "All civvies eat shit" had been the reception accorded the new recruits when they'd got off their train. "We're going to beat up the new guys tonight! Wait'll you get over to sick bay! They're going to give you a square needle that long and that big around in the left nut!" But that was talk. That was just the surface. The real issues to Hendren were issues of honor and morality, of right and wrong, which had always been defined for him in blacks and whites. Hendren met men whose word meant nothing. He met men who bedded strange women, caught the clap, and became engaged, all on the same weekend leave. He met men who got so drunk so regularly that even as a seventeen-year-old recruit not yet wise in the ways of the world you could see that their lives would end in ruin. He met men with tattoos. One had the word *Mom* on his arm and two other tattoos that could be displayed only by dropping his pants, which he was glad to do—there was a spider on the tip of his penis, and a dog chasing a rabbit that disappeared between the cheeks of his butt.

This is not to be believed, Hendren thought. *Where do people like this come from? Where can they possibly be headed?*

From Hutchinson, Hendren was supposed to have gone to pre-flight school, where he would get down to the real business of navigation and meteorology and aeronautics—no more of this gassing planes and placing chocks. But something was happening at the end of 1943 and early 1944. The Allies were pushing back the Japanese. Island by island, battle by battle, the U.S. Navy was retaking the Pacific. Pilot casualties were coming in lower than projected in the doomsday scenarios of those dark days that followed December 7, 1941. Cadets like Hendren were not in such demand as before. Those with less promise were washed out of aviation altogether. The rest, Hendren among them, were sidetracked. They were put into a hybrid program, V-12(a), and sent to college to wait.

For a year, Hendren was at Washburn University in Topeka, Kansas. He did not want to be there; he did not want to be anywhere but in the air. But he had no choice, and he used the opportunity to take premedical courses at Washburn, which he considered an excellent school.

In March 1945, Hendren finally made it to preflight school, in Iowa City, Battalion 3 Able. There was only one purpose to pre-flight, and that was weeding out the guys who didn't have it. In preflight, you studied Morse code, aerology, aircraft recognition, engines, and armaments. You boxed, wrestled, ran, swam, climbed ropes, and crawled through ditches and under barbed wire. In competition with your fellow cadets, you were not graded on the final outcome, on whether you won or lost or according to how many points you posted. You were graded on how fiercely you took it to your opponent, on what was in your eyes when you put on the gloves and stepped into the ring. And in all of that, Mr. Covington's lessons served Hendren well. By the time preflight school was over, he was one of the few boys from that train out of Kansas City who hadn't washed out.

In May, Germany surrendered. In August, two atomic bombs were dropped on Japan, and the war was over. Hendren was told he could get out now or sign up for four more years. It was not a choice he wanted to make. Leave now, and he would never fly. But four more years was four more years' postponement of his goal of surgery, which had never wavered.

You finish what you start. It doesn't matter what gets in your way. That's what Hendren had been taught, at Woodberry and at home in Kansas City.

Hendren called his father, whose advice he didn't always take but which he usually sought.

"Son," W. Hardy Hendren, Jr., said, "I don't know how to advise you."

"Well, Dad, my own thinking is that they're probably bluffing us," the younger Hendren said. "If we complete flight training, I suspect we'll get a choice of what we want to do. We'll probably be able to go into the reserves. Somehow it galls me to have put in this time during wartime to learn to be a military aviator and then to have it stopped. I'm going to take my chances."

Hendren's father agreed. Hendren went to flight school, which was not one school but several: in Norman, Oklahoma; Corpus Christi, Texas; and Pensacola, Florida. Hendren's first plane was a Stearman N2S biplane, a fabric-winged, single-engine workhorse used by both the Navy and the Army Air Corps to introduce cadets to flying. From the Stearman, Hendren graduated to a metal-winged trainer, the SNJ. The hours piled up, and Hendren moved through acrobatics, formation flying, night flying, cross-country flying, gunnery, twin engines, and carrier-landing practice. Pensacola had the infamous Barin Field, known as Bloody Barin for the toll it took on flyers; during Hendren's two months at Bloody Barin, one of his classmates was killed and another suffered a broken arm and leg. But Hendren made it. He wasn't in an advanced fighter yet, nothing like a P-47, but by early autumn 1946 he was a pilot. At the age of twenty, Hendren was ready to earn his wings.

The sky over the Gulf of Mexico was clear and warm on October 1, 1946. Thirty-six cadets hoped to qualify that day on the carrier *Saipan*. Up before dawn, they dressed, breakfasted, and were in the pilots' ready room at seven to hear a briefing by Captain John G. Crommelin, a combat-decorated Navy fighter pilot. Here was the drill: in groups of six, pilots would take off. They would orbit the ship, land, orbit, land, and so forth until each pilot had made six successful landings. Then it would be the next group's turn. Hendren's group would be fourth; if everything went according to plan, they would fly in early afternoon. Before they went up onto the flight deck, Crommelin had one more thing to tell the cadets. One of the 186 landings that day, he said, would be the two thousandth aboard the *Saipan*. Whoever it was would be the captain's dinner guest that night.

Hendren and his five friends spent the morning watching groups one, two, and three. Now it was his group's turn. Now he and DeGroot and Dolmeyer and Grace and Judd and Moore, his buddies, put on their Mae Wests and their parachutes and climbed into their cockpits. *Brakes set. Full throttle. Lock throttle.* Hendren got the takeoff flag, and he was into the air. Straight out he went, then downwind, then abeam of the carrier. As he sat out there, the final leg coming up, he reached into his flight suit for his Kodak camera, a birthday gift from his father. *They'll kick my butt if they catch me*, he thought. But after three years of starting and stopping and being sidetracked and being put back on track, Hendren wasn't going to get his wings without something for the scrapbook.

Now it was his turn.

Hendren watched the landing signal officer, whose commands were law. Disobey the LSO, as one of Hendren's class of thirty-six did that day, and you were out of naval aviation. Three years of training, six landings shy of your wings, and—out! No second chances. No commission. Busted to enlisted.

Hendren came in, closer and closer to the fantail. The LSO gave him a cut. The tail hook grabbed an early wire, and the plane jerked to a halt. The middeck barrier dropped, Hendren got the flag, and he was in the air again.

What a thrill! he thought.

Hendren's second landing was flawless.

On final approach for his third, as he was dropping, as he was coming up the groove, the LSO gave a sudden wave-off! No go! Not cleared for landing!

Instinctively, Hendren looked right, then left. Sitting there off his left wing was another plane, another cadet, out of sequence.

Ordinarily on a wave-off, the pilot would flare left. But left this time would bring disaster. Hendren flared right while the other plane went left. Hendren came around again, got the cut, and brought his SNJ onto the deck without a hitch. Before he could take off again, landings were suspended for a minute or two. A commander ran out to shake his hand. A Navy photographer took his picture. Hendren's third landing had been the two thousandth.

At dinner that night with Crommelin, the ship's cook presented Hendren with a cake. "Congratulations Ensign Hendren. 2000th Landing!" the message in frosting read.

A different message was contained in "A Navy Flyer's Creed," printed on a wallet card Hendren and his buddies received three days later at graduation ceremonies:

I am a United States Navy Flyer. ★ My countrymen built the best airplane in the world and entrusted it to me. They trained me to fly it. I will use it to the absolute limit of my power. ★ With my fellow pilots, air crews and deck crews, my plane and I will do anything necessary to carry out our tremendous responsibilities. I will always remember we are part of an unbeatable combat team—the United States Navy. ★ When the going is fast and rough, I will not falter. I will be uncompromising in every blow I strike. I will be humble in victory. ★ I am a United States Navy flyer. I have dedicated myself to my country, with its many millions of all races, colors and creeds. They and their way of life are worthy of my greatest protective effort. ★ I ask the help of God in making that effort great enough.

Hendren's gamble had paid off. He had his wings. He was naval aviator number P24779. And on October 23, 1946, the Navy would release him from active duty.

. . .

Only once before could Hardy Hendren remember having been so scared.

It was back in Kansas City, and he was nine years old, and he'd been to the movies to see *Rocky Mountain Mystery*, a 1935 thriller that concerns a series of murders at a radium mine. Back home and tucked into bed for the night, Hendren got to thinking about that mine and all those dead people and how dark it was in his room, and pretty soon the venetian blinds were rustling, and there was a scraping sound, . . . and the next morning Hendren found mouse droppings on the windowsill. *I've learned a lesson*, the young boy thought. *Don't let the mind be fooled by fear of the unknown.*

This fear was like that. This was fear he would never experience again, not once, not even in four decades of surgery. It was October 7, 1946, less than a week after getting his wings. A hurricane was approaching Florida. There was a good chance Pensacola would be hit badly and Hendren and his fellow pilots had been ordered to move the planes to Monroe, Louisiana, some 325 miles northwest. Fifteen planes, Hendren's among them, had left Pensacola late in the afternoon. They were still following the designated leader, a pilot who had the only map, when dusk began to fall.

"All of a sudden the guy who's leading us announces that he's lost," Hendren would say years later in retelling the story, a favorite. "How the hell he could have gotten lost, I don't know, but now it's about six-thirty in the evening and the rest of us don't have any maps, and we're depending on the guy who's leading, and he's not sure where he is. So he's going to take us back the way we've just come to look for a place to set down. Well, it was clear that we had not just gone over any major facility, at least nothing that I had seen. Then, without any warning—I guess now it's about seven o'clock; it's just getting dark—the guy that's leading us peels off out of the formation, and away he goes. He doesn't tell us what he's doing, but he's out of gasoline, and he landed—with his wheels down, which is crazy. You don't do that on terrain that you don't know. You land wheels up and skid in rather than land wheels down and nose up. But he did it successfully on the edge of this little town of Tchula, Mississippi, population three hundred, something like that.

"The rest of us saw this guy go down. And if he had said, 'I am out of gas; I am making an emergency landing; you're all on your own,' that'd been fine. But he didn't do that. He was just looking out for his own neck. He just went right down.

"So all of us were looking for where this guy had landed, but there was no visible airfield there. I look around, and here are now fourteen airplanes milling around at five or six hundred feet, and it's getting dusk, and there's no obvious airport around there, and so I said to myself, *Well, you know, we're in trouble.* I took the airplane up to about four, five thousand feet, and I looked down at my gauge, and I was in my reserve tank and the reserve tank is twenty gallons. That isn't a whole long period of time in the air. So I throttled this thing back. This was the first thought of any fuel economy for the afternoon—now that we're lost and it's getting dark.

"I sat up there to just see what's going on. And I saw a set of landing lights go on, and I said, *Thank God, somebody's found a field down there.* Then I saw another set of landing lights go on, and I thought, *That's obviously a field. Two guys have landed.* These guys had seen what they thought was a runway, but it wasn't a runway; it was a community garden. A bunch of black sharecroppers that tilled the cotton fields had a big community garden over on one side of this big cotton field where they grew their peas and their tomatoes and all that sort of stuff. From the air, it looked different from the rest of the terrain there. It looked like a landing strip. And it was October, so the ground was not all mushy from rain or anything, and they'd successfully landed wheels down in these SNJs.

"I made a pass over these guys, and I could see two airplanes on the ground with the guys waving like that and the lights kicked around to illuminate this area that they'd just landed on. So I overflew this, and it looked like a place to land. I thought, *Well, I'm going to land a little bit to the left of them, because I don't want to make a mistake and overrun them and end up plowing into parked aircraft at the end of the roll out.*

"So I put my gear down; I put my flaps down—down to forty-five degrees—I turned on my right landing light and I was looking out the left side, the reason being that in the SNJ, when you're in a very slow flight, the nose comes up, and you can't see straight ahead.

You have to look out the side. That's why you're taught to be watching the LSO when you're coming aboard a carrier and to be turning until you get into the very last bit of the run—so you can see where you're going.

"So I made a carrier approach—slow, right light on, looking out the left side. And I was just about onto the ground, and I saw something go by in my peripheral vision—out there *close*, not at all far—I mean, thirty or forty feet away, right out there. Instinctively, I put the power to this airplane and pulled up.

"Well, this was a house! This was a shanty—one of the sharecropper shanties that was sitting out in the middle of this cotton field. You couldn't see 'em. They didn't have any electric lights, and it was dark enough that you couldn't see the house.

"I pulled my airplane up, and I went over—not fifty feet. And Lester DeGroot was right there, tail up in the air. He'd done the same thing I was doing, and he'd landed in about three or four feet of cotton, and the cotton plants had nosed him up as he came in with his wheels down. And the tail was sitting up there, so close I could have spit and hit it, and I could even see who it was. I was that close that I could see that this was DeGroot hanging on his damn shoulder straps with the tail of the airplane up in the air like this. Fortunately, he wasn't hurt.

"Now I'm thinking to myself, *Damn! This is* real *trouble!*

"So I took the airplane off again, and I'm down to ten or twelve gallons of gas at this particular point, and the logical thing to do is take the airplane up to five thousand feet and jump out. And I was contemplating doing that because that's what you're supposed to do at night if you're over unfamiliar terrain and there isn't clearly a safe place to land. But I'm thinking of those shanties. And all of a sudden I saw a set of landing lights go on, and I watched them. You know, it's funny—that's more than forty-five years ago, and I can just see it today absolutely just like it was. A set of landing lights went on, and I watched 'em. And they flew along, and then they appeared to stop.

"I dropped down again. I'm down to probably ten or twelve gallons of gas, and that's not a safe amount of gas, particularly when those gauges aren't all that accurate. So I flew down, and sure enough it was a highway. And there was an aiplane sitting on the highway, and I said, *Well, if he's done that, that's what I'm going to do*. So I put the gear down again, and the flaps down again, and he left his lights on. He saw me. And I brought that airplane around.

"I thought, *Now, pal, you're doing just what you did last week on the fantail of the carrier* Saipan. *That's your landing target right there, that airplane.* And I brought that airplane down absolutely right over the airplane that was parked there—greased that airplane onto the highway, just like a carrier landing. And as soon as it hit the highway, my right wheel went off onto the shoulder. Off the slab onto the grass.

"I kicked the left brake. It brought the plane back onto the highway, and it stopped, and my feet were shaking. My feet were going just like that—just like that on the brake pedals! I was fine when I was doing the landing, but when that airplane came down and I realized how lucky I was to have successfully landed that thing on a two-lane highway at night—well, then the fear of the situation seized me. I shut the engine off, put the brake on, and got out of that airplane and down onto the ground.

"And from noplace came about, conservatively, twenty little black kids of all sizes. I mean, there were little kids this big, and then there were teenagers, and this one little kid—couldn't have been five or six years old—walked up and tentatively touched the airplane and pulled his hand back and said, 'Woo-wee! Am dis ding big!' Well I grabbed that little kid, and I gave him a hug. . . . I was glad to be alive.

"It was funny because the next day we dragged the three airplanes out of the cotton field and the two airplanes on the highway, and we had these five shiny Navy planes all lined up sitting in the borrow ditch next to the highway. Cars would be coming down this main highway up toward Memphis, and they'd stop, and they'd want to know what was going on. You know, 'Are you guys going to put on an airshow? What's this going to be?'

"The town doctor and unofficial mayor, Dr. J. J. Kazar, recently returned from war duty in the China-Burma-India theater, took us into his house for several days.

"We were all looking forward to flying our aiplanes out of there, but we got word from Pensacola that we couldn't because there was a rule that if an airplane had a forced landing under unusual circumstances, you had to jack it up and test its gear before it could be flown. And they said, 'It's going to be several days before we can get equipment up there to do that, so they ordered us to all return to Pensacola, and the Navy sent up a plane to Greenwood, and they gave us a ride in a JRB, a Beechcraft, back to Pensacola, which was two hours away. Then they had some test pilots fly those planes out.

"And I always regretted that I didn't get to take my own airplane off the highway. After all, if I could set the airplane down on the highway, I surely could have taken it off. That would have been so much fun, you know."

In late October, Hendren packed his trunk, arranged for its shipment home, and left Pensacola on a Harley-Davidson motorcycle. Pulling into Kansas City, Hendren lost his muffler.

"Welcome home, son," Hendren's father said when he heard the noise coming up the drive. "You're selling that tomorrow."

Having missed the start of the fall semester at Dartmouth, Hendren spent much of the next three months at the naval air station in Olathe, Kansas, flying in the reserves and checking out in the F6F Hellcat fighter. One day, his father asked if he'd like to join the family on a trip to Woodberry for a football weekend and biennial reunion. Yes, Hardy said, that would be fine.

That weekend, he shared a room in the gymnasium alumni quarters with Fairfax Aikman, a Woodberry graduate he knew. Aikman had come to Woodberry with Eleanor McKenna, a hometown friend. She was a pretty girl Hardy's age, a girl who laughed easily and had a wonderful singing voice and was fun to be with. Eleanor was a lady, refined but not stuffy, a Presbyterian, a former choir girl, and the only daughter of Scottish immigrants who'd settled in Wilmington, Delaware, where her father was an engineer for Du Pont. Eleanor had been to junior college and was thinking of a career in the theater, but for the moment she was in the mood for adventure. That's the way it was when you'd won a war, and that's why she'd become a stewardess with Trans World Airways. When Aikman suggested Hardy might want to look up Eleanor in Kansas City, where she was based with TWA, Hardy said that would be great.

Eleanor and Hardy were inseparable from the start. On the day just before Christmas that Hardy's older sister, Peggy, announced her engagement, Hardy turned to his steady and said, "You're the girl *I'm* going to marry." In Hardy's mind, it did not constitute a proposal. It was not some possibility or probability. It was merely a statement of fact.

Eleanor laughed. He had his notions, this Hardy Hendren.

"You wait and see," Hardy said.

He told his father next. "Dad," he said, "I've met the right person. We're going to get married. I want to take Eleanor back with me to Dartmouth."

The Hendrens were quite taken with Eleanor—that wasn't the problem. The problem was their son's future. Already, war had interrupted his plans, which had been in the drafting since the Christmas he'd asked Santa for a microscope in order to see germs. You didn't have a say about war. But marriage?

"You can't do that if you're going to become a doctor," his father said. "You're not even through college. You'll have to put off marriage and family."

"Dad," Hendren said, "I'm going to do this."

"How are you going to support yourself?"

"I don't know," Hendren said, "but I'll do it."

The Reverend Trelease, Ben's father, rector of Saint Paul's Episcopal Church, wouldn't marry his former choirboy, although he wished circumstances were such that he could.

"Your father is senior warden," the elder Trelease said. "If I married you without telling your parents, your father would never speak to me again."

"I understand," Hendren said.

But I'm going to get married. We'll cross the state line into Kansas if we have to. There's a Presbyterian church there. The Reverend Jennings will marry us. I know he will.

On a cold day in early February 1947, as the Reverend Ralph H. Jennings and his wife stood witness, Eleanor and Hardy became man and wife.

Chapter 14

As the first patients of the day are being put to sleep in the seventeen nearby operating rooms, people dressed all in green are beginning their day in a lounge at Children's Hospital.

Some drink fresh-brewed coffee, dispensed from two banquet-size percolators that will last until at least noon. Some leaf through a *Boston Herald* that's making the rounds. Most have a copy of today's OR schedule, a computer-generated document that fills two pages. They dissect it, discuss it, mark it up like some sort of medical *Daily Racing Form*, and then tuck it safely into a pocket for consultation throughout the day.

The schedule lists each patient's name, age, procedure, identification number, surgeon, room, and an educated guess of how many units of blood might need to be transferred. Blood is a rough guide to the difficulty and danger of an operation. Another measure is the surgeon's name.

Forty-four cases are scheduled for today, although the day's final tally probably will be bumped up by add-ons, of which acute appendicitis, the quintessential surgical emergency of childhood, ranks at the top. In one operating room, Joseph P. Vacanti, whom Hardy Hendren chose as his first chief resident at Children's, and founder of the hospital's liver-transplant program, is repairing a one-year-old's hernia. In Room 8, the domain of Neurosurgery, an eight-year-old is having the same spinal-cord operation Lucy Moore may need. In another room, three undescended testicles on three boys are being fixed. A deformed penis is being shaped into a normal one. There is some orthopedic work and the harvesting of bone marrow to be transplanted to a leukemia patient and the removal of a thyroid by another of Hendren's ex-chief residents, Robert C. Shamberger, a cancer specialist. In Room 18, Aldo Castaneda is mending a two-year-old's heart. The schedule says he needs six units of blood, much of it to prime the pump, the heart-lung machine.

"Room 17," another item on the schedule reads. "Moore, Lucy.

"Cloacal reconstruction.

"Blood, 2.

"Surgeon, Hendren."

Long after the other rooms have shut down, Room 17 will be in operation. You can bet on it.

As seven o'clock comes and goes, the lounge crowd begins to thin. The men and women in green spread out down the main hall, past locker rooms and shelves of fresh masks, caps, shoe covers, and lab coats. They head toward the operating suites, laid out in three rows separated by corridors containing untold millions of dollars' worth of equipment, instruments, and supplies. Even in the heart of the OR, you cannot forget that you are in the city and that the city is not all goodness and virtue and service to fellowman. Permanent plastic signs warn of continuing thefts of wallets. A hand-lettered sign has been posted offering a reward for the return of a Nikon camera, no questions asked. In the name of pest control—cockroaches, which occasionally are spotted darting into a crack—diners are requested to return all soiled tableware and trays from the lounge to the cafeteria.

Television has helped create a mythology of the modern American OR. The mythology holds that it is a ceaselessly frenetic place, a world of barely controlled confusion where adrenaline is constantly pumped and lives are ever hanging in the balance. *Code red! Anesthesia stat to Room 6! Stand back from the table, everybody, we're going to zap! Holy Jesus, we've got an uncontrolled bleed! Her hematocrit is through the floor!* In reality, much of surgery is mundane. Most of the time, the greatest risks do not arise from emergency or surprise. They are born of monotony and repetition, of lack of concentration, of carelessness and lapse of judgment.

What is not myth is the diversity of personalities in the OR; soap opera characterization is based on some measure of truth. There are quietly confident people in the OR, people who let their work speak for itself. There are spinners of yarns, philanderers, family men and women, silent sufferers, perpetual complainers, and buffoons. There are prissy neatniks, and there are pigs who drop their dirty scrubs and litter on the floor even though a receptacle is never more than a few feet away. "I'd love to catch them someday," says Hendren.

Humor is tightly woven into OR culture, and its woof and weave are cartoons and jokes. For a long time, a cartoon showing a doctor and his patient was taped to the door of one of the lounge refrigerators. The caption: ONE OF THE LEAST ENCOURAGING THINGS A SURGEON CAN SAY TO A PATIENT BEFORE A MAJOR OPERATION: "IF THE TRUTH BE KNOWN, I'M ACTUALLY A FRUSTRATED HOTEL DESK CLERK." But not all OR humor is black. Some is sophomoric and crude. On the inner door to one cardiac operating room there is a bumper sticker with a caricature of a human buttocks expelling a monstrous cloud. A line of prohibition crosses the drawing, and below is the slogan FARTING PROHIBITED.

Ten minutes to eight.

Except for her Pampers diaper, Lucy Moore is naked as she lies on her back on the table in Room 17, her twin stomata staring like bloodshot eyes at the overhead lights. In contrast, the scar from her heart operation last year has faded to pale, and in another few months it will fade to virtual nothingness. Healthy young tissue, which heals so beautifully, is the pediatric surgeon's powerful ally.

Lucy is being put to sleep.

Anesthesiologist-in-charge Veronica Miler, Mary Rabb, and Steven Heggeness, a resident from Brigham and Women's, are preparing her for a journey into unconsciousness and amnesia.

Anesthesia is one of the true marvels of modern medicine, and anyone spending time with Hendren will hear him praise the contribution it has made to what pediatric surgeons can do. Without anesthesia, they would be back in the Middle Ages, when the success of an operation, at least from the patient's perspective, was inversely proportional to the screams.

To see how far the profession has come, Hendren advises surgeons-in-training to read passages by John C. Warren, the nineteenth-century Boston surgeon and Harvard professor credited with introducing surgical anesthesia to the world. "At the first view of this case, I felt very little disposition to meddle with it," Warren wrote of a patient he saw at the Massachusetts General Hospital in 1836, a decade before ether was first used there. The patient, Jabez Wood, Jr., a seaman from the state of Maine, had cancer of the tongue. "Its appearance is that of a foul mushroom fungus," Warren wrote, "of a dark red colour, ulcerated deeply in the middle, and rising above the surface of the tongue a quarter of an inch."

Despite his initial misgivings, Warren decided he could—and should—remove the entire tumor, which he attributed to Wood's tobacco-chewing habit. Warren's chief instruments were forceps and knife. He had nothing with which to kill pain.

"The operation was done as follows," the surgeon wrote.

The patient, having his head resting against a support connected with his chair, I desired him to put his tongue out. As soon as he did this, I attempted to seize it with a double pointed forceps. The instant he felt the forceps, he drew the tongue back. I then thrust the forceps into his mouth, caught the tumour and a portion of the sound tongue on each side of it, in their gripe; drew the tongue out of the mouth, and in two or three seconds removed the tumour, including a portion of sound substance all around and under it. The lingual artery bled copiously. This artery was soon seized and a ligature applied. Then, for greater security, I passed a red hot iron over the surface of the wound. In the afternoon, the patient had some haemorrhage, which was checked by ice. The following day, he was quite comfortable.

Like that of almost everything medical, anesthesia's evolution has been uneven. Many human guinea pigs had to be sacrificed to get to where a Hardy Hendren could open a baby up and patiently piece together her insides without having her experience pain, move, or remember anything when he was finished. Among the earliest substances used as surgical anesthesia were wine, opium, and hypnotism, but the efficacy of each was unreliable. The first great leap, the use of ether, owes less to science than to nineteenth-century hedonism. Ether was not a new substance, having been synthesized (from sulfuric acid and alcohol) as early as the sixteenth century, when it was known as sweet oil of vitriol. Ether was used to relieve colic and bronchial spasms, but by the early 1840s American college students, including many at medical schools, had found another application: getting high. "Ether frolics"—parties devoted to inhaling the substance—became popular across America, and by 1841 they'd come to Jefferson, Georgia, where a young surgeon named Crawford W. Long had set up his practice. Long was invited to several ether frolics, and while he and his hosts stopped short of passing out, they sniffed enough ether to become intoxicated, and like drunken sailors they laughed and stumbled and bumped into furniture and walls. Long noticed that even though they injured themselves—they could show bruises the next morning as proof—taking that abuse didn't hurt. Long was intrigued. *Ether takes away the sensation of pain. Why wouldn't it work during surgery?* On March 30, 1842, Long prepared to remove a cyst from the neck of James Venable, who'd resisted surgery because of a profound fear of pain. Long soaked a towel with ether, gave it to Venable to breathe, and when the patient was unconscious excised the cyst. Venable reported no pain—and was so satisfied with Long's new technique that he returned on another occasion for excision of a second cyst on his neck. Later that year, Long etherized an eight-year-old slave known only as Jack before amputating his toe. Jack, the first child in history to be anesthetized, also reported no pain.

Long, recently graduated from the University of Pennsylvania, did not experiment widely with his new anesthesia, perhaps because he feared his patients would credit a supernatural pact, not scientific principle, with his success. Pain was considered such a natural part of surgery that anyone who could take it away must surely be in league with the devil. Nor did Long publish his experiences until 1849, three years after the first public demonstration of ether at the Massachusetts General Hospital had revolutionized surgery around the world.

Like Georgians, Massachusetts students in the 1840s were getting their kicks at ether frolics. William T. G. Morton, a Boston dentist, began using the substance for the painless extraction of teeth. *Why not in surgery, too?* Morton wondered. He suggested the idea to John C. Warren, who embraced it immediately. On October 16, 1846, Warren, nearing seventy years of age, summoned several physicians and a daguerreotyper to the operating theater of the Massachusetts General. The audience watched as Morton anesthetized a patient named Gilbert Abbott and Warren removed a tumor from Abbott's neck. Abbott felt no pain—only, he later recalled, a vague sort of scratching sensation. "This is no humbug," Warren observed. Only the daguerreotyper was not impressed. Sick at the first glimpse of blood, he'd rushed from the theater without taking what surely would have been one of surgery's most famous photographs.

Unlike Long, the General was not reticent about its accomplishments. Boston newspapers the next day carried accounts of the operation. The next month, the *Boston Medical and Surgical Journal*, forerunner of today's *New England Journal of Medicine*, published an account. Word reached Europe before year's end. To this day, the General annually commemorates the occasion on Ether Day, October 16.

But as good as it was, might not there be a substance superior to ether? That question was the driving force in anesthesiology in the decades that followed the 1840s. Chloroform, oil of turpentine, the puffball mushroom, breathing one hundred times a minute, electricity, chemicals dry cleaners use today—anything and everything was tried in the pursuit of the perfect elixir. In the twentieth century, as science and technique evolved, anesthesiology emerged as an accepted specialty; in turn, it gave birth to a subspecialty, pediatric anesthesiology, with its own professional associations and journals and training programs, such as that at Children's. By the time Lucy Moore was put under, surgeons, once responsible for their patients' anesthesia, could now focus more of their attention on repairing, and less of it on maintaining life.

As the Moores waited in pre-op holding, Hardy Hendren telephoned the OR to give permission to get started. As Beth held her daughter, midazolam had been slipped into Lucy through her IV. Now, as Miler and Rabb move on to the heavy-duty stuff, Lucy is foggy and uncomplaining, just as intended.

Electrodes that will monitor Lucy's heart are attached high on her chest, where they will be out of Hendren's way. A stethoscope is similarly affixed. A blood pressure cuff is put around an upper arm. A flexible, adhesive metal plate that grounds the electric cautery is attached to her upper back. Thiopental, an anesthetic, is given through Lucy's IV. It knocks her right out. Atracurium, a short-acting muscle relaxant, also is administered intravenously; it will prevent Lucy from gagging dangerously during the insertion of a breathing tube into her trachea, which connects to the lungs. The atracurium will also stop independent breathing, and so the anesthesiologist must breathe for Lucy manually, by squeezing a rubber bag that connects to a face mask. To confirm that Lucy is temporarily paralyzed—that it is safe to get the endotracheal tube in—Miler runs a nerve stimulator along Lucy's free forearm. The stimulator administers mild electric current, but Lucy's fingers do not twitch; she is paralyzed.

Through the mask, Miler gives her a few seconds of 100-percent oxygen, which saturates her blood, buying the time they'll need to insert the endotracheal tube. The mask comes off. Miler then threads the tube through Lucy's nose and carefully down into the trachea. The tube is connected to the anesthesia machine, a thirty-five-thousand-dollar piece of technology that will breathe for Lucy, analyze the gases she inhales and exhales, and deliver oxygen and isoflurane gas, a general anesthetic that is a modern replacement for ether. Another machine, this one less complicated, will continuously feed fentanyl, a synthetic relative of opium, through an intravenous line into Lucy's bloodstream. The effect of this delicately balanced cocktail will be immobility, unconsciousness, amnesia, and insensitivity to pain.

For many years, parents of children facing anesthesia feared brain damage. It was not an irrational fear. In an undertaking as complex and precarious as the administration of anesthesia, tubes can become crimped, machine settings can be inadvertently changed—any number of accidents might cut off a patient's oxygen. Unconscious, the brain has no way of crying for help. Continue for too many minutes, and damage, then death, inevitably results. In the old days, about all an anesthesiologist could do was keep an eye on the color of the fingers and blood. Blue meant deoxygenation. Blue meant trouble—trouble that was not always discovered in time to be corrected. The 1980s brought a lifesaver: the pulse oximeter, a simple device that continuously monitors oxygen saturation by reading the redness of blood as it flows through a finger. Because of the pulse oximeter and other sophisticated refinements in the science of anesthesia, malpractice-insurance rates for anesthesiologists dropped in the last decade.

Miler attaches an oximeter probe to Lucy's finger and plugs it into its console. The dial reads 100 percent, which is perfect. Miler, Rabb, Heggeness, and whoever may assist them as the day unfolds will watch that number carefully. To warn of early danger, an alarm will automatically sound if the oxygen level begins to drop.

Dorthy Enos is also busy.

She has scrubbed and gowned, and now she is arranging Hendren's instruments on several wheeled benches and trays draped in sterile cloths.

Most doctors at Children's use the house tools, a common set of thousands of instruments. But even though house tools receive expert handling, you never know who used them last; you never can be certain they're as sharp as you'd like or aren't missing a tooth. Since he was a resident, Hendren has bought his own instruments. They are the finest money can buy—mostly from Germany, with gold-plated handles for easy identification, engraved with his last name, and coded with three bright yellow bands so there is absolutely no question whose they are. Hendren's instruments are built to last. They do not dull quickly. They do not break easily or rust or stiffen up. In your hand, they feel solid, substantial, ready for serious work.

Enos does not merely supervise their cleaning and sterilization; she does not simply arrange for their sharpening and repair. She guards Hendren's instruments, letting no one borrow them, although at Hendren's instruction she will sometimes give one to a visiting surgeon as a memento of the visit. If you know Enos, you know that only a rookie or a fool would dare lay a hand on Hendren's tools, which number in the hundreds. The importance of having his own instruments is another of the lessons Hendren took from Robert E. Gross.

Enos is still in a period of adjustment. Ordinarily, she and her boss work in Room 7, the theater closest to the locker rooms and lounge. Everything is arranged to Enos's satisfaction in Room 7: the boxes of specialized sutures, the catheters, and the instrument cabinet, which also holds cough drops and the Mylanta tablets the chief sometimes requests after eating popcorn on a midnight break. In Room 7, rare is the delay caused by Enos's hunting for anything. Room 7, where Hendren and Enos spend more than half their waking hours in any given week, has been customized in other ways as well. On one wall is a New Yorker cartoon an anesthesiologist modified and presented to the scrub nurse in 1987 on the twenty-fifth anniversary of her employment with the chief. It shows a doctor, a nurse, and an octopus-like organ flying out of a patient into the air. WHOA! WATCH WHERE THAT THING LANDS, DOROTHY, the caption reads. WE'LL PROBABLY NEED IT. On the opposite wall is another sign: IF AN OPERATION IS DIFFICULT, YOU ARE NOT DOING IT PROPERLY. Hendren got that from Gross, who had it on the wall of his operating room.

Enos glances at the clock.

Almost eight.

It's going to be a long one. She wants to get under way.

Chapter 15

On the day he is to rebuild Lucy Moore, Hardy Hendren rises at five-fifteen A.M.

He has had six hours' sleep, a good night for him. So many times in forty years in surgery, Hendren has gotten by on three hours or one hour or no hours at all. He has learned to rely on the catnap, taken on a lounge sofa, a bed, or just flat on his back on his OR floor. As preparation for combat—when your enemy, not your biorhythms, dictates sleep—naval aviation cadets were taught to fall asleep instantly anytime, anywhere. First thing in the morning, fresh from a good night's rest, they'd be marched into the gymnasium and ordered to lie on the floor and force themselves to sleep, without benefit of pillow or mattress. Hendren has found it useful training for the preposterous schedule he keeps. Simply by closing his eyes, he can will himself to sleep.

Hardy breakfasts with Eleanor in the two-bedroom apartment they keep a few blocks from Children's. This is their home during the week, when time is too precious for the commute to their residence in Duxbury, forty-five minutes under the best of traffic conditions, which rarely prevail. Eleanor cuts her husband's grapefruit, pours his juice, fixes his oatmeal and his toast, which he takes with honey. As long as they've been married—through Hardy's years in college and medical school, through his eight-year surgical residency, through the raising of five children, through it all—Momma has fixed his breakfast. And every night, she's had dinner waiting for him, no matter what time he's gotten in. Even in the last two decades, when Eleanor and a friend have run a successful business, a wholesale clothing company called Cycle Venture, Inc., she's happily prepared her husband's meals. Hardy, who can assemble a child, barely knows how to make a meal.

As CNN brings the latest word of the war, Hardy works out on a Nordic Track exercise machine, which Eleanor also uses, more faithfully and more rigorously than her husband does. After shaving and showering, he dresses in a brown pin-striped suit.

"Look at this," he says to his wife. "Unbelievable."

A videotape of what a smart bomb can do is playing on TV.

"Do you see that? Isn't that unbelievable?"

We had .50-caliber machine guns, he thinks. *In the old days, pilots had to dive through a wall of lead, hoping not to get shot down in the process.* These *bombs—they don't have to aim them. Much of it is done with laser beams and computers.*

Hendren cannot break away.

But at seven-thirty, Lucy's appointed hour, he calls the OR to give the word to go ahead, to begin what will be about an hour of anesthesia preparations.

The technology of modern air warfare is mind-boggling, Hendren thinks as the network runs the clip again. For somebody who learned to fly behind the controls of a fabric-skinned biplane, this demonstration the U.S. military has been putting on over Baghdad is incredible. Who could ever have imagined anything like this, almost half a century ago?

Although Hendren's active duty ended in 1946, he flew eight more years in the naval reserves. He flew the SNJ, the plane on which he earned his wings, and he flew the SNB and the F6F Hellcat. All were piston-driven propeller aircraft. He never made it to jets, which were grabbing all the fly-boy glamour in the early fifties, the era Chuck Yeager owned.

"Hardy," Hendren's good friend Bruce T. Bathurst used to say, "you ought to give the jets a try."

But Hendren had done his homework. He'd talked to some full-time jet pilots. He knew that when he'd gone four or six months without flying, he was somewhat rusty in the cockpit. *A little bit off. You have to think your way through it, at least at first. It takes a while to get the feel back.* And that was with props. Hendren had hundreds of hours in props; he could imagine what it would be like tackling a jet on an occasional-weekend basis. *I'd never have the chance to become 100-percent familiar,* he thought. He had a career and Eleanor. They had a daughter, an infant son, and a third child on the way.

"It wouldn't be fair to them," Hendren said to Bathurst.

"You'd love it."

"I don't think it would be a safe thing to do," Hendren insisted.

Bathurst was an old friend, a best-buddy kind of friend. He'd been at Bryant School in Kansas City with Hendren, and he'd gone with Hardy to summer camp in Minnesota, and he'd gotten his Navy wings, just like Hardy. After the war, Bathurst had gone to work for the Prudential Insurance Company, and he'd sold his newlywed friend his first life insurance policy, for ten thousand dollars. Like Hendren, Bathurst had gone into the reserves. The only difference was that Bathurst, still single, moved up to jets.

"Come on, Hardy," he said, "don't be a chicken. You ought to check out in the jets."

But Hendren decided against checking out in the jets. Hendren, in 1954, made his last flight ever at the controls of a plane and then resigned from the reserves.

He was a senior surgical resident at Children's Hospital in June 1956, learning surgery under Dr. Gross, when word reached him that Bathurst was dead.

Navy Reserve Lieutenant Bruce T. Bathurst, thirty, had taken a single-seat F9F-7 jet fighter twenty-five thousand feet over Missouri farmland on a weekend training run when something happened. Maybe he had an aneurysm. Maybe, as his doctor friend would suspect, in his relative unfamiliarity with his jet he'd forgotten to turn an oxygen valve. No one would ever know. As a pilot in a companion jet watched, Bathurst went into a dive. He could not be raised on the radio. Twenty-five thousand feet, straight to the ground, his jet disintegrating on impact in a field.

There but for the grace of God go I, thought Hendren. Sadly, he wrote a letter of condolence to Bathurst's parents. In Kansas City, Bathurst was memorialized at a service conducted by the Reverend Richard M. Trelease, pastor of Saint Paul's Episcopal Church. In time, a playground would be named for the pilot, in honor of his volunteer work with underprivileged children. And Hendren would give his friend's name to his third son.

· · ·

Seven-forty A.M.

Hendren finds a parking space in a Children's Hospital garage. He crosses Longwood Avenue and zips up three flights of stairs and down a hall to his office. Barbara Cosgrove, who sometimes serves as surgical cinematographer, is waiting. So is Paul Andriesse, Hendren's medical artist for twenty-five years. They will be joining the chief in Room 17 today.

"Have you seen the TV?" Hendren asks. "Those bombs? Right down the elevator shaft and then—boom! The sides of the building blow out! Isn't it unbelievable?"

Hendren talks about smart bombs and flying as it used to be and the evolution of aerial combat and America's prospects in the Persian Gulf War, a shade more optimistic this morning. He strides into the inner office, checks the overnight messages, returns a phone call, pencils a note, and leaves his wallet and watch in his desk drawer, where they won't be stolen. When he emerges, Barbara is holding the appointment calendar. She has a question about next week's schedule, and Hendren answers it. And all around are letters to sign, slides to sort, a manuscript to review, a videotape to edit, notes for a lecture on cloacal exstrophy he's giving to a gathering of urologists first thing tomorrow morning at the Harvard Medical School's Countway Library. Even with sixteen-hour days, a staff of six assistants and secretaries, computers, residents to help with the load, and putting in time on weekends and vacations—even with eighty- and ninety-hour weeks as the norm—the work never ends. It never has.

"OK," Hendren says, "let's go."

Briefcase and X rays in hand, he moves at a near trot toward the OR locker room. Down a flight of stairs, through a lobby, down a long corridor, past Cardiology, past the turnoff to Radiology, and into a stairwell that abuts the basement kitchen. The smell of fish frying is a reminder that this is Friday in Boston. Hendren climbs another flight of stairs two steps at a time and pushes past two doors. Punching the combination to the lock on a third door, he enters the men's OR locker room.

Hendren strips to undershirt and plaid boxer shorts. His shoulders and arms, especially his forearms, are muscular. His legs are sturdy. He pulls on support hosiery, which will help control the swelling after he's been on his feet longer than most people have been awake for the day. He dons scrub shirt and scrub pants and, finally, his shoes. Many surgeons operate in Nikes or Reeboks, the footwear of professional athletes and inner-city kids, but not Hendren. He wears old-fashioned surgeon's shoes, which are made of white deerskin and resemble penny loafers. He regularly treats them to liquid polish, just as Robert E. Gross did. And when his shoes are dirtied from blood or iodine-based germicide, universal fluids in any OR, he scrubs them with soap and water in the locker-room sink, then lets them dry on the shoe tree he keeps in his locker. Enos, who orders Hendren's shoes, keeps careful track of their condition. In her locker across the hall, she always keeps a new pair, ready for immediate service.

Hendren puts on his cap and ties the bottom of his mask; made of paper, both are meant to be used once and thrown away. Dressed for work, he goes to the lounge. Hendren used to drink eight or ten cups of coffee a day, a steelworker's ration, but in recent years caffeine began to give his hands a fine tremble. It happened to Gross mid-career, too. Now, Hendren gets through the day with an occasional half cup and sometimes a spot of tea. He drinks a half cup of coffee now, downed in a single swallow. After shooting the breeze with Arnold Colodny, a member of his department who also trained under Gross, Hendren heads down the corridor to Room 17. He secures the top of his mask so that his nose and mouth are covered and walks through the door.

"Good morning," he says.

"Good morning, sir," the two residents who will assist him say. One, Jeffrey Steinberg, is in his next-to-last year of the Harvard Program in Urology, which includes significant time at four hospitals, including Children's. The other resident, Raymond R. Price, is a general surgery resident at Brigham and Women's, and his training includes several weeks' rotation through Children's. Steinberg and Price are among the best young doctors in the land, already in possession of impressive CVs, prosperous and productive futures all but assured. And yet . . . and yet, when they're with Hendren, the legendary Hardly Human, they somehow feel reduced in stature.

Hendren squeezes past a suture cart to get to the light board, where he arranges some of Lucy's X rays. "Good-looking kidney," he says. "No reflux. This is a terrible room, isn't it, Dorothy? There just isn't room to turn around."

"No, there isn't," Enos says. With Andriesse and Cosgrove and Cosgrove's video setup, it is unusually crowded.

I think we should start with her on her belly, Hendren thinks. See what she has for muscle for an anus, then open from behind, mobilize the rectum away from the bladder. That's the difficult part. A hole in that bladder could spell trouble. Then we'll look for a vagina. If we don't find one, . . . we'll probably use colon, and it looks like she has plenty of that. We'll have to turn the baby. Could be several turns in this case. Don't see any way around it. We'll have to build a urethra out of something. This will be a hard one. We won't be out of here before midnight.

No one in his right mind relishes doing cases like this. . . .

Theoretically, it would be possible to accomplish what Hendren plans today in two or more smaller operations. Other surgeons who have taken on a cloaca have done just that. The advantage is virtually all to the surgeon. The surgeon doesn't have to worry about being twelve hours into something with no end in sight. Conceptually, it seems easier to isolate and dispose of problem A first, then problem B, and finally problem C—three separate operations Hendren ordinarily would combine into one. The flaw in the rationale of A-B-C, as some surgeons have discovered to the detriment of their patients, is that in going back for problem B, you may unavoidably damage some of what you accomplished in solving problem A. Before Hendren developed his passion for cloaca, other surgeons had tried reconstructing children by first pulling through the colon and building an anus. But what they found was it was virtually impossible to go back in to work on bladder, urethra, and vagina without wrecking some of their colon work.

From his decades of experience, Hendren has coined a motto, a recurrent theme in many of his lectures: "Small operations for big problems don't work."

It's much better, when you're dealing with adjacent structures, to deal with it all at once and not get into a previous repair when you're doing your subsequent repair. I have preached for the last fifteen years that you don't do that.

For the benefit of his residents, Hendren wants to quickly review Lucy's other problems. He puts films of this week's MRI on the light board and studies black-and-white pictures of Lucy's spinal cord and spine. The films will go to neurosurgeon R. Michael Scott for an opinion. Before talking to Scott, Hendren's pretty sure what his opinion will be.

"Well, that's abnormal," he says. "She needs to be operated on back there. Let's get Dr. Scott to opine. What else do we know about her?"

"She had a VSD, which was repaired," Price says. Yesterday's cardiology workup showed that Lucy's heart has healed nicely since Castaneda's operation last year.

Having seen all of the films he wants to for now, Hendren goes to the phone and calls Robert Lebowitz, a radiologist who, like Scott, works with Hendren on his cloaca patients. They chat a moment about another case.

Eight forty-five.

As the anesthesiologists continue their preparation, Hendren leaves Room 17. Moving toward the waiting room, he observes, "This is probably the only child in the world undergoing this particular procedure on this particular day."

Hendren finds the Moores. He brings them into the office of the surgical-liaison nurses.

"She's going to sleep fine," he says.

Everyone sits, the Moores on two chairs, Hendren behind the desk. On the desk is a bowl of candy. Hendren seldom lunches, not in the usually recognized fashion. What he does sometimes is slip back to his office for a sandwich or some fruit and cottage cheese. Other times, he goes to the lounge for tea or a cup of light cream, straight up. Or he ducks into here for a fistful of candy. Today's selection is M&Ms and candy corn, an overstock from Halloween.

"Anybody want candy?" Hendren asks.

No one but he does. He takes a fistful.

"OK," he says. "Now what is your understanding of what we hope to accomplish today?"

"You're going to do the best possible job to give her a working anus and a working vagina and while you're at it, take out her bad kidney," Beth says.

Hendren discusses the results of Lucy's MRI, how there is a problem with her spinal cord.

"I'm going to push it from my mind today," says Beth.

"We shouldn't be thinking about it today, should we?" asks Jack.

"You can if you want to," Hendren says. But, he cautions, it would only add to today's worry.

He asks the Moores if anyone along the way has mentioned there being ovaries inside Lucy. No, they say. Hendren reminds them that no one has found a vagina, either. But that doesn't necessarily mean there isn't one, he says. Until they've been opened and thoroughly explored, cloaca patients are virgin territory: uncharted, unpredictable, unique.

"In the past year," Hendren says, "I've seen six patients who didn't have a vagina endoscopically or on X ray who turned out to have two. In fact, we call it occult vagina. We're going to do a paper on it."

Hendren explains his game plan. It is a rough sketch, short on detail, long on flexibility. It's not that Hendren doesn't like briefing parents. But how much can you say if you don't know yourself precisely what you're going to do?

"We're going to try to come up with a vagina, rectum, and urinary tract that work," he says, letting it go at that.

He takes a sheet of paper.

"Now," he says, an edge suddenly in his voice, "I've got to do this painful business of an operative permit. I hate it. For thirty-five years I did surgery—probably an average of five hundred cases a year—without an operative permit. Today, we have to do it because behind every patient is a lawyer advertising 'Sue your doctor.' "

Beth says, "We'll sign your permit, and we don't believe in suing."

Hendren doesn't write yet.

Merely pronouncing the word *sue* sends him into the stratosphere, where invariably he will tell his latest lawyer-as-scumbag joke or deliver his five-minute exposition on medical malpractice, realm of parasites. Hendren's three oldest sons are doctors: Douglas Hardy Hendren, an orthopedic surgeon in California; William Grant Hendren, chief of cardiac surgery at the Graduate Hospital in Philadelphia; and Robert Bruce Hendren, a urology resident at the Massachusetts General Hospital. David Fraser Hendren, his fourth son, chose law—corporate law. "If he'd have gone into malpractice," Hendren has said, "he'd have had four people in the family wanting to turn him into a boy soprano."

You're in a room with Saddam Hussein, a cobra ready to strike, and a lawyer. You have a revolver with just two bullets. What do you do?

Shoot the lawyer—twice, to make sure he's dead.

Or, *Have you heard the one about why they're using lawyers instead of rats for laboratory experiments?*

There are three reasons. One, lawyers are in such plentiful supply. Two, people tend to become fond of rats. And three, there are some things rats just won't do.

Hendren didn't expect to be fixing Lucy Moore today.

Until last week, he expected to be in Superior Court. For the second time in his life, he was being sued. A New Hampshire boy whose deformed penis he'd satisfactorily repaired in 1983 had alleged, in a 1985 action brought by the parents, that Hendren had improperly positioned the boy on the OR table. The result, the family claimed, was nerve damage that caused the boy to lose full use of his left leg. According to the suit, the boy has suffered bodily pain and mental anguish and will need continued hospitalization. Because of Hendren, the suit contends, the boy's ability to enjoy life "has been permanently adversely affected."

Hendren was taught to supervise personally the positioning of all of his patients, and it's a lesson he's taken to heart. He remembered this case. He remembered how the New Hampshire boy was laid out on the OR table—in the same position as hundreds of other patients on whom he'd performed similar surgery without complication. There was no conceivable way, Hendren maintained, that the boy's leg could have sustained the kind of pressure needed for that kind of alleged nerve damage. But the boy and his parents were adamant: Hendren had screwed up. They retained a Boston firm notorious for its malpractice litigation, and the firm started blizzarding Hendren with interrogatories and depositions and motions, often part of a strategy of harassment and intimidation to force a pretrial settlement. During the five years the suit was hanging over his head, angering him, making him feel extremely unkindly toward malpractice lawyers, Hendren gave hours and hours to his defense—time that would have been better spent with patients and his research. If the plaintiffs believed they could wring a deal, they'd badly miscalculated, they obviously didn't know the first thing about this doctor. Hendren, to all intents and purposes, was being called a hack. His honor was being besmirched, a matter he did not take lightly.

He would go to trial, just as he had a year earlier in the only other suit ever filed against him. He would trust a jury to uphold his reputation. He would trust them to see this suit for what it was.

This is about greed, nothing more, Hendren thought.

"I had to sit a whole morning giving a deposition to a snide bitch lawyer," Hendren tells the Moores. "The purpose of that was to make me angry."

And he was as angry as he'd ever been, but he controlled his emotions, hid them beneath a cold, full-Harvard-professor-of-surgery veneer. He answered the lawyer's questions during the deposition. But he did not miss the opportunity to signal, in ways subtle and not so subtle, that he was less than awed by the lawyer's intellectual timber. "She is just going around in circles," Hendren said at one point to the lawyer taking his deposition. Leaving, he had some unsolicited medical advice for her. "By the way," he said, "I notice you have a mole on your cheek. You know, those can be precancerous. If I were you, I'd have it removed." The lawyer was not amused, but Hendren was, mightily, and for the first time all day.

The trial was scheduled to begin on January 16.

"We started scrambling," Hendren tells the Moores, "canceling patients like yourself who had been booked a long time."

About a week before the Moores were scheduled to fly to Boston, Paula Zafferes called them to say Hendren had a court case—no more details than that—and it looked as though the chief wouldn't be able to keep his date with Lucy. The Moores already had their tickets. They told Paula they would not seek a refund. In the event something changed, even at the last minute, they'd get to Boston.

As the Moores waited, word reached Hendren through his attorney, John A. Kiernan, a former criminal prosecutor, that the plaintiffs might be willing to settle. A figure was floated: sixty thousand dollars, something in that ballpark—just sign on the dotted line, and everyone could shake hands and walk away.

As settlements go, sixty grand was peanuts.

"I did a perfect job," Hendren told his lawyer. "He's got a normal penis. I don't know what happened to his leg, if anything, but it wasn't anything I did. I've spent probably fifty thousand dollars and the equivalent of a month of my life on this. John, I'm not going to fold like that. Too many doctors do that."

Only once before had Hendren been sued, by the mother of a girl whose diseased urinary tract was slowly killing her. Before Hendren took on the case, Zafferes spoke to the mother on the phone. "She's an angry, hostile, aggressive, demanding woman," Zafferes told her boss, "and you've got rocks in your head if you take this child with that mother." But Hendren does not refuse a patient because of a parent's personality. He went ahead and successfully repaired the problem, and the mother's thanks was a twenty-five-million-dollar lawsuit claiming Hendren had caused the girl to have chronic diarrhea. Hendren couldn't believe it. He knew that whatever had caused her diarrhea, it wasn't his surgery; in fact, as he later learned, she'd been under treatment for the problem long before coming to him. Hendren would not accept an offer to settle. He wiped a week off his schedule and proceeded to trial, in April 1990. It took little more than an hour for the jury to find him innocent.

No, Hendren said to Kiernan, things were no different this time on the case of the New Hampshire boy. *I'll let the jury decide if I injured that boy's leg.*

"Take them to the mat," Hendren instructed Kiernan. "I'll take whatever time I need to defeat that."

Kiernan went back to the plaintiffs. "No settlement," he said.

"What about something even lower?" the other side said. "What about a nominal settlement?"

"No dice," Kiernan said.

Less than a week before the scheduled start of the trial, the plaintiffs folded. No reason was given to Hendren, although he didn't think it was too tough to come up with it. "His injury had a better outcome than we anticipated," one of the plaintiff's lawyers later told a reporter who inquired about the case. "It wasn't as serious as we thought initially."

That's a lie, Hendren thought. *The patient had no nerve weakness at a postoperative visit a month after surgery. As regards disability, the only course he passed in school in the next four years was gym! The truth is they didn't have a case. They weren't going to make any money. They were going to lose, and they didn't have any more money to shell out for costs. And what's more, they never paid their bill for the operation, just like the parents in the other so-called malpractice suit.*

"The family wasn't going to do that," Hendren tells the Moores.

"They answered the lawyer's ad: 'Come see us! It'll cost you absolutely nothing!' " The suit was dismissed. Before it was, Hendren made sure the record stated the reason: "the plaintiffs having decided not to prosecute this action." No one reading it could ever wonder if a settlement, even a measly one, had been struck.

Before writing Lucy's operative permit, Hendren repeats for the Moores his opinion of malpractice lawyers, lest there be any doubt. "They're absolutely scurrilous, unprincipled bastards," he says.

"I'd be angry," Beth says. "I'd be bursting."

"I don't have time to be angry," Hendren says. "But a lot of my friends have quit surgery because of this."

On his complicated cases, Hendren does not use the standard preprinted operative-permit form. Nor does he ordinarily use the words *permit* or *permission*, since they might somehow imply that the surgeon, and not the family, initiated the proceedings. His preferred term is *operative request*. What value that might have in court is untested. Before his two suits, both filed in 1985, he never wrote one, and he hasn't been sued since.

Hendren writes, reading as he goes along, asking questions.

"Do you understand what I'm going to try to do?"

"We read your articles," Beth says.

"How many?"

"Two."

"And did you understand?"

"Yeah, with the illustrations and everything."

"Do you know what the risks are?"

"You could break the bowel."

"It could leak. It could stenose. It could not work. All sorts of things. And we have anesthesia catastrophes. Rarely, but they can occur."

Beth and Jack sign Hendren's form.

"We have asked Dr. Hendren to operate on Lucy's rare problem and to do his best to give her functional anatomy from her cloacal condition. He has explained all aspects of it, we have read and understand 2 of his latest articles on it. We want him to proceed knowing that she can't function 'as is.' We understand the risks involved with surgery and anesthesia. All of our questions have been answered."

From a literary perspective, it is not one of Hendren's better efforts. It does not capture the magnitude of the risk or the trust strangers place in his hands or the great uncertainty of outcome—the fact that not even Hendren, the world's cloaca expert, can make a perfect child every time.

Hendren stands, takes one last handful of candy corn, and heads for the OR door. The Moores, who have been given a beeper, are planning to leave the hospital to shop.

"We'll go down and do our best," Hendren says.

"We have faith in you," Beth says. "That's why we're here, leaving our gorgeous Florida weather."

Does he have any idea when he will be done? the Moores want to know.

"When the last stitch is in," Hendren says.

Chapter 16

It was called Wigwam Circle.

It was 104 units of housing, arranged in rows that resembled the spokes of a wagon wheel. It was prefabricated and cramped, roughly two hundred square feet per unit, smaller than a garage. It was heated by kerosene space heaters that you filled, at a nickel a gallon, from barrels outside the front door. Once used to house workers in a wartime shipyard in Maine, Wigwam Circle had been taken down and rebuilt in Hanover, New Hampshire, where Dartmouth College—like most colleges in 1947—was being flooded with veterans coming back to campus with their new spouses. The war was over. Building futures and starting families were the orders of the day.

In early 1947, when Hardy Hendren returned to Dartmouth to resume his undergraduate education, he and Eleanor lived at Wigwam Circle. It barely would have qualified as a Navy barracks. Their apartment was a single room with two chairs, table, hot plate, sink, and a sofa that converted into a bed. Eleanor cooked on the hot plate. Hardy, enrolled in comparative anatomy, used to dissect frogs late into the night on the table. And if you wanted the latest gossip at Wigwam Circle, all you had to do was knock on the wall. Having gotten your neighbor's attention, you could hold a conversation without raising your voice.

Economically, the newlyweds were struggling. Hardy had the GI Bill, but that was only ninety dollars a month. What would be their salvation would be the Calvinist ethic, whose full meaning had been imparted to Hardy by a Latin teacher at a preparatory school. *We'll just have to work harder*, Hardy thought. *We'll do whatever we have to*. Hardy got a job in the medical library, checking out books for sixty-five cents an hour, barely minimum wage. On reunion weekend, he worked as a dormitory clerk. Eleanor bought fabric at a mill-end store, and turned out drapes, which she sold. Hardy bought fishing flies, which Eleanor sewed onto neckties she'd made, and Mr. Hendren purchased the whole lot, some 250 in all, for Christmas gifts for his customers and employees. Hardy made cobblers' benches and sold them to a Hanover antiques dealer, who advertised them in her window as REPRODUCTIONS BY A DARTMOUTH STUDENT. One year, Hardy and a friend bought a truckload of furniture at an auction, and after painting it green—Dartmouth green—they resold the furniture, at significant markup, to incoming freshmen. Hardy and that same friend bought a cow, had the animal butchered, and filled a frozen food locker with cheap steaks and roasts. Hardy's father sent the newlyweds a check for one hundred dollars every month. Hardy and his bride sold their blood, for twenty-five dollars a pint. *One way or another*, they thought, *we're going to make it*.

By early spring, when Eleanor learned she was pregnant, both sets of parents had been told that their families were now united through the marriage of an only daughter to an only son. "It was too hasty," Eleanor's mother said, to which Eleanor replied, "He's right for me, Mother. We love each other and this is our life commitment." It would take time, but Eleanor's parents would come around. Mrs. Hendren smiled knowingly when her son told her of the wedding. "I am not surprised," she said. Hardy had expected his father to be upset, but he wasn't. "I agree with you that she's the right person," Mr. Hendren said, "and I'll help you in any way I can." In years to come, he would credit Eleanor with much of his son's success, as would his son.

Having children was never a question. Hardy and Eleanor had hoped for a large family, and the beginning of it came soon enough. At 4:02 A.M. on October 22, 1947, Sandra McLeod Hendren was born, three weeks premature, in Hanover. Hardy and Eleanor were both twenty-one years old.

Labor had begun the day before. Hardy had come home from chemistry lab to find Eleanor having contractions. "She's three weeks early," Eleanor's doctor, John Boardman said to Hardy over the phone. Boardman had examined Eleanor only that afternoon. "It's nothing to worry about," he said. "I'm sure it's false labor."

But the contractions did not subside. A neighbor, Ann Reynolds, was timing them. Six minutes between. Then five. Then four. Hardy called Boardman back. Still, he didn't believe Eleanor was in labor. "If it will make you feel better, go to the hospital," Boardman said. "But I can tell you she's going to be home tomorrow without a baby." A friend gave the Hendrens a ride to Mary Hitchcock Memorial Hospital.

Delivery rooms in 1947 were off-limits to fathers, even fathers who soon would be medical-school students required to deliver strangers' babies in order to graduate. Hendren sat in a deserted corridor all night, waiting for word. Shortly after four A.M., the phone rang. "Mr. Hendren?" the voice from the delivery room said. "You have a baby girl."

When he was allowed into Eleanor's room, he gave his wife a kiss. "I love you," he said.

At the nursery window, Hardy saw his daughter for the first time. A nurse held Sandy, wrapped in a blanket.

"I'm so proud!" he said to Eleanor.

That afternoon, he made his wife an apple pie, baking it on the hot plate, inside a metal box that approximated an oven.

Sandy was adorable, the kind of baby strangers feel compelled to touch, with freckles and blond hair and her father's blue eyes. Eleanor and Hardy—twenty-one-year-old Eleanor and Hardy—took Sandy everywhere. The Hendrens did not have a car, but you needn't have had a car in Hanover in 1947. Hanover was a village, the quintessential New England college town, designed for an earlier century. In Hanover, you could walk to the grocer's or to the movie theater or to the Phi Delta Theta fraternity to have a beer on a Saturday night. If you had a baby, you could put her in a carriage and take her along, too. When winter set in, Hardy fashioned a sled out of a carriage and runners. If the snow got ahead of the plows, they could still get where they had to go, this family of three.

Eleanor had Sandy's care during the day, when Hardy was at class, but Dad took over the nighttime changing and the feeding: a bottle of milk warmed on the hot plate. Hardy read to Sandy as she lay on his lap. He sang her to sleep. He cranked the Victrola and

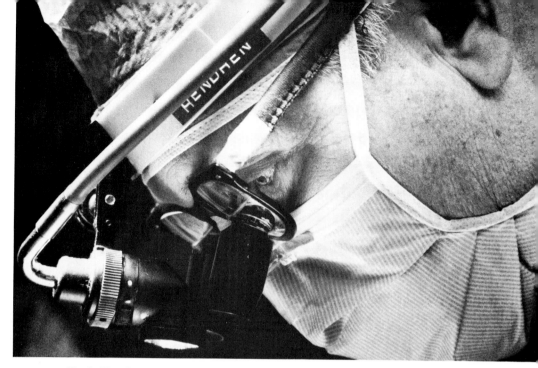

Hardy Hendren concentrates on his work. Sixty-six years old, he has been known to operate more than twenty-four hours straight on some of the most complicated cases ever to face a surgeon, an ability that has earned him the nickname "Hardly Human." (Courtesy: William K. Daby/*Providence Journal-Bulletin*)

Hardy Hendren's great-great grandfather Jeremiah, a Baptist preacher and merchant in Norfolk County, Virginia, in the early nineteenth century. Jeremiah was known for his honesty and intelligence. (Courtesy: John Hendron)

At age two and a half, Hardy Hendren was living in New Orleans, city of his birth. The Hendrens would move to Kansas City, Missouri, the summer after Hardy finished first grade.
(Courtesy: Mrs. W. Hardy Hendren Jr.)

Hendren was twelve years old and an Episcopal choirboy in Kansas City in 1938. The next year, his friend and fellow choirboy Ben Trelease would die of the kind of urinary disease that Hendren the surgeon would be able to cure.
(Courtesy: Mrs. W. Hardy Hendren Jr.)

Home from prep school in Virginia, the teenaged Hardy Hendren poses with his family at Christmas, 1942. His parents are seated; sisters Carol, left, and Peggy, right, are standing with him. (Courtesy: Mrs. W. Hardy Hendren Jr.)

To qualify as a Naval aviator in 1946 at the end of three years in the Navy, Hendren had to make repeated landings on an aircraft carrier. (Courtesy: W. Hardy Hendren III)

New parents Eleanor and Hardy Hendren with their first child, Sandra McLeod Hendren, in 1948, when Hendren was a student at Dartmouth Medical School. (Courtesy: Eleanor Hendren)

In 1959, when her husband was completing his long surgical training, Eleanor posed with their children: Sandy, twelve; Douglas, nine; Will, six; and Robert, two and a half. David, the Hendrens' last child, was born the following year. (Courtesy: Eleanor Hendren)

Sandy Hendren in 1966. Eighteen years old, she had lived more than half her life with diabetes, a disease not even her distinguished doctor father could stop from killing her. (Courtesy: Eleanor Hendren)

Boston's Children's
Hospital in about 1870,
a year after it accepted
its first patients.
(Courtesy: Children's
Hospital, Boston)

The admitting office at Children's Hospital shortly after it opened, in a house
in Boston's South End. In its first five months, thirty patients were treated, several for broken limbs. The hospital's rich surgical tradition was underway.
(Courtesy: Children's Hospital, Boston)

A heart operation on Lorraine Sweeney, seven, at Children's Hospital in 1938 revolutionized cardiac surgery worldwide. The surgeon was thirty-three-year-old Robert E. Gross, the mercurial genius who would be one of Hardy Hendren's mentors. (Courtesy: Children's Hospital, Boston)

Children's Hospital surgeons in 1939. Standing are Chief William E. Ladd, fifth from left, and Gross, extreme right. Gross waited until Ladd was out of town to perform his 1938 heart operation, a move Ladd never forgave. Sitting, seventh from left, is Orvar Swenson, a brilliant surgeon Gross came to consider a threat. (Courtesy: Children's Hospital, Boston)

Children's Hospital surgical staff in 1960, when Hendren, front row extreme left, was chief resident. Gross, fifth from left, had replaced Ladd as surgeon-in-chief. Shortly after this photograph was taken, Gross turned on Hendren, driving him away from Children's. (Courtesy: Children's Hospital, Boston)

Surgeons at the Massachusetts General Hospital in 1961 gather around the chief of surgery, Edward D. Churchill, seated. Hendren is standing in the last row, left; in front of him is George L. Nardi, who more than a decade later operated on Hendren for colon cancer. (Courtesy: Massachusetts General Hospital)

Hendren and Gross in front of the Harvard Medical School on Gross's eightieth birthday celebration in 1985. On that day, the Robert E. Gross Professorship, still held by Hendren, was announced. After being gone more than two decades, Hendren had finally returned to Children's.
(Courtesy: Harvard Medical School)

Children's Hospital today. (Courtesy: Children's Hospital, Boston)

Children's Hospital

Three generations of the Hendren family on Hardy and Eleanor's boat, *Nomo*, in August 1992. The Hendrens' four sons, three of whom are surgeons, and the fourth an attorney, are standing in the rear. Hardy's mother, ninety-four, was not present for this portrait. (Courtesy: Green Photographers, Inc.)

Hendren's operating room at the time of Lucy Moore's surgery. The author, back to camera, is speaking with Hendren. Chief resident Steve Stylianos is standing, while anesthesia technician Winston Woods prepares the room for the next case. (Courtesy: William K. Daby/*Providence Journal-Bulletin*)

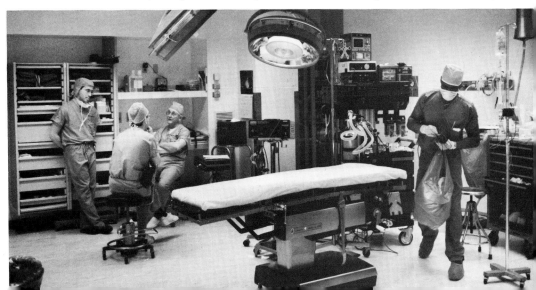

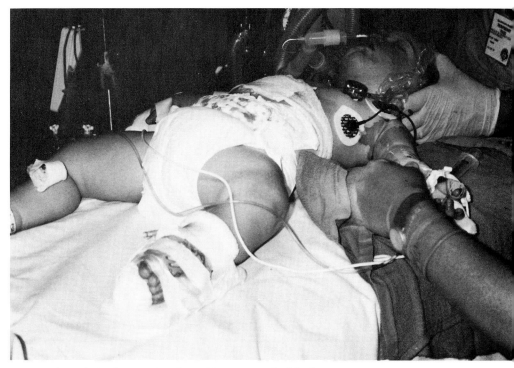

At eight in the morning, Lucy Moore is readied for her reconstructive surgery. Come midnight, she will still be in Hendren's OR. (Courtesy: G. Wayne Miller)

Having cut through Lucy's feature-less bottom, Hendren marks the position he wants for the new organs he is about to build for his fourteen-month-old patient.
(Courtesy: G. Wayne Miller)

Dorothy Enos hands Hendren an instrument. After working so long with him, she almost always anticipates what tools, sutures, or other items he needs.
(Courtesy: William K. Daby/*Providence Journal-Bulletin*)

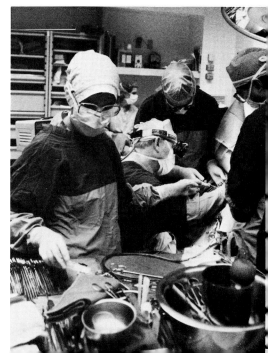

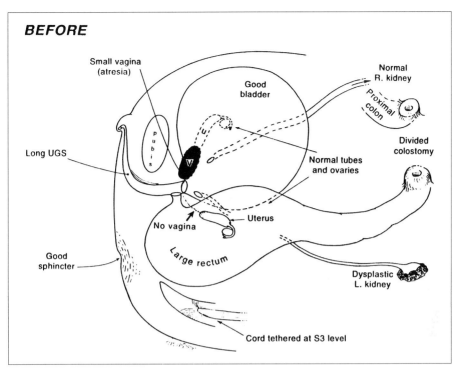

BEFORE

Small vagina (atresia)

Good bladder

Normal R. kidney

Proximal colon

Divided colostomy

Normal tubes and ovaries

Long UGS

Pubis

U

V

Good sphincter

No vagina

Uterus

Large rectum

Dysplastic L. kidney

Cord tethered at S3 level

A diagram of Lucy Moore's lower anatomy before Hendren rebuilt her. Her reproductive, urinary, and intestinal systems are all abnormal, as are her spinal cord and heart, not pictured. The view is from her left side. (Courtesy: Medical artist Paul Andriesse)

After the operation, Lucy Moore's anatomy is almost the same as any little girl's. She no longer has to wear a bag. (Courtesy: Medical artist Paul Andriesse)

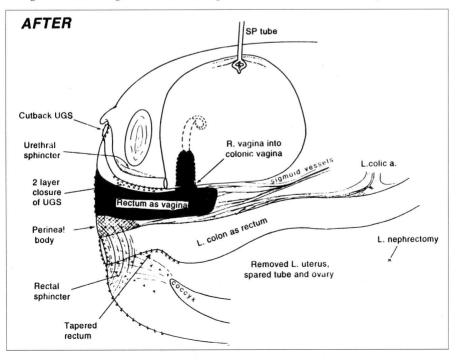

AFTER

SP tube

Cutback UGS

R. vagina into colonic vagina

L.colic a.

sigmoid vessels

Urethral sphincter

2 layer closure of UGS

Rectum as vagina

L. colon as rectum

Perineal body

L. nephrectomy

Removed L. uterus, spared tube and ovary

coccyx

Rectal sphincter

Tapered rectum

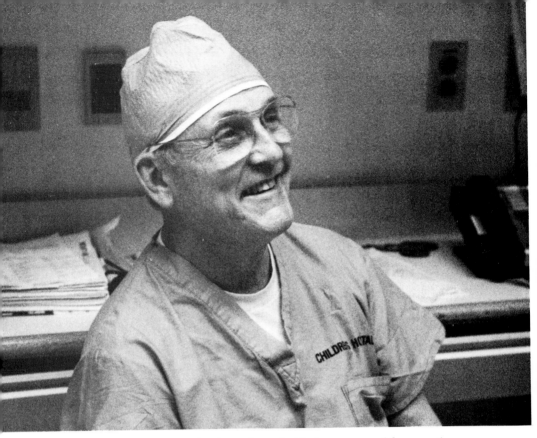

A postoperative shot of Hendren, pleased with the outcome of the operation. (Courtesy: William K. Daby/*Providence Journal-Bulletin*)

Finally normal after almost a dozen operations, Lucy Moore, almost two, poses with the author outside her home in Florida. (Courtesy: *Beth Moore*)

played children's songs for her, and it was apparent, even when she was a baby, that Sandy would love music for as long as she would live, which would be thirty-seven years and thirteen days.

After graduating from Dartmouth College, Hendren enrolled in Dartmouth's two-year medical program, from which he graduated in 1950. That summer, he, Sandy, and Eleanor, pregnant again, drove to Boston in their first car: a 1950 Ford sedan, a gift from Hendren's father. The car did not come with seat belts and shoulder straps, but Hendren wanted them; he'd learned their value while getting his wings. That summer, while flying in the Navy reserves, Hendren scrounged a pair of seat belts and shoulder straps from a wrecked Navy bomber and installed them in the Ford. Eleanor hated the seat belts, but until she had strapped herself in, her husband wouldn't drive.

Hendren was a third-year student at the Harvard Medical School. Hearing Robert E. Gross lecture that fall, Hendren's first semester at Harvard, he knew beyond all doubt he wanted to be a pediatric surgeon, just like Children's chief. This sort of commitment pleased Gross, who took a special interest in students. He remembered the humiliation and embarrassment of being banished from the great Harvey Cushing's operating room when he was at the Harvard Medical School, and he'd vowed he would never treat a student so rudely, no matter how big he got. Gross would nurture a new generation. Gross would welcome medical-school students to his operating room. Ones like Hendren—these were just the sort of young men who had what it took to push the frontiers someday.

Hendren had led the drive to revise the national internship matching system, but that wasn't the only way in which this Dartmouth transfer attracted attention. No one worked harder than Hendren. No one in his class took more quickly to the knife or was more fascinated with anatomy, with the beauty and symmetry of organs and tissues and the supreme logic with which they were put together. Hendren found delight in the dog lab, where he and his classmates performed their first basic operations—appendectomies, bowel resections, splenectomies—on mongrel dogs. At home, his two children asleep, Hendren stayed up practicing his knots. Thousands and thousands of knots, tied inside a training box whose bottom was covered with hooks: surgeon's knots, square knots, one-handed knots, knots using needle holders, knots in tight places, knots with eyes closed.

"Able, vigorous, hard working, intelligent man with good practical sense," wrote a Dr. Dooley, one of Hendren's teachers. Frederick C. Robbins, an instructor in pediatric medicine at Children's (who in 1954 would share the Nobel Prize with John F. Enders and Thomas H. Weller, also of Children's, for cultivating the polio virus) wrote that Hendren was "much better than average in every respect. Seemed unusually mature in his judgement and showed unusual interest. Personality easy and pleasing. Tended to be rather slow but thorough." In July 1951, at the beginning of his senior year, Hendren, twenty-five, spent a month at Children's Hospital. He was taking an elective course in pediatric surgery, and his job, known as striker, consisted of placing IVs and drawing blood and testing urine—surgery's scut work, in which there is no glory.

I love it, Hendren thought. But he loved nothing so much as the opportunity to scrub and go into the operating room with Gross, the number-one pediatric surgeon in the world.

Hendren had not come by his enthusiasm for the OR as naturally as he might have imagined years ago on a spring day in a Kansas City park when he caught and dissected his first specimen with a pocketknife. Real-life surgery was nothing like pulling apart a tadpole, nor was it exactly like the movie he'd seen when he was a student at Bryant School. Dad had made the movie in Fort Worth, Texas, where Mr. Hendren's friend, a surgeon by the name of Herbert Beavers, had invited him and his camera into the operating room to watch a hysterectomy. Mr. Hendren let his son, already so interested in surgery, watch that film, and the boy did, time after time after time on a projector screen he erected in the living room.

No, real-life surgery was cutting into real-life people who bled real-life blood. Actually being there—well, it definitely wasn't a movie. It aroused squeamishness. Hendren had observed his first operation while home on vacation from Woodberry Forest School. His father had a good friend in Kansas City, Lawrence P. Engel, who was a general surgeon at St. Luke's Hospital, where Ben Trelease had died. Would Hardy like to watch him work? Engel wanted to know. Would he ever! The operation was a mastectomy, the removal of a female breast. Hardy scrubbed, gowned, and stood at

Engel's elbow. And when Engel made his first cut, a little bleeder squirted Hardy on his gown. *I feel like I'm going to faint,* he thought. He had had the same feeling in the summer of 1943, when he spent his first semester at Dartmouth. A friend in the medical program, Ed Price from Kansas City, invited him to the anatomy lab, and one lunchtime, Hardy visited. The lab was in the basement. It had a concrete floor and six tables on which were laid out six partially dissected cadavers, including one whose ticket to medical school had been suicide, as was evident from the rope burn around the neck. The sickly sweet odor of embalming fluid filled the room, and while that didn't seem to bother the students, who were taking their lunch break—and were happily eating their sandwiches!—Hardy had to leave the room. "I don't know if I'm going to be able to handle this," Hendren wrote in a letter home to his mother. "This is pretty grim."

But Hardy got used to cadavers. He got used to surgery, came to love it, just as he came to love flying despite slicking himself with his vomit his first time in a plane.

Gross worked in Operating Room 3 of Children's, a cramped, stuffy, street-level room with a window whose bottom half had been painted white so passersby couldn't look in. Gross was a quiet operator. He made no flashes in the OR, told no great stories or jokes to break the monotonous stretches. He did not yell or chew out the residents, not in his OR. He was unfailingly polite to his staff. If he noticed that the nurses were cold, he'd call Engineering and have them turn up the heat. If a dressing needed to be changed, he would change it himself and clean up his mess afterward. Gross kept a toolbox, which residents had painted gold, in Room 3. If an autoclave needed to be fixed or a door oiled or a light bulb changed, Gross did it. It seemed there wasn't anything Gross couldn't fix, in or out of the OR. At home, when the washing machine went on the blink, Gross took care of it, and when his tractor broke, he got that running again, too. When he wanted a barn, he built it with his own hands.

If you watched Gross carefully, as Hendren did, you saw nothing to suggest he was virtually blind in one eye. You saw average-looking hands, strong and graceful when they moved. You sometimes saw one of Gross's little fingers at a peculiar angle, and if you asked, he would tell you this was necessary for the perfect balance of a hand. "The care of children requires a certain indefinable something," Gross wrote, "which might be called the 'art' of pediatric surgery; it cannot be quantified or characterized any more than one can describe adequately the tints of Titian or the bold strokes of Michelangelo."

During one heart operation Hendren scrubbed for in July 1951, Gross kept having trouble with a bulldog clamp. It kept falling in his way.

Hendren had a suggestion. "Why don't you put a ligature around that and then hang a snap on it?" he asked. *It seems so obvious,* he thought. *And he's having such trouble with that clamp.*

The residents in the room looked at Hendren. Where did this striker get off telling the chief his business? Strikers weren't supposed to talk. Strikers were supposed to keep their mouths shut and consider themselves privileged to be breathing the same air as Dr. Gross.

"Hmmm," Gross said. "Good idea."

Hendren, secretary-treasurer of his class, graduated cum laude in 1952 and was matched, through the system he'd had a hand in refining, with his first choice for internship: the Massachusetts General Hospital, where Edward D. Churchill, an early admirer, was chief of surgery. Hendren stayed with Churchill as an intern and then general surgical resident for two and a half years, then studied pediatric surgery and heart surgery with Gross for two years at Children's. In 1957, he returned to the General as senior surgical resident. In 1958, he was an American Cancer Society fellow and Churchill's chief resident on the East Surgical Service, earning fifteen hundred dollars a year—five times what he'd made as an intern. By 1959, when he returned to Children's to be Gross's chief resident for a year, Hendren would have completed seven years of surgery and be board certified in general and cardiothoracic surgery.

Sandy, seven, wasn't herself.

She wasn't eating right, Eleanor noticed. Not like her baby brothers, Doug and Will. She couldn't seem to shake this cold she'd picked up at the end of that summer, the summer of 1955, when Hardy was in his first year with Gross and the family had vacationed in a rented cottage on a hill overlooking the ocean in Wareham.

"And she keeps going to the bathroom," Eleanor said to her husband one Saturday afternoon in September. "Even in the middle of the night, she has to go to the bathroom."

"She's probably got a urinary infection, that's all," Hardy said. "I'll take a sample of her urine and look at it under the microscope."

Hardy took a jar of Sandy's urine to Children's. He expected to find white blood cells, telltale signature of a urinary tract-infection. It would be no big deal.

But Sandy's urine was clean.

My God! Hardy thought. *I hope her urinary frequency is not based on spilling sugar.*

Hendren conducted Benedict's test: boiling urine mixed with a reagent and observing the color of the resulting precipitate. The precipitate was brick red; Sandy's urine was loaded with glucose, an indicator of diabetes. Hardy remembered a course from medical school. *It can't be diabetes,* he thought. *It has to be something else. You can't be cured of juvenile diabetes. Juvenile diabetes slowly kills.*

Hardy went home, and this time, he drew Sandy's blood. When he tested it, back at Children's, he found a blood sugar level of 856. The top normal is 120.

"Momma," Hardy said, "Sissy's got diabetes."

"She can't."

"But she does. Her blood sugar's 856."

"Isn't there anything else it could be?"

Hardy shook his head; there wasn't anything else it could be. He got on the phone to Samuel L. Katz, a resident in pediatric medicine at Children's. Katz, Hardy's Dartmouth and Harvard classmate, had known Sandy from birth. Hardy explained what she had, explained that he and Eleanor would go to any lengths to keep their little girl out of the hospital for as long as they could. Juvenile diabetes meant death, often by age twenty-one or earlier, but while she was alive, Sandy was going to live. Sandy was not going to become the walking wounded. She was going to remain a person, not become a patient. "We don't want Sandy to get onto the hospital track any sooner than necessary," Hardy explained. "A child who starts going to the hospital early can't but have it affect her development. We don't want Sandy to think of herself as an invalid.

We don't want her friends to think of her as sick. We don't want Sandy to have the weight of illness hanging over her head."

Guided by Katz and John F. Crigler, Jr., prominent endocrinologist at Children's, Eleanor and Hardy treated Sandy at home. They administered insulin, and they checked her urine frequently; and on that first weekend, with Sandy's blood sugar so badly out of whack, there was an IV for Hardy to start and more blood samples to be analyzed at Children's. Sandy was in bed, wondering why everything had suddenly changed, worrying about those needles Mommy and Daddy were boiling on the stove. But by Sunday, Sandy's blood sugar had been brought under control.

"Do you want to go to school tomorrow?" Eleanor asked.

"Sure, Mommy," Sandy said. "I'm OK."

Sandy would become accustomed to the twice-a-day shots, the special diet, and the never-ending checks her parents made on her urine. Eleanor and Hardy would inform her teachers of her diabetes and their intention to keep the situation low-key and not restrict Sandy's activities in any way. Daddy's little girl, would learn to play piano from her grandmother. She would appear in school plays. She would take voice lessons and be a happy girl, a girl who always made her own Christmas presents, a girl who was a favorite with her brothers. By 1960, the year Hendren completed his surgical training, the year Eleanor and Hardy's family was complete, she was older sister to four of them.

Even before Hendren's training was completed, his reputation was growing. Churchill, his mentor at Massachusetts General, had played a considerable part. Churchill was a gentle man, and while he had made a huge name for himself in surgery, he considered his greatest achievement the fashioning of so many fine young surgeons. Churchill liked Hendren. He liked his honesty, his manners, his quickness and eagerness to learn, his unquestionable talent, his confidence, which some considered arrogance. During Hendren's first tour at the General, from July 1952 through December 1954, Churchill accelerated his resident's responsibilities until he was doing much more complicated surgery than his peers, with impeccable results. During his second stay at the General, in 1957 and 1958, Hendren only got better. Heart, lungs, veins, urinary tract, liver, intestines, stomach, skin—except for the brain and bones,

Hendren was becoming accomplished everywhere, in children and adults. At Children's, perhaps only Gross had wider range and a more finely developed instinct for the human body. More than just Harvard insiders were noticing. Patients and their families were leaving the General with Hendren's name, and that name was getting around, leading to referrals. A children's hospital in Kansas City offered Hendren a job as chief surgeon, but Gross really wanted him at Children's. Gross told Hendren he could skip the chief residency; it was evident he didn't need any more training. Gross said he would be glad to take Hendren directly onto his staff.

But I'll be a better surgeon if I take the chief residency, Hendren thought.

On July 1, 1959, Hendren began his term as chief resident. He was thirty-three years old.

Like Churchill, Gross believed that when the talent was rich, the way to fashion a surgeon was to pretty much leave him be. Guys like Hendren were self-guided. Guys with seven years' training at two of the best programs in the world hardly ever got into trouble, and when they did, they usually found their way out. Check in on them in the OR every now and again, give advice when they sought it, but otherwise just let them be—that was Gross's philosophy. Hendren took advantage of this freedom. *This is what surgery is supposed to be!* He was busy. He was almost never home. In his year of chief residency, he performed more than three hundred operations and supervised nineteen residents who operated on nearly eight hundred cases of their own. Gross paid Hendren ten thousand dollars for the year—a staggering sum for a resident anywhere, in any specialty, in 1959. Gross allowed Hendren to have his own private patients, an unprecedented privilege. Some speculated that Hendren might succeed Gross someday—which did not sit well with one of the surgeons on Gross's staff, a surgeon who fancied he was the next one in line.

When he had time to think about it, which was rarely, Hendren wondered about Gross. Not the surgeon, but the man. After knowing him almost a decade, Hendren didn't have a clue as to what made him tick. No one else seemed able to figure him out, either. Few had ever socialized with him. Few knew much about his childhood, and no one at Children's knew that he had accomplished so much with a bad eye. "Keep it simple" was Gross's motto, but clearly it applied only to surgical technique. *I wish I had a micro-scope that could show me what's inside his head*, Hendren some-times thought.

Children like Lorraine Sweeney, Gross's first ductus patient, loved Gross, but parents gave him mixed reviews. Nurses were devoted to him, but few could claim to be his close friends. When he indulged them, which was rarely, his recreational pursuits tended toward the solitary: reading, horseback riding, fishing, sail-ing, baling hay, cutting brush in the woods around his estate, which was called Four Winds and was located in Framingham, a Boston suburb. He did not like to be photographed, and when he retired, he would not sit for the customary portrait; he'd seen a colleague's rendering, and the artist had gotten the eye color wrong, an offense Gross found unforgivable. Gross liked classical music and hated TV. He had a wife and two daughters, but it was common knowl-edge at Children's that his marriage was failing. There were rumors, true as it turned out, that he was involved with another woman: Jean L. Lootz, a nurse-anesthetist at Children's, with whom he eventually would live for three decades and who would take care of him in his final days, when Alzheimer's disease had left him incapable of so much as dialing a telephone. Gross was a philanthropic man who gave generously but quietly to many charities. When a resident's wife had a baby or was ill and cash was short, he automatically wrote out a check, never asking to be repaid. But visit him in his office, and you would find every chair but his deliberately piled high with papers—how long would anyone stick around, having no place to sit? Gross issued directives by handwritten note, always signed *REG*. One note Hendren got in the 1959–60 academic year was an order to send all of the residents out for new white shoes. Another note was received by anyone he discovered with blood on a shoe. "Keep them clean," REG wrote, enclosing a bottle of Shinola.

There were other pieces to the puzzle, more disturbing pieces, pieces Hendren did not put into place until early July 1960. Gross was subject to mood swings: up one week, down the next, back up again not long after. He'd had blowups with several of his residents, and some of them had been so shaken they'd left Children's for good. One Gross had in his sights was Orvar Swenson, the distin-guished young surgeon who'd pioneered treatment of Hirsch-sprung's disease. Swenson left in 1950, when Gross made it clear he would never support his work or his advancement through the Harvard Medical School hierarchy.

Gross could even turn on himself, never more destructively than when he failed. He could not bear to lose a patient. It didn't matter if it had been an impossible case, another of his visits to the frontier—a child who had no chance whatsoever in anyone else's hands. When he lost someone, when he believed that he'd botched the surgery—when he believed that if he'd done something differently the child would still be alive—he'd storm from OR to his office, tell his secretary to wipe his schedule clean, and disappear, sometimes for a week or ten days or more. His wife wouldn't know where he was. His secretary would profess no knowledge of his whereabouts. Only a handful of people knew that Gross was off sailing and fishing, was in Florida or the Caribbean. On such trips, he never called in, never wrote. His residents could do nothing but wait for his return and wonder what demons drove a man so great to act so oddly.

Hendren completed his residency on June 30, 1960. Thanks to his father's help and the GI Bill and his and Eleanor's early ingenuity, he had no debt. After a few days in Kansas City, he returned to Children's, where Gross had offered him an office and a position on the staff. On his first morning back, Hendren had two operations scheduled. He went into the OR early. There were his two cases, written in chalk on the scheduling blackboard.

A line had been drawn through each.

"How come you canceled your cases?" said Robert M. Smith, anesthesiologist-in-chief.

"Bob, I don't know what you're talking about," Hendren said. "I didn't cancel my cases."

The OR supervisor had been eavesdropping. "Dr. Gross was here earlier," she said. "He canceled your cases."

Hendren found the chief in his office. Hendren stood, waiting to be acknowledged.

"Yes?" Gross finally said.

"Dr. Gross, I've just been in the OR and my name's canceled off the board, and I'm told you did that."

"Yes."

"Could you tell me why?"

"You're doing too much."

"What do you mean?" Hendren asked.

And he thought, *"Doing too much?" That doesn't make any sense. Two cases isn't too much. Two cases is a light schedule.* Hendren thought about the staff surgeon who fancied himself Gross's successor; over the year, he and Hendren had had their battles. Hendren didn't respect this man and he wasn't impressed with his skills in the OR. *He's jealous,* Hendren thought of this other man, this self-proclaimed heir apparent. *He's probably gotten Dr. Gross's ear.*

But there had been no warning from Gross. Gross had promised Hendren a staff job when his residency was completed. He'd offered Hendren a ten-thousand-dollar annual salary, an office at Children's and the opportunity to continue his research.

"You're doing too much," Gross said. "You shouldn't be able to book two cases like that, just having finished the chief residency." He advised Hendren to take an office down the street somewhere, maybe do some lab work for a while, lie low clinically.

Dr. Gross wants to get rid of me! Hendren thought. *Dr. Gross— the man who confided to my wife, just this spring, how I was the son he never had! I can't stay here under these conditions.*

That afternoon, Hendren went across town to the Massachusetts General Hospital. He told Churchill what had happened.

"Well, Hardy," Churchill said, "you'll recall that when you told me you wanted to do pediatric surgery, I told you to go over and get your training with Bob Gross—but don't plan to stay there with him. Because Bob will never tolerate a young man coming up underneath him. Now I want you to come to the MGH. And I want you to start pediatric surgery here."

Chapter 17

Everyone in Room 17 is busy when Hendren returns from talking to the Moores.

Two circulating nurses, Karen Sakakeeny and Frances Healy McGowan, are busy preparing equipment and supplies. Three anesthesiologists are busy. Two surgical residents are busy. Paul Andriesse is busy with his pad. Barbara Cosgrove is busy with her camera. Dorothy Enos is busy setting up that damn fideo and keeping an eye on Hendren's gold-plated instruments, which for the moment she's wheeled into a corner; God forbid you should brush against them. Four visiting doctors—from Brazil, Venezuela, Mexico, and Taiwan—are busy poring over their copies of today's OR schedule. They have their eyes on Room 17's benches and stools, where they'll perch when the operating field has been established, Hendren is under way, and the busiest things in the room are his hands. Gone, at least at Children's, are the days when chiefs of surgery worked in amphitheaters with visitors' galleries that provided ample room for a medical-school class. If you want to watch Hendren, you must suit up and go in with him.

Hundreds have. Over the past twenty-five years, Hendren hasn't done more than a handful of big cases without an entourage of visiting doctors. Some have come to Boston to see Boston and not Hendren specifically. For others, Hendren has been the principal draw. For a week, a month, or six months to a year in some instances, they attempt to divine the secrets to his success. Some bring patients too difficult for them to fix themselves. Like the host of some inn, Hendren asks his visitors to sign his guest book, and he takes a Polaroid photograph of many of them before they leave. His current guest book, begun in 1970, has nearly four hundred entries, the great majority by doctors from abroad. "Very, very good, try to do it like you," a Swiss doctor wrote next to his name in Hendren's book. "Hope I'll be back," a Parisian doctor wrote. "Many thanks for highly concentrated teaching dose," wrote an Israeli surgeon. "Réunion is an island in Indian Ocean—French," explained a doctor who hailed from there. A Japanese urologist who entered his name in Hendren's book followed his visit with a letter, as many do. "Dear Dr. Hendren," he wrote, "I thank you very much for your kindness. . . . I learned a lot of things from you and I realized that I had performed many operations incorrectly, and after I returned here I modified operation procedure, and I could get much better results."

Hendren steps to the table to survey the situation. "You can start your prep," Veronica Miler says.

"I can't do anything until you're done," Hendren replies.

It's that old bugaboo again: access to Lucy's circulatory system. Like almost everyone who has ever tried to get a line into her, Miler and her team have been having their troubles while Hendren has been talking to Jack and Beth Moore.

Lucy will need four lines, Miler has decided: one to draw periodic blood samples, three for access to her circulatory system, including a backup line should one of the others clog or some emergency develop wherein there would be urgent need to get multiple medications into her at once. Lucy left Nine West with one line already in place, and Miler's team has managed to establish two more, but the fourth is a real problem. They keep sticking her and coming up dry. Another frustration is that their search is restricted: Lucy's legs, which might have promise, are off-limits because Hendren will be working at that end of her body.

"We need one more big IV," Miler says.

"Where do you want it?" Hendren asks. In the worst instances, it takes a surgeon to get a line going. A surgeon can get inside an arm and hunt at his leisure until he finds what they need.

"Anywhere," Miler answers.

Hendren chooses Lucy's lower left foreram.

"Let me have a cutdown kit," he says. Cutdown kits contain

suture material and the handful of instruments needed to place a line surgically.

Hendren unwraps the sterile package, swabs Lucy's arm with Betadine, makes an incision with a scalpel, finds a suitable vein, then tries to get a hold on it with a forceps. Cutdown kits have house instruments. Hendren hates them. He's invested tens of thousands of dollars in his own tools so he won't have to use them.

"This is so stiff you can't close it," he says, exasperated. He would never find a forceps like this in his own set; if Enos ever ordered such an inferior instrument, he would instruct her to send it back. But Enos would never commit such a blunder. She knows instruments, invests considerable time poring through the catalogues to keep current. As you would taste fine wine before pouring it, she personally tests Hendren's instruments before putting them to work.

Hendren squeezes harder on the house forceps, isolates the vein he wants, then tosses the tool onto the end of the table.

"Try it!" he says to one of the circulating nurses. When he's turned back to his work, she good-naturedly rolls her eyes. Boy, is he demanding.

Hendren cuts the vein, threads a cannula into it and closes the skin with stitches. "There," he says. "You've got a good central line." The cutdown has taken ten minutes.

"Thank you," Miler says. "Thank *you.*"

Like most who have worked with Hendren for any time, Miler knows there is a foundation to most of his complaints. She's learned how to tell his bark from his bite, when to spar with him, when it's in everyone's best interest to back off and remain silent. But her assistants today—Heggeness, a resident, and Rabb, a fellow— haven't had the benefit of Miler's experience. They haven't been around long enough. They're not too sure about W. Hardy Hendren III, this man who routinely operates for eighteen hours straight. For whatever time they're in Room 17 today, they'll keep a low profile and hope for a smooth sail. No one ever wants problems, but with the chief of surgery, you want them even less. A chief has the power to make life truly miserable.

"I'm just trying to remember if I ever saw Dr. Gross doing a cutdown," Hendren says. "I don't think I ever did. OK. That's my annual cutdown. I'm not doing any more this year."

Lucy is finally ready.

Hendren and Miler lift her to the foot of the table, remove her diaper, and gingerly position her legs in infant stirrups, a jury-rigged assembly of tape, pins, and poles. Her legs are spread wide. Except for her single hole, her bottom is blank. Certain that no part of her leg is resting on metal—don't want any nerve damage—Hendren gets his Nikon. It is a veteran of thousands of operations, just like its owner.

He focuses on his virgin canvas and snaps several shots. He always enjoys comparing them to post-op pictures, when the finishing strokes have all been applied.

"OK, Barbara," he says, "come set up with your camera behind me. Put a light on baby's bottom here. That's good. How close can you zoom? Is this a closeup lens? Is it in focus?"

"It's an autofocus," his secretary says.

"That looks good, Barb. Go ahead and hit it."

Hendren begins his narration. "OK. This shows the baby's typical cloacal bottom. There's where the anus should be," he says, touching his finger to a featureless patch of skin. "And it's a totally blank bottom with one small opening right up here under the clitoris. Cut." Barbara's footage will be combined with endoscopic views to make a training film. Surgeons might not be able to duplicate Hendren's results merely by watching, but at least they'll get a basic understanding. Over the years, nineteen of his edited, illustrated, and narrated productions have been acquired by the film libraries of the American College of Surgeons and the American Urological Association.

Jeffrey Steinberg, who has scrubbed and gowned, is ready to paint Lucy's bottom with germicide.

"OK. Good. Go ahead, Jeff," Hendren says.

Steinberg drapes towels and a sheet over Lucy, leaving only a small circle of exposed skin. Hendren scrubs and gowns and rejoins Steinberg at the foot of the table.

"Stool, please."

Enos rolls one to him. Hendren sits. He does not like the way Steinberg has arranged the sheet. The circle, his work area for this stage of the operation, is too small.

"It's an automatic habit of doing without thinking," Hendren says.

"I think they teach us not to leave the rectum anywhere near what we're working on," Steinberg says.

"I see," says Hendren. "Even when the rectum doesn't exist?"

"No, sir."

"Stimulator, please."

The stimulator consists of a battery box, wires, and a disposable probe that resembles a large blue pen. It activates muscle tissue according to the same principle of electricity that high school biology students demonstrate when making frog legs twitch. Enos hands him the probe.

"Veronica? You're nonparalyzed?"

By varying the anesthesia, Miler can control how far under Lucy is. Knowing Hendren, she deliberately has kept Lucy somewhat light—light enough for the muscles in her bottom to be responsive to mild electric shock.

"Nonparalyzed."

"Thank you. You're so good to me! All right. Zap it."

Hendren zings here and there, searching for the exact center of the sphincter and levator, muscles that act as a thick, powerful clamp around the normal rectum. He is scouting a location for the anus he'll build today. As with most cases of cloacal reconstruction, the margin of error is slim. A millimeter or two off, and Lucy's chance of continence will decline.

Beneath Lucy's smooth white skin, you can see puckering: strong muscle contraction, a promising omen. Without native muscle, there's nothing much you can do for continence—nothing you can plug in, no artificial valve, no muscle from leg, arm, or abdomen you can transplant. The choice presented by absence of good muscle—a choice several of Hendren's patients have had to make—is between constant soiling and a bag. Most go for the bag. But some children, having reached the age of reason, have decided a life in diapers is a lesser evil than a stoma and a bag. This is the sort of conundrum Hendren has devoted a career to erasing from the surgical agenda.

"Film this, Barbara. OK. See? There's the center of her anus." He touches an area a little higher. "Her vagina's going to go right up there. OK. Cut."

No matter how many earlier endoscopies he may have conducted, no matter how many illustrations his artist may have drawn, no matter how precise and detailed his notes from earlier examinations and operations are, Hendren never opens up a cloaca patient without a good, long look through his scope. If he were a resident today, not the chief, there are those who would criticize him for taking too long with the scope. *You can never know too much about your patient's anatomy,* Hendren believes. *There's no such thing as taking too long familiarizing yourself before you open a little baby up and go to work.*

The endoscope has been resting in its protective plastic case, the Scopeholder, which was designed by Hendren and his oldest son, Douglas, an inventor before attending medical school and becoming an orthopedist. Hendren holds a patent on the Scopeholder, but it has never brought him riches because he's never devoted the time to serious marketing or sales.

Steinberg hands the scope, Hendren's personal instrument, to the chief. Enos is ready with the fideo. She attaches its camera to the eyepiece.

"Let's film, Dorothy."

"Recording."

Hendren starts up into Lucy, narrating as he proceeds.

"We're going up the urogenital sinus. . . . All these funny little doodads—I don't know what they are. . . . They could possibly be entrances to the vagina. . . . Here's the bladder neck. . . . Now we're in the bladder. . . . See where the bladder's pushed forward by the rectum? . . . There's a ureteral orifice over there. . . . This telescope is a bad telescope. Can't you give me a telescope with a better lens? Cut the filming! Take the TV off! Let's see if we have a better scope. It's a shame to spoil a good video with a lousy scope. . . . OK, Dorothy, let's shoot this again. . . . good . . . here are those little things again. . . . OK . . . stop filming. Cut it. Cut it!"

"Cut," Enos says.

"That's all the filming."

"Promise?"

"Nope!"

In Hendren's book, a cardinal rule is *Thou shalt fear germs.*

Hendren does, and not only when he's working. At home, a dispenser of Dial antibacterial soap is next to the kitchen sink. At home, a flyswatter is never out of reach, and Eleanor and Hardy think nothing of interrupting a sitdown dinner to go on the offensive against the latest insect threat. Knowing that public rest rooms are rife with germs, Hendren has devised a system of minimizing his contact with their dirty surfaces. The trick is paper towels. After using the toilet, you flush with a clean towel. With a second clean towel, you turn on the faucet, dispense soap, and wash. With a third towel, you turn off the faucet. With another, you dry. And with yet another clean towel, you open the door and leave. What if there is only an electric hand dryer? one might ask. That's easy. To open the rest room door, reach into your suit-jacket pocket and use the fabric as protection as you pull on the door handle.

Hendren knew of a surgeon who ordered his residents to move their bowels in the evening, not the morning, when they would head directly from lavatory to operating room. Hendren is not quite so fanatic, but he rigidly controls the behavior and dress of anyone in his room. In four decades in surgery, he has seen many patients breeze through long, tricky operations only to die later of massive infection—*complications* is the euphemism commonly used—that could be traced to sloppiness or inattention to detail in the OR. It is a senseless, stupid way to go: death from a speck of dust or a piece of dandruff or a droplet from a sneeze that escaped someone's improperly positioned mask.

"Sterility is being aware every second," Hendren tells his residents. Sterility is not going into the OR in scrubs you've worn on the street. Sterility is not bumping into things, no matter how crowded the OR gets. Sterility is turning one's head from the table when one coughs or sneezes. Sterility is not resting one's hands under one's arms, where a surgical gown has only a single layer of fabric, not the double protection that is provided over the chest and lower arms, which are in closest proximity to the open wound. When hands are idle, sterility means practicing Hendren's "prayerful posture"—hands clasped close to chest, like the stance of a choirboy. In years to come, in patients as yet unborn, sterility will derive from the memory of a Hardy Hendren rebuke that young surgeons carry with them.

Hendren is obsessed with hair, and his male residents are always clean-shaven, no matter how many hours they've gone without sleep. Hendren likes their hair cut as short as his, the female residents' hair not much longer. "Who's walking around here like Goldilocks?" he said once to a male urology resident who had beautifully thick hair. "You will either get a haircut or wear one of those girls' hats." To a resident he caught with arms crossed and hands nestled tightly under his arms, he said, "So when you scrubbed this morning, you scrubbed all the way up to your hairy armpits? Hmmm? Go change!" Another time, a bearded male nurse from one of the wards came into Hendren's room. He was wearing the standard mask and cap, inadequate for such a full growth. "Bacteria jump off those things like rats off a sinking ship!" Hendren said. He ordered the nurse to return to the locker room and get into more elaborate garb.

Worse than hairs are flies, which would be a disaster in an operating room. To get anywhere near the surgical suite at Children's, a fly would first have to get inside the hospital, no mean feat considering almost none of the windows open, and the doors all close automatically. It would have to negotiate three flights of stairs, several corridors and corners and fire doors, all the while slipping past dozens of people with a profound professional interest in pest control. It would have to evade the Flintrol insect electrocutor that guards the entrance to the OR suite. But somehow, on the day in 1990 that Hendren was rebuilding Katie Brinegar, a fourteen-month-old Vermont girl who had a cloaca, one made it: a big, black, buzzing fly, separated from Hendren's OR by but a single door.

Hendren spotted it in the corridor as he was on his way to his office to eat a bowl of fruit. He took chase, swatting with his hands and shouting—in English and in Spanish—to two Hispanic attendants who happened to be walking by.

"Fly!" Hendren shouted. "Fly! There's a fly loose in here! *La mosca!*"

Pam Spinney, whom Hendren had recently hired to help with his medical writing and who had come—with some trepidation—to see her first cloaca, joined the effort. Now four people were after the fly, running, swatting, closing doors, trying to head it off, raising a ruckus.

"*La mosca! La mosca!*" Hendren yelled.

The fly escaped. But at least they'd managed to shoo it away from the surgical suite and back toward the lounge.

Ten-fifty A.M.

"Let me have a Q-tip," Hendren says.

Lucy has been released from her stirrups. She is flat on her back on the table. Now Hendren is beginning a total-body prep, a life-saving ritual that can take fifteen minutes and will allow working on the patient from either the back or the front.

With germs, the threats are not only external. Improperly handled, the patient's worst enemy can be himself or herself; if your handlers are not vigilant, you may be responsible for your own death. Before it's cleaned, the skin is potentially lethal, as is the gastrointestinal system, especially its lower end: the rectum, colonized by all sorts of bacteria. Other surgeons let residents or assistants prep, but Hendren rarely does, making exceptions only with those whose technique he implicitly trusts.

Steinberg rolls Hendren a prep cart. Hendren takes a long-handled Q-tip, dips it in Betadine, and begins a thorough cleansing of Lucy's navel. Microbes are fond of navels, too.

For the moment, Enos's services are not needed. She is over on the phone, updating a friend on her workday. "We're going to be here all night," she says.

Miler overhears the conversation. "All night?" she says to Hendren, who always appreciates a good barb about how long his big cases go. "You said six hours!"

"That was before all of Anesthesia's fiddling," Hendren jokes. "You know, like what Johnny Most used to say: 'fiddling and diddling.' "

Most, for decades the colorful radio voice of the Boston Celtics games, has been in the news a lot lately. Last month, on the occasion of his retirement, a ceremony in his honor was held at the Boston Garden. A longtime heavy smoker, Most is in failing health. During much of the ceremony, he had to sit in a chair on the Garden's famed parquet floor. From the balconies, he looked awkward and frail.

"You know why Johnny Most's not saying that anymore?" Hendren asks.

No one answers.

"Cigarettes."

Smoking killed Hendren's father. It killed Eleanor's father and Enos's father. It killed so many people Hendren knew—relatives, neighbors, fellow surgeons, hospital friends, childhood acquaintances. Once a smoker himself, Hendren never passes up a chance to deliver dire warnings.

Satisfied there cannot possibly be a live germ still lurking down in Lucy's navel, he discards the Q-tip, dips a cotton sponge into the Betadine, and begins to paint her body a yellowish brown. Belly, sides, thighs, chest, perineum, down to the ankles, up to the neck— Hendren paints a wider area than some surgeons would consider necessary. He carefully cleans around each stoma, entryway to the intestines.

"OK, let's turn her," he says.

With so many wires and tubes to watch out for, turning an anesthetized baby, a baby now on total life-support, is no simple job. Hendren assigns the posts—this person on this limb; that one over there; you come and take this leg, please. "Turn halfway up this way. . . . Go ahead . . . halfway . . . OK . . . good . . . thank you, everybody. . . . Can this electrode move a little higher?"

Hendren bathes Lucy's backside with Betadine. Again, he issues instructions: Price to hold one leg; Hendren himself to take another; Miler to get a grip on Lucy's shoulders. They lift Lucy free of the table and hold her while Hendren preps her belly and perineal area one more time.

Enos is standing off to the side. Already in place on the table are a heating pad, a sheet of lamb's wool, and a jelly pad, each soft and cushioning, designed to prevent mischief with circulation and nerves. They are not sterile, but the drapes and towels Enos has ready to cover them with are. Some doctors use disposable fabrics for their draping, but not Hendren. He likes the feel and thickness of traditional cloth. Somehow, paper just doesn't seem right.

"There's a little spot over here, Dr. Hendren," Enos says.

Hendren paints where he's missed.

"OK, come under with your big drape, Dorothy" he says. "Everyone stay away from Dorothy. Perfect. OK. Chest down. Do not put the legs down yet."

Hendren starts painting Lucy's legs, feet, toes.

"It'll give us a little extra protection," he says. "Wrap that. Perfect."

Lucy's legs are encased in towels, which will simplify midoperation turning, when you don't need the aggravation of fussing with nonsterile limbs. Miler erects the ether screen, a drape that forms a barrier between the surgical field and the head of the table, the anesthesiologists' station during most operations not involving the face, brain, or neck. Lucy's eyes have already been taped shut, to prevent the corneas from drying, and now her head is encased in a clear plastic bag. The bag will help her tiny body retain warmth. It quickly fogs, creating the impression of a character in a bad horror movie.

Lucy is on her stomach, her butt propped up. If you watch closely, you can see the slight rise and fall of her upper body, synchronized with the hiss-whoosh, hiss-whoosh of the ventilator bellows. But soon, you can't see even that. Hendren and Enos cover Lucy with drapes until all that's visible is her bottom.

Sakakeeny hands Hendren his loupes, surgical telescopes that provide three-and-a-half-power magnification, essential for surgery this fine. He puts on the loupes, which resemble eyeglasses, and above them he fastens his headlamp, which delivers intense but cool illumination. Leaving Enos to roll the instruments into position at the foot of the table, Hendren adjusts his loupes and lantern and leaves the room to rescrub. Next to Room 17 is a trough. Over the trough is a window with a view of the OR, and as Hendren washes, vigorously scrubbing for several minutes with a brush and antiseptic soap, he scrutinizes everyone in the room. It's an easy way to catch a slip in sterile technique.

Hands clean, Hendren returns to the OR. Enos helps him on with a fresh gown and brown gloves, size eight. Hendren moves to his customary spot to the left of the patient, as seen from the foot of the table. Circulating nurse Karen Sakakeeny plugs the cord to Hendren's headlamp into a freestanding power source. Enos takes her place, which is directly at Hendren's right hand. She is now sandwiched between him and her instrument trays, which occupy more space than the operating table. For three decades, this has been the customary setup—Hendren, Enos, instruments, never varying from that order. Lord help you should you violate the proportion of Hardy Hendren's room.

"That spot is sacred ground," Hendren said one day to an Asian resident who, on his first visit to the chief's room, had innocently claimed Enos's place while she was busy elsewhere in the room. "It's like a Shinto shrine. Dr. Choi would join his ancestors if he stood there too long!"

Hendren wants one last check of where he'll put Lucy's anus. With the nerve stimulator, he probes the baby's bottom, blank but for that single hole.

"Toothpick."

Enos hands him a sterile wooden toothpick, one with a fine point. He dips the toothpick into brilliant green dye and draws a horizontal line, from cheek to cheek across Lucy's buttocks. Exactly in the middle, exactly in the center of anal muscle contraction, he makes a circle.

"That's going to be our mark for the anus."

"I like that," says Enos, the only one in the room who would venture an opinion. Hendren doesn't simply welcome his scrub nurse's opinion; he often seeks it, then gives it weight. Many times in their three decades as a team, Enos's advice has led Hendren to lengthen an incision, choose a different suture material, take a break when he's worked himself into a tight corner and needs to gain perspective. "She's my conscience," he says.

In his mind, Hendren is imagining the final product, the completed canvas. *She has to be functional,* he thinks. *But she has to look right, too. We won't have done our job if she doesn't look normal. She has to be able to look at herself and think she's no different from any other little girl.*

Hendren turns his attention to Lucy's single hole—her cloaca. Its entrance is framed by a normal-looking clitoris and two labia, also normal. He puts a suture through each, then clamps a hemostat to each of the three sutures. One by one, he gently pulls on the sutures to widen the cloacal opening. The weight of the hemostats, which he positions out of the way, keeps the cloaca open.

"Now we'll make this perineal body," he says. "Then vagina, perhaps from here to there."

With his toothpick, he's drawing again. The line for the vagina, about an inch long, is perpendicular to the more substantial line he drew to locate the anus.

"I think that's about where the urethra should be, back there. That's pretty good. Let me take a picture of that."

He changes gloves and snaps a few frames with his Nikon.

"OK," he says when he's changed gloves yet again. "Let's have a knife."

Chapter 18

Edward D. Churchill, chief of surgery at the Massachusetts General Hospital, was a young surgeon's dream. There were no storms beneath that gentle, quietly brilliant surface, no whipsaw emotions or hidden agendas. Fresh from the humiliation by Gross, Hardy Hendren couldn't have asked for more on his arrival at the General in the summer of 1960.

At the age of sixty-five, Churchill had achieved all he'd hoped to with the knife. He'd made impressive contributions to thoracic surgery. He'd established research laboratories at the General. In the Second World War, he'd been a surgical consultant in the North African and Mediterranean theaters of operation, and he'd received a Distinguished Service Medal for his work. He understood well, from study and firsthand experience, that over the centuries war, as horrible as it was, had provided the science of surgery an incomparable opportunity to advance. But the battlefield was more than a laboratory for Churchill. He believed that the wounded soldier deserved the same compassion and quality of care as any patient in a civilian hospital, a belief not universally held by his peers. These were brothers and sons, husbands and fathers, not so much cannon fodder. "Military surgery is not to be regarded as a crude departure from accepted surgical standards—an 'awful business' as it has been called," Churchill wrote. "Military surgery is the surgery of trauma encountered in massive proportions." An injured soldier, he wrote, "is not like a box of ammunition or crate of rations that can be deposited at the boundary of an echelon and responsibility dismissed."

By the 1950s, when Hendren trained under him, only one item remained high on Churchill's agenda: heading the next generation on its way. Churchill was a listener, a man to whom you could unburden yourself, and the chairs in his office were not all crowded with papers. Sitting with him, you did not get the feeling a stopwatch was running. You got the feeling that this man, a giant in his own right, genuinely cared about you.

Although there had been pediatric surgery at the General before Hendren, it was catch-as-catch-can. With Hendren's appointment, Churchill gave it formal status as a service. He gave Hendren, thirty-four years old, responsibility for its development. And then, typically, he left Hendren alone.

During the first year after the completion of his residency, when the outside world had no knowledge of what had transpired with Gross that summer, Hendren operated at both Children's and the General. Families still requested him, still wanted him to operate on their sons and daughters at Children's. Pediatricians on the staff of Children's still referred cases to him. Among them was Sidney Farber, the cancer scientist, doctor, and chief of staff whose office was in the Jimmy Fund Building. Occasionally on his visits to Children's, Hendren would bump into Gross, but the older man never had much of anything to say, not until July 1961. Hendren was in the scrub area of old OR 7 one day that month, preparing to remove the right kidney from a girl named Theresa, who was awaiting him on the operating table, when Gross walked in.

"Good morning, Dr. Gross," Hendren said.

"You don't have any right to operate here," Gross said.

Oh, no, Hendren thought. *Here we go again.* "What do you mean?" he asked.

"You didn't get a letter the first of July renewing your appointment," Gross replied.

"I didn't get a letter from the MGH, either," Hendren said, "but I would think it would be supposed that I would continue to have operating privileges unless notified to the contrary."

"Nope," Gross said. "You have no business doing this case."

Gross relented—but only on that case, already prepped and ready to go. When the last stitch was in, Hendren left Children's. He would not operate there again for twenty-one years, nor would he see much of Gross, although they would find themselves at the same surgical meetings from time to time. One such occasion was in July 1963, in Sheffield, England, at a meeting of the British Association of Paediatric Surgeons, whose guiding force was Sir Denis Browne. Gross, honored overseas guest and speaker, attended. So did Hendren, who was being considered for membership in BAPS. In a meeting closed to him, Hendren's name was placed in nomination. He had several supporters, including David Waterston, preeminent heart surgeon at London's Hospital for Sick Children, Great Ormond Street, England's finest pediatric hospital. Waterston had invited Hendren to work with him for three months in 1962, and he'd been greatly impressed by this new young talent from Boston. But Gross wouldn't hear of Hendren being elected to BAPS. He took Hendren to breakfast that morning, and then, behind closed doors, he argued against making his former chief resident a member of the organization. A man of great influence on both sides of the Atlantic Ocean, Gross prevailed. Hendren would have to wait until the next year's meeting, in Edinburgh, when Gross was not in attendance, before being admitted to BAPS.

There was plenty of work at the General, too much work at the General, and only Hendren to do it. For almost a decade, until 1968, when he brought an associate on board, Hendren was on call twenty-four hours a day, 365 days a year. He routinely operated six days a week and often, with emergencies, on Sundays, too. He started his own research lab. He wrote for professional journals, and beginning with the maiden issue in 1966, he served on the editorial and advisory board of the *Journal of Pediatric Surgery*, whose editor-in-chief was C. Everett Koop of Children's Hospital of Philadelphia. Hendren lectured before professional audiences. He made sixteen-millimeter films of his most noteworthy cases and went to conferences, spreading the word about new procedures he'd devised. He trained residents and interns of his own. He took pains to place postoperative calls and write postoperative thank-yous to referring physicians, who returned the courtesy by sending more patients and advising other doctors to do the same. In 1961, his first full year under Churchill, Hendren operated 322 times, an average of almost a case a day. The next year, he performed 371 operations. One of these was on Christine, a two-and-a-half-month-old girl.

Christine was a cloaca baby, number 1 of the 113 that Hendren would rebuild by the summer of 1992, thirty years later. She'd been admitted to Children's Hospital at the age of eleven hours, and the surgeons there had performed a colostomy, put a tube through her abdomen into her bladder, and left another tube in her vagina. While those procedures had saved Christine's life, they were far short of the reconstruction she would need if she were ever to have a normal life. Knowing Hendren would try to figure out a solution to Christine's problems, then attempt to implement it, her pediatrician referred Christine to him at the General. Of his first endoscopic view of her insides, Hendren wrote:

> This opening runs in through a rather narrow passageway for a full 2 centimeters and then it balloons into a large vagina. Passing upward in this vagina in the midline one can see a single small opening, undoubtedly her rectovaginal fistula. At a point just superior to that, there is a midline septum and as one looks at the septum it is just like looking down the barrel of a double-barrel shotgun, with each hole representing the entrance to a uterus. . . .

On Christine's record, the Children's surgeons had predicted that the tube in the baby's vagina, which drained urine, "will probably need to be kept in place for several years." In his first operation on Christine, in September 1962, Hendren enlarged her vaginal opening in such a way that there no longer was any need for the tube. He repaired her colostomy, which, like Lucy Moore's, had badly prolapsed before she'd come to him. Christine would need several more operations over the years, but when Hendren was done, she would be continent of urine and feces and capable of sexual relations.

In 1964, Hendren performed more than 500 operations. In 1969, the year he separated the Siamese twins, he logged 679 cases, an average of more than two operations a day on the six-day-a-week schedule he was regularly keeping. Some surgeries were ditzels, his word for circumcisions or appendectomies or similarly routine cases. But many were behemoths: cloacal reconstructions, the rebuilding of wasted urinary tracts, the undoing of bags. They were cases that went from morning to night or longer, cases that would constitute Hendren's major contributions to surgical science. His schedule was crazier than an intern's. He was a man who would not stop to eat until hunger gnawed at him. And still, he felt there was never enough time.

In 1960, when Hendren arrived at the General, there was no board-certification procedure for pediatric surgeons; as a recognized specialty, it was yet to be born. Hendren had boards in general surgery and cardiothoracic surgery for both children and adults. Encouraged by Churchill, who believed no specialist should ever lose his bearings as a generalist, he roamed all over the disease and birth defect spectrums. He developed a special interest in cancers— rhabdomyosarcomas, sacrococcygeal teratomas, and other rare tumors that are as intimidating as their names suggest. Hendren was also fascinated with trauma, marveling at how childish mischief could have such devastating consequences, all in an instant. He rebuilt children who had survived car wrecks. He saved a boy who'd been run over by a horse-drawn wagon. He operated on children who were injured when they fell off bicycles and out of trees. He restored the normal functioning of children who had swallowed lye and sulfuric acid and drain openers—substances that eat all tissue in their path. He became expert at treating children with burns— burns that resulted from playing with matches and gasoline, from lighting candles at church, from houses that caught fire and space heaters that exploded and bathrobes that went up in flames as a child leaned over the kitchen stove. Hendren couldn't save every victim, but by careful excising of burns and grafting with skin, he saved most, even ones with 60 and 65 percent of their body surfaces destroyed by flame. This is the technique used today at the Shriners Burn Institute in Boston.

Hendren had been trained in cardiac surgery by the original pediatric heart surgeon, Gross, and he'd trained under David Waterston. But Hendren's heart work at the General never really took off. He did eight cardiac operations in 1962, fourteen the next year, and seventeen in 1965, but by 1969 he was down to only six. To no small extent, Hendren's limited heart work was due to Children's Hospital, which had developed a network of clinics throughout New England to attract patients in need of cardiac surgery. The fact was, the mighty General, earliest of Children's detractors, could not compete with its smaller neighbor on this score. Another reason was internal: an issue of turf. The General's heart surgeons felt they should get all the cardiac cases there, even children, even though their principal focus was on adults. Faced with the politics of that situation, Hendren concentrated on pursuits that, years later, would give him the expertise he'd need to fix Lucy Moore.

Hendren's interest in the genitourinary tract had been piqued at Children's, where cardiac work at the time of his training overshadowed all else.

Open-heart surgery had arrived on the scene in the 1950s, bringing with it new pumps and new machines and new materials to enthrall surgeons who lived on the frontier. Open heart was where the excitement was. Gross was no longer the lonely pioneer, the daring young resident waiting for his chief to take a vacation so he could try a bizarre new operation few but him believed could succeed. Now Gross had competition, in Minnesota and Philadelphia, among other places. Never captivated by the genitourinary tract, Gross, by the late fifties had lost interest in it altogether. Instead, he was busy trying to keep his name out front in the field he'd given birth to, pediatric heart surgery. At Children's, urology was all Hendren's. He'd learned the usual way to alleviate upper-urinary-tract disease: disconnect the bladder, and dump the ureters into a piece of small intestine, which emptied through a stoma into a bag. At Children's, he saw the consequences of the kind of life such surgery allowed: not only an appliance perpetually glued to your belly, but recurring infections and stones and, in some cases, death. At Children's, he spared his first two children bags with his initial success with megaureter repair.

Based on his work at the General in the sixties and seventies, some would proclaim Hendren preeminent in pediatric urology, but not every urologist in the land would anoint him; there were those who resented this surgeon who hadn't formally trained as a urologist, didn't define himself as a urologist, didn't believe, as Churchill didn't believe, that the best surgeons forsook their generalist bearings. Hendren sought to appease the dissenters. At the urging of Harvard professor Wyland F. Leadbetter, the General's chief of urology from 1954 to 1969, and one of his strongest supporters, Hendren decided to seek board certification in urology. He wrote to the American Board of Urology stating his intention and was informed by return letter that he was not qualified to take the exams. First, he would have to complete a three-year residency.

Forget it, Hendren thought. *If that's how they play the game, I'm not in it.*

But sniping only went so far. In medicine, good results become good advertising, attracting those who ultimately determine a doctor's success: patients and their families. In 1961, Hendren's first full year at the General, 57 of his 322 cases were genitourinary. In 1965, 212 involved kidneys, ureters, the bladder, the urethra, or genitalia. By 1969, more than 350 cases, better than half his total load, were genitourinary. Hendren was perfecting megaureter repair. He was repairing cloacas and infants with ambiguous genitalia, a wide selection of surgery's true basket cases. He was writing about his solution to the problem of urethral valves, the defect that he concluded probably was responsible for the death of his childhood friend, Ben Trelease. He was devising a way to restore the functioning of lower urinary tracts that had been left fallow when ureters were diverted through a piece of small intestine into a bag.

"Undiversion," as Hendren termed this restoration, represented a dramatic strategic shift. No one wished a bag on a child, that went without saying. But in certain circumstances, bags saved lives. Hendren saw fewer circumstances; that was all. He saw that while bags were lifesavers over the short haul, because of complications they could claim lives in the long run—lives like Ben Trelease's. To his mind, that was a devil's deal. *The surgeon should go to any length to avoid giving a child a bag*, Hendren thought. *Bags should not be the easy way out, and for some surgeons, they are.* So what of the veteran—the child who came to Hendren already wearing a bag? The child whose bladder had shriveled like dried fruit from years of nonuse? What could be done for her or him?

In Hendren's hands, they could be made normal.

One of his early successes was Wayne Hinckley, a Massachusetts youth who had been born with an obstructed urinary tract, which had resulted in a diversion operation at the age of three. The operation had saved the child's life, but he'd been left wearing a bladder bag, which had subjected him to the taunts of schoolmates. At the age of eleven, Hinckley had considered suicide. "He is now happily rid of the embarrassing bag," stated an article and diagram about Hendren's new procedure that were published in the May 26, 1975, issue of *Newsweek*. Even urinary tracts left fallow for years and years could be coaxed back into function, Hendren had proved.

Some urologists doubted it was possible, but once again, there were Hendren's results—documented, duplicable, available for all to see. Hendren did not receive plaudits only in the public press. In recognition of his contributions to pediatric urology, he was made a full voting member of the American Urological Association. In 1970, he became the first American elected to membership in the Society for Paediatric Urological Surgeons, an elite group of predominantly European doctors. And in 1974, despite a strenuous effort by some to keep him out, Hendren was made an honorary member of the Society for Pediatric Urology, an American group. When he presented one of his first papers on undiversion at the 1974 annual meeting of the American Surgical Association, he received a long ovation. Several senior urologists and surgeons stood to speak in praise of his accomplishment. Among them was the recently retired Robert E. Gross.

As his practice grew, Hendren increased his secretarial and support staff. He brought other pediatric surgeons on board. The first was Bruce Henderson, who'd trained in Cincinnati under Lester Martin, Gross's chief resident two years before Hendren. The second was Samuel Kim, a Harvard Medical School graduate who'd trained at Boston Children's and at the Alder Hey Children's Hospital in Liverpool, England. The third was the person who succeeded Hendren as the General's chief of pediatric surgery, Patricia K. Donahoe, named one of *Ms.* magazine's Women of the Year in 1987.

The Hendrens could afford to buy a succession of three houses in Brookline, where one neighborhood was so popular among physicians it was known as Pill Hill. Later, they could afford to buy a summer cottage in Duxbury, an old oceanfront community south of Boston. Eventually, they could buy a year-round place there. The Hendrens weren't in Hanover anymore, selling their blood and cooking on a hot plate, but neither were they becoming rich. Hendren was plowing much of his income back into his practice, into research and free care. The Hendrens believed their best personal investment was in educating their children, and they believed the best educations were private ones—preparatory schools and Ivy League colleges. And when it was time for advanced schooling, for law school and medical school, they believed it their responsibility to underwrite that, too.

With his days so long, Hendren insisted the family join him for breakfast every morning. When he got home, as often after midnight as before, he woke his children so together they could say their prayers. Nights and weekends, he and Eleanor painted and hung wallpaper. He built a backyard patio, working after dark with the help of floodlights. He borrowed a sander from the General and refinished the hardwood floors. He taught his children to swim and fish, his boys to hunt. Sometimes, he'd bring one or more of the kids to the hospital, get them scrubbed and gowned, and bring them into his OR to watch him work. But Eleanor bore the brunt of raising four sons and a daughter with a terminal disease. She was chauffeur, cook, seamstress, dishwasher, disciplinarian, hostess to visiting surgeons and to the occasional patient her husband invited to recover in their home. She supervised homework, arranged for music lessons, and made sure the children learned typing, a skill she believed would pay dividends no matter what profession they pursued. To Sandy, she was nurse as well as mother. This was what Eleanor had envisioned the day in Kansas City she'd agreed to marry Hardy Hendren: being wife and mother to their children. This was how she wanted to live—as a pillar supporting them all, five children and her man.

Sandy was growing up. Sandy was a tease to her brothers, a girl who played the piano and sang in a voice that reminded Eleanor of her own. In grammar school, her love of music nudged her to the stage. She liked musicals, and she was in several productions presented by The Vincent Club, a century-old Boston charity that supports the training of gynecologists, research in gynecology and the care of women at the Massachusetts General Hospital. Sandy, who was on many other stages around New England over the years, had a favorite role: Agnes Gooch in *Mame*. She had a favorite song, the theme song from the musical *Annie*.

Sandy was handling her disease like a Hendren—without self-pity. Those insulin shots, so painful at first, became just another part of the day. And really, what was so bad about having your urine tested regularly? How terrible could a disease be when you felt fine most of the time, when you never had to go to the hospital—except to visit Daddy? Besides, how many people outside of the home knew? Only a few close friends had been told. Not until high school did Sandy start to delve into the mechanics of her disease. Not until she was a teen did she begin to read everything she could find on juvenile diabetes. Not until her health began to fail and there was no way to keep the secrets anymore did Sandy understand that not even her father, her famous surgeon father, could save her. She was dying, and she would have to summon enormous strength to stave off death for as long as she could.

Sandy's first hospitalization occurred while she was at The Winsor School, a private girl's school the Hendrens had chosen, in part because it was only three blocks from Children's. A hypoglycemic reaction put her in Children's, but she came through that crisis intact, graduated, and went on to Colby Junior College in New London, New Hampshire, with the idea she'd be a teacher. That's when bad things started happening, around Sandy's twenty-first birthday. She began to put on weight, and her face, always lean, became puffy. She was hospitalized with pancreatitis, and her retinas began to hemorrhage. Her eyesight began to go, and the thinking then was that removing the pituitary gland might save a diabetic's vision. A surgeon friend of Hendren's removed the gland, and blindness was averted, at least for a while, but endocrinologically Sandy was a cripple. She needed cortisone and thyroid now on top of the insulin. In the late 1970s, when she was changing careers, she had a reaction to her medication and lost circulation in two toes, which were amputated at the Massachusetts General Hospital. That stay was a long one, because her foot was so slow to heal.

Like three of her brothers, Sandy was interested in medicine, what her father did. While at the Boston University School of Education, from which she graduated in 1970, she'd worked for her father in the OR as a scrub technician. She taught at a grammar school for a few years after graduating from BU, but teaching lacked something. She wanted medicine. She wanted, in whatever time she had left, to become a doctor. She took a job as a technician in a laboratory at the Dartmouth Medical School, near the place of her birth, and she enrolled at Dartmouth as a postgraduate student, taking premedical courses. When she was ready, she applied to only two medical schools: Dartmouth and Harvard.

"You really ought to think twice about going into something as fierce as medicine," Hendren said.

"It's what I want," Sandy said. "I'm going to do it."

Harvard and Dartmouth rejected her.

"I'm so disappointed, Dad," she said.

"Sandy," Hendren said, "I really am not disappointed. You

really shouldn't go to medical school, because it's too physically demanding on you."

Why not try nursing? her father suggested. Sandy liked that idea. She enrolled at BU's School of Nursing, and when she graduated, with honors, in 1980, she went to work in the gynecology department of her father's hospital, the Massachusetts General, where she would die.

One day in late 1969, a pediatrician on Boston's North Shore called Hendren. A woman had just given birth to Siamese twins, Lawrence Essember said. She and her husband wanted them separated, if that was possible. Would Hardy be willing to try?

With his assistant for the day, Sandra McLeod Hendren, the chief of pediatric surgery at the Massachusetts General Hospital drove to Hunt Memorial Hospital in Danvers. Hendren had never attempted a separation before, but he'd done his reading. He knew that one in about every fifty thousand births produced Siamese twins, many stillborn. He knew that there were five basic variations: chest to chest (thoracopagus) and belly to belly (omphalopagus), accounting for the majority of cases; buttocks to buttocks (pygopagus), the next most common; and two rare configurations—head joined to head (craniopagus) and perineum to perineum (ischiopagus). He knew that on sixteen previous occasions, Siamese twins had been successfully separated, success being defined as the survival of both babies. But never in Boston. Never such a complicated tangle as the girls he saw in a nursery that day in November.

The North Shore twins were unique. At least, Hendren could find nothing like them in the literature. They were joined from their lower sternums (xiphoid) to the center of their bottoms—chest to chest, face to face, frozen in twisted embrace. With Sandy's help, Hendren examined them. He heard two heartbeats, saw four legs and four arms. One head, he noticed, was slightly smaller than the other. He found only one small anus, but nature had given the twins four vaginas. On such a cursory look, Hendren couldn't figure out much more about the other major organs. Theoretically, the twins could have two bladders or a single bladder or no bladder. They could have a single liver, a single kidney, a shared large intestine.

They probably could live together, Hendren thought, *but it wouldn't be a very good existence.*

The parents agreed. Would Dr. Hendren be able to help?

"Yes," Hendren said, "we'll do our best."

His instincts told him he should go ahead immediately, while their insides were still sterile from the womb. He knew that massive infection had killed Siamese twins in earlier attempts at separation, and he could greatly reduce that risk by taking up the knife before their gastrointestinal tracts were colonized with bacteria.

The twins were transferred to the General, where a preoperative workup brought encouraging news. The girls had four kidneys and two bladders. There appeared to be but one colon, but it was a good length. It probably could be divided, one half doled to one girl, the other half to her twin. The girls had two livers. They were fused, but each half had a good blood supply, and Hendren probably could get them apart. Hendren gave the conjoining a name that would have made Mr. Covington, his Woodberry Forest Latin teacher, proud: xipho-omphalo-ischiopagus-tetrapus twins, the tetrapus describing four legs. He assembled a team of five anesthesologists; three surgeon assistants, including an intern; his scrub nurse; several circulating nurses; and Sandy, who assisted the circulators. Toward the end of the operation, watching from the gallery were Eleanor and the boys and Eleanor's mother. "Why didn't you bring the family dogs?!" Hendren teased at one point.

Even before he began, word was out. The administrator of Hunt Memorial Hospital had announced the twins' birth, and the General had confirmed their transfer there. But the parents had not been identified in early news accounts, and publicly no one was saying anything about whether a separation would even be attempted. Hendren wanted it that way. He knew word about the doings in OR 12 eventually would leak out; medicine was not so cloistered that it could keep such a big secret, but until he'd operated—until he had an outcome, one way or the other—the last thing he wanted was the outside world hanging on his every move.

I don't want this to be a medical spectacle was his thinking. *I don't want to be seen as seeking publicity.*

On the morning of November 26, baby A and baby B were put to sleep. Hendren opened them along the line where they came together, from sternum to pubic bones, which were fused, an incision that gave ample access to the Byzantine anatomy within. Working as he always did—unrushed, thinking several steps ahead—he began to sort out what he had: two good stomachs, two good upper lengths of small intestine, a common colon, a common lower length of small intestine, two bladders but with a bizarre hookup to the kidneys. Instead of each baby having her both left and her right kidneys drain through ureters into her own bladder, the right kidneys connected to one bladder, the left kidneys to the other.

"All right," Hendren said when he knew what he was dealing with. "Let's go to work. Let's see what we can do."

He began by sorting out, then tying off, the blood vessels of the twins' single umbilical cord, which connected the girls in such a way that they'd shared a common blood supply. Then Hendren divided the colon, giving baby B the top half and baby A the bottom. He gave each baby a temporary colostomy, which he'd be able to get rid of at some later date, after he'd constructed an anus for each girl. He rearranged the urinary tracts so that a right kidney and a left kidney in each baby drained into the bladder he'd assigned to each. Then he started cleaving the livers, a delicate and bloody business.

Hendren sped up. He cauterized the small vessels with electric cautery and tied off the vessels too large for cautery to close—and still the bleeding, particularly from baby A's liver, was brisk. Suddenly, baby A's blood pressure dropped. You could see it on the monitor. She'd lost too much blood. Baby A's heart was in arrest.

Hendren reached through her diaphragm, opened her pericardium, and touched her heart. It had no blood; it was not beating. Hendren started massaging it with his forefinger. The anesthetists infused baby A with blood. The heart started. The heart beat normally again. The operation continued on.

It was along about this point that the news came on the radio, which Hendren had on in his room for background music.

"In a historic operation this afternoon at the Massachusetts General Hospital," the newscaster crowed, "Siamese twins were surgically separated with success."

Hendren was amazed. "Isn't that something," he said. "We haven't said a word to the press. And here we are, only halfway through, and the successful outcome is being announced on the radio."

It gives you some idea of what you can believe of the press, Hendren thought, *when something is being announced as successful when it's not even a fait accompli.*

Hendren continued. He would later learn that the leak had been through a recovery-room nurse whose boyfriend was a reporter.

When he was done with the internal organs, Hendren covered

baby B with warm towels and began closing baby A. The wound was a huge thing—four by six inches of exposed intestines—with nothing to cover it, no way in the world to stretch skin over that large an area. The solution was a synthetic patch. Hendren sewed it over the wound with just the slightest bit of tension to begin stretching the tissue of the abdominal wall, what little tissue there was. Later, Hendren would bring the baby back to the OR, remove some of the patch, stretch the tissues some more, until, in stages, he had a suitable abdominal wall. Done with baby A, he sewed the patch into baby B.

After twelve hours in the OR, the twins were individuals.

That's pretty good! Hendren thought. *And Sandy was here to help us.*

Reports of the operation went worldwide. The daily progress of the girls' recovery made headlines for weeks. The two girls came to be known not as Siamese twins, or conjoined twins, but simply as twins. TWINS FACING NEW SURGERY! MGH DRS. REVEAL ONE TWIN REVIVED AFTER HEART FAILURE! TWINS 'EXCELLENT' AFTER 2D FOLLOW-UP SURGERY! TWINS DUE FOR THIRD OPERATION! SURGEONS AID TWINS FURTHER! TWINS MAY GO HOME FOR HOLIDAY! It seemed almost Arthurian, that anyone could turn a monster into two beautiful babies. It was magic, the answer to a mother's prayer. It was Christmastime 1969, the year astronauts had walked on the moon, a year in which it was still OK to believe that a doctor could perform miracles.

Whatever his private thoughts on celebrity, and his uneasiness was based less on principle than on a concern with what his colleagues might think, Hendren knew he had to ride this one. And if he had to ride, he would go with class. He granted interviews and was gracious in his dealings with the press, although he insisted reporters read back to him the remarks of his they planned to quote. He patiently explained his own role, but he made sure the reporters promised to include in their articles his unqualified praise for the anesthesia team and his surgeon assistants and his pediatrician friend Larry Essember, as well as the rest of the doctors at Hunt Memorial Hospital who'd got the ball rolling. He agreed to have his photograph taken, but only if the entire team could pose, too. He even agreed to go on a Boston TV show.

The show was *Garroway*, a Boston talk-variety show hosted by

Dave Garroway, the first host of NBC-TV's *Today,* which premiered in 1952. Hendren, primed to discuss the surgical intricacies of separating Siamese twins, arrived at the studio and discovered that programmers, in their infinite wisdom, had selected Tiny Tim as his fellow guest. Tiny Tim was soon to marry Miss Vicky on Johnny Carson's *Tonight Show.*

I know Tiny Tim, Hendren told the producer before they went on air. He's the one who plays a ukulele and sings "Tiptoe Through the Tulips," isn't he?

Yes, he is.

I don't have a ukulele, but I can sing that song, Hendren said. Would you like to hear me?

In his best falsetto, Hendren sang "Tiptoe Through the Tulips."

Pretty good, huh? Hendren said when he was done. I think it's good enough to sing on the air. In fact, before we get to the surgery stuff, I think I will!

The producer didn't know Hendren was kidding.

Halfway into January 1970, the twins went home. One, the one whose head was smaller, was learning disabled, and she has lived at home, confined to a wheelchair. But her sister had normal intelligence and has led a normal life. Hendren operated to get rid of her colostomy and bag, and he performed various plastic surgeries, and by the time she was in her twenties, she had a job, an apartment, and a boyfriend.

By 1967, the practice of cardiovascular surgery at Children's had grown to the point where not even the legendary Gross, now sixty-two, could meet its demands and the demands of general surgery, which had remained under his purview. The hospital's trustees split Gross's service, leaving him in charge of heart surgery and bringing on board M. Judah Folkman to be the surgeon-in-chief. Administratively, the position gave Folkman control of all surgery at the hospital. But practically, his turf was general surgery only. Cardiovascular, once launched, would remain a powerful force on its own, independent of all other surgery.

Only ten years out of the Harvard Medical School, Folkman was a brilliant surgeon with an interest in tumors and the mechanism by which the body creates the blood supply that feeds them. It was a perverse concept, strikingly at odds with the fundamental law of

survival: the body sowing the seeds of its own destruction by providing tumors with the one thing they must have, a steady supply
of blood. No one else was studying angiogenesis of tumors; in the
1960s, few could conceive the promise Folkman's research would
hold for the victims of cancer. One group that did was the National
Institutes of Health, which began to funnel the first of millions of
dollars to Folkman. For more than a decade, Folkman managed to
juggle OR with lab. But by the late seventies, angiogenesis research
was fulfilling its promise. Folkman was unlocking secrets. He believed science could find a way to stop the formation of blood
vessels in tumors—maybe even reverse it in already established
cancer. Not even a brilliant man could juggle both jobs, surgery and
angiogenesis research. In 1981, Folkman decided to drop his full
commitment to surgery. He would occasionally return to the OR,
but from then on he would concentrate on the lab.

The new surgeon-in-chief was Aldo R. Castaneda, who'd been at
Children's for almost a decade, having succeeded Gross as chief
cardiac surgeon in 1972, when Gross retired to Vermont. Although
his title gave Castaneda administrative responsibility for all surgical
matters—budgeting, promoting, personnel—clinically, he had little interest in anything but the heart. Children's needed someone to
take over general surgery, which Folkman had decided to give up.
An international search began. A committee was formed. Daniel
Tosteson, dean of the Harvard Medical School, asked Hardy Hendren, chief of pediatric surgery at the General and full professor of
surgery at Harvard Medical, to join the committee. Hendren suggested writing to the heads of all pediatric surgery departments in
the world, asking who they would recommend. The committee
thought that was wise.

In the responses, Hendren's name was the one most frequently
mentioned.

Would you consider the job? the committee asked him.

I'd have to talk to the dean first to learn his mind, Hendren said.

Said Tosteson, If you would consider accepting the job if it were
offered to you, then you should take yourself off the committee.

Hendren did. A number of other people were also considered for
the job, but none was chosen. With the strong support of Castaneda, Hendren was invited to return to Children's.

"I'd very much like to," Hendren said.

There were, however, a few matters that needed to be settled first.

One was Hendren's personal staff, which included his department manager, Paula Zafferes; secretary Linda Lapham; Constance Bova, who handled billing; and Dorothy Enos, with him since 1962. His assistants would be no problem, Hendren was informed by the hospital's administration. But Miss Enos? Children's didn't have personal scrub nurses. Nurses at Children's were partners in healing, not handmaidens.

We come as a package, Hendren said, or we don't come at all.

The administration had no choice but to agree. Hendren would not only lend prestige to Children's. He would bring a surgical practice that generated millions each year for the hospital.

Another matter was Hendren's title.

In academic medicine, titles are not simply something that happen your way. Titles are your coat of arms. They reflect stature within your field, position on the pecking order within your institution. Like European royalty, academic doctors do not take titles lightly.

We'll call you pediatric surgeon-in-chief, the administration told Hendren.

Not good, Hendren told the administration. "All the surgery over there is pediatric surgery," he said.

What about surgeon-in-chief for general surgery?

No, Hendren said. "Two thirds of what I do is urologic reconstructive surgery," he said. "If I'm going to come over here, it's got to be with a title that does not indicate that I don't do one thing or another."

Chief of surgery was the title everyone agreed on, in the spring of 1982. Under Hendren would be general surgery, plastic surgery, urology, and gynecology. Cardiovascular surgery would remain separate, as would orthopedics, otolaryngology, and neurosurgery.

Hendren was at his mother's in Kansas City when the announcement was made. The first to call with congratulations was Robert Gross.

Chapter 19

With one single, unhesitating slice, Hendren cuts Lucy's blank bottom along a line from the spot where he's drawn her anus down to the base of her clitoris.

Lucy flinches.

"The baby's reacting to what I'm doing," Hendren says.

He is annoyed but not angry. He understands. In order to allow Hendren to electrically stimulate Lucy's bottom, anesthesiologists could not paralyze her. Now that Hendren has marked out his spot for her anus, they can be heavier with the isoflurane gas. Rabb, who's manning the station, turns it up. She will not use an intravenous paralyzer, in case Hendren needs to stimulate the baby again; intravenous paralyzers are slower to reverse than gas. Nor will she use nitrous oxide, which can bloat the bowel, making it difficult to work down in there and very difficult to close the wound when the operation's done. One of Hendren's standing orders whenever he's entering the belly is no nitrous. With the constant flow of new residents through Children's, his order is not always obeyed, much to his annoyance.

"Let me have the little needle-point cautery, Dorothy," Hendren says.

Electric cautery is another of the great innovations of surgery. Its roots are in the 1890s, when French doctors discovered that a spark gap current generated at high frequency could cut and coagulate tissue and when used with care would not fry it. In the 1920s,

W. T. Bovie, a scientist at the Massachusetts Institute of Technology, working with the neurosurgeon Harvey Cushing, developed the basic design of the modern cautery. In the right application, cautery is a powerful and efficient tool. It gives a fast, bloodless cut through most tissues. It saves time, sparing a surgeon from frustration.

Enos hands Hendren the cautery. For the next few minutes, he alternates between it and the knife.

Hendren makes no false starts, no wasted movements, no mistakes. Down through skin he goes—through two layers of fat, yellow and globular like fresh-killed poultry—through muscle, fibrous and stringy but no match for cautery and blade—deeper and deeper into Lucy, toward major organs and anatomic confusion and a series of decisions that will fundamentally affect this fourteen-month-old baby for the rest of her days. Like sap from a tree being carved, droplets of blood appear on the cut edges of tissue. These are the bleeders: capillaries and small vessels that individually couldn't do much harm but cumulatively could bleed a patient to death. Large vessels must be tied off, but small bleeders can be sealed with the cautery, which produces a blue spark, makes a distinctive zapping sound, and sends up a wisp of sweet-smelling smoke. Hendren zaps here and there. Blood pools in the bottom of the incision, getting larger by the minute. With her suction tube, her "sucker," Enos cleans it out. A surgeon has to be able to see.

That's about the right size, Hendren thinks. *That's about as much as we'll need from below.*

Lucy's open wound is the size of his fist, a deep valley of brilliant red, glistening in the glare of Hendren's headlamp and the room's twin ceiling-mounted lights. Hendren keeps it open with two locking clamps called Weitlaners. Steinberg helps by precisely positioning two pronged retractors according to Hendren's instructions.

"There's the sphincter," Hendren says. "I want you all to see this because this is a very nice sphincter here. See that thick muscle there? See it? It runs all along there."

Hendren cuts again. He's into tricky territory now. He's opened the urogenital sinus, or cloaca, which many hours later he'll refashion into a urethra. He's down to the region around the bladder, where Lucy's rectum ends in an abnormal attachment to the bladder neck. He has to separate the two, rectum from bladder. Doing so will require the most meticulous work. Straying from the proper plane of dissection—where tissue layers meet—could result in an inadvertent hole in the bladder, and even if the hole were seen and closed, it could reopen later, becoming a fistula, a difficult complication that could cause leakage and infection.

No matter how careful he is as he works on and near the rectum, and he's always very careful, Hendren would not take a chance with dirtiness. Unlike a bladder, a dirty rectum is rife with germs— germs with the potential to contaminate the entire operating field—and that is why Hendren is so demanding when it comes to preoperative bowel cleansing. "You could eat your dinner off that one, it's so clean," he joked during one operation. For Hendren, who's found dirty intestines more than once on his table, it was a high compliment to the ward nurses, who prepare patients for their trip to the OR.

Before starting on Lucy's rectum, Hendren stops to ponder those tiny pits on the wall of the cloaca that he saw through his endoscope. Again, he tries to maneuver a tiny probe up into them to see if they lead anywhere. The probe won't go.

"What are they?" one of his visitors asks.

"I don't know," Hendren says. "They look like little holes. Of course, the thing we want to be careful of is that they don't represent vaginas."

Separating rectum from bladder is too delicate to use the cautery. Even a meticulous hand could cause unwitting damage with cautery. Delicate tissues could be imperceptibly burned, and a burn could hinder healing and thus lead to a fistula. Hendren puts the cautery away, at least for now. For this phase, he'll use only scissors and knife, even though they'll slow him considerably. As he works on the rectum, Hendren is on the lookout for a vagina. One could be almost anywhere. It could be fully formed or vestigial, a worthless caricature of what nature intended. There could be two vaginas or none. So far, everything points toward none. Faced with this kind of anatomic puzzle, less gifted surgeons might be tempted to walk away. Those who stayed might putter. They might work a bit on this piece of the puzzle and then move over to that other piece there and maybe sidestep over to this third major problem here. And while they might or might not have a clear picture of the final product, getting there would be serendipity. Not with Hendren. He's still facing some significant unknowns, the vagina question being most notable of those, but he's done enough by now, almost noon, to be able to envision Lucy's postoperative anatomy clearly. This may be Hendren's greatest gift—his ability to conceptualize, to assess correctly the consequences of his every move before he makes it, to know with strategic certainty how so many hundreds of steps will come together in the end, all without benefit of blueprint or manual, only what's in his head. It is a talent grandmasters of chess have, almost a four-dimensional ability, something that cannot be taught or gleaned from *Gray's Anatomy.* "His technique is second to none, but what's unique to Dr. Hendren is this vision," said Hendren's chief resident for the 1991–92 year, Steven Stylianos, a surgeon who's studied under many chiefs.

We have to mobilize the rectum, being careful not to injure any nearby structures, Hendren thinks. *We have to search for a vagina. Plenty of colon. Seems to have good blood supply, which will help if we have to make a vagina or extend a high-placed occult vagina, if that's what we find she has. We have a functionless multicystic kidney to get rid of, but we'll do that when we turn her over. We'll take that ureter out as well.*

With a final snip, Hendren separates the end of Lucy's rectum from her bladder. Now he must free up a substantial length of rectum from the tissues wrapped around it. This mobilizing will take time. At the very least, Hendren will need enough length to reach down to where the anus will be. He may very well have to take an additional piece for use as a vagina. At this stage of the operation, he can't sacrifice any rectum. He has to preserve the blood supply, its lifeline, throughout its entire length. Knife, small scissors, large scissors, forceps—taking his cues from how the tissues are aligned, Hendren segues through his instruments as he frees up Lucy's rectum. He's not speaking now. Enos isn't, either. But when he extends his hand, there she is, placing the next tool he needs softly into his palm, not a second wasted.

Hendren sometimes communicates to Enos with hand signals, and sometimes he makes a verbal request, but their ordinary relationship is characterized by this wordless harmony. After three decades at his right hand, Enos nearly always anticipates Hendren. Almost without exception, she knows which instrument he'll want next, what kind of suture material, which size needle, what particular solution to wash out a wound. She knows where the spare batteries for the stimulator are kept, where the catheters only Hendren uses are stored. She knows how to work the video. She serves as Hendren's second set of eyes, tracking those who enter and leave the room and apprising him of their purpose if she thinks he ought to know. She is Hendren's guardian of sterility. She continually monitors his performance, suggesting a break when she sees him getting frustrated or fatigued. On a break, she pops the popcorn.

In forty years in the OR, since he was an intern doing his first appendectomy in Room 5 of the Massachusetts General Hospital in July 1952, Hendren's passion for surgery has not dimmed, but it is tested when Enos is on vacation. Nothing is quite the same when she is away; nothing goes quite as smoothly. "It's like trying to fly a 747 with a different crew every time you take off," he said once when he was without the help of his scrub nurse. Hendren will not schedule a big case if Enos is not going to be around, and he's been known to cancel one already on the books when an emergency has taken her away. No wonder only a few of the other nurses volunteer to step in for Enos when she's gone. No wonder her annual compensation, when benefits and overtime are factored in, is that of a middle-level manager at a major corporation.

"Dorothy is the best scrub nurse I have ever worked with anywhere in the world," Hendren says, not gratuitously. He's incorporated his belief into a title: World's Best Scrub Nurse, or WBSN. Hendren's always making such a big deal of the title—a visitor cannot be in his room long before hearing it—that Stylianos had a fake citation made, only partly as a gag. Enos takes her title with good humor, although she would never call herself WBSN; she prefers the title she came up with, Saint Dorothy. Of course, WBSN could not go unanswered. If he was going to have an acronym for her, then she needed one for him. What she coined was SOH, for Sweet Old Hardy, but only in this context, the context of teasing and fun, will she use his first name at Children's. In all other hospital situations, he's Dr. Hendren. Only away from Children's, only at the Hendrens', where Enos is sometimes a guest, does she ever address her boss as "Hardy."

Everett Enos, Dorothy's father, was the son of a fisherman who left the Azores for Gloucester, Massachusetts, at the turn of the century. Dorothy Esther Smith, her mother, was the daughter of a

Maine carpenter. The Enos's only child was born in Boston in 1937. The family moved several times while Dorothy was growing up, from town to town in the Boston metropolitan area, where Everett drove a truck. Dorothy graduated from Dedham High School, where she'd been on a college-preparatory track. But Dorothy doubted she'd be going to college. In the Enos household, there was never any serious discussion of college for her. Dad didn't buy the idea of higher education for girls.

For a year after graduating, Enos was a clerk for the John Hancock Life Insurance Company. She earned thirty-two dollars a week, and she had the notion that maybe someday she'd be an airline stewardess—until a friend was accepted into nursing school, and Enos decided she'd like to give that a crack. She saved her money, and in the fall of 1955 she entered the only school to which she'd applied: the Children's Hospital School of Nursing. Except for giving needles, Enos loved nursing, and she loved nothing as much as her rotation through the operating room. This, she knew, was where she wanted to be.

Enos met Hendren during her first year at nursing school. He was twenty-nine, serving his first residency under Robert E. Gross, and he was supremely confident but not cocky, like some of his less talented peers. Hardy Hendren always said "please" and "thank you" and he had a sense of humor. He had his own instruments: two needle holders, two scissors, and a pair of forceps, each with gold-plated handles. No other resident had his own instruments, never mind a gold-plated set. In 1959, Enos was out of nursing school and on the staff at Children's when Hendren returned from his training at Massachusetts General to be Gross's chief resident. That year, Dr. Hendren often requested Miss Enos and her roommate, Maggie Knapp, to scrub in on his cases. That year, Dr. Hendren did something very few doctors ever did: he invited two nurses, Enos and Knapp, to have Thanksgiving dinner with the Hendren family.

Enos stayed at Children's when Hendren left for the General in July 1960. By early 1962, Hendren was busy enough to be able to afford his own scrub nurse, long a tradition at the General. He asked Maggie Knapp first, but she declined. She was engaged to be married.

What about Miss Enos? Would she like to join her old chief resident across town?

"Maybe I'll try it for a little while," Enos said.

"Help has arrived!" Hendren wrote onto his calendar on March 12, 1962, the day Enos came to work with him. In years to come, Hardy and Eleanor would faithfully mark the anniversary of Dorothy's arrival, which is two days before her birthday, with a card and a gift. On her twenty-fifth anniversary, they hosted a black-tie dinner at The Country Club in Brookline. An entire surgical department joined together to pay tribute to Dorothy Enos. Several of Hendren's former chief residents presented her with an opal pendant and a plaque recognizing her contributions to their development as surgeons.

At twenty-five, Dorothy Enos had no idea what she was getting into. She had no idea of the hours Hendren kept, of how many cases he would schedule, of how complicated some of the reconstructive surgeries he was starting to get into were. But she was game. Not just anyone was doing what Hendren was doing, and not just any nurse was given Enos's responsibilities. She scrubbed for Hendren, but she also joined him in the dog lab. She helped with formulating statistics, combing records, lining up slides and notes before his lectures. When the day was done, typically not until nine or ten at night, she'd often go back with Hendren to his home on Chestnut Hill in Brookline, where Eleanor would have a steak or chicken dinner waiting.

Hospital medicine is an intensely cooperative venture, the coming together of departments, divisions, and disciplines to make a sick stranger well. But in academic medicine, the fraternity the patient and family see belies the political reality. Children's is less one big, happy hospital than a collection of fiefdoms, each with its own ruler, loyal foot soldiers, spies, jesters, revenue sources, and turf to defend—and, sometimes, to expand. "The Holy Roman Empire," says one of Children's brightest minds, immunologist Fred S. Rosen: "many bodies politic under one roof."

You would never guess this perusing Children's official publications, unless you are skilled in reading between lines. Official publications that emanate from Anne Malone's Development and Public Affairs Department reflect an extraordinary effort at presenting balance and fair play. There are no Lone Rangers in the official view, no Top Guns, only selfless women and men of talent who could not have gotten where they are without a diverse supporting cast. No one specialist or department is allowed to hog the ink. Colleagues are always complimentary of their brethren. Never is heard a disparaging word. Rarely is there a glimpse of ego, that great motivator.

But beneath that carefully maintained image are some respectable rivalries. The fiercest, at least in word, is between surgeons and nonoperating physicians, between surgery and medicine. Surgeons, in the prevailing view of some medical people, are technicians who earn too much money and get by on less than maximum brainpower. Medical people, say some surgeons, are intrinsically lazy snobs who would have to call a conference before changing a light bulb. "You don't want to stand in front of the door at five, when the medical service lets out—you'll get stampeded," Hendren said once at suppertime, when he was only halfway through a case. Retorts Rosen: "Surgery is boring. You sit there, snip snip, cut cut. I am not a seamstress. The thinking doctors go into medicine." Incidentally, it was Hendren whom Rosen asked to operate on him to remove a pilonidal cyst when Hendren was Gross's chief resident.

During one of Hendren's long surgeries, a medical student was scrubbed in with the chief. All day, Hendren went back and forth with her over her knowledge of anatomy. She impressed him, correctly naming the five important structures—potentially dangerous to the surgeon—near where he was working, which was on the larynx: subclavian artery, subclavian vein, phrenic nerve, thoracic duct, and recurrent laryngeal nerve. She lost points, however, when she could not name a single one of the Marx Brothers. "My goodness!" Hendren said in mock horror. "What's wrong with your generation?"

Mostly, Hendren tried to steer the student into surgery. She was planning to follow a medical track.

"Are you *sure* you don't want to go into surgery?" he asked.

"I could never rise to such heights," the student said.

"Why, any trained ape can do this," Hendren replied, mimicking a gorilla. "Eeee-eeee-eeee!" he screamed, hunching his shoulders and scratching near his sides with looped arms. "We're nothing but a bunch of technicians! Isn't that what the medical people teach you?"

Surgical and medical services have been on each other's cases for so long their competition has been incorporated into an adage: *The*

*surgeon does everything but doesn't know anything; the medical
man knows everything but doesn't do anything; the psychiatrist
doesn't know or do anything; and the pathologist knows everything but it's too late.*

Another division is between physicians and nurses, who have
emerged as a powerful political force in the modern hospital.

During the decade Hendren trained, nurses were subservient to
physicians in most respects, nowhere more so than in the OR, where
the surgeon was the unquestioned captain of the ship. Nurses handled instruments, emptied bed pans, took blood pressure, temperature, and pulse. They held the children's hands and rocked the
babies to sleep—important members of the health-care team, but
not fully vested partners. Some considered them handmaidens, a
role increasingly at odds with the feminism of the sixties and seventies. In those decades, nurses wanted a share of power, and they got
it. It was an era when patients were becoming consumers and cost
an issue, when specialty spawned subspecialty and the physician
was taken off his pedestal. It was an era when professions allied with
nursing—social work and activities therapy—got their share of
power, too.

Hendren liked much about the old ways, and he speaks of that
era as a sort of golden age. He believes some nurses today spend too
much time in meetings and doing paperwork and too little time
caring for patients and helping physicians. He thinks that some
nurses take too many coffee breaks and work too strictly by the
clock. He does not believe all nurses need advanced degrees and
professional associations and complicated management structures,
although he goes to lengths to point out the sophistication they need
to be an accomplished scrub nurse and to run specialized units such
as the recovery room and intensive care. He believes that many of
the jobs done today by nurses with advanced degrees could be done
by nurses' aides and nursing assistants at great savings. Nursing is
the largest single item in the Children's Hospital budget today.

Hendren is not shy about his opinions—not to his fellow physicians, not to nurses, not to nurse managers or the administration. His
sentiments evoke varied reactions. Some surgeons, typically those of
his generation, agree with him. Some nurses become less than eager
to work in Hendren's OR. Some lie low when he is around. Others
trade jokes and banter with him. Despite his beliefs, Hendren is fond
of many nurses, and they, in turn, of him. They see a paradox:

Hendren's most trusted associate is Dorothy Enos, one of them. This tells them he recognizes individual merit. They know that his daughter was a nurse, as is one of his daughters-in-law. And they know that he is a perfectionist, that there is no one else they would have cut open their own children. "I used to hate working with him," says Lisa Small, one of the nurses who has scrubbed in for Enos. "I respect him now." Another circulating nurse says of his perfectionism, which cannot be compromised, "He's traded his whole life for this. He used to bother me. He doesn't now. I understand he has to be this way."

Once a year, at the graduation dinner party for Hendren's departing chief resident, Children's surgical nurses put on a skit. For one night, no one is sacred. At the 1991 party, the nurses on Eight West parodied *The Wizard of Oz*. The biggest laughter came at the end of the skit, when a nurse playing Dorothy, who was carrying her stuffed dog, Toto, went in search of the wizard.

"My dog, Toto, just needs a quick cloaca repair," the Dorothy character said, "but we can't find the way to the wizard. Nobody can show us the way."

"Oh, that's easy," several munchkins said, "just follow the yellow brick road."

But Dorothy hadn't gone far before a wicked witch appeared. "Well, my pretty one," the witch said, "it's no use. *If* and *when* you find the wizard, he will have trouble fitting Toto into his God-almighty schedule!"

The wizard came onstage. "I am the Wizard Hendren, the closest thing you can get to God!"

"I . . . uh . . . I . . . " Dorothy said.

"Speak!"

"My dog Toto, . . . he has a cloaca. . . . I was told you're the best to fix it—"

"I am the best! Does the dog have insurance?"

"Well, no," Dorothy said, "but I heard you were a good man—"

"No insurance, no surgery! Do you think I pay for my waterfront home with my looks?"

"No, but . . ."

"No *what*?"

"No, *sir*! But I thought you could write it up in the journals and be famous and—"

"*I am famous!*"

The audience roared. Hendren's entire department, their spouses, the nurses who work with him, residents and interns and friends—all roared, none more loudly than Hendren himself.

"A movie! What a production!"

Having completed the first of his two heart operations for the day, Aldo R. Castaneda has dropped by Hendren's room. Surgeons are curious sorts. At Children's, they're always popping into someone else's room to check out the action.

A visiting doctor gives Castaneda his place on a gray stool. Castaneda looks down at Lucy's guts.

"Aldo, this is one of your patients," Hendren says. "Lucy Moore. You did her VSD last year."

"Oh yes," Castaneda says. He gets off the stool and threads his way past Barbara Cosgrove's videocamera to the light board, where Lucy's films still hang.

"The big thing is her rectum," Hendren explains. "The little thing squished up there is her bladder. It's probable she doesn't have a vagina. But I've been fooled and found two before. Get back up, and I'll show you something."

Castaneda returns to the stool.

"Here's her muscle," Hendren says. "This mark here is where we're going to put her rectum. See it?"

Castaneda nods.

Hendren describes what he's doing: mobilizing Lucy's rectum. "Then we're going to turn her over, open her up, and see what's inside. We'll try to fashion something for a vagina. I think she'll end up having a pretty nice bottom."

On his way out the door, Castaneda hams it up.

"Since I did the VSD," he says, "can I be in the movie?"

"Go ahead," Hendren tells Cosgrove. "Get a shot of him. I can edit it out later!"

It's a minute before noon. Karen Sakakeeny is over at the counter, hunting for news on the boom box someone has brought into the room. She finds what she wants and turns up the volume. At a Washington press conference, George Bush is praising Israel's restraint in the wake of Saddam Hussein's launching of several Scud missiles.

Hendren wants a still photograph of the wound he's opened. He asks Sakakeeny for his Nikon.

"But the president's on," she says.

Hendren laughs. "Down there, he's the boss," he says. "In this here room, I'm the boss."

"He's mental!" Sakakeeny whispers jokingly.

But Hendren is interested in what the president has to say. All day, he wants updates on the war.

Steinberg sneezes. Standing there, holding his retractors, he *sneezes*.

"Turn your head, Jeff," Hendren says. "Have you ever seen a photograph of that?" A photograph of the trajectory that sneeze droplets take when launched from behind a surgical mask?

"It comes out the sides?" Steinberg offers.

"Out the front, as well," Hendren says. "Now, turn your head as far away from the field as you can."

Chastened, Steinberg turns far away on his next sneeze.

Hendren has freed up as much of Lucy's rectum as he can reach from this side; he'll have to finish the job when he goes in through her abdomen. But before they turn her, Hendren intensifies his hunt for a vagina. With a forceps in one hand and a tiny retractor known as a rake in the other, he separates the planes of tissue that surround the bladder. He probes the urogenital sinus, which he's already split open. Those tiny pits—those still intrigue him, although their significance remains dubious.

"I wish I knew what those things are," he says. "I think developmentally they were close to being vaginas."

No use concerning ourselves with them anymore. Whatever nature had in mind, they are of no use to Lucy now.

"All right," he says. "Now, what do you guys want me to do?"

Sometimes when Hendren tosses out a question like this, a resident may offer a suggestion, but any who know Hendren understand that doing so can be risky. If you come up with the wrong idea, you'll hear about it. Usually, it's best to let Hendren do all of the talking.

No one answers.

"We need a urinary output," Hendren says.

He inserts a catheter into Lucy's bladder and attaches a bulb syringe to the free end. The syringe will collect urine, which Enos will periodically empty and measure, calling out the volume for all to hear. Urinary output is one of many carefully monitored measures of homeostasis, the patient's state of well-being, useful to surgeon and anesthesiologist. It tells them especially about hydration. Opened on an operating table for hour after hour, a baby can lose a tremendous volume of vital fluids. There is loss from bleeding, loss through evaporation from the open wound, loss from weeping—the lymphatic system's supercharged response to the massive trauma of extensive surgery. There is temporary loss when fluid accumulates in tissues, a process called sequestration, or third-space loss (the three spaces being intravascular, intracellular, and interstitial, or between cells). And there are the normal losses through perspiration and respiration. One of the great balancing acts of surgery is maintaining fluid and electrolyte balance. In concert with the surgeon, the anesthesiologist accomplishes this by the careful monitoring and infusions of fluids, including whole blood or blood components and lactated Ringer's, a solution of sodium, potassium, calcium, chloride, and lactate.

What's this?

Hendren surveys the wound, the question of a vagina still paramount in his mind. With scissors, he starts dissecting in an area to the right side of the rectum. The tissue there looks different.

It looks thickened, Hendren thinks. *Let's see what's there, if anything.*

He's found something! It's definitely an organ of some kind. Pinkish and about three centimeters long, the width of Hendren's little finger.

Vagina! Not a very good size, but it's vagina. Ending blindly. I wonder if it's connected to a uterus up above? Have to keep dissecting to find out.

"Dorothy happens to be a person devoted to our patients," Hendren tells his guests. "You didn't hear her, but she was muttering to me, 'Don't forget about the possibility of a vagina.' Now, I'd already been talking about that. She was just being doubly certain. She gets three points!"

Hendren snips off the blind end of the vagina. Thick, gray mucus drains out. This is hydrometrocolpos, characteristic of a vagina or uterus that has been sealed at the lower end.

"That's a very small vagina," Hendren says.

If we find another one equally small, we can sew them both together. We've done that before, and it's worked nicely. Or there's

*always colon. We can always use colon to extend it. Thank good-
ness, she's got plenty to spare.*

"We'll figure something out," he says.

With his scissors, Hendren moves up toward where a uterus will
be if there is one. After several minutes of dissection, he's rewarded.
Hendren hasn't been this excited today since watching his first
videos of smart bombs over Baghdad.

"There's a little cervix up there! Oh, yeah! *Oh, yeah!*"

One-fifteen P.M.

Finding the vagina and dissecting it away from the bladder neck
has taken an hour.

But the hunt is not over. It's not time to turn Lucy, not yet.

When they're like this, vaginas often come in pairs, Hendren
thinks. *I bet there's another one in there.*

"All right," he says. "I think I'll come around to the other side
and look for the other vagina." He will have a better angle if he
moves from his customary spot.

Relocating from one side of the table to the other is not as easy
as it sounds. The cord to Hendren's headlamp must be unplugged.
The visitors' stool must be moved. The visitors and circulating
nurses, who are not sterile, must give Hendren a wide berth. A path
must be cleared through the instrument trays and camera setup so
that neither Hendren nor Steinberg, who also will switch sides,
touches anything dirty. Nothing is more annoying in the middle of
a tough operation than the hassle of changing gowns because of
someone's stupid mistake.

Sakakeeny unplugs Hendren's cord and follows the chief to the
other side. She plugs him back in. In passing Price, the other
resident, Hendren takes notice of his gown. It's looser around the
neck than the chief would like. If it continues to loosen, it could
expose his unsterilized skin.

"Will someone tie Ray up here?" Hendren says. "He's got *droo-
pus* of the gown."

Hendren steps to the table and reorients himself. With his
fingers, he feels what he's done. Fingers are a surgeon's finest
instrument, useful for holding, retracting, pushing, joining, measuring, exploring, analyzing texture. For all their accomplishments,
Hendren's fingers are not perfect. When he was six and living in
New Orleans, his sister Peggy one day was playing with paper dolls.

She asked her brother to get her a pair of scissors. He got a kitchen knife instead. He was whacking around with it when it slipped and cut deeply into the base of his left thumb. A surgeon fixed Hendren, but not well: he forgot to sew a tendon back, leaving Hendren's left thumb forever without full range of movement. To qualify for Navy aviation, Hendren not only had to gorge on bananas and water; he had to hide his handicap. But it has not affected his surgery.

"Here's the rectum," he says. "Here's the bladder neck. Here's the vagina we just found. I'm going to look right over here for another vagina. Right down in here, there's probably another one. There's got to be, because Dorothy said so. Because basically all I know you taught me, anyway, right?"

Enos doesn't answer. But her look is a familiar one. *Let's stop the small talk*, it says. *We're going to be here half the night as it is.*

"All right, Dorothy. Let's go to work."

Chapter 20

Hardy Hendren would never describe himself as passionate. That might imply emotional tempestuousness, a quality he does not believe a surgeon should possess. But Hendren is passionate. He has never done anything halfheartedly or with hesitation. He has never started something he didn't intend to complete with his absolute best effort, a lesson he learned from his father. Hendren has an opinion on most things, and he has rarely felt compelled to keep those opinions to himself. There are few dark corners or grays in his world, whose axis is the Kansas City of his Depression-era childhood.

Predictably, Hendren is politically conservative. "I wouldn't vote for a Democrat if it were my key to heaven," he has said. He does not like Kennedys, especially Ted, the senior U.S. senator from his state; almost a quarter of a century later, Chappaquiddick still angers him. Hendren believes the American Civil Liberties Union is made up mostly of weirdos and creeps. He cannot comprehend political correctness, doesn't understand why someone would ever call one of his patients "differently abled," or some such. He believes that able-bodied people should work and that their wages should be what the free market will pay them. He prefers the structure of the fifties family to its nineties counterpart, although he will support a woman with talent and ambition who seeks to be a doctor. He blames liberals for high taxes, inefficient government, welfare abuse, and high crime, a Republican's standard litany of complaints.

Hendren believes that what America needs is Islamic law, whose punitive principle is an eye for an eye.

One day a few weeks after Lucy Moore's reconstruction, Hendren was in his operating room examining a boy whose bladder cancer he'd cured. In a nearby room, a sixteen-year-old high school student was losing his battle for life. There was little Hendren's chief resident, Jay J. Schnitzer, could do. The sixteen-year-old had taken one bullet in his right leg. Another bullet had entered the groin and torn up his intestines before lodging in his lung. Schnitzer, an experienced trauma surgeon who honed his skills on the Gaza Strip, worked for six hours on the boy. Fifty units of blood were used, but still the boy could not make it. The lines on the monitors went flat, and he died on the table, the operating floor still slippery from his blood.

During the morning, Hendren had periodically checked in on Schnitzer to be sure he was OK. When word of the boy's death reached the chief, it was accompanied by a rumor that the sixteen-year-old had been the random victim of a drive-by shooting as he'd walked to school. The assailant had not yet been arrested.

"You know what they ought to do with the bastard when they catch him?" Hendren said. "Let him swing from the yardarm. In Copley Square." Public executions, Hendren argued, would be a deterrent. Why, just look at Islam.

"Do you know what they do when they catch a thief?" he asked.

"Cut off the hand that did the thieving?" a resident scrubbed in with Hendren offered.

"Cut off the right hand, which they eat with," Hendren replied. "That way, they have to eat with the left hand, which is traditionally used after the toilet." This makes them social outcasts, Hendren contends, effectively deterring theft.

No person has annoyed Hendren as much as his governor for many years, Michael Dukakis, the liberal's liberal. Hendren blames legislation Dukakis supported for allowing third-party insurers, notably Blue Shield of Massachusetts, to delay their payments to surgeons. He blames Dukakis for high taxes, inefficient government, welfare abuse, and high crime. He believes that Dukakis, son of a Harvard-educated doctor, dislikes physicians because his own dream of becoming one was dashed by a poor grade in physics at Swarthmore College. When Dukakis ran for president against George Bush, fellow naval aviator, Second World War veteran, and

Republican—Hendren couldn't stand it. He does not have a bumper sticker personality, but this time he put one on his car: DUMP THE DUKE AND KITTY LITTER TOO. When informed of the possibility that Dukakis might teach at Harvard's John F. Kennedy School of Government, Hendren wondered what the title of his course would be. "How to Screw Up Government?" he mused.

During one operation, when the discussion had turned to politics and the 1988 presidential election, Hendren said to a circulating nurse, "Did you vote for Dukakis?"

One wiser in Hendren's ways might not have admitted that she had. But the nurse was frank. "Yes, I did," she said.

"How could you vote for Dukakis?"

The nurse laughed. Yes, she conceded, his campaign had turned out to be a bomb. His defeat had been humiliating.

"Are you embarrassed you voted for Dukakis?"

"Yes." She laughed again.

"All right," Hendren said, a familiar twinkle in his blue eyes. "You're forgiven!"

Hendren believes passionately in the power of medicine to heal, a belief he enthusiastically promulgates.

In July 1990, on one of his rare television appearances, Hendren discussed a recently concluded Suffolk Superior Court case on a current-events program, Channel 7's *Boston Common*. Joining him were a professor, an attorney, and a spokesman for the Church of Christ, Scientist. Over its eleven weeks, the trial had generated a tremendous amount of ink. Ginger and David Twitchell stood accused of manslaughter in the death of their two-and-a-half-year-old son, Robyn, who'd suffered for five days from a bowel obstruction before expiring. As Christian Scientists, the Twitchells had relied on prayer to treat their child, not medical help. They were convicted. Hendren was a figure in the trial, testifying as an expert witness for the special prosecutor, John Kiernan, his medical malpractice attorney.

"I think that certainly prayer can be of help," Hendren said on *Boston Common*. "It certainly is synonymous with the power of positive thinking. When I faced cancer myself a number of years ago, I prayed. But I also saw a very good surgeon to do what he did well."

The Christian Science spokesman, Nathan Talbot, presented his position: that individuals and parents have a responsibility to seek the kind of care that conscience and religion demand.

"Well, Nathan," Hendren said, "I fully respect your right to believe what you do. But let me ask you a practical question: if you were, God forbid, to drop over here with a coronary right now, would you like for me to do CPR to try to resuscitate you and get you two blocks down the street to the Mass General? Or would you like for us all to fold our hands, bow our heads, and pray?"

Talbot was quick. "I think I'd like what most people would," he said. "I would want the most effective treatment. And from twenty years in practicing spiritual healing, my preference would be spiritual treatment. Not that I would necessarily ask you to do that, but I would want to be in touch with a Christian Science practitioner."

Hendren shot back, "But you see—there isn't time. If you were to fall over with a coronary now, somebody would have to do something very effective very quickly to resuscitate you."

Medical healing, Hendren believes, should be available to all. He applies no test to his prospective patients, none but the Hippocratic oath, whose tenets are incorporated into the more contemporary International Code of Medical Ethics: "*A doctor must always maintain the highest standards of professional conduct. . . . A doctor must practice his profession uninfluenced by motives of profit. . . . A doctor must always bear in mind the obligation of preserving human life. . . .*

It doesn't matter where you live, what religion you practice, for whom you voted in the last election, how complicated your case is, or whether you have the ability to pay. If you need Hendren, Hendren is there. Ask, and he will take care of your child. In his practice, all patients are equal.

On March 6, 1990, a baby girl was born in a hospital in Texas. Abby's father was an intravenous drug abuser; her mother, sixteen, already had two children. Even before seeing her daughter, she'd decided to put the newborn up for adoption.

Abby came into the world with dark eyes and thick black hair. A closer look showed problems—multiple, life-threatening problems. Abby had no outer ears. She had a bad heart and no anus. Her esophagus ended blindly before reaching her stomach, and what truncated length she did have connected by a fistula to her trachea. Her spine was defective, and she had a cloaca. Like Lucy Moore,

Abby was a VACTERL association baby. If she were to live, she would need an emergency colostomy so that her intestines would not back up and kill her. She would need the urgent repair of her esophagus so that she could take nourishment and her lungs would not be at risk from the fistula. If she were ever to come close to being normal, more surgery would be needed down the line. Abby would be expensive and a risk. She would be a project.

The hospital's general surgeons were divided. Some felt whatever could be done for Abby should be done for her.

Others didn't want to perform the colostomy. They felt it would be better not to operate, to let Abby die.

Look at her social situation, they reasoned. *What kind of life could she have? Wouldn't it be better for everyone if she were allowed to die? Wouldn't that be most humane? To let her quietly fade away, here, where no one need ever know?*

Susan, a woman from a small town in Missouri, was a resident in pediatric medicine at the Texas hospital. She was present when Abby was born. She was in the neonatal intensive care unit when the staff began to sort out Abby's deformities. She heard that the surgeons were bitterly divided. She thought the possibility of not operating was morally reprehensible—a violation of the Hippocratic oath, if not a violation of the law—so she joined the opposing faction and several others at the hospital who, similarly horrified, brought the case to the hospital's ethics board. Also joining the cause was Susan's lover, a pediatric nurse named Anne.

Ethics was firm. "We do not know what the exact social circumstances will be in the future for this child," a board member wrote in Abby's record. "We also cannot predict the child's own evaluation of those circumstances. . . . Despite this neonate's deplorable family situation and potentially (socially) difficult future, I feel that we should not withhold full therapy on the basis of social considerations. . . . I recommend full, aggressive surgical and medical therapy."

Abby was saved.

And when no one else stepped forward to take her, Susan did. Susan had fallen for Abby, this poor little darling who'd come into the world with two strikes against her. Susan would seek legal guardianship of Abby. Susan would give Abby a home—her home, which she shared with Anne. They would make it their mission to make Abby whole. When they heard about Hardy Hendren, heard he was the world's expert on cloaca, they brought the child to Boston from Pennsylvania, where they had relocated.

Hendren took Abby to his table and examined her endoscopically. He was not pleased with how her colon had been handled during her colostomy. But the hitch wasn't surgical. The hitch was money. Susan's insurer, Blue Shield of Pennsylvania, would not pay an out-of-state surgeon, and Susan, fresh from years of medical training, wasn't in a position to pick up the tab. That was all right, Hendren said; he would take care of Abby for free. Since Blue Shield would not pay Children's Hospital, either, Hendren convinced his administration to waive their charges. On April 26, 1991, he reconstructed Abby, the baby other surgeons would have thrown away. Ordinarily, Hendren would have waited several months before reversing her colostomy, before getting rid of her bag. But Susan's circumstances were changing. She'd broken up with Anne, changing hospitals and moving back to Texas. She asked if Hendren could possibly fit the operation in before August 1?

He could, and did. "Evidently Sue now has a new friend and has discontinued largely her relationship with Anne, . . . [who] is now dating men again!!!" Hendren noted in the record. "I am totally unable to understand all these social situations."

As someone with a professional interest in strangers' bowels, Hendren long ago learned the wisdom of being familiar with his own. After using the toilet on Tuesday, December 10, 1974, Hendren saw a spot of red in the bowl. *Tomato skin* was his initial thought. But it wasn't tomato skin, a closer look revealed. It was blood, and blood could mean many things. It could mean a harmless polyp or a hemorrhoid. It could mean cancer. Declining his usual breakfast, Hendren immediately began a bowel prep, which would clean his intestines for examination.

After hours that evening, Hendren asked George L. Nardi, a surgeon friend at the Massachusetts General, to perform a sigmoidoscopy, an endoscopic examination of the rectum and sigmoid colon, the section of large intestine—roughly a third of its total length—starting above the rectum. Nardi did. Nothing was found to explain what was going on. But healthy bowels don't bleed. Hendren had a bad feeling about things. He wasn't going to let it pass, as some might. On Wednesday, he asked another doctor friend, Stanley Wyman, for the next logical test: a barium enema. It was done quietly in an office across the street, so that the whole staff at Massachusetts General Hospital wouldn't find out about it. This time, evidence of a tumor was found. Hendren wanted no doubt. He wanted a colonoscopy, which would provide a view of his bowels from his rectum all the way to the place where the small intestine connects to the large, and he wanted his colleague, the surgeon Stephen E. Hedberg, to perform it on Thursday morning.

Hedberg and Hendren had known each other for some two decades. They were friends, neighbors, mutual admirers, fathers of large families, graduates of the Harvard Medical School and the Massachusetts General Hospital residency program. Hedberg was an outdoorsman and marathoner, a conservationist and Army veteran who belonged to the Harvard Club of Boston and The Country Club in Brookline and the Duxbury Yacht Club, just like the Hendrens. Hedberg had operated on one of Hendren's sons for a bowel problem. In turn, Hendren had fixed a serious urologic malformation in one of Hedberg's close relatives. Like Hendren, Hedberg was a surgical pioneer, having played a considerable role in the development of colonoscopy.

A patient undergoing a colonoscopy is ordinarily given an intravenous sedative. Sedation brings a patient to the point of unconsciousness, blunting pain as the colonoscope, a long, flexible tube, is steered through the twists and turns of the large intestine. But sedation leaves the patient drowsy, typically for the day. After a colonoscopy, patients are advised not to drive or operate machinery. They certainly should not perform surgery. But Hendren had a full schedule the day of his colonoscopy. He could not afford the luxury of sedation. A colonoscopy would hurt, but Hendren didn't see that he had a choice. Hedberg worked the scope into his intestine. There, about halfway up, in the transverse colon, was a saucer-shaped lesion measuring about two centimeters across. Hedberg brought the eyepiece around so Hendren could have a look.

Typical appearance of cancer, Hendren thought. *Nothing else it could be.* And then: *I can't have cancer. I take care of cancer!*

Hedberg suggested a biopsy, which involves taking a tissue sample for laboratory study but is not without risk.

"No biopsy," Hendren said. "That's a cancer. You know it and

I know it." He did not want to risk introducing cancer cells into the bloodstream, where they might travel to some other part of the body, taking seed and growing and killing him, assuming his colon didn't first.

The operation was scheduled for the next day, Friday the thirteenth. Hendren had his pick of anesthesiologists, and he chose John F. Ryan, the pediatric anesthesiologist with whom he regularly worked. He had his pick of surgeons, and he chose Nardi, who'd graduated from medical school at the age of twenty-one and had been a Navy officer in the Second World War. Nardi was a renowned researcher at the General, coeditor of a major surgical text, *Surgery: Essentials of Clinical Practice*, and he was a pancreas and colon man. Like his friend, he had a firm foundation in general surgery. To assist Nardi, Hendren asked a second-year surgical resident, Mark S. Hochberg, and Robert W. Sloane, Jr., one of the General's two chief surgical residents. Sloane gladly interrupted a brief vacation to come in for the operation.

Hendren had his pick of scrub nurses, but he did not choose Dorothy Enos. *It wouldn't be appropriate,* he thought. Instead, he asked the OR supervisor who besides Enos was the hospital's best. Marion Freehan, known to her colleagues as Bunny, the supervisor told him. He then asked Freehan, not telling her at first who the patient was.

"What's wrong with Dorothy?" Freehan asked.

"I don't want her to scrub on this particular case," Hendren said.

"Why not?"

"Because I'm the patient."

On the morning of his surgery, Hendren called Eleanor, home with their children, and his mother, in Kansas City. He was taken to the OR. Bunny Freehan scrubbed. And while he hadn't thought it proper for Enos to assist officially, Hendren wanted her in the room. She stayed in the background. Only when Nardi got ready to begin work with house tools did she intervene. Quietly, without any fuss, she brought him a set of Hendren's own instruments.

The operation lasted three hours. Hendren was opened down the midline, with a one-foot-long incision extending from the lower sternum to the lower abdomen. Nardi palpated Hendren's liver, gallbladder, pancreas, kidneys, stomach, and spleen; all were normal. Hendren's bowel was mobilized, its blood supply identified, the vessels ligated. Nardi removed the right and transverse colon, more than half the total colon length, plus three inches from the end of Hendren's small intestine. With Hendren still open, a pathologist friend, Robert E. Scully, came into the OR to fetch the colon. Back in the laboratory, Scully examined it and two dozen abdominal lymph nodes to see if the cancer had metastasized. It hadn't. Hendren was probably cured.

"Did they get it all?" Hendren asked while waking up in the recovery room.

"Yes," Enos said.

But there was other news as well. In reconnecting Hendren's intestines, a procedure known as anastomosis, Nardi had used staples. Hendren thinks staples are a shortcut, producing a join not always as good as what a skilled surgeon can accomplish by the traditional method: sewing with sutures.

"You're not going to like it," Enos said. "They put you together with staples."

"I don't care what they used," Hendren replied, "as long as they got it all—and it works!"

In his hospital room on the fourth post-op night, when he was given the OK for clear liquids, Hendren and two young doctor friends, Toby Cosgrove and Matt Donnelan, made inroads into a bottle of Chivas Regal; for the first time since his surgery, Hendren slept well that night. On the fifth post-op day, Hendren dictated letters and saw patients from his hospital bed. On the seventh post-op day, in accordance with Massachusetts General policy, Hendren was wheeled in a wheelchair to the hospital door. He got out of his chair and walked to his office, where, after lying down, he managed to put in half a day's work. The next day, he took two of his sons skeet shooting at The Country Club. Two days after that, he went duck hunting with Arnold Colodny, a pediatric surgeon and longtime friend.

Cancer has been the bogeyman in Hendren's life.

His father, a smoker throughout adulthood, died of cancer. A grandmother and an aunt died of cancer. So did Eleanor's father and Dorothy Enos's father, both smokers. One of Hendren's good friends at Children's has cancer. The first wife of Hendren's best friend, Al Zeller, was cured of breast cancer only to die of ovarian cancer. Zeller himself had cancer.

Hendren met Zeller at Dartmouth, where they were tight from

the start. Zeller was Sandy Hendren's godfather; Hendren, Zeller's best man. Zeller went into surgery, but his career path zigged and zagged and never led him to academia, where his friend had landed with such a splash. During most of the sixties, Zeller was a general surgeon near Portland, Maine. By 1969, the year Hardy Hendren was separating the Siamese twins—and more than a few Americans were becoming free spirits—wanderlust caught hold of Zeller and he shipped off to Kabul, Afghanistan, where an international relief agency supported him in establishing a surgical training program. Zeller did more than one thousand operations a year in Kabul, and many were not run-of-the-mill cases, the sort he'd encountered in Maine. Health care in Afghanistan in the sixties and seventies was a pitiful affair, and by the time many of Zeller's patients came to his attention, they were ready for membership in some medical monstrosity hall of fame. There was the man with bladder stones as big as golf balls, the three-hundred-pound woman who thought she was pregnant but really was carrying a two-hundred-pound ovarian cyst, the patient with tuberculosis of the spine. And tumors—tumors like Zeller had never before seen and hoped never to see again. Tumors that had started on the knee, the breast, the shoulder, the sternum, the skin and had consumed their hosts by the time Zeller saw them. The only treatable case of breast cancer he saw in Kabul was that of his wife, Barbara. The mastectomy he performed saved her life.

The Zellers had moved to Africa when, in October 1975, Al decided to attend a meeting of the American College of Surgeons. On the first leg of his trip to San Francisco, Zeller's back hurt, and when he used the bathroom, there was blood in his urine. A kidney stone, he thought. On his stopover in New York, he visited his mother, who had codeine, left over from a trip to the dentist. Zeller took some, then flew to San Francisco, where he renewed his acquaintance with Hendren.

Over breakfast, Zeller mentioned the blood and the pain.

"You'd better have it checked," Hendren said. "Here. Now."

"I'm going to," Zeller said.

He went to San Francisco's Kaiser Foundation Hospital, where radiography disclosed a kidney tumor. Back in Boston, Zeller showed Hendren the films. Hendren offered to refer him to the urologist of his choice, but that wasn't the way he wanted to go.

Some years ago, he'd watched Hendren remove a large kidney tumor from a child. It had been a large, invasive thing, the kind of tumor not every victim survived.

"I want an operation like that," Zeller said. "And I want you to do it."

Bringing Zeller into the General as Hendren's patient was a potential political problem. Hendren didn't need a crystal ball to predict that the chief of urology would not cotton to the fact that the chief of children's surgery was planning to operate on a grown man for a urologic condition. Hendren, after all, was a *pediatric* surgeon. But with the backing of the General's chief of surgery, W. Gerald Austen, who was the Edward D. Churchill Professor of Surgery at the Harvard Medical School and another of Hendren's supporters, Zeller was admitted as Hendren's patient.

"I very lightly palpated the kidney," Hendren wrote in the record, "and really could not tell much about the nature of the mass in the upper pole except it was a good-sized affair, about the size of a baseball. I felt that by far the safest thing to do was a radical removal of the kidney without handling it at all, and so that is what we proceeded to do." The operation included cleaning out all of the surrounding fat and lymph nodes, into which cancer could have spread. When he had everything out, Hendren gave the rest of his friend's abdominal organs a thorough look. For some reason, there were adhesions around a section of colon, a possible prelude to intestinal obstruction. Hendren cut them away. For good measure, he took Zeller's appendix, too. Before he closed the patient up, Hendren took some photographs.

"I want you to see that we did a thorough job," he told his friend postoperatively. "Look for yourself."

Zeller was cured. Two years later, his wife would die of cancer.

Hendren was six and living in New Orleans when he had his first cigarette. Next door lived a boy whose older brother smoked, and one day Hendren took a surreptitious puff. He got sick. And that was enough to keep him from cigarettes until he was a teen, until it was cool and he was at Woodberry Forest School. Woodberry sanctioned smoking only at the age of seventeen or in senior year, whichever came first, and only with the written permission of the boy's parent. In the fall of 1942, the fall that P-47s buzzed the school, Hendren arrived back on campus with his father's signature. All senior year, Hendren was a regular visitor to the Smokehouse, the designated smoking room in the basement of the school's main dormitory.

Through his Navy years, through medical training, through his early career, Hendren was an off-and-on smoker. When he was on, he'd light up three, four, five times a day, usually a Salem menthol cigarette. By 1974, when Hendren was forty-eight, he'd been intermittently inhaling carcinogens for three decades.

It took his own cancer to put the fear of the Lord in him. His own cancer highlighted his hypocrisy, which could no longer be excused by the fact that when he started, smoking was not widely known to cause cancer. By 1974, the dangers were well publicized. A man who cured cancer had no business flirting with a case of his own.

I have to quit, he thought.

He did. And became the worst—or best—kind of reformed smoker: someone out to make the rest of the world quit, too. In 1975, Hendren went beyond passion. He became a zealot. Eleanor gave him one thousand pens customized with a logo that Joseph P. Vacanti, Hendren's resident at the time at the General, had suggested: DR. HARDY HENDREN "SAYS SMOKING WILL KILL YOU." Hendren handed them out to smokers, and when that batch ran out, Eleanor bought him another, and then another, four thousand pens in all. Hendren lectured to community groups, and to his lectures he brought the inevitable slide show. The slides cited statistics and death rates and parodied popular cigarette ads. YOU'VE GONE THE WRONG WAY, BABY! one read. Another showed the Marlboro man and next to it a cemetery named Marlboro Country. NO FLAVOR HERE! was the inscription over a tombstone. Hendren couldn't stop sermonizing. It wouldn't matter if the smoker were a stranger on the street or a longtime OR colleague. During the reconstruction of a boy's urinary system that went on for twenty-three hours, a nurse Hendren hadn't seen in some time came into his room. "Well?" Hendren said. "I can't lie, Dr. Hendren," the nurse said, "I'm still smoking." Hendren turned to a second nurse and said: "Do me a favor, will you? Take his measurements—height, weight, width, all of that so I can order up the appropriate box."

Another time, Hendren was set to operate on Mohammad, a Saudi boy. Mohammad had been born with his bladder on the outside of his body. Beginning when he was a newborn, when his family first brought him to America on a Concorde jet, Hendren had systematically rebuilt him. Over the years, Hendren and the boy's family had become close. Many times, Hardy and Eleanor had had them as houseguests. And Hardy had arranged for the best heart surgeon in town to care for the father, a three-pack-a-day smoker, when he had a heart attack that caused a ventricular aneurysm. In turn, Mohammad's family had brought the Hendrens gifts, including a video camera and an oil painting of Sandy and a winter coat the father gave the surgeon off his back when Hardy, momentarily forgetting Saudi custom, complimented him on how it looked. The families were so close that Hendren called Mohammad "my son."

On this occasion, Hendren had just finished an endoscopy of the boy. Tomorrow, he was set to do a few hours of final surgery. He found Mohammad's father in the recovery room.

"Have you been smoking this morning?" Hendren asked.

"No," the father said.

"Let me smell," said Hendren.

He took the man's left hand and sniffed. Then he took his right. Finger by finger, he smelled, stopping when he got to the space between middle and index fingers.

"You *were* smoking," Hendren said. He was not amused. His voice had that Harvard edge to it. His voice was a knife.

"It was just one," the father said.

"Promise me you'll quit—or I won't operate on Mohammad."

"I promise."

"It would make me sad to see you die," Hendren said. "There would be no one to raise your lovely daughter and 'my son.' Promise me you'll quit. Swear to Allah you won't smoke."

The father swore, but he would not be able to quit. Hendren, of course, fixed the boy.

Hendren's most extraordinary performance came in March 1991, after he had brought a boy, not yet two, into his OR. The previous year, Andrew had suffered from cancer. Specifically, he had grown a huge rhabdomyosarcoma, a malignant tumor, throughout his bladder and prostate. Chemotherapy had shrunk it but could not make it disappear. By late 1990, Hendren had decided that if he did not operate, the boy would die.

"If he's alive, not in pain anymore, and you get the cancer, we'll have our miracle," Andrew's mother said as she handed her son over to Hendren.

As he began an eleven-and-a-half-hour operation that would save the child's life at the expense of his virility and bladder, Hendren observed, "When they find a way to cure cancer without cutting people all up, I'll be the first one standing here cheering on the sidelines."

Hendren got the cancer. All of it, as he discovered when he performed an endoscopy that March. He found Andrew's mother in the waiting room, which, as usual, was full. With a high degree of confidence, Hendren could say Andrew probably was cured. The boy's mother was overjoyed. How could she ever thank Dr. Hendren? A year of hell had come to an end.

"Are you still smoking?" Hendren asked.

"Yes," the woman said. It was so hard to quit, she explained, especially given that her husband smoked, too.

"You know about secondary smoke, don't you?"

"Yes."

"You know that it could kill Andrew."

"I know."

"And it could kill you," Hendren said. "You know, I've never met a smoker diagnosed with lung cancer who didn't immediately quit, as if that could redeem him—get him down off the cross— which of course it can't."

Hendren told Andrew's mother about his own smoking habit, how he'd quit when his colon cancer was diagnosed. He did not lift his shirt to show her his foot-long scar, although he sometimes does to drive the point home.

By now, a dozen people were watching. Andrew's mother was confessing to Hendren that she was a recovering alcoholic, that she hadn't had a drink in a decade, that she was a faithful at Alcoholics Anonymous but that smoking—smoking was tougher than booze.

No it's not, Hendren said. Look at the facts. You've stopped drinking! Stopping drinking takes being involved in dawn-to-dusk therapy, admitting how rotten you are, an expensive and intense regimen. Not so for smoking.

"So, how do you do it?" the woman asked. "From an ex-smoker to a smoker, what's the secret?"

"It's one hour at a time," he replied. "Don't worry about tomorrow or next week or next month. Just focus on one hour. And when one hour's up, focus on the next hour. And in three or four days, it'll get easier."

By now, two dozen people were watching.

"Celebrate the good news that your son is cured of cancer," Hendren said. "Quit."

"I'd like to. . . ."

"Open that bag," Hendren said. "Go on."

The woman opened her handbag. There on top was a pack of one-hundred-millimeter cigarettes.

"Take them in your hand."

She did. Her hand trembled.

"Now crush them."

She couldn't.

"Go on."

Still, she couldn't.

Hendren gently took the pack from her, mangled it, then dropped it in the trash barrel.

"Do you have another pack?"

"No."

"Where's that lighter?"

"I don't have one."

"What do you have?"

"Matches." She rummaged in her purse. "These."

Hendren took them and tossed them away, too. "See?" he said. "Now you've quit."

"It's almost a feeling of relief," the woman said.

Hendren hugged her, kissed her on the cheek. "I like kissing women who don't smoke," he said.

Hendren did not follow up on Andrew's mother to see how long lasting her resolve was. But ex-smokers have called to brag about their success. Ex-smokers have sent thank-you cards and flowers.

"Doctor! Doctor!" a janitor said to Hendren late one night when he was making his way from the operating room to his office. "I quit! I quit!"

"How long?"

"Two weeks!"

"Good. Wonderful! Keep up the good work."

But not all are so deferential to the chief. Hendren worked hard on the mother of one cloaca patient he'd successfully reconstructed, but, like Mohammad's father, she was still a smoker when she went home from Children's.

"Dr. Hendren," she wrote in a letter, "please know there is not a day I look at that child I do not thank God for you and your talent. Her life would have been a nightmare without you and you are remembered in my prayers always. Thank you again for your talent and interest in Cheri.

"P.S. I don't drink, I'm not rich or good-looking anymore, I don't screw, I want to smoke!"

Chapter 21

This new angle doesn't yield much. Hendren finds a small pouch-like thing near Lucy's freed-up rectum, but it's nothing he recognizes, nothing he can use. It's not a second vagina, which is what he'd really like to find.

"I don't see one over here," he says.

Not much chance now she has another. Looks like we'll have to use intestine to give her the length she needs.

Dorothy Enos points to an area of pinkish tissue Hendren has been exploring.

"Is that rectum?" she says, less as a question than a statement of fact.

"Pretty much," Hendren says.

I'm not getting anywhere over here, he thinks. *I've done about all I can do for now with her on her belly.*

"We've got to go above," he says. Then, to Karen Sakakeeny, "Can you please call Veronica Miler?"

Turning a patient can be tricky. Hoses can become crimped, lines disconnected, monitors unhooked. You need several people to turn a patient properly. You need everyone to be in sync. You want every one of your ducks lined up before you begin.

In September 1990, Hendren was preparing to rebuild a cloaca patient from Florida. Like Lucy Moore, the little girl's anatomy gave Hendren no choice but to open her from below and then from above. He'd prepped the girl's abdomen and chest, and now he needed access to her bottom and back. "I've got the front painted," Hendren said. "We're going to put a towel on and turn her."

The turn seemed to have been successful. Hendren got to work, prepping the girl's bottom and back.

Suddenly, the anesthesiologist, a young resident, announced in a less-than-reassuring voice, "The patient's not ventilating!"

Translate: *The patient's not breathing. The patient's not getting any oxygen to the brain.*

Hendren stopped what he was doing. He looked at the anesthesiologist, and what he saw did not inspire confidence: a young doctor frantically checking hoses, lines, anesthesia-machine settings, and monitor leads. The monitor said the patient's lungs were not releasing carbon dioxide. The girl's upper chest was not gently rising and falling, rising and falling.

Hendren trained in an era when anesthesia was cruder, when good surgeons automatically became old hands at OR emergencies. This was an emergency. This activated a basic instinct in Hendren. As the anesthesiologist dithered, he calmly pulled down the ether screen, turned his patient onto her back, removed his surgical mask, disconnected the hose from her endotracheal tube, put his mouth to the tube, and began breathing into it. Meanwhile, a nurse had called senior anesthesiologists, who were quickly in the room and who quickly identified the problem: in turning the patient, a hose had become unplugged. They reconnected, it and oxygen flowed again to the lungs. The patient, who had been without air for no more than half a minute, was fine. The pulse oximeter, which measures oxygen saturation of the blood, never dipped below 100 percent, the normal reading.

For the rest of the operation, Hendren insisted a senior anesthesiologist remain in the room. The younger resident surely expected a reaming, but Hendren did not deliver it. Instead, he complimented everyone on the way the incident was handled: the resident for promptly sounding the alarm, her superiors for immediately correcting the problem, the entire room for staying calm.

"As soon as people get excited," he said, drawing the lesson of the day, "they don't work well. You can't think when there's bedlam going on."

"Veronica," Hendren says, "we have to turn little Lucy."

Miler, a veteran of many of Hendren's big cases, sizes up the situation. She and Hendren decide on the posts: Enos will be here, the chief over there, the anesthesiologists up north, where most of the potential danger is. Lucy will be lifted, rotated, and gently placed back down.

"Are we ready to flip?" Miler asks.

"Yup," Hendren answers.

The turn is smooth. Hendren redrapes Lucy and repaints her belly with a fresh coat of Betadine. Without having to be asked, Enos hands him a knife. Hendren opens Lucy's abdomen with a four-inch incision from navel to pubis. Down through skin he cuts, through a blanket of fat, through a layer of tissue called the midline fascia, finally piercing the peritoneum, a thin but tough membrane that lines the abdominal cavity.

"Can we have a ring?" Hendren says.

Enos hands him a circular stainless steel ring, notched to hold a set of retractors known as blades, which are elbowed at one end to hook onto the edge of an incision. Hendren positions the ring. One at a time, he fastens six blades to the ring, ratcheting back on them, adjusting the ring until the incision has been pried into a wide-open wound, one Hendren is satisfied will be large enough to allow instruments and hands room to maneuver inside. The basic blades-and-ring concept was the genius of Sir Denis Browne, England's pioneer pediatric surgeon, the European equivalent of William Ladd or Robert Gross. Like Hendren, Browne had a passion for correcting birth defects, and his success was so great that after his death, in 1967, the British Association of Paediatric Surgeons memorialized him with the Denis Browne Gold Medal, presented once a year to the surgeon who best exemplifies Browne's pioneering spirit. In 1968, Gross was the first recipient of the Denis Browne medal, which in later years was awarded to C. Everett Koop (1971), Orvar Swenson (1979), and Hendren (1991). Like Browne, Hendren has his name on several instruments he designed. The Hendren pediatric blade, which fits the Browne ring, is one. Also in use around the world are the Hendren cardiovascular clamp, which comes in two models, and the Hendren megaureter clamp, for megaureter repair. He also designed a heavy-duty reinforced adult ring, which had its maiden run during the surgery on Hendren's best friend, Al Zeller. But he has not tried to market it.

Hendren reaches through the ring and, with his hands, pushes aside Lucy's omentum, a free-floating apron of fatty tissue rich in blood vessels. The omentum overlies much of the intestines but is attached to the stomach, situated higher in the belly. It is not the most majestic of organs, but it is remarkable. Answering some primitive immunologic call, it can travel anywhere in the lower abdomen in a matter of hours—to a foreign body, a burst appendix, an area of infection, or a nascent tumor, sealing off the offender and concentrating the might of the body's immune system on the threatened area. Respectful of its unique ability, surgeons have accorded the organ the title Policeman of the Abdomen.

Omentum out of the way, Hendren has a clear view of Lucy's abdominal cavity. Human hands have been here before, but they have left barely a trace. Lucy's colon has been divided, but otherwise this is virgin tissue.

That's not always the case. Sometimes surgeons open up an OR veteran and find adhesions: scar tissue that has formed as the body healed itself after the trauma of the earlier operation. There is no way to prevent adhesions or predict who will get them or how severe they will be. Adhesions can be nothing but a few filaments of transparent tissue stuck to a bowel; a couple of snips with a pair of scissors, and that's that. At the other extreme are massive adhesions, where the entire contents of the abdomen are stuck together as if a large quantity of glue had been poured over everything. Bad adhesions look like something off the set of a low-budget science-fiction film, but they are more than aesthetically unappealing. They can be dangerous—they can cause intestinal obstruction, sometimes years after an operation. Encountering them, a surgeon goes nowhere with his operation until they are out of the way, and getting them out of the way can be bloody and slow. Bad adhesions all but blind the surgeon. You can't just get down in there and whack away at them. No telling what lies just underneath—more adhesions, or maybe a major blood vessel or a vital nerve. Hendren tells his residents, "What you always have to be saying to yourself as a surgeon is 'What tiger lies in the woods just beyond where I am?' " With bad adhesions, it's proceed with caution.

Two forty-five P.M.

For the nurses—all but Enos—the day shift is drawing to a close.

A nursing supervisor pokes her head into the room. She gets Karen Sakakeeny's attention. "To add insult to injury," the supervisor whispers, "do you want overtime?"

"My God, no!" Sakakeeny jokes in a whisper. "I don't want to be here until Sunday!"

Unimpeded by adhesions, Hendren is exploring Lucy's belly. He is completely absorbed. He could be doing this for the first time, so intense is his concentration. "This is bladder shoved all the way forward," he says, more to himself than to anyone else. It is a small organ: smooth, thin walled, thankfully normal, shaped like a little girl's silk purse. He runs his fingers along Lucy's large intestine, familiarizing himself with its mesentery, an apron of tissue—reminiscent of the omentum—that carries the intestine's blood supply. The large intestine is sturdy looking, coiled like a hawser and lined with capillaries. The small intestine is thinner and longer, resembling a nest of snakes, plum to pink in color. And everywhere there is blood: strawberry red and free flowing when fresh, gooey and darker red when beginning to clot.

Hendren moves Lucy's intestines aside. Steinberg keeps them out of his way with a retractor.

"There's a little dysplastic kidney down there," Hendren says. "The other one has function. This is nothing."

"Birth defect," the Yale doctor had said to Beth Moore so long ago. "Multicystic kidney."

To the touch, the bad kidney is knotty and hard, a mutant. Hendren sets about tying off the vessels that feed it. When he's satisfied it won't hemorrhage, he cuts it out and with a forceps drops it into a plastic specimen cup Enos holds for him. The kidney is a useless-looking thing, no bigger than Hendren's thumbnail. Theoretically, he could have let it be. "But it could cause hypertension," he says. "Conceivably, it could also become malignant. It would have small potential for that, but now it has no potential."

Hendren returns to his exploration. Six hours into the operation, and he has yet to set about the actual repair.

On Lucy's right, he makes a promising discovery: an ovary. Next to it, he finds a Fallopian tube. With his fingers, he traces the tube down to a uterus. Connected to the uterus is the undersize vagina that he mobilized from below. What luck! It is not a normal female reproductive system—the scale is wrong—but it has all of the right elements connected in the right sequence. Assuming Hendren gets the vagina problem solved, Lucy's body should be able to deliver an egg to the place where it can be fertilized and grow. The Moores have prayed for this, but it will be hours before they learn the good news.

"See the uterus?" Hendren says to his residents and foreign visitors. They nod. "See the ovary? And the tube? And there's a vagina down in here, too. Give me a spatula, Dorothy. A right angle. OK. Now hold this apart, Dorothy."

Hendren is working on Lucy's left side. He's found a second ovary, a second Fallopian tube, a second uterus. But below it, nothing. No second vagina.

"See there? It's a blindly ending uterus."

The second uterus is abnormal in other respects. It is misshapen and shrunken, barely an inch long. Hendren slices a cross section to see if it has an interior space, or lumen.

"It's a solid core."

Even if somehow he could connect it to Lucy's single vagina, it would serve no useful purpose: it has no uterine cavity, no chance to allow for menstruation or conception. It must come out.

"Look very closely, Dorothy. Make sure I don't commit any mayhem."

A surgeon must always consider the consequences of what he does and—just as importantly—what he doesn't do.

Enos agrees with her boss that the uterus is useless. But she wonders why Hendren is going to take only it, and not its Fallopian tube, too. Isn't he leaving Lucy with the risk of a tubal pregnancy?

"She won't get a tubal pregnancy because the sperm won't be able to get there," Hendren says. "That would be quite a jump! But I'm glad you're thinking, Dorothy. There's nothing I like better than a thinking woman!" He chuckles. He likes teasing his scrub nurse every now and then. Sometimes Enos teases back. But this time she ignores him.

Hendren ligates the bottom of the Fallopian tube and snips out the uterus. It, too, goes off in a plastic container to Harry Kozake-wich, a pathologist, who gets to examine every specimen from the OR. With a microscope, Kozakewich will confirm Hendren's description. When he has done so, Lucy's useless uterus will be discarded, or it will become a teaching tool, preserved in a jar that could sit on a laboratory shelf for generations.

Hendren again turns his attention to Lucy's intestines. Having failed to find a second vagina and knowing that by itself the first is too short to reach her bottom and too small for normal sexual function, Hendren has no choice but to make the vagina larger and longer.

Reconstructive surgeons are clever in the new uses they find for body parts. Especially innovative are the orthopedists and craniofacial specialists. Good orthopedists can make a toe into a finger, a knee out of an ankle. The craniofacial experts can take a piece of skull to reshape a forehead, using a rib or two to substitute for the purloined skull. Plastic surgeons can harvest smooth forearm skin and roll it into a penis, although not a very good penis, functionally or aesthetically. Hendren's ingenuity has been mainly with soft tissues and organs. He has found stomach good for enlarging bladders. He's used scrotum to make the shaft of a penis, flaps of buttocks to make a vagina. He's used scrotum to make labia for genetic males he's transformed into females because they were born without a penis. He's used bladder lining for a male urethra. He's also used buttocks skin for a male urethra, and he's used buccal mucosa, the inside lining of the cheek, for the same purpose. Heading the other way, he's used rectal mucosa to rebuild a mouth destroyed by a burn. Hendren has found large intestine—colon—to have extraordinary utility. A section of colon can be patched onto a bladder to make it larger. A section can be swung up to make a substitute esophagus. A section can be swung down to make part or all of a vagina.

Hendren runs his fingers along the length of Lucy's rectum he freed up working from below. It is a grossly dilated section of rectum, too dilated to propel stool to an anus properly.

"I'm going to use a little segment of this dilated lower colon to extend the vagina downward," he says.

Working from below several hours ago, Hendren began separating the rectum from the bladder and adjacent tissues. Now he finishes the job. The rectum is finally free, but it is not free floating. It remains tethered to the body wall by its mesentery, whose blood vessels are thinner and more numerous the farther they get from the major arteries, which deliver the blood that keeps colon alive.

Hendren tries pulling the end of dilated rectum down to where he wants Lucy's vagina to be. "It won't quite reach," he says. "I'm going to have to lengthen the mesentery."

The trick to elongating mesentery is cutting while maintaining blood flow. Slight bleeding from capillaries at the end of the rectum means you've preserved a good blood supply. A darker, bluish hue to the rectum—and no bleeding from the end, meaning nothing is getting to the capillaries—is bad. It means your new vagina proba- bly will necrose: it will die. *Even with the most careful attention, with years of experience, you can lose a blood supply.*

Before cutting, Hendren maps out his route. He identifies the arteries and veins he cannot afford to lose. Lucy is fortunate to have an abundance of large intestine, even if nature did not place it where it belonged, and Hendren could probably work his way out of a jam by throwing away a badly separated piece and starting over. But only the most reckless sort would proceed on that assumption. The reconstructive surgeon sacrifices nothing he might use, even if he cannot at the moment predict what that use might be.

Hendren starts into the mesentery. He isolates a large vessel, clamps a smaller vessel branching off from it, ties the smaller vessel, cuts it, moves ahead a bit, clamps the next small vessel, ties and cuts it. With the electric cautery, he cuts through the membrane holding the vessels. Like a sheet being carefully torn into two unequal strips, a smaller section of mesentery is slowly separated from the main membrane. The part Hendren cuts free contains the network of vessels that supply blood to the length of colon he needs.

Four-twenty P.M.

The bad kidney is out. The useless uterus is out. The vagina issue has been settled. Bladder and rectum have been separated. The rectum has been mobilized.

Hendren's done about all the taking apart he'll have to do today. It's time to turn Lucy once again and start putting her together.

With moist gauze protecting the intestines, Hendren temporarily closes Lucy's belly with two heavy sutures. The team turns her without incident. Once again, her bottom is exposed to the surgeon.

Hendren's next task is making a urethra. He'll fashion it out of Lucy's cloaca, the long, thin passageway he opened at the start of the operation.

"Now, Barb," he says to his secretary-cinematographer, "you might get a little of this. Are you in close?"

Again, Hendren explores. He takes note of the good, thick band of muscle just below the bladder neck: urethral sphincter muscle, responsible for urinary continence. As with the anus he'll build, Hendren wants to be sure muscle properly envelops the urethra. He needs to determine the muscle's center. With the nerve stimulator, he finds it. Then he threads a small catheter into the bladder, laying it on the bed of the opened cloaca. The catheter will give him the caliber he wants for Lucy's urethra. He'll sew the cloaca loosely around it.

"Let's see, Dorothy," he says, "how do we want to start—a five-oh?"

Enos agrees with her boss's choice of suture. She opens a package. Sutures are manufactured with needles attached; there's nothing to thread. She loads the needle into a needle holder and hands it to Hendren.

"I'll do a running, locking stitch," he says. Rather than tie a knot at each loop, he'll sew all the way to the end.

"That's a watertight stitch?" Steinberg asks.

"Right."

Hendren runs the stitch up the cloaca. He positions sphincter muscle firmly around it and sews that with interrupted stitches.

Lucy Moore now has a urethra.

It looks pretty good, Hendren thinks. *A little longer than normal, but that's OK. That'll reduce her risk of urinary-tract infections, which many girls are susceptible to.*

He sews the end of the catheter to Lucy's clitoris. He does not want that catheter to move. He does not want to risk having it mistakenly pulled out later during healing when it will be an outlet for urine. One good yank, and Lucy would be back in the OR.

Satisfied with the urethra, Hendren needs access through the belly again. Again, Lucy is turned.

"Want to take a quick break?" Hendren asks. "Let's take a quick supper break."

Hendren has been standing for more than eight hours, and until now, when he finally gives it some thought, he hasn't been hungry or thirsty or in need of a trip to the bathroom. Capable of going fourteen or more hours without stopping, without feeling any bodily calls, he tries to make a point of taking a break if he thinks a case will go into another day. It's not good for him or the help to get too carried away. Have to keep the blood sugar at a respectable level. Have to empty the bladder.

The phone rings. It's Janet Hamilton, surgical-liaison nurse whose shift will be ending before long. Beth and Jack Moore have come back to the hospital from their shopping, and they want an update.

Jean Kiernan, the evening circulating nurse, Karen Sakakeeny's replacement, holds the phone to Hendren's ear.

"Things are going well," he says. "We're getting ready to take a break. The whole group. We're just partway through. . . . I don't know. I don't know. All right, 'Bye."

To the room, Hendren says, "The minute you tell them how long you think you're going to be, they immediately begin to worry at the end of that time."

Hendren covers Lucy's abdomen with a wet sponge. He places a blue towel over the sponge and asks a surgical resident who's come into the room to stand watch. As Hendren's crew leaves, the resident and Heggeness stand guard over Lucy's unconscious body, covered by towels and sheets. The team will sup in the OR lounge, down at the end of the hall, only seconds away.

"We've got the back of this one broken," Hendren says on his way out. Sometimes, Eleanor brings dinner for everyone, has it waiting in the lounge—sandwiches or Chinese takeout or McDonald's burgers and fries. Hendren is grateful when Eleanor does that, because it's a chance to be with her for a few extra minutes in the busy week. But tonight, she's busy. Supper's on the chief. It will be brought up on trays from the Children's Hospital cafeteria.

Five-thirty P.M., Friday, January 18, 1991.

There is an old saying among surgeons: "Eat when you can, sleep when you can, and don't mess with the pancreas." The caution about the pancreas relates to its location in the body, a dangerous crossroads of vessels and nerves. The eating and sleeping derives from a surgeon's years of training, when bodily needs take a backseat to the demands of a residency.

Thirty years out of his training, and Hendren hasn't changed. He eats with gusto, as if somebody were standing over his shoulder, awaiting an opportunity to snatch his food away. He eats whatever strikes his fancy, and what typically strikes his fancy is foods rich in carbohydrates, readily converted into energy. Hendren loves Enos's popcorn, even though it often gives him indigestion. He likes candy, ice cream, pies, cakes, and sodas, and none of the diet stuff, thank you. This evening, he has a salad followed by a slice of apple pie and a glass of lemonade. His break lasts as long as it takes to use the bathroom, get his wallet and an update on the war, eat, and scrub back in—about twenty minutes.

Back to work.

Lucy is lying on her back exactly as Hendren left her. He uncovers her, then spreads her legs and positions them up and away, giving maxiumum exposure of her bottom. If he wanted to, he could reach down through her open belly with one hand. With the other, he could reach through the bottom incision and touch fingertips.

He pulls Lucy's colon through the bottom. He leaves a little extra—about two inches—hanging out, so there's no question that it will be long enough. Guided by the marks he made this morning with toothpick and green dye, he positions the colon where a normal vagina would be: between Lucy's freshly constructed urethra and her anus, which does not yet exist, except in Hendren's mind.

"How's that?" he says.

"Looking good," Steinberg says.

"Dorothy?"

Enos nods in approval.

Hendren inserts a stainless steel dilator several inches into the colon-vagina. The presence of the dilator will preclude closing the surrounding muscle too tightly around it. Steinberg holds the dilator, roughly the thickness of a Magic Marker, as Hendren sews the colon to the nearby structures—with carefully placed stitches, to prevent Lucy's new vagina from prolapsing. Wordlessly, Enos hands Hendren loaded needle holders. Thanks to Hendren's care with the mesentery, this piece of colon is well supplied with blood, and Enos must be nimble with the suction in order for Hendren to see. When he has the colon anchored, he trims off its final inch and with cautery stops the bleeding. Kozakewich, the pathologist, has his third specimen, a knob of rectum once attached to the bladder neck.

At Enos's request, the boom box has been tuned to a station that plays classical music. A Strauss waltz is on. Hendren hums along as he tacks the opening of Lucy's colon-vagina to the skin of her perineum—which, only twelve hours ago, was blank white bottom.

It has to look good, he thinks. *It can't just be functional.*

The rectum-vagina joins neatly to the surrounding skin. After it heals—after Hendren has worked on Lucy's labia—it will be almost a normal vagina.

"All right!" Hendren says. *That looks very good.*

He turns his attention to the stunted vagina Lucy brought with her into the world. He must join it to her rectum-vagina if sperm are to have any way of getting to her uterus and Lucy is to have her period, just like other girls.

Before he can start, there is an interruption. Lawrence Hatchett, Children's chief urology resident for the 1990–91 year, has dropped by. He's gone directly to the boom box, still broadcasting the Strauss waltz.

Hatchett and Hendren have their differences. Hatchett is not always as deferential to staff surgeons as Hendren and others think he should be. Hendren is not always as easygoing and understanding as Hatchett would like. Hatchett is black, and blacks remain underrepresented in the Harvard medical world. At a period in their education when many premedical students have made themselves prisoners of organic-chemistry labs, Hatchett was a philosophy major at Marquette University in Milwaukee, and he played four years on the school's nationally ranked basketball team. Hatchett speaks his mind. He doesn't believe a physician knows everything just because he has a Harvard title. Nor is he in awe of everything Harvard as some of his colleagues are. Neither Hendren nor Hatchett will shed tears when Hatchett leaves Boston in June for private practice, an uncommon, if lucrative, career track for a chief resident from Children's Hospital.

"What do you say, you guys?" Hatchett says. He's come into Hendren's room bearing one of his favorite tapes: *Brazilian Romance,* a Sarah Vaughan recording.

Hendren lifts his head out of the operating field and says: "Is this how you address the Robert E. Gross Professor of Surgery at the Harvard Medical School: 'you guys?' "

Hatchett laughs.

"Now *I* might call *you* 'you guys,' " Hendren says, "but *you* ain't supposed to call *me* 'you guys.' "

"Do you like Sarah Vaughan?"

"Yeah."

It is a feeble endorsement but an endorsement nonetheless. Without further ado, Hatchett starts the tape. "If you get tired of that," he says, "I have *Reggae's Greatest Hits* here!"

Some surgeons demand mausoleum quiet in the OR—as Gross did. Some need classical music in the background. Others, mostly the younger generation, won't lift a scalpel until they have rock and roll on the boom box, not necessarily at low volume. Whatever works, works.

Hendren is mercurial, his mood determined in no small measure by the job at hand. During periods of intense concentration or when there's a potential for trouble, as infrequent as that may be, the only movements are his hands, the occasional blink of his eyes, the shifting from one leg to another to keep the pins and needles at bay, the pulse in his carotid artery, which travels through the neck to feed the head. The only sounds are the ratcheting of the needle holder, the hiss-whoosh of the ventilator bellows, the electronic pulse, the hum of the ceiling exhaust, an autoclave buzzer in a distant room. No one speaks when Hendren's like that, never mind request permission to listen to Sarah Vaughan.

When the going's easier, the mood's lighter. In Hendren's tape collection, which Enos oversees, are Pachelbel, Vivaldi, Strauss, Handel, a broad selection of Christmas music, and opera. He is a Pavarotti fan, and he likes singing along with his recordings. "Next time around," Hendren says, "that's what I want to be."

When there are foreign visitors in the room, he likes to try out his German and Spanish and French, each a bit rusty but not too rusty to prevent basic communication with native speakers. He enjoys listening to jokes and telling jokes, especially jokes about lawyers and Kennedys. Possessed of a prodigious memory and an innate sense of timing, he is a tireless storyteller. Even in his teenage years, Hendren had recognizable talent with a tale. In the one-paragraph blurb beneath his picture in the Woodberry Forest yearbook, mention is made of academic excellence, success in wrestling, and "wit and ability to tell tall stories."

Hendren has stories about famous doctors, wacko patients, off-the-wall parents, monstrous operations, dynamic nurses, prominent philanderers, cancer victims, baseball players, national politicians,

Saudi sheikhs. He has stories about Eleanor, their deceased daughter, their four sons, their seven grandchildren and four daughters-in-law, his mother, his mother-in-law, the boatload of drunks he rescued one day on the waters off Duxbury, the former Catholic nun who used to live with the Hendrens to mind the house during the long week. He has stories about squirrels, which he plugs with a .22 rifle when they get into his bird feeders. He has stories about pigeons, "flying poop factories," which he plugs when they mess on his boathouse roof. He has stories about the family dogs over the years, including Pippi Longstocking, the German shepherd he operated on at the Massachusetts General Hospital for an esophageal defect. He has stories about his days in the Navy, his days at Dartmouth, growing up in Kansas City.

Hendren brings his stories to life with accents, occasional animal imitations, and a falsetto operatic voice. His characterizations often have a forties feel: this good-looking girl is "the prettiest kitty in the city"; that uptight woman is a "nervous Nellie"; this talkative sort is a "chatty Kathy"; that surgeon who shoots off at the mouth is a "quick-draw McGraw." But while Hendren may add a splash of color where needed to a favorite story, he does not play with the facts. That would be dishonest. And it would be unnecessary. His memory leaves him no holes to fill in.

The quintessential Hendren story is an illustration of human folly—and often his own. One favorite concerns Enos and his loupes, his surgical magnifying glasses. For weeks, his old pair hadn't been fitting quite right. Hendren had tried adjusting them and keeping them up with tape, but still they kept slipping down his nose. He needed a new pair, and with Enos's prodding, he finally went to be fitted. The day came when the new loupes arrived. Enos handed them to him when he was in the operating room, about to scrub in for his first surgery of the day. He took the glasses, worth almost a thousand dollars, and examined them. They looked fine. He hooked the headband around the back of his head and settled them over his eyes. So far, so good. But when he extended his arm to focus on his hand, his ordinary preoperative check, everything was a blur. "They've screwed up the damn prescription," he said. He was not amused, not at that kind of money. And he was ready to pick up the phone and tell the surgical-telescope people exactly what he thought of them when Enos looked over and pronounced, in a most casual voice: "You're still wearing your glasses." Hendren had put his loupes on over his regular spectacles.

Hendren laughs when he tells these stories—he laughs and laughs and laughs, so that you know it's OK to laugh, too.

Hatchett's experiment in broadening horizons lasts one song. When it's over, Hendren asks someone to please get rid of Sarah Vaughan and her *Brazilian Romance.*

"Don't you like it?" Hatchett asks.

"I like it fine," Hendren says. "It's just not the right background for what we're doing."

"Maybe closing music." Maybe when the operation's done.

"Maybe."

Kiernan silences the boom box.

"Thank you," Hendren says.

Seven forty-five P.M. Lucy's been asleep twelve hours.

Only one other room is still going: Room 15, where Robert Shamberger, Hendren's best tumor specialist, has spent most of the day removing a cancerous thyroid gland from a four-year-old girl's neck. The neck, so crowded with vessels and nerves, is a treacherous place in which to operate. Only the reckless would try to set speed records while working in the neck.

Hendren is working inside Lucy's belly now. Although the colon-vagina is securely anchored within Lucy's pelvis, it is not its own organ yet. It is still the lower end of her large intestine, most of which is needed for something else. Hendren must decide on a proper length and divide that piece from the rest of the colon. But first he will connect her natural vagina to it.

With a needle-point cautery, he fashions a small opening into the top surface of the colon-vagina at a point about four inches up from its attachment to Lucy's bottom. The secret here is to make the opening large enough so that when her surgery is complete, Lucy's body won't close it during the healing process. Given the diameter of Lucy's natural vagina, the biggest Hendren dares go with the opening is about two and a half centimeters. Even then, he has to flare the open end of the natural vagina. It fits perfectly. Hendren sews it on.

It should be big enough, he thinks. *It shouldn't stenose.*

"It's really a good anastomosis," he says.

An inch higher on the rectum is where Hendren decides the back wall of Lucy's colon-vagina should be. Satisfied that the mesentery is still delivering good blood, he grasps the rectum with his left hand. With a pair of scissors in his right, he cuts clean through the intestine. After cauterizing the little bleeders, he closes the inner end of the colon-vagina with a single layer of synthetic sutures.

"Let me have a little stitch," he says. "I'm tacking that left ovary over here up against the pelvic wall because it seems to want to fall down into the pelvis."

The phone rings. Kiernan answers it. It's Eleanor Hendren. She's home.

"Let me talk to her," Hendren says. "I thought she'd abandoned me. Tell her I'll be there in a minute. I'm looking for a needle." He searches inside the wound and on the drapes before finding the needle on his gown. "I see it. Good. Thank you."

Kiernan holds the phone to Hendren's ear.

"Hi! Yes, Mom, . . . I'll be a while . . . fat chance! . . . OK . . . call me at ten, would ya? All right. Good-bye." Rare is the evening that Eleanor doesn't call Hardy, or Hardy, Eleanor.

Hendren has now used the lower four inches of the large intestine for the vagina. There's more than enough colon left for Lucy's new rectum, which will meet the outside world through the anus Hendren will create. But first, he has to get that colon to reach down to Lucy's bottom. Needing more length, he must divide the mesentery again. It is tedious work, separating the sheets of tissue with the blunt edge of the scissors, identifying vessels, deciding which must be ligated, which preserved.

Twelve hours into the operation, and Hendren's movements are as steady and smooth as when he began. This is not only because he is a sixty-four-year-old man still blessed with stamina; at any age, even the best surgeon's hands may tire or tremble slightly during a long operation. Sooner or later it is a physiological inevitability, no matter how you are constituted. But a smart surgeon can take steps to minimize this. One trick Hendren has learned is resting the wrist of the cutting hand lightly on the patient. Another trick is holding the scissors as Hendren is holding them now: across the palm, like chopsticks. Held this way, the surgeon does not have to raise his arm and lift his shoulder to reach inside a wound. An arm uplifted in that fashion tires more easily.

Hendren asks Steinberg to tie a few knots.

Hendren is as exacting about knots as he is about sterility, and for much the same reason. A bad knot, like dirty technique, can kill a patient, especially in the bowels, one of the most germ-laden parts of the human anatomy.

After Steinberg ties the knots, Hendren gives a few pointers on doing it more smoothly and with better rhythm.

"Tie with the tip," he says, not with the middle of the suture, where you must drag six inches through the knot. "And don't jerk on it. It's not necessary. Try it. It works."

Steinberg is actually a respectable knot tier, and Hendren holds him in very high regard. But in the chief's view, you can never be too proficient in tying knots. You must never slip into mediocrity, never consider such a mundane task mundane. When you leave Hendren's room, he wants you to take with you a memory of perfection. Long after he's gone, he wants you to imagine him there, looking over your shoulder. It's a concept he has not confined to his pupils. In advising his growing sons on questions of conscience, Hendren told them to imagine a miniature of him actually sitting on their shoulder. When the real father was not there to consult, the sons were to turn to that make-believe one and ask: "Is what I'm about to do the right thing?"

With knots, no one escapes Hendren.

During one operation in 1990 that went seventeen and a half hours, Hendren was helped by a female surgeon. Throughout the morning and all afternoon, she stood across from him, observing, holding retractors, picking the brain of the master himself with carefully rehearsed and intelligently articulated questions.

As Hendren was closing up the boy's bladder, he asked the doctor if she would like to tie. Would she like to tie? Why, it would be an honor! But hers was a nervous honor, and her hands trembled just a little. She knew all about Hendren and knots. Struggling a bit, she managed to tie one knot, and two, and three. Hendren watched, and an experienced observer of the chief could see that twinkle in his eye.

On the fourth knot, Hendren cocked his head and said, "Who taught you how to tie?"

The female surgeon looked at Hendren. What did he mean?

"That's an air knot," Hendren said. "You could fly an airplane through there."

He beckoned to a nurse and said, "Air gauge, please."

The surgeon was mystified. She didn't know what was going on, only that it wasn't shaping up in her favor.

The nurse went to Enos's instrument cabinet and returned with a sterile green package. Enos unwrapped it. Inside was a tiny plastic triplane. Hiding it in the palm of her hand, she slipped it to Hendren. Imitating a sound he knows well, the sound of an airplane engine, he made several passes through the open wound.

"See?" he said. "You could fly an airplane through the loose loops of that knot!"

The surgeon was greatly relieved when she realized Hendren was pulling her leg and her knots were just fine, after all.

At eight-fifteen P.M., the phone rings again. It's a nurse from the recovery room. The surgical-liaison nurse has gone for the day, and the Moores, who have left the hospital again to spend what may be a long night in their hotel room next door, have been instructed to call recovery for updates. Beth is on the other line now, looking for the latest word.

"Tell her everything's going fine," Hendren says to Kiernan, who answered the phone.

Ten minutes later, Hendren's chief resident, Jay Schnitzer, drops by to report on the day. After a long twelve hours, Shamberger is finally done with his neck dissection and radical thyroidectomy, Schnitzer says.

"It's about time Room 17 was the last one in business," Enos says. "We want to uphold our reputation!"

Hendren listens to Schnitzer, then updates him on Lucy Moore.

"What's her blood pressure?" Hendren asks Steven Heggeness, the resident anesthesiologist, when Schnitzer has moved on.

"Ninety-five over forty-seven."

"What has it been?"

"About that. We've got a very good pulse in here."

"How much fluid have you given?"

"Sixteen-hundred ccs of lactated Ringer's plus two hundred cc's of blood." Heggeness has calculated his fluid replacements based on laboratory analysis of regular samples of Lucy's blood, what his monitors say, what has been collected in the suction jars hooked to Enos's sucker, and the blood-soaked sponges the circulating nurses have weighed.

"I'd give her more blood," Hendren says. On his big cases, experience has taught him that it's better to err on the side of generosity than frugality.

Hendren has freed another six inches of good colon, more than enough to reach the place where Lucy's anus will be. But he's having trouble bringing it down. Lucy's pelvic cavity is crammed.

With a clamp in one hand and colon in the other, he wriggles it down. But in doing so, he's concerned that the colon may be slightly twisted. The color is not bright red. He pulls the intestine back through, back up into the belly.

"You're going to have to pull it through and I'm going to have to feed it down to you," he says to Enos.

Together, they get it right this time.

"That's good," Hendren says.

"It's nice to see good color," Enos says.

Nine o'clock.

There's little left to do with Lucy's abdomen but close her up and turn her over one last time, to finish her bottom.

Chapter 22

The prostate gland is headlining at the eighty-sixth annual meeting of the American Urological Association, being held this first week of June 1991 in a convention center next to Toronto's Skydome, home of baseball's Blue Jays. Never in history have so many urologists, more than four thousand, gathered in one place. Rarely has there been such intense publicity surrounding the prostate, a small, undistinguished-looking organ that produces the major component of male ejaculate. Excitement about the prostate this year is eclipsing interest in the penis, ordinarily the celebrated organ when urologists convene. And it's overshadowing interest in urology's other charges: kidneys, ureters, testicles, bladder, and urethra.

In press conferences, during formal presentations, in hallway chats, over lunches, between innings at the Blue Jays–Angels game, scientists and salesmen and physicians are atwitter about new advances in the treatment of benign prostatic hyperplasia, or BPH—"prostate trouble" in the lay vernacular, a nonmalignant enlargement of the prostate that affects a majority of men over fifty. Lasers are being conscripted in the fight against BPH, which can make urination difficult and traditionally has been correctable primarily through surgery. Heat treatments have been devised. Also a technique called balloon dilatation, whose long-term efficacy has yet to be established. And development of Proscar, Merck and Company's experimental new drug, which a *Wall Street Journal* staff writer features in an on-scene report from AUA Toronto. "Merck has touted Proscar as its next major-selling drug," writes Michael Waldholz in the June 3 *Journal*, "and analysts have argued that it must eventually garner annual sales of $500 million to $1 billion for Merck to retain a 20% or more yearly gain in profit, a rate that has kept Merck a darling of the investment community."

Prostate cancer, second-leading cancer killer of American men, is also big at AUA Toronto. Early detection is the message, and one who is energetically spreading it is hockey great Maurice "Rocket" Richard, the Montreal Canadiens hall-of-famer, a prostate-cancer survivor. Richard speaks at a press conference, hands out autographed photographs of himself, hangs around the booth belonging to the Prostate Cancer Education Council. Old-fashioned rectal exams, the subject of so many bad jokes, remain important in detecting this cancer. But a relatively new technology, testing the blood for prostate-specific antigen, or PSA, is rapidly gaining acceptance as a screening tool. No fewer than thirty presentations of one sort or another at AUA Toronto concern PSA. No fewer than ninety are devoted to BPH.

Hardy Hendren has come to Toronto, but not to get up to speed on prostate problems, seldom seen in children. Hendren has come bearing news of his latest innovation: the bowel nipple, a surgical creation too complicated to ever become a fad. The nipple can give urinary continence to certain children whose badly deformed anatomies once left little choice but bags.

On Sunday, the day he is to present his paper, Hendren takes a stroll through the upstairs exhibition hall. He attends perhaps a dozen meetings a year, and he makes a point of bringing himself-up-to date on new technologies, new pharmaceuticals, new techniques. He meets old friends and catches up on the latest surgical gossip.

The exhibition hall could hold the Blue Jays and Angels, it is so cavernous. Most of the big names in medical and pharmaceutical manufacturing are represented here, and many of the little ones as well. The hall is thick with salesmen and saleswomen, carefully coiffed, conservatively attired, persistent but not pushy. If you are a doctor, they want to give you free pens, tote bags, literature, and samples. They want you to buy their endoscopes, computers, lasers, X rays, books, cameras, ostomy bags, steel catheters, plastic catheters, balloon catheters, and suprapubic catheters. They want you to stop a moment at their booth. Have you seen our new drug

Aphrodyne? It's used to treat a certain kind of impotence, "when diabetes dims the flame of love." What about our new uro-ultrasound machine? Watch the screen as we illuminate the actual bladder of our live model, this bleached-blond woman with the orange lipstick and breast-hugging white camisole who's lying on our table. Please check out our new laser cautery. Watch as we demonstrate it on beef liver and a chicken breast! Have you seen our vacuum erection device, which comes with our patented constriction rings? Here—watch as we demonstrate it on our mannequin, Clyde. See how perfectly that ring fits? Notice how our vacuum erection device won't pull out Clyde's pubic hair, as many of our competitors' models would!

In Booth 2022, a smiling young saleswoman for Meadox Surgimed of Oakland, New Jersey, is demonstrating her company's automatic biopsy system. The automatic biopsy system is a disposable spring-powered gun that shoots a long needle into the body for precision biopsy. It is suitable for use on liver, kidney, breast, pancreas, lung, and prostate gland. Sausages and Red Delicious apples are typically used to demonstrate biopsy guns, but the Meadox Surgimed team has found that kiwi fruit provides superior realism. "It's more like necrotic tissue," the saleswoman says. She holds one of her flashlight-shaped guns against a kiwi fruit and pulls the trigger. Voilà! A scientifically precise biopsy! "They say it's not painful," she says. "I'll never know."

"I know," Hendren says. "I've had it. And it's unpleasant."

Hendren is nosing around the videotapes. At no charge, you can check a film out of the video library and watch it on one of the dozens of VCRs that have been set up. For your viewing pleasure, there's even fresh popcorn.

"*V-7*, please," Hendren says to the woman in the checkout booth.

More than one hundred videos, many new, are available at AUA Toronto. You can watch how to remove a prostate surgically or see how rats who have undergone a vasectomy have had their vas deferens rejoined with surgical microclips. You can learn how to do your own scrotal sonography, how to dissect the groin, and how to perform balloon dilatation, about which Hendren remarks, "In five years, no one will be doing it." Jesun Lin, from Taiwan, would like you to view his "cocktail technique for repair of hypospadias,"

hypospadias being a deformity of the penis. A Brazilian team has done a film on the many foreign objects they have removed from bladders and urethras. It is a bizarre piece of cinema verité, something Monty Python might well have come up with had the comedy troupe decided to parody urology training films. It is narrated in embarrassingly bad English with Handel's *Water Music* playing in the background as scissors and alligator clamps do battle with sutures, catheters, gauze, a syringe cap, and even a pencil that disappeared inside a woman during masturbation.

V-7, a film by Michael E. Mitchell of Children's Hospital and Medical Center in Seattle, and Paul H. Lange of the University of Washington Medical Center, is a far more polished production. Mitchell trained under Hendren and is writing a book on reconstructive surgery with him. Mitchell also played a major role in developing gastrocystoplasty, the technique of enlarging bladder with stomach—a technique he taught Hendren, who has used it many times since. The video, which features a thirty-eight-year-old man who lost his bladder and prostate to cancer, demonstrates the creation of an entire new bladder from only stomach. Like Hendren's, Mitchell's philosophy is to avoid sentencing a patient to a bag whenever possible. Hendren happened to be a visiting professor at Seattle's Children's Hospital during the surgery, which was performed at a nearby adult hospital. At the operation's end, Mitchell and Lange asked Hendren to scrub in briefly for a cameo appearance in their film—an invitation intended as a bit of a joke on those who would eventually be viewing it. *Is it really Hendren?* they might wonder. *What's he doing in a film on an adult out of Seattle? Isn't that Mitchell's operation?*

Near the film's end, Mitchell is sitting in his office, summarizing the results. "Paul, I think it looks pretty good," he says. "We should get the opinion of someone else."

The film cuts back to the OR—to a gowned, gloved, and masked Hardy Hendren standing at the operating field. Hendren looks the camera straight on, smiles, and pronounces, "Looks very good, don't you think?" Then he giggles.

"Well, thank you," Lange says. "We agree. And we've been very pleased with how the patients have done."

Hendren has not yet seen Mike Mitchell's finished film. He won't today. *V*-7 is a hot number at AUA Toronto.

"I'm sorry," the clerk says, "that video's out."

"Thank you," Hendren says. He's disappointed. He was tickled to have a part in Mitchell's production. He enjoyed being on the inside of the little joke.

Hendren strolls. He doesn't get more than a few feet before he runs into a doctor he knows. And after an exchange of pleasantries, he advances only a few feet more before running into someone else. For the half hour he's on the exhibition floor, this is how it is—the hellos, the handshakes, the stories, the unsolicited offering of opinion, working the crowd like a veteran politician, operating in what another protégé, Patricia Donahoe, Hendren's successor at the Massachusetts General Hospital, calls his godfather mode. There's the Mexican doctor who lets Hendren in on a secret: a private party will be thrown for him when he visits Mexico later in the year. There's the thrice-married colleague from California whose son is a resident and might like someday to train at Boston Children's. There's a urologist from Utah who'd like Hendren to operate out there, an Irish doctor who says he'd travel anywhere to see Hendren work, and an Air Force general and urologist whom Hendren engages in a discussion of shooting carrier landings. There's Gudrun Ch. Koller-Storz, whose father owns the company that makes the endoscopes Hendren buys. John Lattimer, a past president of the AUA who was an Army doctor at the Nürenberg trials. A doctor who sent Hendren a boy close to death, in part because he'd failed to move decisively on the boy's severe birth defect; feeling guilty at the sight of the chief, he seeks Hendren's forgiveness and receives it. "No one has a memory like yours!" says another doctor. It's not clear if this is intended as a high compliment or acknowledgment of a fact that should make one calculated and cautious in Hendren's company.

Not everyone is a huge friend and admirer. Lawrence Hatchett is here. So is the assistant editor of a medical journal who turned down one of Hendren's manuscripts—not because the science was suspect but because he didn't like the writing. "It is the consensus that this is an enormous and valuable experience but the vehicle in which it is carried is disappointing," the editor wrote in his rejection letter.

A dozen or more times a year, Hendren takes to the road, a missionary with a simple message: *Never give up. Every kid can be helped, no matter how hopeless it seems.*

He lectures and presents papers most places he goes, and often he's presented with a medal, citation, or honorary citizenship at a banquet. But the real excitement for his hosts is when he goes into the OR. In thirty-five years, Hendren has operated in virtually all of the major cities in North America. He's operated—without financial remuneration—in Shanghai; Peking; Vellore, India; Panama City; Rio de Janeiro; Warsaw; Moscow; Medellín, Colombia; Dublin; Liverpool; London; Lyons; Sendai, Japan; Rotterdam; Salzburg; Bern; Damascus; and Blantyre, Malawi, among other places. He's operated in a 110-degree room without an interpreter, without Dorothy Enos, with bad instruments, under bad light, with primitive anesthesia. He's operated in amphitheaters and on closed-circuit TV, an arrangement he no longer allows because he believes it's not in the best interest of the patient for the doctor to be simultaneously operating and narrating to a live TV audience.

He's invited many of the doctors he's met to come to Boston to visit, first at the Massachusetts General, then at Children's. Eleanor has accompanied him on most of his trips; they provide a chance for the couple to be together for extended periods, an opportunity rarely afforded in their day-to-day lives. Hendren has brought his own instruments with him, some of which he has donated to his hosts before he's gone home. He is sometimes distressed by the mentality he finds, particularly in surgical backwaters. Meaning to be most gracious, his hosts will give him his choice of difficult cases. "It is up to you, Professor Hendren. Take as many or as few as you'd like. And don't forget, tonight we host an official dinner in honor of our most distinguished guest, Professor Hendren."

They don't have it quite right, Hendren will think. *This isn't about celebrity. This is about fixing kids.*

Hendren is a great reader of surgeons. One whose words have stuck with him is Sir Charles Bell, the nineteenth-century Scotsman known for his contributions to the mapping out of the central nervous system and brain. Bell understood how, by its very nature, surgery provides its practitioners great leeway in what they do—and why. Bell knew the shield behind which surgeons engage in their profession. "The Public, who are so ready to determine on the merits of our Profession," Bell wrote in 1821,

and even the patients who are to suffer, are surprisingly ignorant both of the Surgeon's motives for what he does, and the propriety of the methods he puts in practice. He is continually operating in secret as a matter of necessity; the most sensible give the decision up to him; so that he is answerable to his own conscience, and to that alone. Nor is the Public aware of the temptations which men of our Profession withstand. Credit for great abilities, gratitude for services performed, and high emoluments, are ready to be bestowed for a little deception, and that obliquity of conduct, which does not amount to actual crime. This is precisely the situation in which a man requires a thorough devotion to the principles of honour and right conduct, to preserve him from the commission of error.

In late 1991, Hendren, Eleanor, and Dorothy Enos joined a group of eight doctors, three nurses, and a respiratory therapist that traveled to Damascus, Syria, to provide free care for children and adults from Syria and Lebanon. The group was sponsored by Physicians for Peace, a nonprofit, nonpolitical association that arranges medical missions to countries that have not enjoyed domestic tranquillity. Founded in 1985 by one of America's preeminent plastic surgeons, Charles E. Horton of Norfolk, Virginia, Physicians for Peace has sponsored missions to Iraq, Turkey, Israel, Jordan, Egypt, and Greece. Like Hendren, many of the doctors who have gone abroad are reconstructive surgeons, skilled at rebuilding faces, hands, legs, genitourinary systems, skeletons, and skin mangled by violence or defective at birth. Missions include lectures and contact with host physicians, who are keen to learn the latest from the U.S.A. But the emphasis is on healing. By the time Hendren went to Syria, nearly four thousand patients had benefited from Physicians for Peace—physicians and other professionals who are compensated only for their travel and lodging expenses, not for their services.

The Hendren party arrived in Damascus on a Friday evening. On Saturday, Hendren and Enos made rounds at the city's Children's Hospital and were shown eight children. One was a prune belly child, victim of a disfiguring and incapacitating abdominal and urologic disorder. Another needed a megaureter repair. A third had exstrophy of the bladder. Most had been operated on several times before, and the previous attempts had only made them worse. Hendren was their last hope at normalcy. "Keep a running tab on these kids," Hendren said to Enos "so I can keep them straight. Then we'll work out a timetable."

When he'd seen all eight children, Hendren asked the doctors what OR time would be available for him.

Tuesday and Wednesday, from nine o'clock to two o'clock, he was told.

A man less well mannered would have snickered. "There's no way we're going to be able to do all these kids," Hendren said, "from nine o'clock to two o'clock on two operating days."

Then take however many children you can fit in, he was told. Chose whichever ones you'd like.

"Why can't we operate on Monday?" Hendren asked.

Well, Monday was a national holiday, commemorating President Hafez al-Assad's ascension to power.

"I'm not going to be attending that celebration," Hendren said.

"Sorry, Professor Hendren, but no one will be working in the OR on Monday."

"If they want me to fix these kids, they will be," Hendren said. Well, if he insisted . . .

"Now why can't we operate all day Wednesday?"

Because the U.S. ambassador was hosting a reception for Physicians for Peace. *Surely*, Professor Hendren would not miss the ambassador's reception.

"I think the ambassador won't know if I'm not there," Hendren said. "So let's forget about that. We're going to have four full operating days, and we're going to operate until we get all of these cases finished."

I'm not going to choose this one over that one, Hendren thought. *We are not going to have a kid come in the hospital and look forward to getting fixed and go out without being done. I'm going to do them all.*

And he did, squeezing in sixty hours of OR time over four days, including one thirty-six-hour stretch in which he operated, to his hosts' amazement, for thirty hours.

Surgery is craftsmanlike in its perpetuation, passed from one generation to the next less through academe than by being at the master's side. In his travels, Hendren enlightens. He inspires. But his greatest contributions as an apostle come not on the road but home in Boston. To really follow Hendren, you must be apprenticed to him.

Although they have been operated on for as long as there has been surgery, and there has been surgery since prehistoric times, only in this century have children become universally accepted as separate surgical citizens. Historically, surgeons considered children miniature versions of adults. The fact that their developmental status profoundly affects surgical outcomes was not widely understood until the nineteenth century, when, in France in particular, a growing number of surgeons began to concentrate on children. The twentieth century has seen the emergence of a group of physicians others would hail as the Fathers of Pediatric Surgery—Max Grob in Switzerland, Denis Browne in England, William E. Ladd at the Children's Hospital in Boston, Robert E. Gross, who studied under Ladd and then succeeded him as chief of surgery. While Ladd is the most legitimate contender to the title of American Father of Pediatric Surgery, no one's influence in the United States has been as broad as Gross's. Gross was the first president of the American Pediatric Surgical Association, holding office in 1970 and 1971; of the twenty presidents from then until 1991, only four had not been trained by Gross or by someone Gross trained. And of the twenty-four advanced pediatric-surgical training programs in the United States and Canada in 1991, eighteen were headed by surgeons trained by Gross or by a Gross trainee.

Of the surgical specialities, pediatric surgery is among the most elite. Of the 51,690 fellows of the American College of Surgeons in December 1990, 43 percent were general surgeons. Next in popularity were the urologists, accounting for 4,744 members, or 9 percent. Only 542, or barely 1 percent, of the fellows were board-certified pediatric surgeons. Each year, there are fewer than two dozen board-eligible graduates of advanced programs in all of North America. Hendren's—the chief general surgical residency at Children's—receives sixty applications annually. One is chosen, for a two-year fellowship. When the two years is up, the surgeon, finally fully trained, is at least eight years out of medical school. Thirty-five years old, and just beginning.

Medievalism provides a metaphor with which to describe the relationship between Hendren and the surgeons in training under him: chief resident, assistant chief resident, senior residents, junior residents, and interns, in descending order. It is a hierarchy based on experience and three qualities that experience develops in the achiever: judgment, competence, and responsibility. The hierarchy is reminiscent of a tenth-century abbey, with Hendren the abbot. The codes of public behavior he dictates to those below are rigid, formal, and unwritten but acutely understood by all. Hendren is Sir or Dr. Hendren, never Hardy. Dr. Hendren enters and leaves all rooms first. Dr. Hendren leads any group proceeding down any hall. At Surgical Grand Rounds, the weekly in-house lecture series, Dr. Hendren sits in the first seat of the first row on the right; when he is absent, his seat is left empty. Unless you are in the OR, your attendance is required at Grand Rounds and at the weekly diffi-cult-case conference, Morbidity and Mortality, or M&M. No matter how far behind you may get when you're seeing patients, you strive never to be late for Grand Rounds or M&M. And finally, it is Dr. Hendren, and no one else, who permits your entry into his OR.

It is a tremendous and sometimes frustrating paradox—such subservience expected of men and women who could not have made it so far, all the way to the master's side, without supreme self-confidence, ego, and ability. Hendren knows well. Like every sur-geon who's become chief, he's been there himself.

The rewards can be substantial. If you are good, if you are experienced and trustworthy, Dr. Hendren will give you great lati-tude with your own patients. You will have your own room, where you will be in charge—albeit under the ever-watchful eye of the senior staff, a situation Hendren's mentor Churchill called "the practice of surgery in a goldfish bowl." You will be buried in the commodity you value most: OR time. Dr. Hendren will fund your research, guide it, invite you to coauthor a paper with him, a credential you will proudly claim. You will be like a fine racehorse, an analogy he also borrowed from Churchill. Hendren's job will be letting you go—free, fast, reigned in only when you're at imminent risk of leaping off the track.

Like the Harvard name, Hendren's recommendation will help launch your career wherever you may go when your residency is finished. His invitation to join the permanent staff of Children's Hospital, extended to but a few, will do more than that. You will be assured of steady work, which will help build your fledgling prac-tice. You will have a good chance of eventually becoming a profes-sor of surgery at Harvard Medical. You will be backed in your research and have a high-profile platform from which to announce its results. You will have Hendren's unwavering support in the swirl of hospital politics. Hendren will counsel and advise you, and he will listen to what you say. He may help you with your medical-school debts, which can be enormous. He may help you in buying a house. In Hendren's decade at Children's, five of ten chief residents have graduated to a position on the staff: Joseph P. Vacanti, the liver-transplant surgeon whose promising research (jointly with the Massachusetts Institute of Technology) someday may give medicine the ability to grow new organs; Robert C. Shamberger, the cancer surgeon; Craig W. Lillehei, who performed Children's first double-lung transplant; Jay M. Wilson, whose chief concern is badly damaged lungs in newborns; and Dennis P. Lund, interested in trauma and transplanting intestines. Like the chief, all are qualified to operate across a broad spectrum of the anatomy, although among none is the spectrum quite as broad as that across which Hendren himself operates. Like the chief, these men are passionate. They believe there can be no higher calling than academic surgery.

Once during an operation, a urology resident had scrubbed in with Hendren. He and Hendren were going back and forth over the relative merits of general pediatric surgery versus pediatric urology. Hendren, a general surgeon first, commented on the erratic and fiercely demanding schedule of his chosen calling. The resident conceded that part of the attraction of pediatric urology was its more predictable schedule, particularly in private practice.

"You don't want to work nights?" Hendren said.

"No."

"Or weekends?"

"No."

"Or on vacations?"

"No."

"Or in emergencies?"

"No."

"Tell me something," Hendren said. "What do you hope to accomplish in the next thirty, thirty-five years?"

The resident paused, then said, "I don't know. I haven't thought about it."

"By and large," Hendren said, "people who haven't thought about it by your age never do get around to thinking about it."

"When did you know what you were going to do?"

"Well," said Hendren with a laugh, "in second grade I walked up to my teacher and said, 'Miss Wally? I'm going to fix cloacal exstrophies!' "

Hendren has announced no plans to retire; in fact, he expects to operate and teach through at least his seventieth year. But when he does retire—when his presence on Longwood Avenue has been reduced to a cubicle in the Countway Library of Medicine—Death Row, as some professors emeriti in residence there have dubbed it—his legacy will be those he's influenced, those who can draw a line from him to Gross and from Gross back to Ladd. Every pediatric surgeon is unique, if only by most minute degree; in a decade of training, he or she is influenced by many hospitals, many operating styles, many teachers. But nearly all can point to a single individual and call that individual their mentor.

Since starting to practice at Massachusetts General in 1960, Hendren has been associated with hundreds of surgeons-in-training. Some have barely brushed by him in the OR, but others have spent months, years learning from him. Today, many of his protégés are heading their own departments, chiefs at their own hospitals in cities across the continent: Seattle, New York, San Diego, Chicago, San Francisco, Atlanta, and Saint Petersburg, among other places here and abroad.

Several hundred urologists and fellow travelers are in the auditorium at AUA Toronto when Hendren takes the podium.

"I'd like to present an experience in using an ileal nipple for continence in selected cases of cloacal exstrophy," he says. A slide appears on the screen. It shows a ten-year-old girl who has been opened from chest to bottom.

The girl came to Hendren in 1985. She had been born with cloacal exstrophy, a defect resembling Lucy Moore's but compounded by the absence of an abdominal wall, a situation that had left her organs spilling out of her belly. Until about 1960, cloacal exstrophy was a universal death sentence. At birth, this girl's life had been saved—by one of Hendren's friends, Judson G. Randolph, surgeon-in-chief at Children's Hospital National Medical Center in Washington, D.C. Randolph, another of Gross's chief residents, had referred the girl to Hendren to reconstruct her bladder so that she might be continent.

"We have been asked to review it to see if that might produce any additional thoughts about just how all of this might be worked out," Hendren wrote a week after Valentine's Day, 1985, when he first examined the girl. "This is of course an exceedingly complex set of decisions that need to be made."

In a sixteen-and-a-half-hour operation, Hendren fashioned order from chaos. He was initially slowed by severe adhesions, which required three hours to take down. He removed the smaller of the girl's two vaginas, both of which entered the bladder. He brought the good vagina to the surface, using two flaps of skin: one from her perineum and another swung in from her buttocks. He moved each of her ureters, which had been connected to her bladder at bad locations. He enlarged her bladder with a length of small bowel.

Then he did something no one had ever done before.

He substituted a lower section of small bowel, known as the ileum, for the bladder neck and urethra, which in the normal anatomy work in tandem to maintain continence. It was an experiment—but what choice did he have? There was no good tissue with which to build a urethra, nothing for a bladder neck. He could give her a bag, but that would be conceding defeat. That would be the easy way out for the surgeon, a lifetime of misery for the girl. Hendren had an idea, cooked up the first time he'd examined her. He would take a ten-centimeter length of small intestine, and he would fold it back onto itself to create a five-centimeter sleeve. With a bit of luck, it would be a watertight nipple, projecting up into the bladder, sufficient to keep her dry but not so tight that a catheter could not be inserted, the only way the bladder could be emptied whenever she had to urinate. The little girl already had a bag for solid waste, and her anatomy wasn't going to be forgiving on that point. If only Hendren could get her dry, could do away with the necessity for bag number two . . .

Why wouldn't it work? Give it a good blood supply, fold it back carefully, sew it in carefully, instruct her on how to catheterize— why wouldn't it work?

Hendren made his ileal nipple, sewed it inside the bladder, then closed the bladder up. He filled the bladder with sterile water to test his latest idea. "The results were no leakage at the patient's urethra," Hendren wrote in the record. "This was exciting!"

An Andriesse drawing of the girl's postoperative anatomy is projected onto the screen at AUA Toronto.

"This shows her completed repair," Hendren tells his audience, "with the augmentation, the nipple and reimplants, and the vagina. And subsequently, we've used that piece of colon to enlarge the vagina."

Next on the screen is a photograph of a little girl voiding into a cup.

"This shows this youngster emptying by catheterization using a metal cannula. She was done in 1985, is now six years post-op, is totally dry, has normal preservation of her upper tracts, and leads an essentially normal life in her own view."

On through subsequent successful bowel nipples he goes. On through children who were born genetic males but, lacking no male genitalia, were surgically transformed into females.

"This shows this little kid to illustrate that although she has been raised in the female role, she is a genetic male, and she's the toughest little kid in her class and beats up all the boys and has a mouth on her with a vocabulary just like a sailor. . . . You can't escape the male imprint that she demonstrates, . . . but she's dry. . . . This was a particularly formidable one. . . . There wasn't much to work with. . . . We used three different pieces of small bowel to do three different things. . . . This patient is dry, and she regards her fate as much better than it had been before."

Case 6 is a little girl from a northeastern state.

Like the others, she is a cloacal-exstrophy patient. Born a genetic male, she was transformed by Hendren, after consultation with her parents, into a female.

"Now sooner or later," he tells his audience of urologists, "you will fall on your face with a new technique. And this is one I show because it illustrates that."

Chapter 23

The little girl from a northeastern state was a first child. Mom was in the computer field. Dad managed a warehouse. For months, they'd tried to have a baby. Finally Mom had conceived, and her pregnancy was uneventful. Not a hint that something might be wrong with her first baby. And so when she went into labor five weeks early, she figured, *It's no big deal. Maybe our baby will be a little small; that's all.*

The little girl was naturally born, and she came into the world the way normal babies normally do, kicking and screaming. But she was not a normal baby. She had clubfeet. Her lower legs were crooked. The lining of her spinal cord protruded through an opening in her back, and the cord itself was abnormally aligned in her spine. She had a single kidney, not two, but two appendixes, not one. Her abdominal wall had not formed properly, and her intestines spilled out of her belly. Her small intestine was abnormally joined to her large intestine. Her bladder was open and in two halves, as if surgically cleaved. She had no anus. She had two testicles but no penis, only a nodule that sort of resembled a clitoris. Even the surgeon who would fix her, Hardy Hendren, a man who has seen the worst deformities nature can serve up, would later write into his notes, "This is a terrible sight to behold."

With an incidence calculated at as low as one in four hundred thousand, the average hospital may never see see a case of cloacal exstrophy. When one does come along, there is no standing etiquette for greeting the arrival. The little girl's doctors and nurses reacted the way any layperson, any parent would react. They were stunned. Who had ever seen such a horrible thing? Was this a boy? Or was this a girl? How could this infant survive, never mind ever come close to being normal? They laid the little girl on the delivery-room examining table, and they stood there, staring, shaking their heads, murmuring among themselves, getting on the phone to call in the specialists, who at least might be able to give this monstrosity a name. They did not let Mom or Dad hold their little girl. After allowing them one quick look, she was rushed to intensive care.

Maybe it's better if she dies, thought Mom, a good, strong, decent woman who would later experience the most terrible guilt at her initial reaction.

But the little girl did not die. Alongside scrambled anatomy was good anatomy: a normal circulatory system, a normal pulmonary system, and a normal brain that would, in due time, allow this baby to develop into an intelligent, sunny, and lovable little girl. The little girl needed immediate surgery, but it was well beyond what any average hospital could handle. She would have to be transferred to a pediatric hospital. Philadelphia had an excellent one. Johns Hopkins in Baltimore had a fine pediatric service. And there was Boston's Children's. The little girl's doctor knew the chief of surgery there. "If this were my child," the doctor said, "I'd go Hardy Hendren." Hendren, the little girl's doctor knew, had unsurpassed experience with cloacal exstrophy patients—having reconstructed, by the summer of 1992, twenty-four of them (in addition to his 113 cloaca patients).

The next morning, the baby went by ambulance to Children's, where Hendren examined her. He could tell, looking at the little girl's ambiguous genitalia, what the chromosome tests would quickly disclose: genetically, this was a male.

Making a penis is not impossible. Men wounded in war, adult transsexuals, victims of sadistic sex crimes and violent accidents— all have come to the surgeon seeking help in making what they do not have. The surgeon has done the best he can, roving throughout the body in search of suitable tissue. One technique involves taking a graft of skin from the lower abdomen and rolling it into a tube. Skin from thigh, shoulder, and upper foot has been used. By the

1990s, the preferred operation was the cricket-bat flap, so named because of the shape of the flap, taken from the nearly hairless inner forearm. Aesthetically, the results of phalloplasty vary: from only fair to quite poor. The best man-made penis looks something like a normal penis, but it would never be mistaken for one; the worst only compounds an already difficult situation. Functionally, a well-made penis allows normal male urination—that is, when standing. But compared with the natural organ, even with the best results it is a disappointment in sexual relations. It is in fact easier to make a realistic vagina than a realistic penis. With estrogen at the onset of puberty, it is possible to produce secondary sex characteristics such as breast development in a genetic male. Faced with patients like the little girl from a northeastern state, most physicians, Hendren among them, advise assigning a female identity—immediately, while the psychological slate is still blank.

Before meeting Hendren, the little girl's parents were put on alert by a nurse at Children's. As gifted as he was with the knife, she confided, Dr. Hendren's bedside manner can be, well . . . perhaps *brusque* is the polite way to put it. But Mom and Dad didn't find Hendren like that when he met with them before taking their little girl into his OR. It seemed he didn't have another patient in the whole world, he was so understanding.

"What sex is our baby?" they asked. Until they knew, they didn't want to give their baby a name, and they didn't want to settle for something gender neutral, a Pat or a Chris.

Hendren explained.

"It would be best to raise her as a girl," he concluded. "I have many patients like that. And they are good, happy kids."

In his first operation on the little girl, only hours after her birth, Hendren managed to close her bladder. He removed the two testicles, repaired the juncture of small intestine and large, returned her bowels to her belly, and closed her abdominal wall. To give everything a chance to heal, he left her with a temporary ileostomy, which required a bag at the end of her small intestine.

The operation was a complete success.

His next surgery on the little girl was not.

Most of the surgical failures Hendren deals with are someone else's. Someone else who tackled a problem without the talent to solve it. Someone else who took a chance he or she shouldn't have taken. Someone else who was dishonest with himself or herself, or who, in the name of advancing science, put the prospect of professional accomplishment ahead of a patient's well-being. Roughly a third of Hendren's biggest cases involve trying to reverse someone else's bad outcome. As a professor, the chief tries to impart to his pupils skills that will spare them such outcomes, skills that will give them uniformly good results.

Once, in the middle of a case that went nearly fifteen hours, Hendren quizzed two residents, as he often does, about the qualities they thought a superior surgeon should possess.

"Judgment," one said.

"Compulsiveness," said the other.

"Technical skills," said the first.

"You've said judgment," said Hendren. "You've said compulsiveness. I know what Dorothy will say."

"Persistence" is what Enos said.

"Caring," the first resident added.

"All right," Hendren said. "We've got down judgment, technical skills, persistence. Steve wants compulsiveness. And you want caring. Caring about what?"

"My patients," the first resident said.

"Creativity," the second one said.

"No one mentioned one of the most important attributes," Hendren said. "Honesty. *Honesty.* How often have you heard a surgeon finish something and say, 'I *think* this will be all right.' "

"Many times."

"And how many times *has* it been all right?"

Silence in the room.

"Usually, when a surgeon says that, he has a doubt in his mind. And when he has a doubt in his mind, there's usually a dubious result. Would you say that's a fair statement?"

Everyone did.

Except perhaps in his head, Hendren would never compile a list of his salvage operations. He would never confront a colleague because he does not believe it is his responsibility to stand in judgment. He does not get his kicks from criticizing others. The damage is done; his job, Hendren believes, is to repair it so a child can move on with life. But were such a list ever compiled, it would include a girl named Allison, a psychiatrist's daughter. Allison came to Hendren from California. She had been born with abnormally located ureters, which should have been fairly simple to correct. But two failed surgeries left her with two bags, which had put her, at the age of six, in psychological therapy—where she continued until she was twelve, when Hendren got rid of her bags.

The list would include a boy from New York who came to Hendren with one kidney dead and the other near death, a complication of a tortuous urinary tract that had not been surgically corrected. The list would include Elizabeth, a young woman who was born with a cloaca. Surgeons at a prominent hospital had tried to fix her, but when she came to Hendren, her vagina was still hidden away inside her, she was incontinent of feces, and her marriage was in trouble because it could not be consummated. Hendren would fix Elizabeth, and after he did, she would become a mother.

The list would include George, a boy from west of the Mississippi River. George was born with bladder exstrophy: his bladder spilled out of him through a hole in his abdominal wall. Instead of opening at the tip of his penis, his urethra ended in a hole at the base of its shaft. Surgeons had managed to get the bladder back inside, had closed the boy's belly, and had made an attempt at repairing his penis, but their intervention from then on had done more harm than good. George had had at least thirteen operations before coming to Boston Children's Hospital. At least fifteen surgeons had participated in his care. By the time Hendren saw him, his life had become a cycle of fever, vomiting, and pain. Urine seeped out of a hole in his lower abdomen, and at the age of nine, he wore diapers. His penis was split open in two ugly halves, base to tip. His testicles were not properly located in his scrotum. His bladder had been enlarged with a patch of intestine, but the patch was poorly positioned. His right ureter was blocked, and as a result, his right kidney was not working properly and thus was making him sick. George had many scars: on his bladder, penis, and belly. And he was full of adhesions.

We'll have George healed by the time he's six or eight, the surgeons out West had told George's parents early on. *You won't even remember this. It'll all just seem like a bad dream.*

For George's parents, the last straw was the artificial sphincter. In an attempt to make George dry, surgeons in 1989 had sewn a prosthesis into him. It clamped around his bladder neck, and you were supposed to be able to open and close it, almost like a faucet. The squeeze-bulb mechanism that was to activate it was implanted in his right scrotum. But the artificial sphincter never worked. One day in the fall of 1989 when George's mother, Susan, was washing her son, the skin on his scrotum perforated, and there it was—the squeeze bulb, in plain view. That day, Susan had had it. That was it with the surgeons out West. She would let them remove the sphincter surgically, but after that they would never perform another operation on her son. Susan wanted a referral to someone else, someone who knew what he or she was doing. One of George's doctors had trained for a time with Hardy Hendren. Maybe he'll see George, the doctor told her. Susan took Hardy Hendren's name to the library, to her gynecologist, and to the family pediatrician, who'd heard Hendren lecture and observed, "He wrote the bible on this." Said another doctor: "It would be like going to see the pope." A devout woman whose strength comes from prayer, Susan was sold. One of George's doctors wrote a letter of referral, but when weeks passed and there was no answer from Boston, no acknowledgment that the letter had ever been received, Susan picked up the phone. It was the spring of 1990.

"Please, I'm begging you," Susan told a secretary, "I want to talk to Dr. Hendren."

But Dr. Hendren was not available that day. Dr. Hendren would review George's records, and he would get back to her. And when he finally did—when he finally told Susan he thought he could help her son, at least he was willing to try—Susan already had a plan. She was taking George on a plane, and they were flying to Massachusetts to stay with her in-laws. The next time her son got so sick—she figured it wouldn't be long—she was bringing him to the emergency room at Children's.

"I'm going to be in Boston tomorrow," she told Hendren on the phone. "I'll take anything you have. I don't care if it's midnight. I'll take any cancellation. Anything. *Please.*"

With his schedule already badly overbooked, as it always is, Hendren said that what George needed—a major reconstruction, an operation that would last a day—would have to be toward summer's end.

Susan couldn't wait. She flew east, and the next time George was sick, on June 13, she brought him to the emergency room and introduced him as a patient of Dr. Hendren's.

"Welcome to Children's!" said Hendren when reached by phone. He liked Susan's pluck. It spoke eloquently of her love for her son, what ultimately would be the child's saving grace.

"We will go to work today and do what seems reasonable, with no limit of time imposed on us," Hendren wrote in George's record on the morning of his surgery. The reconstruction was gargantuan, lasting twenty-three hours and requiring more than two gallons of fluids, including two pints of blood and blood components. As he operated, Hendren was astounded that so much could have gone so wrong on one kid. "I don't understand what they've done to this penis," he said as he set out to fix it and George's other problems.

At one point nearly twelve hours into the operation, Hendren's colleague Alan B. Retik, chief of Children's Division of Urology, came into Room 7.

"Is it as difficult as advertised?" Retik asked.

"It's a tricky one," said Hendren.

"It looks like a mess."

"Well, it is."

The two discussed the relative virtues of artificial sphincters. Hendren allowed as how he'd used one only once.

"How many times have you used one, Alan?" he asked.

"Once," Retik replied. "The kid was incontinent by the time he got to the recovery room."

"Everyone knows a sphincter doesn't work for this kind of patient," Hendren said.

George's recovery at Children's took almost four months, in part because scar tissue does not heal as readily as the virgin stuff. It took George many tries before he was able to catheterize himself whenever he had to void. But when he went home, he was dry. He was no longer sick. His penis, so deformed when he flew east, was nearly normal.

Before Susan and her son left, Hendren had a long talk with George, who was in the habit of raising his voice to his mother, as nine-year-old boys are wont to do. "I've heard you yell at your mother many times while you were here," Hendren said, "and I want you to stop that. She's your best friend. If it weren't for her persistence, you wouldn't be fixed. She's the one person you must never speak harshly to again in your whole life. Promise?" George did. A month later, Hendren wrote George a letter. In it, he told him not to let a day pass without giving his mother at least one hug and a kiss.

Hendren's first surgery on the little girl from a northeastern state lasted eight hours. Four months later, R. Michael Scott repaired her tethered cord, the same spinal cord defect that Lucy Moore was born with. Four months after that, in April 1989, Hendren closed her ileostomy and got rid of the bag on her belly. Just before Christmas, her clubfeet were corrected at another hospital, one that had as strong an orthopedics department as that of Children's but was closer to home. By the end of that surgery, the little girl had spent nearly twenty-four hours in the OR. But much remained to be done. She was still wet. Her bladder was still too small, and she needed genitalia. She needed what other little girls had. She needed liberation from this intersex zone to which nature had sentenced her.

I know she may always have some handicap, and her life will be different from that of other children, her mother was thinking, *but I think and pray she will be happy, confident, and able to enjoy life without feeling sorry for herself. I want her to be an independent young woman. I want her to go to college and do something she finds stimulating and rewarding. I will never tell her she can't do something because of her handicaps. I've seen people with problems worse than hers do amazing things.*

And later, when the family had grown with the birth of two healthy boys, the little girl's mother would think, *She will have two brothers, and I hope they all love each other and that the two boys will always look out for her. I don't know if she'll ever get married. I don't want her to be lonely, so I'm glad she'll have her family if she doesn't.*

Some parents of children like this little girl have gone to great lengths to keep the genetics a secret. *What purpose would be served by telling the whole truth?* they have rationalized. *What difference would it make to our daughter? Wouldn't it just create a whole new set of psychological problems?* Their girls have been told that they were anatomically deficient when they were born. They've been told they will not be able to have children. But they have been told nothing about their XY chromosomes.

The little girl's mother was of a different mind. *Sometime, I will tell her her complete medical history. I think she should hear it from me. It's in her medical records, and I wouldn't want her to find out another way. This is something I didn't tell anyone except my parents. I don't want anyone to think of her as anything other than a little girl. I will be certain this information doesn't get into her school or any other public records. As for when I will tell her, it will depend on her. I will tell her everything, except this sex subject, as soon as she asks and can understand. To tell her she was supposed to be a boy is going to take more confidence and maturity for her to handle. I will probably send her to therapy when she is young to help her handle all that has gone on in her life. I will go first, though, to find out the best way to present this information to her.*

In 1991, Hendren brought the little girl back to his table. All the groundwork was in place; it was time for the major reconstruction. In seventeen and a half hours, Hendren took a piece of small intestine and used it to make a vagina. He took half of the little girl's stomach and used it to make a bladder of adequate size. He reimplanted her ureter so that urine would not back up in her lone kidney. Faced with insufficient tissue to make a proper urethra and bladder neck, what could keep her dry, he made his sixth bowel nipple.

He started with a four-inch piece of small intestine. Satisfied that he'd divided the mesentery properly, that the intestine had a good blood supply, he brought the piece of intestine down to the bladder. Hendren sewed one end into the base of the opened bladder. It fit nicely. Then he took the free end and—much as one would cuff a pant leg—folded it back over its base to create a nipple.

"It's a ridiculous-looking arrangement," he said as he stitched, "but it's worked well before."

The nippled bloated. It was a sign that despite the care Hendren had taken, perhaps the blood supply was not adequate. Having come this far, he had no choice but to close the little girl up and wait to see if he'd succeeded. "I was somewhat disappointed that it seemed to get very congested and was quite large," he wrote in his operative note, "but it did bleed when I incised it and so I thought it was probably viable. In each of those that we have made before, this bowel segment becomes very congested, but I have not lost one previously."

He lost this one.

As the little girl recovered from her operation on Nine West, Lucy Moore's floor, her stomach-grafted bladder and the vagina Hendren had made healed nicely. But the nipple, designed to keep her dry—wasn't keeping her dry. Urine was seeping out of it, inflaming the skin on the child's bottom.

Three weeks after the reconstruction, Hendren took the little girl to the OR and put a scope up into her. "I honestly don't see a good nipple there, and I am concerned that the nipple may have sloughed," he said. "I think we will simply have to wait and see until things have healed up further whether we still have all or part of our nipple remaining or have lost the entire thing."

Hendren explained again to the little girl's parents the nature of this kind of surgery.

"There are some problems that can be solved easily, quickly, now, as a quick encounter, and that's the end of it," he said. "For example, a kid comes in with appendicitis. OK, quickly you make the diagnosis. Then you take the patient to the operating room, and you do an appendectomy. Unless it's ruptured and caused peritonitis, it's over. The patient leaves the hospital in a day or two, and that's the end of it. That's not the way it is with cloacal exstrophy. We can't wave a wand over the baby and make it all normal in one fell swoop. And therefore philosophically we must persist until we get it all right. Pediatric reconstructive surgery is no place for somebody who must rely on being able to go up and do one quick slapdash and have it work out fine and flamboyantly walk away and say, 'Well now, let's on with the next thing.' That's just not the nature of it."

The little girl went home, wet. Three months later, back in Boston, another endoscopy confirmed Hendren's fear. The nipple hadn't survived. Deprived of an adequate blood supply, its cells had done what cells do without proper nutrients: they'd died. The nipple tissue had become necrotic. Soon, white blood cells would finish the job. The body would completely absorb the nipple, and there would be nothing left. Hendren would give the little girl's body time to heal completely. He would let the scar tissue soften where the nipple had been attached to the bladder, soft tissue being more conducive to surgery than hard tissue. He was sorry, he told the little girl's parents, sorry for them and for their daughter. But he would try again. He would not give up. "In this type of surgery," he said, "persistence is a requisite. The adage 'If at first you don't succeed, try, try again' is what we must follow."

The little girl's parents were disappointed but not shattered. Any shattering had come when the little girl was born. And Hendren was right. They'd come a long way.

Good surgeons do not take failure lightly. Failure can bring a lawsuit. Failure does not enhance a reputation, except, perhaps, when presented as a caution for all. Failure does not widen the referral network. Failure can leave a patient worse than when he or she came into the OR. In the extreme case, failure can kill.

In the wake of failure, bad surgeons may be dishonest. They may imply that the patient was somehow at fault, that anesthesia somehow screwed up, that pre- or postoperative care by any of the dozens of other health-care professionals typically involved in a big case was deficient. They may skew their published results by not reporting their failures. Worst of all, they may lie to themselves.

The best surgeons confront their failures. They admit them to their colleagues and students. Putting aside pride for the moment, they are brutally direct in their self-criticism. What were my mistakes? Did I commit an error of judgment—say, operating when the patient was too sick to withstand the trauma of surgery? Did I go too fast? Did I cut a corner? Did I leave the OR with even the slightest nagging doubt that I didn't do my best? Was there an error of technique—a knot improperly tied, a sterile procedure violated? Or was this an unavoidable consequence of working on the frontier, where the territory is largely uncharted?

In failure, there is always a lesson, if only a reminder that even the best can fail, even the best should never allow themselves to be lulled into expecting unbroken perfection in an endeavor as complicated as building bodies. From failure can come knowledge. It is as true in surgery as it is in computer programming or auto-body repair. Only the stakes are different.

One of the worst failures Hendren can recall occurred when he was Robert E. Gross's chief resident.

"I remember doing a baby at Children's Hospital with a big neuroblastoma," Hendren has said. "It was in OR 1, and we were using cyclopropane anesthesia—which we don't do anymore because it's explosive and can depress the heart—and the baby was failing. The heart was not doing well, and I was caught in this circumstance and faced with: What am I going to do? I'm halfway through removing this big tumor, and the heart is petering out; we're having trouble with anesthesia. And I suppose in retrospect the thing to do would have been to pack the belly and get out as fast as I could. In other words, that you would do better to stop, back up, let them get the vital signs stable up there, even come back later. But I started trying to finish the operation under very bad circumstances: low blood pressure and the anesthesiologist sounding the alarm that the vital signs were slipping.

"I cut the aorta. The aorta was surrounded by the cancer.

"The baby lost a lot of blood before we could control the bleeding and resuture the aorta, which was imbedded in tumor. The baby died later. Her outlook was dismal, anyway—this was the era before chemotherapy—but I felt bad that the urgency of the situation pushed me into inadvertently cutting the aorta while trying to hurry to get out of the situation. I think years later I would not get myself pushed into going at such a pace because we're having trouble with something else."

In reflecting on the little girl's failed bowel nipple, Hendren was reminded of a fact: surgery is a human enterprise.

"Why if you turn out one hundred automobiles may you have one that is a lemon?" he asked.

"Because even in something that should be as standardized as putting together an automobile, you may get a flaw in material, you may get a flaw in workmanship, you may get some fluke that nobody can understand. But it happens. I mean, it happens in something that is as precise and predictable as engineering and manufacturing—even with careful quality control. So that when you then put in the variables of surgery, the people involved in it, the chance for infection despite antibiotics, differences in the tissues of a particular patient—there are so many variables that it's a small wonder more things don't go wrong."

In August 1992, when he felt the little girl's body had done all the healing it would do, Hendren brought her back to his OR. He found no trace of her bowel nipple, only hardened tissue at the bladder outlet. It was not tissue suitable for another try at a nipple, and so

Hendren again had no choice but to improvise. After closing the old bladder outlet, he transformed the bowel-vagina he had created before into a catheterizable conduit—a new outlet that was situated somewhat higher, and would accept a catheter (inserted through a stoma) to empty her bladder. Having used her previous bowel-vagina for the conduit, Hendren made a new vagina from a fresh length of small bowel. With yet another fresh piece, he further enlarged her bladder. She would leave the hospital dry, for the first time in her life. Her parents were pleased that Hendren had persisted and that they had kept faith in him.

Chapter 24

Nine-fifteen P.M.

With a sharp-pointed hemostat, Hardy Hendren pierces Lucy Moore's lower left abdominal wall. He pulls a tubular rubber drain through the hole, leaving the business end inside near her new rectum and vagina, where serum can accumulate as her body heals. The drain will give fluids an easy way out and prevent their building up in the pelvis, a development that could cause an abscess, anathema to the surgeon and a threat to the patient.

Before he closes her belly, Hendren carefully inspects Lucy's bowels. He wants to be sure their color is good. He wants to be sure that in all the activity inside his patient, there hasn't been an inadvertent twist that could block her intestine, which would mean a return to the OR at the worst possible time: when her body was trying to recover from the shock of an operation of this magnitude.

"I'm laying the bowel back in serially," he announces. He expects his residents and visitors to pay particular attention. This little step saves lives.

He starts at the top of the small intestine, at the juncture of bowel to stomach. With both hands, he traces the bowel downward, feeling for crimps, laying it into the abdomen according to the correctly coiled course. He could be a conscientious fire fighter, winding and examining a length of hose. Not all surgeons are so finicky when closing a belly. Some just stuff the intestines in. Some have never heard of such a thing, laying bowel back in serially. Other surgeons believe Hendren's method is superfluous, the sort of thing only the most nit-picking, old-fashioned kind of guy would waste his time on. But Hendren has seen the results of bowels carelessly stuffed into bellies.

It was Max Grob, the Father of Pediatric Surgery in Switzerland, who inspired Hendren to examine the intestine so carefully before closing up the patient. One of Grob's favorite subjects was malrotation of the bowel, a congenital intestinal defect about which he'd written extensively. In 1970, the year after Hendren had separated the Siamese twins, Grob and his wife were houseguests of the Hendrens on a visit to Boston. On the day he arrived, a baby with a malrotation was admitted to the Massachusetts General Hospital. Would the distinguished Professor Grob be willing to operate on the baby with us? Hendren asked. It would be very instructive to see the Swiss master work. Grob said he would be flattered. And that was the day Hendren learned the procedure he has honored with a name: the Grob maneuver.

That was also the day Hendren learned from Grob the virtues of a midline incision: opening a patient down the exact center of the abdomen. Hendren had been schooled in the transverse incision— side to side—and the so-called paramedian incision, parallel to the midline and theoretically stronger when closed. The midline incision is more sparing of muscle, Grob asserted. Since then, Hendren has always used it and has taught his residents to do the same.

Whenever I watch anybody operate, I can learn something, good or bad. Surgery is such a synthesis from so many people.

In the summer of 1962, the Hendrens went to London. For three months he was visiting surgeon at the Hospital for Sick Children, Great Ormond Street. He worked with David Waterston, and from him Hendren learned a new way of holding scissors: across the palm. Making use of his free time, what little there was of it, Hendren spent hours in the Hunterian Museum, which commemorates the contributions of John Hunter, the eighteenth-century British surgeon and anatomist. Hunter, born in Scotland, was an extraordinary scientist, a short but strong man who got by on four or five hours' sleep. In an era when ribaldry was a popular characteristic, Hunter was a temperate man, a gifted storyteller who used anecdotes to illustrate scientific points. His medical interests spanned the anatomical spectrum: from the digestive and circulatory systems to nerves and the reproductive organs. His philosophy, like that of other great innovators, was simple: don't stand still; take chances.

"In pursuing any subject," Hunter wrote some two hundred years ago, "most things come to light as it were by accident, that is, many things arise out of investigation that were not at first conceived, and even misfortunes in experiments have brought things to our knowledge that were not and probably could not have been previously conceived."

The large intestine—the colon—is not as long or tortuous as the small. A visual check is sufficient for Hendren to see that Lucy's colon is in good shape. He does not need to touch every inch.

He examines her bladder, the blood supply to her new vagina, the configuration of her ovaries, Fallopian tube, and uterus. Satisfied that everything is in good order, that the belly can be safely closed, he removes the ring. The edges of the wound close back in. Using a retractor at each end of the incision, Hendren's residents straighten it. He draws the edges together to be certain they fit, which they do. With four layers of sutures, Hendren rejoins the peritoneum and fascia, muscle, fat, and, finally, skin. He lavishes special attention on the skin, joining the edges with a subcuticular closure—a closure just beneath the surface. A subcuticular closure, made with absorbable sutures, gives a finer scar and avoids something children fear almost as much as needles: taking out the stitches, a week or more later. Hendren could close the skin with staples, but he does not like them. He thinks a subcuticular closure looks better.

Hendren is tired.

If he chose to pay attention to it, he could hear a part of his mind urging him to hurry up, to get the job done and get out of this confining, bright, windowless room. But he doesn't listen to that voice. "Dorothy and I could set track records," Hendren has said, and maybe that would be OK on some kinds of surgery—surgery in which the prime objective is only to remove something, for example. But when organs are being repaired, the goal is accuracy, and accuracy is not always consistent with speed. "A case like Lucy's," Hendren says, "doesn't allow you to put in a single mistaken stitch. Not a one. One bad stitch in here, and you have a leak.

One leak, and you can have a dead patient—or a hell of a complicated, protracted course."

Lucy's belly is closed.

Looks pretty good, Hendren thinks. *But you can never tell what a scar will eventually look like. Some become a hairline. Others become prominent and quite raised.*

The chief asks Jeff Steinberg to apply Steri-Strips to seal the skin edges. Steinberg gets to work.

Over on his stool, Jin-Cherng Sheu, Hendren's Taiwanese visitor, is getting nervous. Midnight is approaching, and in Puritan Boston the subways and trolley lines close at one A.M. on weekends. Sheu knows the ribbing visitors may get from the chief if they try to sneak away before a case is completed, but what can he do? He has no car. Taxis are expensive. He's got to get home!

"I take subway," he says softly.

Hendren hears him and is concerned. At this hour, people have been stabbed, robbed, shot, raped, and murdered not far from the hospital. Catching a trolley means a three-block walk, almost certainly followed by a long wait.

"I'll drive you," Hendren tells Sheu.

"A subway at this hour is not safe," Enos says.

"No problem," Sheu says. "I take subway."

"No, no!" Hendren protests.

"We'd feel terrible if anything happened," Enos says.

"Subway OK."

"You're not taking the subway," Hendren says firmly. "No subway."

Sheu gives up. There's no arguing with the chief. Reluctantly, he'll accept a ride.

Veronica Miler comes into Room 17 to assist with the turn.

"This is going to be OK," Hendren says. "Every time she goes to the bathroom, she's going to say: 'Thank you, Veronica!' "

"No, she's not," says Miler. "She's going to say, 'Thank you, Dr. Hendren, *sir!*' "

The turn is smooth. Hendren paints more Betadine on Lucy's bottom, then slides a Hegar dilator into her colon-vagina. Lucy's urethra is completed, and her vagina is completed, but behind them is a still-open wound. Sticking out is the free end of Lucy's large intestine. The rectum and anus will be located in this last part of the open wound, but first Hendren must fashion a perineal body: that narrow but necessary bridge of skin and muscle that separates the vagina from the anus in the normal girl. He cannot simply bring the two sides of the wound together. How he makes the perineal body will affect the front of the anal sphincter and the entrance to Lucy's vagina, the appearance of her labia. Hendren places several traction sutures through the labia and hands the sutures over to his residents, who hold them until the labia have opened like a lily in bloom. Hendren sews the wound together to make the perineal body.

"Lower the table please," Hendren says. "OK. Lower it a bit more. OK. That's good."

He kneads Lucy's lower colon between his fingers. The last three inches are too thick and too dilated to function as a normal rectum and he cuts it off. Another specimen for the pathologist. Now he's back to good colon, colon with normal caliber and a good blood supply. Colon that is better for fashioning an anus.

Guided by the green markings he made on the skin, Hendren positions the colon in the precise center of muscle. The colon's lower edge is resting against the perineal body, and Hendren anchors it there with several stitches. But he does not close the skin around the colon yet.

"That's right in the middle, isn't it?" he says. "All right, let me have a Hegar. What do you think, Dorothy, a twelve?"

Enos dips the right size dilator into mineral oil and hands it to Hendren. He slips it into the colon. With toothpick and brilliant green dye, he marks an inch-long inverted V on the colon's upper surface.

"I'm going to take it right up to the coccyx," he says.

"Taper it?"

"Yes. It's too big."

Tapering—narrowing the end of Lucy's rectum—will make for a snugger anus, which will improve the chance of continence. With a pair of scissors, Hendren cuts out the V. He sews the edges together, the dilator still in place to prevent making it too narrow. Then he tacks the upper lip of the rectum to muscle and skin. Two inches of wound remain. He closes it, taking care to fit the muscle properly around Lucy's anus—taking care to adjust the tension so that when he's done, Lucy even has a proper cleft between the cheeks of her bottom.

"Big wet, please, Dorothy," Hendren says.

Enos dips a large sponge into a tray of water and hands it to her boss, who washes the baby.

Twenty to midnight.

Lucy's anatomy looks astonishingly normal: urethra *where it belongs*, vagina, *where nature should have put it*, anus, *perfectly positioned*.

"It's a very good one," Hendren says. *A tough one, but I'm pleased.*

Hendren inserts a drain into Lucy's rectum. Another goes into her vagina. With a couple of quick stitches, he sews each in place. He places a dressing over Lucy's bottom, and for the final time she is turned, onto her back.

"Sponge count?" Enos says to Carol DeLash, the circulating nurse who's pulling the graveyard shift tonight. Jean Kiernan, the nurse on three-to-eleven, has gone home.

Sponges are dispensed from sterile packages of ten, and every time a new package is opened, the previous ten are counted. After being counted, nine dirty sponges are tied with the tenth and left in a pile on a table. Working by this decimal system, the circulators keep a running tally.

Occasionally, preoccupied with other business, circulators lose track. The decimal system breaks down, and at operation's end the count is off. Except for emergencies, nothing energizes an OR like a missing sponge, which can cause an abscess or block an intestine if left inside a patient. The circulating nurse goes on the hunt. Visitors and anesthesiologists join in. Hendren usually tolerates about three or four minutes of this before he breaks sterility and joins in, too. Onto his hands and knees he will go, looking under the table, under Enos's instrument trays, sifting through the bags of dirty laundry and trash. Hendren has a nose for a missing sponge, and only a novice would accept his wager that the newcomer can't find it first. More often than not, Hendren finds it in one of the trash bags. In his career, only once can he remember ever closing with a sponge inside a patient. It was almost forty years ago, and he was chief surgical resident at the Massachusetts General Hospital, and he'd operated on a man to remove a cancerous lung. He'd closed the chest when the male nurse who'd done the sponge count announced they were one short, and they'd looked everywhere. It had to be in the patient; it just had to be. "I'll buy you a case of beer if there's a sponge in there," Hendren said. But the sponge eluded them. Hendren had no choice but to reopen his patient—and there it was, in the apex of the man's chest. Grateful to have got it, Hendren bought the nurse his case of beer.

As Enos observes, DeLash counts: ". . . five, six, seven, eight, nine, *ten*."

Every sponge is accounted for tonight.

Hendren, Enos and Miler uncover Lucy. Miler removes the plastic bag that's encased her head to prevent heat loss and peels the tape off her eyes, which have remain closed, the corneas safe from drying. Lucy's face is swollen, her hair a matted, soggy mess, her skin muddy brown from the Betadine. She is unconscious and may remain so for a day or more. But she's definitely a little girl, anatomically correct now, all except for the two stomata Hendren will remove in the spring, stomata that for the time being will necessitate continued wearing of a bag. Hendren takes another big wet and cleans Lucy further. He puts a dressing over her belly.

"May I have some one-inch tape, please?" he says.

He secures the dressing and the catheter coming from her urethra. Nothing left now but to transfer her to her bed and take her up to intensive care.

"Have you got a nice warm blanket we can put the baby on?" Hendren asks. DeLash fetches one from the blanket warmer. Hendren lifts Lucy and lays her on it.

"She says, 'I feel better already!' " Hendren says.

Miler and company roll Lucy's bed to the OR table. A portable pulse oximeter and oxygen tank are placed at the foot of the bed, along with Lucy's X rays and chart and the post-op orders Steinberg wrote. An IV pole is hung. Lucy is disconnected from the anesthesia machine. Heggeness breathes for her by squeezing an ambu bag, which will substitute for the OR ventilator until she's connected to one in intensive care. Wires and tubes are sorted out, and on the count of three Lucy is slid from table to bed.

Hendren removes his gown, headlamp, and loupes and fishes around on the side counter for his eyeglasses. "That's a hard operation," he says to himself.

Hendren finds pen and paper. Sometimes after an operation, he will pick up the phone and dictate, entirely from memory, his operative report to a machine. But tonight, he's too tired. He will dictate Lucy's report, which will run to five single-spaced typewritten pages, on Monday. For now, he scribbles a few sentences and a diagram that will refresh his memory.

"Today's the eighteenth?" he says. His strong suit is not workaday numbers. Hendren can remember the name, school, hair color, and weight category of a wrestling opponent from half a century ago, but not always today's date or the combination to the OR locker-room lock, a number that's been unchanged for years.

"Nineteenth now," says Steinberg.

Twelve-twenty A.M., Saturday, January 19, 1991.

Sixteen hours and thirty minutes after Lucy was brought into the OR, she is wheeled out into a deserted corridor. The room empties. Hendren and Sheu are left alone.

One hundred and five regular sponges have been used on Lucy, along with thirty smaller ones known as peanuts. Five thirty-gallon plastics bags have been filled with dirty linen. Five thirty-gallon bags marked INFECTIOUS WASTE have been filled with sponges, packaging, and fluids. Four smaller bags are also full. Hundreds of instruments have been used. No one has counted every stitch, but there are easily several hundred. Taken from Lucy in Room 17 were two hundred cubic centimeters of Lucy's blood, a multicystic kidney, several inches of intestine, a malformed extra uterus, and a useless piece of ureter.

One of the nurses has left a note with the number of the Moores' hotel, next door to Children's. Given how long a case like this can go, many parents of cloaca patients wait in their hotel rather than the waiting room, a depressingly lonely place in the midnight hour.

Hendren dials. Jack comes on the line.

"Hi," Hendren says, "everything's fine. We just finished. She's going up to the intensive care unit on the fifth floor. I feel good about it . . . yes. . . . Give them about half an hour; then it'll be OK. . . . When you look down at her, don't be concerned. Number one, her face is all puffy. Number two, she's got a tube coming out of her bladder, a tube coming out of her vagina, a tube coming out of her urethra and rectum. Just don't expect her to be waving at you when you come in."

Jack asks if they will see him tonight.

"Not if I can help it," Hendren says with a weary smile. "I'll see you sometime. Righto."

Jack thanks Hendren.

"All right," Hendren says. "'Bye."

Two weeks ago, Hendren had a bad cold. He didn't cancel any cases, but he dragged himself through several days. Now, he's sniffling again. His legs are killing him. His shoulders, back, and neck hurt. So do his knees, particularly the right knee, which required arthroscopic surgery after a skiing accident in 1989. He's hungry and thirsty, and he needs to use the bathroom. He takes off his glasses, and with two tight fists he rubs and rubs until it seems he'll become a danger to his eyes.

In nineteen days, Hendren turns sixty-five.

Enos has taken care of her instruments and put away Hendren's loupes, and now she returns to fetch her boss. He puts on his glasses, stands, picks up his Nikon camera bag, and beckons to Sheu. Followed by his Taiwanese visitor and his nurse of twenty-nine years, Hendren leaves Room 17.

I feel optimistic about what we were able to do, he thinks. And then: *I wonder what Eleanor's cooked for dinner. I wonder how the war's going.*

Chapter 25

As he's leaving Children's Hospital, Hardy Hendren calls Eleanor to say he's on his way. With Sheu, he escorts Enos to her car, as he does without exception whenever it's so late. He waits to be sure her car will start, and when it does, he goes to his own. He leaves the garage and drives onto Longwood Avenue, where the only signs of life are a young doctor seeking nourishment and caffeine at Sami's twenty-four-hour restaurant. Hendren takes a right onto Brookline Avenue, which is deserted and cold. He drives fast but not recklessly. At red lights, he leaves plenty of distance between himself and the car in front, and he keeps an eye on his rearview mirror. He does not want to be boxed in, nor does he intend to become the victim of some stoplight-holdup scheme. He does not want to have to use the loaded .38-caliber revolver that he has a permit to carry and which he sometimes has in his pocket this late at night.

It is after one A.M. when Hendren finally gets to his apartment. Once upon a time, Hendren regularly made the forty-five-minute drive to his home in Duxbury. It didn't matter the hour or how long he'd been up or how tired he was. But snapping awake a split second before he would have rammed a bridge abutment in the wee hours of the morning changed his thinking.

Eleanor is cooking bacon and scrambled eggs when Hendren arrives. Bacon and eggs are quick and easy, and Hendren, whose blood cholesterol has somehow stayed abnormally low, has eaten them all his life—with gusto, just as his father did. Sometimes on a Saturday evening, Hendren will cap his day with a beer or a bourbon old-fashioned, but not on any other day, not on a Friday. He switches the bedroom TV to CNN to catch the latest on the war.

Through all the years they have been husband and wife, the Hendrens have applied to their marriage but a few simple rules. They never start or end the day without setting aside time exclusively for each other. They never go to sleep angry at each other. They never allow household tension to escalate beyond control. And they make sure to compliment each other.

Eleanor can do anything, you know. She's about the most solid human being you could ever look for: just so nice and natural and unaffected with the right sense of family and country and responsiblity and accomplishment.

Eleanor's job for many years was raising the Hendrens' five children. But even before their youngest, David, was in high school, Eleanor and her buddy Annette Browne, a mother of six, were looking ahead, toward the time when their children would be grown, toward some other big undertaking into which they could throw their energies. They came up with a clothing company, Cycle Venture, Inc., a name that was a pun on this new phase of their lives and the company's chief product, a hand-sewn skirt for bicycling, golf, or tennis. Cycle Venture got its start in 1972, when Eleanor and Annette designed identical skirts and wore them to doubles matches on the courts at The Country Club, in Brookline. Several women told them they should be in business, which is exactly what they had in mind. Eleanor and Annette put together a mailing list and a brochure, borrowed ten thousand dollars, and found professional seamstresses to make their skirt. Improving on the original design, Eleanor and Annette were soon marketing the wrapped and pleated Cycle Kilt. Eventually, L. L. Bean and Talbots were buying the kilts. In 1977, Eleanor and Annette incorporated their new company and began establishing new accounts around the country. Today, Cycle Venture has seventeen national representatives. It employs seven and annually turns out thousands of kilts, skirts, and jackets, sold in pro shops and department stores and wholesale to suppliers of tennis and field hockey teams.

The Hendrens fall asleep with the television on, but not before saying "I love you" to each other. Eleanor and Hardy have always tried to live by that rule, too. They've tried not to let a day slip without saying those three words at least once.

Sometime around three A.M., Hendren stirs. He shuts the television off and goes back to sleep.

Like those of Thomas Alva Edison, whose body seemed to have found a way around sleep, the rhythms of Hendren's life are beyond the bounds of normal. The calendar and clock have not given Hendren enough time to accomplish all he wants to accomplish. As a surgeon, he is controlled and methodical, but there is an urgency driving his work that he can answer only with more work.

Friends frequently beseech him to slow down. "Dr. Hendren, one of these days you're going to drop if you don't take care of yourself," an OR nurse will say.

To which he will invariably reply, "Don't forget, there's a great big rest at the end!"

In 1991, Hendren allowed himself a week of vacation, but he timed it to coincide with the jury duty he'd been notified that he might be called for. When he wasn't called, he scheduled a couple of small operations, caught up on his paperwork, polished his bowel-nipple manuscript, and visited the dentist to have several of his teeth capped, a repair that consumed six hours over three sessions. It was August. When Hurricane Bob walloped Boston that month, Hendren, assured that the emergency generators at Children's would deliver uninterrupted power to the OR, went ahead with his scheduled cases, although nearly all of his colleagues canceled theirs.

The only conditions that have ever slowed Hendren down are sickness and exhaustion, rare but not unexampled. Lucy Moore's surgery took place during such a knockout period, a period when the chief's schedule and a lingering cold combined to beat him down. During the preceding week, he put in sixteen-hour days. He worked the entire weekend after Lucy's surgery. The next week brought another round of sixteen-hour days, capped the following Friday by another major reconstruction, one that went twenty-one and a half hours. By Monday, January 28, having averaged no more than four hours' sleep for more than two weeks, Hendren was fatigued. *I shouldn't operate like this*, he thought. *I don't have my edge.* He had another difficult reconstruction booked for that day, but he would not do it. Apologizing, he told the parents that he would rather deal with their disappointment than what could happen if he was too tired to do a good job. He canceled the case. *And good thing.* When he got to it, a month later, he was in the operating room eighteen hours straight.

At about the time Hendren was making Lucy Moore into a girl with the potential for having children of her own someday, his reasearch assistant, Pam Spinney, was beginning a project. She was setting out to track down each of the 105 cloaca patients Hendren had at the time, some of whom, in need of medical attention no more, were no longer in contact with him. She was attempting to see how they had made out as they moved from childhood into the age when sexual relations and reproduction joined continence and appearance as concerns of the cloacal patient.

Of Hendren's 105 patients, Spinney succeeded in tracking down 98. They ranged in age from infancy to thirty-two years old. Twenty were from Massachusetts, with the remainder from twenty-four other states and twelve foreign nations. Sixty-five were primary cases—patients for whom no reconstruction had been attempted before Hendren operated. Of the forty secondary cases, the extent of earlier surgical intervention was largely limited to attempts at bringing the rectum through to the bottom. These efforts, well-intentioned as they may have been, complicated Hendren's job.

Constant wetting remained a problem for only three patients, for all of whom Hendren planned further work. Forty-seven patients had normal bowel control; another twenty-seven remained continent with the use of a soapsuds enema every day or every other day; and only seven could be said to be truly incontinent. (Of the remaining seventeen, some had occasional soiling while others were too soon out of surgery to accurately assess.) Eight patients who had reached adulthood reported satisfactory intercourse. Two patients who had married were not having intercourse, in one instance because of psychological problems unrelated to anatomy. In the other case, the woman had married a man whose penis was defective. Hendren planned to repair it and also enlarge the woman's vagina, which he discovered during examination was not sufficiently large.

Two of Hendren's cloaca patients delivered babies by cesarean section. One was Elizabeth, a woman who was born in the 1960s, a time when her abnormalities still defied most who had ideas of correcting them. She did not have an anus. She did not appear to have a vagina or a urethra, only a single opening on her bottom, into which her urinary and reproductive tracts emptied. Somewhere deep inside her, her rectum was connected to her vagina. Doctors at the small-town hospital where she was born were baffled, and in their bafflement they broke a cardinal rule of good medicine: they attempted to fix a problem without understanding what it was. They took the newborn to the operating room, and they cut into her pelvis through her single opening, apparently in an attempt to find her rectum. Failing in their hunt, they committed another blunder. Closing their incision, they sutured Elizabeth's bladder outlet and vagina shut. She still had that single opening, but only at the surface. Now, feces and urine had no way to escape her. Now, she was dying.

I don't have a clue as to what they were thinking, thought the surgeon who would operate on her twenty years later, Hardy Hendren.

Elizabeth's life was saved at a larger hospital when separate incisions were made in her belly to allow feces and urine to escape. Later, an emiment surgeon built an anus and made an opening so that she could urinate. Her bags, at least, were gone. Elizabeth would not completely grasp the perversity of her anatomy until the first time she attempted to have sex, but there was no hiding the wrongness of her rectum. The eminent surgeon had made an anus, all right, but it wasn't in the center of the sphincter muscle and she had constant fecal soiling. All through grammar school, all through high school, Elizabeth had accidents. She had accidents on the playground, in the classroom, at home, on the softball field. Sometimes, she'd make it to the bathroom before anyone knew. Sometimes, she was too late.

"You're only being lazy," her mother would say.

"But, Ma, I'm trying," Elizabeth would say, "I'm really trying. I can't help it! Honest, I can't!"

But her mother didn't believe her. Her mother spanked her and made her wash her panties in the toilet. Her mother made her wear diapers one time when she was thirteen years old.

"I didn't have any friends," she told Hendren in 1987, the year she finally got to Boston. "I don't like myself very much, not at all. I mean, people are like, 'Oh, you look nice' or 'You have a nice body,' and I just—I don't like myself. And that's wrong, because you can't have anybody like you until you like yourself. But I know what my body's gone through, and it's hard to deal with, especially going through what my Mom and Dad's done to me growing up."

Elizabeth had married by the time she came to Hendren, but because of her anatomy, her marriage could not be consummated. A man could not get inside her. "This young lady represents a very formidable surgical problem," Hendren wrote of Elizabeth, cloaca number 74 in his series. She needed a urethra. Her vagina needed to be freed up, pulled down, and put in the normal position. Her anus needed to be moved. In an eleven-hour operation that November, Hendren accomplished everything.

A month after returning home, during which time the tissues had had time to heal, Elizabeth and her husband consummated their marriage. Elizabeth became pregnant but miscarried two months later. In April 1988, she was pregnant again. The following January, the daughter she'd wanted since she was young was delivered by cesarean section. Her daughter was a normal girl, a healthy girl, smart and inquisitive. Except for the scars, Elizabeth's anatomy was similar to that of any other woman's. She was continent, although she still soiled once in a great while, and Hendren would need another try before she would be completely normal in that respect, too.

"I have a beautiful baby girl," Elizabeth wrote to Spinney. "She just turned two in January! Every day of my life, when I look at my daughter, I just thank Dr. Hendren so much for making this all possible! She is such a smart baby, she has a *very* large vocabulary for her age! I'm sorry to go on about her, it's just I'm so grateful!"

Although it is customary for chiefs at Children's to leave at age sixty-six, no one is trying to push Hendren out, as Robert E. Gross was pushed out when he was sixty-six. Hendren intends to continue as long as his health and vigor will allow, probably about five or more years. When asked about his decision to keep working, he makes reference to a passage from the book of Matthew, chapter 25, verses 14–30. It is the parable of the servants who are entrusted with their master's money. The two who are given the greater sums invest the money, and their sums are doubled; the third servant hides the money he is given. And at last their master comes to settle his accounts with them.

And so he that had received five talents came and brought another five talents, saying, Lord, thou deliveredst unto me five talents; behold, I have gained beside them five talents more." His lord said unto him, Well done, thou good and faithful servant; thou hast been faithful over a few things, I will make thee ruler over many things; enter thou into the joy of thy lord. He also that had received two talents came and said, Lord, thou deliveredst unto me two talents; behold, I have gained two other talents beside them. His lord said unto him, "Well done, good and faithful servant; thou hast been faithful over a few things, I will make thee ruler over many things; enter thou into the joy of thy lord. Then he which had received the one talent came and said, Lord, I knew thee that thou art an hard man, reaping where thou hast not sown, and gathering where thou hast not strawed. And I was afraid, and went and hid thy talent in the earth; lo, there thou hast that is thine. His lord answered and said unto him, Thou wicked and slothful servant. . . .

Having slept five hours after rebuilding Lucy Moore, Hendren is awake by six-thirty A.M.

By eight, he is at the office, going over the details of the talk on cloacal exstrophy he is giving this morning to a gathering of physicians at the Harvard Medical School's Countway Library of Medicine. An hour and a half later, after speaking and fielding the inevitable questions, he is back at the office to meet with a urology resident, Bill Larchian, who is seeking career advice. When the meeting is over, Hendren slips onto the wards to make his rounds. Lucy is in intensive care, still heavily sedated and on a ventilator. Hendren fills in the Moores on the details of her operation and sees his other patients and their parents. Back at the office, he works, alone, on papers and a book in progress until well after dark. *Always behind.* Tomorrow, he will be in the office again, from two P.M. until eleven P.M. And on Monday, Martin Luther King Day, he will work from nine A.M. to seven-thirty P.M.

But now it's time for a break. Time for Duxbury.

He locks his office door and walks down the corridor toward the elevator, which he will take tonight rather than the stairs, his customary means of leaving the building. The lights are low, the TV off, the waiting room empty. Even busy hospitals have their quiet interludes, and a Saturday evening in the middle of January is one of them. Hendren does not wait for his car to warm. Moving as fast as conditions allow, he pulls onto Longwood Avenue and drives south, zigzagging along an elaborate shortcut he's blazed over the years to circumvent the Southeast Expressway, which is snarled at most hours. On Route 3, it's a straight shot south. On his car phone, he apprises Eleanor of his whereabouts. Then he calls Kansas City and talks to his mother. Every Saturday, no matter where he is, he updates Mrs. W. Hardy Hendren, Jr., who has followed her son's career as if it were her own. Just before Plymouth, Hendren leaves the highway and heads past frozen cranberry bogs to Duxbury, a town married to the sea for almost four centuries.

Since Sandy was a toddler, the Hendrens have been in love with the water. For many years, Hendren's parents rented a cottage in Wareham, near Cape Cod, and it was there that Eleanor and the children spent some of their summers, there that Hendren sneaked when he could. Later, Hardy and Eleanor bought a second home in Duxbury, which the family used in the summers and rented out for the rest of the year. In 1976, confident that Hardy was cured of cancer, they bought the home in Duxbury, where they have lived since. Built in 1901, the house is white shingle with a slate roof and a patio along the back, the side that faces the Atlantic Ocean. It was built on the highest spot of land around, which is not high by any absolute standard but high enough to keep the cellar dry during hurricanes and nor'easters. There is a flagpole on the lawn, which ends at a seawall that drops off to rocky beach. The Hendrens have a pier and an early-twentieth-century boathouse, recently restored to perfection by Frank Gigliotti, a craftsman whose skill with wood, metal, and mortar Hendren greatly admires. Someday, the Hendrens may convert the boathouse to guest quarters, but for now the biggest concern is the pigeons that roost on the roof, making a terrible mess. Hendren hates pigeons. For a while he was plugging them with a shotgun, but then he discovered he was putting holes in the roof's copper flashing. Ever ingenious in his solutions to problems, Hendren switched to a .22-caliber rifle with scope and short-range hollow-point bullets.

Off the top of his head, Hendren could not tell you how many rooms his house has, only that there are enough to sleep four sons and four daughters-in-law, seven grandchildren, and Barbara Frain, the former nun who was then living with the Hendrens, minding the place while they were in Boston during the week.

Hardy stops outside the driveway gate, secured with an old fan belt. Only one vehicle is parked in the drive tonight: the red Toyota pickup truck Eleanor bought him as a Christmas gift one year, used mostly to take the trash to the dump or drive to the beach. He swings the gate open, drives into the garage, and shuts off the ignition. The Hendren dogs, a German shepherd and a black Labrador on her last legs, greet him.

Eleanor's in the kitchen when he opens the back door.

"Momma," he says, "I'm home."

Chapter 26

The Moores see their daughter for the first time at twelve-fifty A.M. Saturday, half an hour after she left the OR.

There is nothing pretty or dainty about Lucy, Beth and Jack's little Lucy, unless it's that faintest trace of a smile that seems to flicker across her lips every now and again. Lucy has been washed, but her face and ankles and wrists are swollen, her eyes are shut, and she is not responsive to anything or anyone around her. Being in the intensive care unit of a children's hospital is not an uplifting experience. Almost no patient here would last more than a few minutes without machines. Some, even with the machines, don't get out alive. Intensive care is a beeping, hissing, hushed place—a medical war room where crisis management is the daily drill.

Beth and Jack have seen it all before.

And as they get approval to see their daughter, they're not taking in the technology. The time to be shocked by that is long past. The Moores are quietly rejoicing, for once again Lucy has safely been there and back.

"You can kiss her if you'd like," a nurse says.

"As if I needed an invitation!" says Beth.

Beth and Jack bend over their baby, bestowing on her the lightest of kisses, whispering wordlessly into her ear, smoothing her brow, stroking those chubby forearms of hers, so stubbornly unyielding of blood.

Since nine o'clock yesterday morning, the Moores have been

.

shiftless, wearing a beeper and wandering Boston in an effort to
unburden their minds, as if such a crazy thing were possible at a
time when a man they barely know has their baby in pieces in a
room they are forbidden to see. They have window-shopped, and
they have eaten, and they have come back to Children's, and they
have gone to their hotel room to try in vain to sleep. They have
spoken on the phone to their two other children, to their parents,
and they have wished desperately they were all back in Florida,
sunny Florida, not nomads in this city locked in the dead of a New
England winter.

Finally I can believe she's not going to die, Jack thinks as he
kisses the new person Hardy Hendren has made. Beth is thinking
about the possibility of Lucy's having children someday. Beth assumed Hendren would be able to fix Lucy's urinary tract, but she
had not dared to hope he would be able to put together a reproductive system, too.

That's what's unbelievable about all this, she thinks.

For Lucy, the next six days are days in limbo.

Try as they might, the staff cannot wean her from the ventilator.
Their first attempt is on Saturday, post-op day one, the day patients
recovering from even the longest surgeries ordinarily can begin to
breathe on their own again. Lucy's endotracheal tube, which connects her lungs to the machine, is slowly removed—extubated.
Lucy coughs and flails, and her attempt to breathe independently
collapses in blue-faced failure. Her airway, the passage by which air
enters and leaves her lungs, is badly swollen, is too narrow to
support unassisted respiration. The tube is reinserted quickly. Second and third attempts at extubation come on Tuesday, with the
same results. Lucy's medication is adjusted in an attempt to bring
down the swelling. After the fourth unsuccessful try, on Wednesday, a smaller endotracheal tube, hopefully less irritating to her
airway's delicate mucous membranes, is inserted.

Lucy, meanwhile, is in a chemical haze. Morphine is sitting on her
pain, and a sedative is preventing her from thrashing wildly, which
would be a disaster considering the wires and tubes needed to keep
her alive. The point is to dull her, not to put her out of commission
entirely. Whenever the heavy-duty stuff is rolled out, it's best to use
as little as possible to get the job done. But whatever it takes to
ensure relative comfort, Lucy will get.

Not so many years ago, she wouldn't have. The prevailing view in medicine was that infants and children should not receive the same consideration regarding pain that was accorded adult patients. At some institutions, although not at Children's, that attitude carried over into the OR, where surgeons routinely operated on infants with little—or even no—anesthesia. Many reasons were cited. "Children don't have well-developed nervous systems and therefore don't experience pain" was the most common. "Children can too easily become addicted to painkillers" was another. "Pain builds character" was a third. Perhaps most widely expressed was the belief that medications to dull pain would produce complications in children, especially in small children, that adults would not experience. Long a neglected area of research, pain in children only recently became the subject of numerous studies. Researchers at Children's and elsewhere now have demonstrated beyond any doubt that even in utero, babies respond to—and experience—pain. They have shown that children, like adults, rarely become addicted to painkillers when they are used for their intended purpose. Far from building character, the stress associated with pain can complicate postoperative healing, studies have shown.

For six days, Jack and Beth do the best they can. They tie a balloon to Lucy's bed, tuck Lucy's favorite stuffed doggie in with her, cover their baby with the quilt Beth made—attempting to create "a sense of home," as Jack calls it. They prop Lucy's radio–tape player next to her pillow and softly play lullabies. "I don't know how she'll feel about these tapes when she gets home," says Beth, "the association." Sometimes, Lucy sleeps. Sometimes, that flicker of a smile. And sometimes, her eyes well with tears, her body stiffens, and her head bobs from side to side. Jack and Beth wonder if their ministrations are having the intended effect—to reassure and comfort—or are only serving as a cruel tease to their Lucy, who surely is still there somewhere beneath the surface of this netherworld.

"If we can just get through the next month . . ." Beth says.

On Thursday, post-op day six, Lucy is given dexamethasone, an anti-inflammatory drug. For the fifth time, her endotracheal tube is slowly removed. Through a stethoscope, Andrew T. Strigenz, an anesthesiologist who's been helping with Lucy's care, listens to her lungs; they sound raspy but not dangerously so. A mask is placed over her mouth so that she can breathe moistened oxygen laced with another anti-inflammatory medication that should help keep the airway open. A nurse threads a small catheter down her throat to elicit a good, strong cough. Coughing helps move mucus, which can impede breathing.

"OK, sweetie," the nurse, Diane McAleer, says. "Oh, I know. Say, 'Ouch, meanie!' There. Give a good cough."

Lucy coughs and cries.

"Real tears," Beth says. She's holding Lucy's hand. "Oh my darling! I love you so much! I love you so much!"

The minutes pass. After an hour, Lucy's breathing is labored, but she's making it.

"She looks a little better," Strigenz says.

"I think she sounds better," McAleer says.

Two hours pass.

"That's the longest she's gone," says McAleer. "She looks good."

On Thursday night, Beth has a dream. In it, Lucy's trip to Boston has not had a happy ending. She has not come home a normal little girl. She has not come home at all. She has checked out of Children's by way of the morgue. . . .

Beth flies awake. She does not remember details of the dream, only that *Lucy's dead. My precious little girl, dead.* She snaps on the light. Jack has returned to Florida to be with the other kids, and she is alone in a room in a hotel. When she left her this evening, Lucy was fine. *But Lucy is not fine now,* her mind is screaming at her.

Lucy's dead.

Beth dials intensive care.

"Mrs. Moore," the nurse says over the phone, "everything's fine."

"Are you sure?"

"I'm sure."

"Oh, thank God!"

The next morning, Friday, January 25, one week after Hendren's reconstruction, Lucy is transferred from intensive care back to Nine West. The swelling is receding, leaving proof that all along there really was a Lucy face beneath the puffiness. Theoretically, now that her endotracheal tube is gone, Lucy could engage in her baby talk and laugh. But she does neither. She is reasonably alert, she is processing everything around her, but her face betrays only one emotion: a sort of sullen displeasure, as if she were angry with Beth.

As if she blames me for all this, Beth can't help but think.

After her last major surgery, Aldo Castaneda's heart repair, Lucy's personality disappeared. Gone without a trace, as if surgically removed. Normally a smiling, giggling baby, for weeks she was a grim caricature of herself. She refused to laugh or smile. She refused even to make eye contact with members of her family. If Beth had been forced to make the diagnosis, it would have been clinical depression.

"My goal is to make you laugh by Tuesday," Beth says when Lucy is settled back on Nine West.

She gets right to work.

For the next who-knows-how-long, Lucy's world will be a stainless steel crib, and while it will be a prison, Beth won't let it look like one. She puts up balloons, tapes to the rails the get-well cards that have started piling in, and arranges stuffed animals. She puts Madeline, a doll with a realistic appendectomy scar, within Lucy's reach. She puts Lucy's play-doctor kit in the crib and lines up her books.

"You can develop your vocabulary this month because you're not developing your muscles," Beth says.

Perched on a stool that brings her to Lucy's eye level, Beth reads to her daughter. Her first selection is a book that Beth, day-care center director, made before leaving Florida. *Who Loves Lucy?* is the title on the cover, a sheet of red construction paper that features Lucy's picture. Inside are pictures of her family, a picture of Mickey Mouse.

"Who loves Lucy?" Beth reads as she flips through the pages. "Daddy loves Lucy. James loves Lucy. Mommy loves Lucy. Mary loves Lucy. Mickey loves Lucy. We all love Lucy!"

Lucy doesn't smile. She doesn't laugh. But after repeatedly pulling away, repeatedly reacting to Mom as if she were some loathsome stranger, she finally allows Beth the privilege of planting a single kiss on her cheek.

The day-to-day management of Lucy's postoperative care falls to her parents, nurses, and residents. Hendren gets frequent briefings on her care, sometimes in a phone call to his OR, and each evening, when the chief resident, Jay Schnitzer, drops by his office for the daily update on all patients on Hendren's surgical service. But during Lucy's stay, Hendren will actually lay eyes on her only occasionally.

Not everyone sings the praises of this system.

"A doctor should spend more time at bedside," some nurses and parents—a minority—have complained. "Since when does healing stop at the operating table?" "Who does he think he is, this W. Hardy Hendren the Third, M.D.?" "What we'd really like to know is just where is he all this time, anyway? No one could possibly spend *that* much time in an operating room!"

Access is an issue not only to those in-house. Whenever Hendren's patients and their families get together, stories of efforts to reach him are invariably swapped: stories of calls not immediately returned, of letters that take weeks to turn around, of strategies to pierce the defense thrown up by Hendren's staff. The wall, some have called it—the wall, whose function is to screen the constant bombardment of Hendren so that what gets through is that which only the chief must settle personally.

"I realize how busy you are and appreciate your taking the time to read this letter," wrote one father of a young girl Hendren had rebuilt. "I'm sure that I am just one of hundreds of patients who bother you with their child's problems but I am concerned about my little girl and want her to have the best medical care, which I feel only you can provide. I have tried calling you at your office several times but have had no luck in reaching you, and I don't want to bother you at home because your only time to rest is at home and you don't get much of that, I'm sure." The father ended with his phone number and an invitation to call collect, "anytime you are free."

Hendren is surprisingly sensitive to this criticism. He repeatedly apologizes for being so busy. Repeatedly, he explains his work ethic: that his talents are best utilized in the OR, not on the ward, that every hour at bedside is an hour lost at tableside. As for post-op care—well, Children's has an outstanding staff, he explains. His residents are the best young surgeons in the world, and it isn't always necessary to deal personally with the chief. When it is, there are ways. Dropping by his office early in the morning before he takes off for the OR is one way. Dropping by on a Saturday, when he's usually busy with a paper or paperwork, is also a way. For outpatients, calling his home early on Sundays is a way. His answering service puts through calls to him whatever the hour, seven days a week, and he never signs off call when he's in Massachusetts. His card has his home phone number on it, and when he hands it out, he encourages families to take advantage of his numbers if they have a question or a problem.

Most understand. "I don't care about the social aspects. I just want him to fix my kid" is how one mother put it. "We appreciate the man and the skill and accept the fact that he's usually in the OR, not bedside," Beth writes on the Patient and Parent Survey.

What Hendren doesn't advertise is that on occasion he's paid travel costs for those who have not had the money to come to Boston or that on his out-of-town trips he typically sets aside time in other cities to see patients, thus sparing them the time and expense of coming to Children's for a checkup. He does not make a big deal of the times he's opened his house to patients convalescing after surgery. Hendren cottons to parents who have persevered in the struggle to see sons and daughters through extraordinarily difficult times. He knows, from his own Sandy, the strength they have summoned.

He saw this strength in Susan, the mother of George, the boy from west of the Mississippi River who came to Hendren with a very scarred urinary system. George's operation took place in December 1990, but he was still in Children's that March. George's tissues were healing slowly, and Hendren was having trouble catheterizing the boy. One day, he brought George into the OR and electrically cut some scar tissue from his bladder outlet to clear the way. Finally, success! When he was done, Hendren had Susan suit up, and he brought her in to teach her how to catheterize, a skill she would need at home. She caught on easily. Hendren told her to wait in the hall while they woke George.

A few minutes later, when Hendren left the OR, Susan was in tears. Her youngest son had flown east to be with her, she explained through sobs. They were staying at her in-laws, but the house was small, and there had been mounting tension and bickering. Susan went to her parents, but yesterday tests had disclosed that her father had terminal cancer. Today, Susan's own mother told her they could not continue to stay with them.

"I'm sorry to be like this," Susan said. "It's just that every-thing—"

"Shh," Hendren said. "You're a very strong woman." He hugged her. "Sometimes what we need is a good cry," he said. "Go ahead. Let it all out."

When Susan had cried herself out, Hendren called Barbara Cos-grove in his office and asked her to arrange accommodations at Gardner House, which has rooms that Children's provides at low cost to needy families.

Slowly at first but soon with speed, Lucy returns.

On her second day back on Nine West, she takes her first sips of water. On her third day, she is taking fruit juice. On Sunday, January 27, she takes four ounces of formula. By Monday, she's moved on to Cheerios, vanilla yogurt, and nibbles of an egg-salad sandwich. Her urine output, an indicator of kidney function, is satisfactory. Her bowels are back in action, and Beth is busy once again changing her bag, which she will not need after Hendren's next operation, scheduled for spring. When Lucy's bandages from the surgery are changed, the wounds are clean, dry, and infection free. She's healing very nicely.

On Monday, Beth finally gets that smile from her girl.

"I'm not going to be satisfied until I get a laugh!" she says. "Give me a kiss! I love your kisses! One more kiss! Thank you!"

Tuesday is the changing of the guard: Jack back from Florida, Beth headed down for a week. Lucy is able to leave her crib and be wheeled into the playroom and up and down the halls in one of the hospital's custom-made wooden carts. Lucy the itch, the real Lucy, is back now. She's chewing on her IV line and trying to pull out her catheters and drains. She is fascinated again with her colostomy bag—she wants to pull it right off if she can! One day during Jack's watch, she succeeds. When he's out of the room, she gets her bag off, spreads its contents all over herself, and has her finger inside her stoma when Jack returns. He's used to this. Doesn't faze him at all. "She's into exploring—like any kid her age," he says as he cleans up after his daughter.

On Friday, February 1, two weeks after Lucy's reconstruction,

Hendren sneaks out of his operating room to examine her. He looks under her dressings, reviews her chart, discusses with Jack details of the spinal cord operation Mike Scott will do. On her trip back to Boston for the surgery, in April or May, Hendren will get rid of her colostomy bag. With luck, that will be the last of Lucy Moore's major surgeries.

On its preadmission authorization, the Moores' insurance company, the Prudential, has approved benefits for Lucy for nine postoperative nights. Such pronouncements alternately amuse and infuriate Hendren, who has spent three decades trying to enlighten insurers about what he does, without notable success. On the billings for all of his big cases, Hendren writes the insurance company a lengthy letter of explanation and encloses operative notes and before and after illustrations by his artist, if they have been drawn. His secretaries have spent hours on the phone trying to explain what it is the chief does. Hendren himself has made many calls. He's invited insurance executives to meet with him, invitations they have declined.

And still—letters like Lucy's preadmission authorization speak more to ignorance than the ongoing battle doctors and insurers wage in this, the era of skyrocketing health-care costs. Hendren's letter will explain the operation and conclude with a comparison even a claim processor ought to be able to understand:

> In terms of its duration and difficulty, this operation is equivalent to performing five complicated open-heart operations one right after the other, or five total hip replacement operations. A difference might be, however, that five heart or hip operations would include a lot of opening and closing time, and this baby's case is all operating time, and there are many surgeons trained to do the open-heart cases, but very few who are prepared to tackle a complex cloacal malformation. I believe that the fee listed is a fair one for this long and complex case. The nicest part of all this is that we now have a little girl who has a normal life expectancy, who should have good urinary control and good bowel control, and who probably will be able to have children as well. Please let me know if there are any questions about this claim.

Nine days!

In his experience with cloacas, Hendren has never been able to discharge a patient like Lucy in nine days. For this sort of recon-struction, a full two weeks would be a remarkably swift recovery. Twenty-one days is closer to the norm, and a month is not unusual. At least the Prudential (whose preadmission letter stated "condi-tion—digestive system" as the reason for her hospitalization) was in the ballpark. Sometimes insurers are ludicrously low. "Based on the generally accepted criteria we employ for these reviews," wrote the insurer of another of Hendren's patients before a cloacal reconstruc-tion, "we expect the length of stay will be four days."

Hendren never sends a patient like Lucy home without bringing her back to the OR for endoscopic evaluation. On Monday, Febru-ary 4, Lucy is anesthetized, and Hendren looks inside her with a scope. Her new vagina looks good, as do her new rectum and urethra. Hendren is able to easily pass a catheter, important in view of urinating. As sometimes happens after a major operation like hers, the nerves that control Lucy's bladder are temporarily para-lyzed, and it may be weeks before their function is restored, weeks before her bladder is able to expel urine spontaneously. Until it is, Jack and Beth will have to catheterize her. "Thus far," Hendren says, "I am very pleased at the way things have worked out."

The next day, Beth returns from Florida to Children's. She will stay with Jack and Lucy until all three go home. What a change, in just a week! Lucy is walking again, albeit with assistance. Her IV is gone. She is not tethered to a pulse oximeter any longer. Her drains are out. She doesn't have any tubes going into her anywhere, only a capped line into a vein on her neck so that medications can be easily administered and blood samples taken.

And she is laughing. *Laughing!*

"You have parts!" Beth says when she changes her daughter's diaper.

On Tuesday, February 12, twenty-six days after admission, Lucy Moore is discharged from Children's Hospital. She spends one night with her parents in their hotel room and the next day flies home with them to Florida, to the island of Longboat Key.

Part III

HOME

Chapter 27

Many weeks after Lucy Moore has left Children's Hospital, on a day when the sky is clear, the grass is green, and Eleanor's rose gardens have returned to life, Hardy Hendren is at home.

Today is Sunday. Nothing is on the schedule, and there is an incongruous laziness in the air, as if all that energy during the week followed some secret law of physics, producing by the seventh day an equal but opposite effect. The Hendrens love clocks, and over the years they have collected grandfather clocks and wall clocks and alarm clocks, but Eleanor and Hardy pay scant attention to them on this kind of a Sunday. The passage of time is marked only by when the dogs need to go out, when the Hendrens' favorite fried-chicken place closes, and by the tides, which dictate when and where Hardy can use his boat. On this kind of Sunday, even speech patterns loosen. There is less Harvard professor in Hardy's voice than the Missouri—*Missoura*—of his youth, back before the world went to war.

"This is where I recharge the batteries," Hardy says. His face bears witness. With eight hours' sleep behind him for the first time in a week, he does not look his age.

He is wearing boat shoes, a short-sleeved madras shirt, and a pair of knockabout cotton trousers, clean but rumpled. The Hendrens have no houseguests this weekend, no visiting surgeons. The family calendar is clear, too, so there will be no grandchildren to take out on the water today, no mother and mother-in-law to entertain, no sons with which to swap stories from medicine and the law. Breakfast is grapefruit, bacon and eggs, and decaffeinated coffee, from a machine Hardy professes not to know how to operate.

After the table is cleared, Hardy putters for a while in the cellar. Frank Gigliotti is building him a woodworking shop, which, when finished, will house his lathe, drill press, saws, planer-jointer, sander, router, and Frank's custom-designed sawdust-collection system, which provides a suction port for each tool so that Hendren's lungs will stay clean. A skeletal hand scrounged from an anatomy laboratory years ago has been hung over the toolbench with a handwritten sign: FROM A CARELESS WORKMAN.

On the other side of the cellar, a cavernous space that runs the length of the house, Hardy has stored the overflow of documents produced by his practice: file cabinet after file cabinet filled with inactive patient records; carton after carton packed with reprints of his published papers and notes; chest after chest of custom slides, plaques, letters, journals, books, sixteen-millimeter movies, and videocasette recordings. Hardy has never thrown anything away. Even as a boy, he didn't. He has every letter he received when he was away at Woodberry Forest School and in the Navy. He has lecture notes and textbooks dating back to when he was fourteen.

Done with his basement puttering, Hardy returns to the first floor, the public space when he and Eleanor entertain. Hardy has no framed certificates on the walls anywhere in the foyer, dining room, parlor, library, kitchen, or sun room—no eleven-by-fourteen color photographs of high honors being bestowed, no ceremonial gavels, no gold-plated scissors. The only overt evidence of his forty years in surgery is in the library, which became Sandy's room temporarily, while she recovered from the amputation of her leg near the end of her life; there, occupying two shelves, are the maroon-bound notes from every operation Hardy Hendren's ever done, starting with the first, an appendectomy he performed on July 17, 1952, fresh from Harvard Med. But ask, and you will learn that many of the adornments and furnishings in the Hendren household are testimony to Hardy's career—testimony of a less obvious kind. They are presents from patients and their families whose surgical experiences are chronicled in those maroon-bound notes. From all over the world, they have been sent to him: ivory carvings, china, scimitars, afghans, music boxes, pottery, paintings, jewelry, brassware, icons, and needlepoint. And the perishables, consumed, not displayed: Scotch whisky, Swiss chocolates, French wines, home-made jellies and jams.

Family is the evident motif on the first floor. The living room piano is crowded with photographs of weddings, christenings, anniversaries, and birthdays. A photograph of Sandy at her debutante ball is on a table. An oil painting of Eleanor, done when she was thirty-four and pregnant with David, hangs on the wall of the dining room. On other walls are oil paintings of Hardy's father; Hardy's grandfather, the first William Hardy Hendren; Hardy's great-grand-father, Jeremiah Hardy; and Hardy's great-great-grandfather, the Reverend Jeremiah Hendren. Attached by magnets to the refrigerator door are snapshots of Eleanor, the four boys, and Hardy, fast asleep in a crib outside his OR after a brutally long case. In the dining room, there is an example of Hardy's handiwork on display, but it is not from surgery; it's a three-leaf cherry table that he made at Dartmouth working nights in the college woodworking shop so many years ago.

Hardy heads toward the second floor. On the stairway wall, in ascending order of birth, are pastel drawings of each of the children, commissioned when they were six or seven years old. On the second-floor landing, still more family: annual photographs used as Christmas cards, the first from 1947, when Sandy was a baby and Hardy was a Dartmouth undergraduate.

Hardy gets to his study and throws the windows open to the ocean breeze, warm and inviting today. The cries of seabirds and the smell of salt air reach inside. Hardy's study is a comfortable room, and there are times during the roughest stretches of his longest surgeries when a part of him wishes he were here. His study has a light box for viewing slides, a Dictaphone, and the latest copies of some of the professional journals to which he subscribes. Hardy can work here, and sometimes he does, but other times he reads or simply sits and lets the mind wander. On one wall, he has hung paintings of every plane he's ever flown. On a shelf, he has a snapshot of Sandy, taken after she lost her leg: she is in her wheelchair, smiling and holding Eleanor and Hardy's first grandchild, Sarah Grace Hendren. On the desk, there is a gold pen set customized with an inlaid picture of a smiling Dr. Hendren with Jessica, a girl whose esophagus he reconstructed. In the closet, he stores his collection of human hearts, removed during autopsy and preserved in wax. On the bookshelves, antique surgical texts and the family Bible share space with shotgun shells. In a file cabinet, he has his Boy Scout merit-badge sash and locks of hair from his dead grandmother, father, and daughter, contained in yellowing envelopes.

Here, in this study, Hardy Hendren plans to write a book. He has no definte plans for when he will finish it, but he's sketched out an outline and put together several hundred typed pages of notes. He has a tentative title: *Inside Number One.* He knows what some people think when he tells them the title, but he explains that's not the meaning at all. *Inside Number One,* he says, will be a firsthand look inside some of the institutions where he's worked. Children's Hospital, Boston, will be featured. So will the Massachusetts General Hospital, the Harvard Medical School, Great Ormond Street in London, the Queen Elizabeth Central Hospital in Malawi, the Children's Hospital in Damascus, the Central Surgical Institute in Moscow. And so forth.

At least one chapter of Hardy's book will concern Robert E. Gross, the man who turned on him in the summer of 1960. It will be a difficult chapter to write, for time has not eased the humiliation Gross caused that year, not entirely. Time has not given Hardy all of the answers he's sought about the great surgeon he thought was a supporter but whom he never trusted completely, knowing what he'd done to Orvar Swenson and others.

Should Hendren follow strict chronology in his book, the chapter on Gross will conclude with Gross's death in a nursing home on October 11, 1988, at the age of eighty-three, a victim of Alzheimer's disease. But for the purposes of *Inside Number One,* perhaps a better end to the chapter would come earlier, in May 1974, when both Hardy and his onetime mentor happened to be in Colorado Springs to attend the annual meeting of the prestigious American Surgical Association. Gross, who'd retired from Children's two years earlier and would never attend another meeting of the ASA, was presenting no papers. Hendren, a new member, was presenting to his widest audience yet his results with undiversion—the process of restoring the functioning of urinary tracts left fallow by earlier surgery and getting rid of bags, a procedure that would rank with megaureter repair and cloacal reconstruction as his crowning achievements.

On the day before Hendren was to give his paper, he ran into Gross. Gross had seen the next day's program, and he asked Hendren if he could could read what Hendren was to present. Certainly, Hendren said. Then Gross asked if he could join Hardy and Eleanor for dinner that night. They would be honored, Hendren said. Over dinner, Gross complimented his former pupil on his paper. Tomorrow, he said, he would comment publicly on it.

Hendren's presentation was flawless. It featured the usual slides of medical drawings, X rays, and postoperative photographs of healthy, smiling children, Hendren's hallmark. In the twenty-minute discussion period, Gross, elder statesman of pediatric surgery, was the first of several prominent surgeons called to the podium to comment.

Gross complimented Hendren's achievement. "As I get to the end of an academic surgical career," he concluded, "it has been a tremendous satisfaction to me on many occasions to find young men who have been through the residency training program and on our staff who have taken a new look at things in this field, and other areas in children's surgery, and with vision and thought have made new approaches and new techniques. They have accomplished things which we thought before were impossible. It's a great pleasure to let them have the ball and go toward new goals and get far ahead of us. As I reflect on these things, it is very appropriate to recall the words, uttered so long ago by Leonardo da Vinci when he said, 'The brilliant student will certainly outshine his teacher.'"

The audience stood in applause, an unusual event at an ASA meeting. Hendren was stunned. When others had finished their comments, Hendren rose to thank his former teacher. *The slate,* he thought, *has now been wiped clean.* Later that morning, as the meeting was ending, another Harvard professor confirmed Hendren's interpretation of Gross's remarks. "You may have thought that Bob was discussing your paper," said the professor, who'd known Gross for decades, "but that isn't what he was doing. He was giving you a public apology."

Sandy's room is around the corner from Hardy's study. It is a spacious and cheerful room, decorated in pinks and whites and subdued blues. A portrait of Sandy at about the age at which her diabetes was diagnosed graces one wall, along with her nursing diploma, earned from Boston University when she was almost thirty-three. The Hendrens sometimes use Sandy's room as guest quarters, and a crib has been brought in for the nieces and nephew Sandy never lived to see, but little else has changed since the last day Eleanor and Hardy's firstborn was home.

"Sandy was a brave girl," her father says. "Sometimes I come in here, and I can still hear her voice."

Forced to give up her dream of following her father in his profession, Sandy threw her energy into acting and, later, becoming a nurse. Her disease clawed at her, but it could not pull her down, not yet. While in nursing school, she had a bad reaction to a medication, and her circulation was compromised. She lost two toes to amputation, but despite a long hospitalization, she graduated with her class, and with honors. She took a job at the Massachusetts General, where her father was chief of pediatric surgery. She was a nurse in the Division of Gynecology, and she had three good years, but then her health started to slip again. Her vision was deteriorating, and there was laser surgery to forestall blindness, but the tide could not be stemmed forever. In early 1983, her leg became badly infected. Antibiotics couldn't beat the infection. By June, she required daily debridement—removal—of dead and dying tissue. She was in a wheelchair.

Sandy was almost thirty-six years old. She'd long since used up the time the actuarial tables had given her. *You can see the writing on the wall,* Hardy thought, and the terrible irony and cruelty of it brought tears to his eyes.

In June 1983, a year after his appointment as chief of surgery at Children's, Hardy was to travel to France to receive an honorary doctoral degree from the Université d'Aix-Marseille. It was a great honor: Hendren was only the second American to be so selected (Swenson was the first), and Sandy wanted to be there with her dad. She was crestfallen at the thought that her leg might prevent her from going.

"I don't care about my leg," Sandy insisted. "I want to be there."

Hardy thought about that. He thought about what his friend Samuel Katz had said when Sandy's diabetes had been discovered so many years ago, when his little girl was only seven: that her life expectancy was at most only twenty more years.

"Sissy," he said, "we're going to take you."

Hardy packed gauze and antiseptic and ointment and some of his instruments, and he and Eleanor took turns with Sandy's wheel-chair. They got her to the airport, to Paris, onto the connecting flight to Marseilles. Morning, noon, and night, Hardy boiled his instruments in a pan on a stove, and when they had cooled, he removed the dead tissue from his daughter's leg. Three times a day, Sandy gritted her teeth and didn't complain.

Sandy saw her dad, dressed in his Harvard academic robe—crimson with ermine trim—receive his degree.

The day after their return to Boston, Sandy's left leg was amputated below the knee at the Massachusetts General Hospital.

This amputation got to Sandy. For a while, she wouldn't let herself laugh, wouldn't have anything to do with her prosthesis, wouldn't venture far from the library, where a hospital bed had been placed. But with the help of Eleanor and Pat O'Connor, a woman the Hendrens had found to help with their daughter's care, Sandy came out of this uncharacteristic depression. So she had lost a leg. That didn't mean she wouldn't be able to play the piano or sing or make her Christmas gifts, just like always. It didn't mean she might not be able to return to work in some capacity. It certainly didn't mean she had to stay in a hospital bed in the library. The house had an elevator. From now on, she was going to sleep in her second-story bedroom, where she belonged.

Sandy would need her renewed resolve to get through what happened next. What happened was that one of her doctors, anticipating eventual kidney failure in his patient, decided Sandy needed a shunt for renal dialysis. The shunt would connect an artery in her forearm to one of her veins, increasing the pressure in them, dilating them to provide easy access to her circulatory system. Hendren wasn't sure a shunt was indicated, but he deferred to his colleague. His colleague was an expert in such affairs. Sandy consented, and the shunt was made. After the operation, Sandy's right hand felt perilously cool to Hendren's touch. He wondered about her circulation, wondered if the shunt were too severely reducing the blood supply to her fingers and hand. No, he was told, everything was all right. Sometimes shunts do that.

Hardy was in his OR the following Saturday night, about to operate on a newborn with a large sacrococcygeal teratoma—a tumor of the buttocks region. The phone rang. It was Sandy.

"Daddy," she said, "my hand is turning black."

That night, the shunt was removed. The next morning, there were arteriogram X ray studies and then a thoracotomy—the opening of the chest to cut sympathetic nerves, a procedure that might improve blood flow to the hand. But the fingers were dead; there was no choice but to remove them. Sandy was left with a hand like a lobster claw: only a shiny, stiff thumb and forefinger were left. Never again would she play the piano.

That was medical malpractice, Hardy thought, *but I would never sue. He thought he was doing right, trying to help our daughter.*

He was proud that Eleanor and their children felt the same way.

On the Thursday before her thirty-seventhth birthday, Monday, October 22, 1984, Sandy realized her driver's license was about to expire.

"I need to renew it," she told Eleanor, even though she had not driven for two years.

Eleanor brought her to the Registry of Motor Vehicles. By herself, Sandy walked into the registry, steady and sure despite a prosthesis for a lower left leg and foot and no toes on her right foot. Squinting and taking her time, taking advantage of a kindly clerk, Sandy passed the vision test. She did not show her bad hand. And when she was asked if she had any handicaps, Sandy said no, certainly not.

She got her license.

For her birthday, her parents gave Sandy a videocassette recorder. It was just what she'd wanted. The very first thing she would do was record *Dallas,* her favorite TV show. On Saturday, Eleanor and Hardy flew to San Francisco, where Hardy was due at a meeting of the governors of the American College of Surgeons. On Sunday, with Pat O'Connor's help, Sandy threw herself a thirty-seventh birthday party. Friends and brothers and fellow actors and actresses came. Everyone ate fried chicken. A singing telegram was delivered. That night, Sandy went to bed watching a *Dallas* rerun.

"A perfect end to a perfect day," she told a friend.

At nine o'clock on Monday morning, six o'clock San Francisco time, Eleanor called to wish her daughter a happy thirty-seventh.

"I can't wake her," the nurse on duty in Duxbury said.

Eleanor put Hardy on the line.

"She must have had an insulin reaction," he said to the nurse. "Quickly, go down to the refrigerator and get some glucagon, and give her a shot. I'll stay on the line."

The shot didn't work.

"Go get another one," Hardy said. "Be sure you give it deeply into a muscle and not subcutaneously."

It didn't work.

"Go to the medicine cabinet, and get a rubber tube out of there, and pass it down into her stomach. Go mix some sugar in water and syringe that down the tube into her stomach."

It didn't work.

"Call the fire department," Hardy told the nurse.

When the Duxbury ambulance arrived, the nurse explained the situation to the lieutenant, who agreed to take Sandy directly to Mass General instead of to the nearest hospital, a community facility in Plymouth. Just before the ambulance pulled into the General, Sandy's heart arrested. In the emergency room was her brother Douglas, who was a resident in orthopedics. The ER team managed to start Sandy's heart, but she was irreversibly comatose.

When two weeks had passed, when a senior neurologist, a family friend, said there was no hope Sandy would ever recover, her family gathered around her bed at the Mass General. One by one, the people she loved whispered their private farewells. Everyone held hands around Sandy as Douglas recited the Twenty-third Psalm.

> *The Lord is my shepherd; I shall not want.*
> *He maketh me to lie down in green pastures: he leadeth me beside the still waters.*
> *He restoreth my soul: he leadeth me in the paths of righteousness for his name's sake.*
> *Yea, though I walk through the valley of the shadow of death, I will fear no evil: for thou art with me; thy rod and thy staff they comfort me.*
> *Thou preparest a table before me in the presence of mine enemies: thou annointest my head with oil; my cup runneth over.*
> *Surely goodness and mercy shall follow me all the days of my life: and I will dwell in the house of the Lord for ever.*

Sandy was disconnected from the ventilator.

Slowly, she turned her head to the left, toward her father. Her eyes opened and locked on Hardy. They stayed on him as he stroked her hair and the life went out of her.

Today is too beautiful to stay indoors, even in his study, and so Hardy goes outside. Eleanor is tending her roses. Yesterday, she mowed the lawn, using the Hendrens' John Deere tractor, and the smell of fresh-cut grass is strong and sweet.

"You know," Hardy says, "Eleanor and I were standing out there on the seawall a couple of weeks ago, looking around and thinking how fortunate we were to be here and to have each other and to have a nice family and to have all of the grandchildren and all that. And Eleanor said, 'You know, we have a lot, and we've done a lot, and we've never stepped on anybody else to get it. We never have.' And she's right. You know, there are some people who climb over the backs of others to get where they're going. We've never done that."

Hardy compliments Eleanor on her roses and goes into the boathouse, which is next to the compost pile and vegetable garden. In the boathouse are water skis, life preservers, the grandchildren's float toys, and gardening tools. Hardy's twenty-year-old BMW 750 motorcycle is there, too.

"Let's go for a ride," he says to a visitor, handing him a helmet. Hardy enjoys giving visitors rides, on his motorcycle and on *NOMO*, the larger of the Hendrens' two motorboats.

Hardy puts on his own helmet and a pair of leather workman's gloves. He turns the key. The engine catches.

"OK. Hop on."

Hardy drives out into the afternoon, into the salt breeze and the sun, strong and hot and casting crisp shadows. He drives through Duxbury, smiling and waving to people he knows. He is a cautious driver, and he would never take his BMW onto the highway, but when he has a good stretch of open road, he gives it gas.

After driving a few miles around the town, Hendren takes a left.

"This is a special place," he says.

He is at the Church of Saint John the Evangelist, where seven years ago he paid his last respects to a dear friend, Steve Hedberg, the man who diagnosed his colon cancer. Five days before Sandy died, Hedberg died, too, the victim of a case of hepatitis B he contracted while amputating the leg of a motorcyclist injured in an accident.

Hardy walks around to the back, to a grove of tall pines. It is shadowy and cool and quiet, palpably quiet, and the air has the faint scent of pitch.

Sandy's grave is marked with a small stone bearing only her name and the dates of her birth and death. Hardy stands silently a moment, his head bowed, then stoops to examine the lily he and Eleanor placed there a week ago, Easter Sunday.

Three of the four blossoms are gone, and he snips them off. Leaving the good one, he turns to face the warmth and light of the sun.

Chapter 28

The town of Longboat Key, Florida, is a barrier island, not quite eleven miles long and no wider than one-half mile at its widest. Those who inhabit its western shore, where the Moores built their house, can watch the sun set over the Gulf of Mexico. To the east is Sarasota, where Lucy was born.

The legend of Longboat tells of Indians and pirates and buried gold, but it took air-conditioning and insecticides and a prosperous circus owner, John Ringling, to transform Longboat from an obscure fishing village into the upper-crust community it is today. Dreamers have come to Longboat, and their dreams, at least their financial ones, have mostly come true. Nearly 45 percent of Longboat households have incomes over $75,000. Waterfront house lots, what few are still left, start at $200,000 and go to $1 million or more. Gardeners, caretakers, interior decorators, and burglar-alarm companies do a lucrative business here. Longboat is what lured the Moores from Westchester County to Florida, the state Beth swore she could never call home. In the end, the beach sold her, as it has so many others. The beach and the temperature of the Gulf, which averages sixty degrees in the coldest month, January. During Beth's pregnancy with Lucy, the Moores worked with an architect to design a five-thousand-square-foot house with pool, patio, and boardwalk leading to the beach. The house was built on 150 concrete piles, to survive hurricanes.

For a few weeks after Lucy comes home to Longboat, life at the

Hardy walks around to the back, to a grove of tall pines. It is shadowy and cool and quiet, palpably quiet, and the air has the faint scent of pitch.

Sandy's grave is marked with a small stone bearing only her name and the dates of her birth and death. Hardy stands silently a moment, his head bowed, then stoops to examine the lily he and Eleanor placed there a week ago, Easter Sunday.

Three of the four blossoms are gone, and he snips them off. Leaving the good one, he turns to face the warmth and light of the sun.

Chapter 28

The town of Longboat Key, Florida, is a barrier island, not quite eleven miles long and no wider than one-half mile at its widest. Those who inhabit its western shore, where the Moores built their house, can watch the sun set over the Gulf of Mexico. To the east is Sarasota, where Lucy was born.

The legend of Longboat tells of Indians and pirates and buried gold, but it took air-conditioning and insecticides and a prosperous circus owner, John Ringling, to transform Longboat from an obscure fishing village into the upper-crust community it is today. Dreamers have come to Longboat, and their dreams, at least their financial ones, have mostly come true. Nearly 45 percent of Longboat households have incomes over $75,000. Waterfront house lots, what few are still left, start at $200,000 and go to $1 million or more. Gardeners, caretakers, interior decorators, and burglar-alarm companies do a lucrative business here. Longboat is what lured the Moores from Westchester County to Florida, the state Beth swore she could never call home. In the end, the beach sold her, as it has so many others. The beach and the temperature of the Gulf, which averages sixty degrees in the coldest month, January. During Beth's pregnancy with Lucy, the Moores worked with an architect to design a five-thousand-square-foot house with pool, patio, and boardwalk leading to the beach. The house was built on 150 concrete piles, to survive hurricanes.

For a few weeks after Lucy comes home to Longboat, life at the

Moores' settles back into something resembling a normal rhythm. Day-to-day, the nature of Lucy's care has changed, but not the investment in time. If anything, things are worse. Lucy still has a bag. Urine no longer seeps out of her second stoma, but the new urethra requires regular catheterization while the tissues heal tight and her bladder, still lazy from surgery, recovers. To keep her new vagina and rectum from narrowing, Beth has to insert a metal dilator deep into each opening once a day, a temporary regimen. Lucy screams the first many times, and her screams unsettle her brother and sister. Beth calls Hardy Hendren to plead for some other way, a smaller-caliber dilator, anything.

With my luck, the smart aleck in Beth thinks, *Lucy will be gay, and all this will have been unnecessary.*

"Just do it," Hendren says.

"But—"

"Either you do it, or I have to operate again," Hendren says, and Beth keeps doing it, and eventually the screams stop, as Hendren assured her they would.

In late April, Lucy returns to Children's for two more operations. The first is to correct the neurological abnormality known as tethered cord, disclosed in the MRI she had in January. Normally, the end of the spinal cord floats freely within the spine at the level of the first lumbar vertebra, a structural feature that accommodates growth and body movement. A tethered cord is anchored too low; untreated, tension is created as the child grows, possibly resulting in a variety of problems, including numbness, poor coordination, bowel or bladder incontinence, and weakness of the leg muscles. In a three-hour operation on April 28, neurosurgeon Mike Scott, whose work Hendren greatly respects, opens Lucy's spine to expose her cord. Working under a microscope, he isolates the band of fat anchoring the cord and slowly peels away the nerves that entwine it. It is extraordinarily delicate work, with potentially severe and irreversible consequences for the slightest mistake: lower-body paralysis, the loss of bladder and bowel control, which Hendren has worked so hard to achieve.

Scott's work is flawless. A week later, Lucy is back in Hendren's room for the last major surgery she will need.

With his endoscope hooked up to the video, Hendren examines Lucy and pronounces satisfaction with her new parts. He trims her new rectum, which has prolapsed slightly. In an operation called a colostomy takedown, he frees up her two stomata, removes their ends, sews the two pieces of her large intestine together, and then brings everything back inside. Lucy now has a colon that ends in an anus, not a bag. Hendren closes the wounds.

Five hours have elapsed.

Hendren finds Beth and Jack in the waiting room.

"Everything's fine," he says.

Half an hour later, the Moores visit their daughter in the recovery room. There has been no problem with extubation this time, and there will be no trip to intensive care. This afternoon, she will return to Nine West, and tomorrow she will be walking again. In two days, Wednesday, May 8, she will have her first bowel movement. On Thursday, she will be back on a regular diet. On Saturday, after Hendren examines her, she will be discharged.

Lucy is drifty as Jack and Beth lean over her in the recovery room. She cries softly.

"You did it again Lucy!" Jack says.

"No more stomata!" says Beth.

"Do you miss them?"

"Close your eyes, sweetie."

"Go to sleep, Lucy."

By the time her reconstruction is complete, Lucy Moore has visited an operating table on ten occasions.

She's had an emergency colostomy.

Two revisions of a prolapsed stoma.

Open-heart surgery.

Endoscopy.

Cloacal reconstruction.

Endoscopy.

Spinal cord repair.

Colostomy takedown.

Endoscopy, on a routine checkup at Children's in the fall of 1991.

Starting at birth and including all of her hospitalizations and care, the cost to rebuild Lucy has been over $250,000, borne largely by the Moores' insurer. The greatest percentage has gone to cover expenses associated with her January 1991 reconstruction. The costs for nursing services, intensive care, tests, the operating room, anesthesia, and surgery for that reconstruction have totaled nearly

$100,000. Less than 20 percent has been for physicians' fees, a percentage Hendren asserts is in line with national health-care costs.

Nothing has gone directly into Hendren's pocket. In accepting an academic position at the Harvard Medical School, Hendren agreed to participate in a Harvard financial system that regulates the income of everyone on the faculty of the university. Like the general surgeons who work with him, Hendren belongs to the Children's Hospital Surgical Foundation—in essence, a group practice. His income and that of his surgeons is pooled, and out of the pool come pension benefits, medical and disability insurance, travel and conference expenses, and money for journals, books, artwork, and the like. Each foundation member's salary is also drawn from the pool, as are salaries and benefits for secretaries and support staff. Hendren's salary, which falls within guidelines that the Harvard Medical School suggests for its professors, reflects his administrative and teaching responsibilities, his patient load, and his academic productivity—largely measured by his publications, which are ample testimony to the academic dictum "publish or perish." After salaries and expenses are paid, foundation funds go to support surgical research and other activities that benefit Harvard and Children's Hospital.

Hendren does not discuss his salary, some of which is used for Hendren family philanthropy, including the contributions he makes to a fund his father established: the W. Hardy Hendren Scholarship at Woodberry Forest School. But Hendren makes less, substantially less, than what his skills and reputation would bring on the open market—as surgeon to the stars, to pick a ludicrous example. Money has never motivated him.

What has are children like Lucy.

On an afternoon in autumn 1991, just before her second birthday, Lucy Moore waddles across her living room to French doors that open onto the patio and pool. Beyond the pool is the Gulf of Mexico, warm and inviting and dappled by the sun.

Lucy peers through the glass. Sometimes, when all is quiet, a blue heron appears by the pool. He's a big bird, bigger than Lucy, and one of these days she's going to catch him. But the bird is not there this afternoon. Maybe he's down by the beach, where many times Lucy's watched him eat his dinner.

"Beach!" says Lucy, "Beach! Beach!"

Beth and Jack gather the shovels, buckets, beach chairs, and a bottle of spring water. Mary wants to stay in her room, but James joins the expedition, and he and baby sister follow their parents onto the beach. There is no one else for miles in either direction, nothing but pure white sand and noisy gulls, scavenging on the incoming tide.

Right away, James starts building a sand castle down by ocean's edge. Beth and Jack discuss Jack's new wine business. Now that Lucy's care is so much less demanding, he's finally getting things off the ground.

"Wa-wa!" Lucy interrupts.

"Water?" her father asks.

"Wa-wa!"

Jack hands her the bottle of spring water. Lucy drinks deeply, splashing some down the front of her swimsuit.

"That's a manly drink, Lucy!"

Lucy laughs, that easy, contagious baby laugh of hers. She sets off down the beach, down toward her brother, but gets sidetracked by shells halfway there. Always a million shells on Lucy's beach, black shells and blue shells and pretty red shells, each one worth a look. Chattering to herself, smiling back at Mom and Dad, Lucy sits on the sand. She is a fair-skinned girl, with bright eyes and hair the Florida sun has made strawberry blond. Not five months have passed since a knife last touched her body, but already her scars have faded to pale imperfections. Lucy wears a diaper now. Recently, she has started to show some interest in using a toilet.

The farther away you get from the beginning, from the pain, Beth thinks, *the more you forget. You forget what we went through, just how bad it was. Life has become so simple and so normal—I mean, the bad stuff just kind of recedes. Now she's into her terrible twos, and sometimes I want to kill her, not say, "Poor baby! Look at all she's been through!"*

We talk about how we were really lucky, lucky that her problems could be dealt with with surgery rather than chemotherapy or radiation or any of those other treatments that sometimes go on and on without end. We feel lucky when we think of her future— although I'm guarded, I keep telling myself chances are she's going to have problems. I mean, she has only one kidney. And her genitalia are different.

*But it's percentages. Most of me is forgetting it. And Lucy—
what will she remember? Probably nothing. We've saved an album
with pictures and some of her records, and someday she'll look at
it. But for now, she's just a normal little kid.*

Lucy leaves her shells and goes to James, who's sculpting a turret
for his castle. Reluctantly, James hands over the spare shovel, but
he won't let Lucy anywhere near his creation. She ambles back to
her parents and starts to dig. She doesn't see the blue heron, but
Jack does. He's settled in the surf.

"Lucy," says her father, "the heron's back. Big bird."

"Buh! Buh! Buh!" she says.

"Want to see how close you can get?"

Lucy is atwitter now. Maybe if she runs fast enough, this will be
the time she'll catch him. Followed by her mom, she scampers after
the bird, but the bird stays several paces ahead.

"That heron is scared of you, Lucy," Beth says.

"Buh! Buh! Buh!"

The big bird stays out of reach. Beth wraps her arms around her
daughter and lifts her off the sand.

"I love you," she says.

"I-luv-you!"

Just before Thanksgiving 1991, Beth writes a letter to Hardy
Hendren.

Dear Dr. Hendren,

Lucy turned two yesterday. As is our (Jack thinks obnoxious) tradition, I went around the table videotaping the family talking about Lucy.
My mother got too choked up to talk. My sister and babysitter cried.
My uncle called her a Miracle Baby. My son says she has the best table
manners in the family. Eight other loving comments and then it was my
turn.

I took the opportunity, as I have countless times before, to pay
tribute to YOU. "If it wasn't for Hardy Hendren . . ." Well, before you
knew it, there were cheers of HARDY! HARDY! HARDY! spilling out
of our living room. I figured you probably heard us and wondered what
the fuss was all about. . . .

I have tried to explain how strange it is to figure so small a part in
someone's life (yours) who plays so GREAT a part in our lives. It's a
kind of unrequited love, I'd say. So this is a full-fledged love letter. I'll

shout your praises from a mountaintop, I'll pay tribute to you at an awards ceremony, I'll treat you to the best dinner in Sarasota or I'll simply remember to thank you quietly every so often.

We owe our Lucy to you. Thank you again.

Beth.

Acknowledgments

More than two years went into this book. Along the way, many people who could have thrown up roadblocks didn't. Oh, there were a few detours along the way, mostly to meet the concerns of a hospital that is ethically and legally bound to protect the confidentiality of its patients. But we made it.

I want to thank Alexis Magner Miller, my wife and fellow journalist, who transcribed many of the dozens of interviews that I taped. She also came up with the title, carefully dissected the first draft, and, as usual, made dozens of suggestions that improved the book.

I am extremely grateful to my parents, Roger and Mary Miller, who watched our children on many of those long weekends when the heat was on. And to Andy and Martha Kinnecom, my hosts in Florida; Andy was my traveling partner on my trip to the Woodberry Forest School.

At *The Providence Journal-Bulletin,* I first must thank Joel Rawson, who was as enthusiastic as I was throughout this project. Also, Jim Wyman, the executive editor, and Carol Young, metro managing editor, who have long encouraged me; Brian Jones, who knew when to nudge me back on course; Tom Mooney, whose instincts are sharp; and our publisher, Steve Hamblett, who supports these curious employees of his, the writers.

Several people made important contributions in the early stages, long before this book was a book. Milton Henderson, general surgeon, storyteller, and friend, got me thinking surgery. Pediatrician

Arnold Fiascone helped put me in touch with Hardy Hendren. As always, Kay McCauley, my agent, knew just how to get where we had to go. And of course, a nod to my sister, Mary Wright, R.N., who's long helped me to understand medicine.

A project like this one doesn't go anywhere without librarians, and none was more helpful than Linda Henderson of *The Providence Journal-Bulletin;* nearly all of the research she did for a newspaper series I wrote on Children's was essential to the book. I spent many, many hours at the Countway Library of Medicine in Boston and found its reference department to be absolutely topflight. The Countway's Rare Books Department, managed so expertly by Elin L. Wolfe and Richard J. Wolfe, true bibliophiles both, was a tremendous resource. I am grateful to the librarians who assisted me at Brown University, the *News-Journal* of Daytona Beach, Florida, *The New Orleans Times-Picayune,* and *The Kansas City Star.* Also, to the public libraries of Boston; Providence, Rhode Island; Kansas City, Missouri; and Richmond, Virginia. And for help with research pertaining to New Orleans, I am indebted to Andrea Ducros, library associate in the Louisiana Division of the New Orleans Public Library.

My journey took me to several schools. I am grateful to Barbara L. Krieger, archives assistant, Dartmouth College Library; Fred Kaplan, a Charles Dickens scholar and professor of English at Queens College of the City University of New York; Nancy H. Courtney, news director, Tulane University; P. Steven Thomas, reference librarian, Washburn University of Topeka; Eric Hillemann, college archivist, Carleton College; Mark Johnson, sports information director, Marquette University; William I. Bunnell, director of library and information services at Mercersburg Academy. Richard F. Barnhardt of the Woodberry Forest School was extraordinarily generous with his time, advice, and long-term loan of source documents. And thanks to Principal Donna F. Burch and her staff at Bryant School in Kansas City, who opened up their school to me and shared their archives.

Also in Kansas City, Mrs. W. Hardy Hendren, Jr., was a gracious hostess with a memory as sharp as a tack. Her daughter, Carol Robb, shared home movies shot during the Hendrens' childhood that captured the era and the family in a way no other medium could. The Reverend Murray L. Trelease, recently retired from

Saint Paul's Episcopal Church, and his sister, Rosemary Trelease Day, now a Rhode Islander, gave me a vibrant picture of a vibrant child: their deceased brother, Ben Trelease. Thanks also to Paul Koontz, a Kansas City surgeon and longtime friend of Hendren's. I also am indebted to Virginia Major Thomas, Hardy Hendren's girlfriend in the 1930s, now married and a mother and living in Texas.

I was well served by numerous media outlets, including WLUK-TV, Channel 11, Green Bay, Wisconsin; WHDH-TV, Channel 7, Boston; *Parents Magazine Expecting; The Greenwood* (Miss.) *Commonwealth,* which kindly sent me a microfilm account of Hardy Hendren's 1946 near-crash landing; the *Peshtigo* (Wisc.) *Times;* and Gannett Suburban Newspapers, White Plains, New York.

Many in the medical community were resources: C. Everett Koop, former U.S. surgeon general; Judson G. Randolph, recently retired surgeon-in-chief of Children's National Medical Center in Washington, D.C.; Michelle Marcella, assistant to the director of the Massachusetts General Hospital's Office of News and Public Affairs; Charles A. Lankau, Jr., chief of pediatric surgery, Miami Children's Hospital; Janusz Bohosiewicz, a pediatric surgeon in Katowice, Poland; Winston E. Harrison, a urologist in Columbia, Missouri; and Joshua A. Copel, associate professor of obstetrics and gynecology at Yale University School of Medicine. Also of help were the American Urological Association, whose public relations person, Bill Glitz, went out of his way to assist me during the two AUA conventions I attended; the American Academy of Pediatrics; the American College of Surgeons; the American Pediatric Surgical Association; Physicians for Peace; and the Society for Paediatric Urological Surgeons. And, at the Harvard Medical School, the late Carl W. Walter, clinical professor of surgery (emeritus); Dwight E. Harken, clinical professor of surgery (emeritus); Patricia K. Donahoe, professor of surgery and chief of pediatric surgery, Massachusetts General Hospital; Francis D. Moore, Moseley professor of surgery (emeritus); Daniel D. Federman, dean for medical education; Claude E. Welch, clinical professor of surgery (emeritus); Barbara A. Steiner of the Harvard Medical School's Office of Public Affairs; and Susan Vomacka-Decker. Also, the public relations departments at Mercy Hospital, Wilkes-Barre, Pennsylvania; the University of

South Florida College of Medicine, Tampa, Florida; Sarasota Memorial Hospital; and All Children's Hospital in Saint Petersburg, Florida.

At Children's Hospital, Boston, Saira Moini of the Department of Development and Public Affairs went well beyond the call of duty in handling my million and one needs; she was always uncomplaining and efficient. Also in that office, Peggy Slasman, Phil Lotane, and Vice President Anne Malone were of great assistance. David S. Weiner, president of Children's, took a chance by allowing my project to proceed. Two of his top administrators, Vice President for Medical Affairs Michael F. Epstein and Vice President for Nursing Eileen M. Sporing, were also cooperative. Physician-in-Chief David G. Nathan was always willing to meet with me. His insights into the workings of a major teaching hospital were invaluable to me, an outsider.

Dozens of nurses at Children's gave of their time; thank you all. I'm especially indebted to four women who manage four wards—with great pride and professionalism—and who opened those wards to me, cheerfully and with the only precondition that I get it right: Joanne Geake, Carole Arenge, Dorothy Mahoney, and Jayne Rogers. I also want to thank Doris Fina, Janet Hamilton, Anne Jenks Micheli, Lenny Mendoza, Jackie Hamblet, Gerry Barringer, Kathy Caponi-Russell, Jean Kiernan, Pam Garavano, Peggy Knowles, Diane Puleio, Dotty Jenkins, Karen Sakakeeny, Carol DeLash, Lisa Small, Jane Mulhall, Joan Simpson, Valerie Miller, Beth Bardizian, Rosemary H. Grant, Joanne McCarthy, Mia Graham, Sara Jones, Colleen C. Torrice, and Corinne Kiernan.

At least as many physicians allowed me into their world. I could do a separate book with Gerald B. Healy, otolaryngologist-in-chief, and maybe someday I will; his ideas about reforming health care are intelligent, seemingly workable, and deserving of a wider audience. Neurosurgeon-in-Chief Peter McL. Black is that rarest of people: a gentleman and a scholar. Besides having a marvelous sense of humor, surgeon Joseph P. Vacanti is a keen student of human behavior. Many anesthesiologists shared their knowledge, none more willingly and helpfully than Interim Anesthesiologist-in-Chief Mark A. Rockoff and Robert S. Holzman, assistant professor of anesthesia; without Mark, my passages on the history of anesthesia would have been woefully incomplete. Radiologist-in-Chief, Emeritus, John A. Kirkpatrick, Jr., opened up his department to me, and two members of his staff, Jane C. Share and Rita L. Teele, were extremely helpful. Thanks also to Orthopedic Surgeon-in-Chief John E. Hall, Steven Stylianos, Michael G. Caty, Jay Schnitzer, Dennis P. Lund, Howard J. Weinstein, Marian Craighill, Elof Eriksson, John B. Mulliken, Alan B. Retik, Fred S. Rosen, Arnold H. Colodny, Craig A. Peters, Anthony Atala, Neil R. Feins, Angelo J. Eraklis, Robert C. Shamberger, Jay M. Wilson, Craig W. Lillehei, Melanie S. Kim, Lewis R. First, Bruce R. Korf, Gary R. Fleisher, Charles B. Berde, Neil L. Schechter, Philip J. Spevak, William Berenberg, Edward J. O'Rourke, John P. Cloherty, Bill Larchian, Steve Ruyle, Paul R. Hickey, and Betsy Tuttle.

Thanks also to Bob McGarvey, Paul Williams, Louis M. Kunkel, Myra D. Fox, and Nancy Majors, all of Children's. Also, my gratitude to Theresa J. Clark, assistant to the chief surgical resident.

John Hendron, whose ancestors are also Hardy Hendren's, despite the variation in the spellings, saved me days of research with the meticulous family genealogy he's compiled over many years. Jean L. Lootz and Elizabeth Lank were not the only sources on Robert E. Gross, but they were two of the most important. Another was M. Judah Folkman, the brilliant surgeon-scientist, and a fourth was Orvar Swenson, who invited me to visit him in his retirement in Rockport, Maine. Hillard Hughes, a childhood friend of Hardy Hendren's, filled in some gaps, as did Al Zeller, who became Hendren's friend at Dartmouth and who welcomed me to his home near Portland, Maine.

For information on Lyme disease, I was assisted by the Westchester County (N.Y.) Department of Health and by Betty Gross, founder of the Westchester Lyme Disease Support Group. Demographic help came from Mark E. Malo, an economist with the Florida Department of Labor and Employment Security; the Longboat Key (Fla.) Chamber of Commerce; the Westchester County (N.Y.) Office of Tourism, and the New York State Department of Economic Development. Thanks also to the Embassy of Guatemala, Washington, D.C.; the Virginia Air National Guard; Dean C. Allard, director of the U.S. Navy's Naval Historical Center, and Roy A. Grossnick, head of the center's aviation history branch; Kevin G. Meer, public affairs officer, Richmond (Va.) International Airport; and Linda Wiseman of The Vincent Club in Boston.

A special thanks to Lorraine Sweeney Nicoli, the patient in whom Robert Gross first successfully ligated a patent ductus arteriosus. Wife, mother, and grandmother, Lorraine Nicoli is alive and well more than a half century after her historic surgery.

Thanks to Sharon Kay Light for permission to quote from her book.

I received information on medical technology from MDT Corporation, Rochester, New York, manufacturers of the Bovie electric cautery; COBE Laboratories, Lakewood, Colorado; and E. I. du Pont de Nemours and Company, Wilmington, Delaware.

Many, many thanks to Stephanie and Jonathan Warburg. They helped me understand the strength of the bond that forever joins the parent to the child; so commendably, they made the Max Warburg Award for Courage, the Max Warburg Memorial Program, and the Max Warburg Fund realities. The fund's address is c/o The Boston Foundation, 1 Boston Place, Boston, Mass. 02108.

When it came crunch time, I couldn't have made it without Pam Spinney, Hardy Hendren's research assistant. Pam has been a delight to work with, and I could never say enough good things about her professionalism. She is living proof that courtesy and competence can go hand in hand.

I am deeply indebted to Jon Karp, my editor at Random House. Jon gambled on me and my ideas when he had no reason to. There is no editor I respect more. Thanks so much, Jon.

Finally, I'd like to extend my deep appreciation to many, many families across America and a few from overseas. During 1990, 1991, and 1992, I spent hundreds of hours on the wards and in Hardy Hendren's office and operating room, learning how Dr. Hendren made their children normal. The rules of Children's Hospital's required that I obtain written permission from each of these families. They graciously granted it. Without them, this book would have been only an idea.

Bibliography

The following books were helpful in understanding surgery, particularly reconstructive surgery, and Hardy Hendren's position in his field:

Abrams, Jerome S. *Abdominal Stomas: Indications, Operative Techniques and Patient Care.* Boston: Wright-PSG, 1984.

Arciniegas, Eduardo. *Pediatric Cardiac Surgery.* Chicago: Year Book Medical Publishers, 1985.

Bell, Charles. *Illustrations of the Great Operations of Surgery, Trepan, Hernia, Amputation, Aneurism and Lithotomy.* London: Longman, Hurst, Rees, Orme and Browne, 1821.

Bodenhamer, William. *A Practical Treatise on the Aetiology, Pathology and Treatment of the Congenital Malformations of the Rectum and Anus.* New York: Samuel S. and William Wood, 1860.

Bogdanich, Walt. *The Great White Lie: How America's Hospitals Betray Our Trust and Endanger Our Lives.* New York: Simon and Schuster, 1991.

Bosk, Charles L. *Forgive and Remember.* Chicago: University of Chicago Press, 1979.

Castleman, Benjamin, ed. *The Massachusetts General Hospital, 1955–1980.* Boston: Little, Brown, 1983.

Catherine Louise, S.S.M. *The House of My Pilgrimage: History of the American House of the Society of St. Margaret, 1873–1973.* Boston: privately published, 1981.

Churchill, Edward D. *To Work in the Vineyard of Surgery.* Cambridge, Mass.: Harvard University Press, 1958.

Clark, John O. E., ed. *The Human Body.* New York: Arch Cape Press, 1989.

Converse, John M., J. William Littler, and Joseph G. McCarthy, eds. *Reconstructive Plastic Surgery.* Philadelphia: W. B. Saunders, 1977.

Dripps, Robert D., James E. Eckenhoff, and Leroy D. Vandam. *Introduction to Anesthesia: The Principles of Safe Practice.* Philadelphia: W. B. Saunders, 1988.

Earley, Laurence E., and Carl W. Gottschalk. *Strauss and Welt's Diseases of the Kidney.* 3d ed. Boston: Little, Brown, 1979.

Edgerton, Milton T. *The Art of Surgical Technique.* Baltimore: Williams and Wilkins, 1988.

Ferrari, Bernard T., J. Byron Gathright, and John E. Ray, eds. *Complications of Colon and Rectal Surgery.* Philadelphia: W. B. Saunders, 1985.

Forfar, John O., and Gavin C. Arneil, *Textbook of Paediatrics.* Edinburgh, Scotland: Churchill Livingstone, 1978.

Gardner, Kenneth D., Jr. *Cystic Diseases of the Kidney.* New York: John Wiley and Sons, 1976.

Gower, Catherine A., and Patti L. Lowery, *Bone Marrow Transplantation.* Bethesda, Md.: National Cancer Institute, 1989.

Gross, Robert E. *The Surgery of Infancy and Childhood.* Philadelphia: W. B. Saunders, 1953.

Guersant, M. P. *Surgical Diseases of Infants and Children.* Philadelphia: Henry C. Lea, 1873.

Handlin, Oscar. *Boston's Immigrants, 1790–1865: A Study in Acculturation.* Cambridge, Mass.: Harvard University Press, 1941.

Holmes, T. *The Surgical Treatment of the Diseases of Infancy and Childhood.* London: Longmans, Green, Reader and Dyer, 1868.

Johnson, Stephen L. *The History of Cardiac Surgery, 1896–1955.* Baltimore: Johns Hopkins University Press, 1970.

Kelley, Samuel Walter. *Surgical Diseases of Children: A Modern Treatise on Pediatric Surgery.* St. Louis, Mo.: C. V. Mosby, 1929.

King, Lowell R., Anthony R. Stone, and George D. Webster, eds. *Bladder Reconstruction and Continent Urinary Diversion.* St. Louis, Mo.: Mosby Year Book, 1991.

Kirklin, John W., and Brian G. Barratt-Boyes. *Cardiac Surgery: Morphology, Diagnostic Criteria, Natural History, Techniques, Results and Indications.* New York: John Wiley and Sons, 1986.

Kolata, Gina. *The Baby Doctors: Probing the Limits of Fetal Medicine.* New York: Dell, 1990.

Koop, C. Everett. *Koop: The Memoirs of America's Family Doctor.* New York: Random House, 1991.

Lapides, Jack. *Fundamentals of Urology.* Philadelphia: W. B. Saunders, 1976.

Lawrence, Peter F. *Essentials of General Surgery.* Baltimore: Williams and Wilkins, 1988.

Lyman, Henry M. *Artificial Anaesthesia and Anaesthetics.* New York: William Wood, 1881.

Moore, Keith L. *Essentials of Human Embryology.* Burlington, Ontario: B. C. Decker, 1988.

Netter, Frank H. *Atlas of Human Anatomy.* Summit, N.J.: Ciba-Geigy, 1989.

Norfleet, Elizabeth Copeland. *Woodberry Forest: A Venture in Faith.* New York: Georgian Press, 1955.

Peebles, Rhonda J., and Diane S. Schneidman., eds. *Socio-Economic Factbook for Surgery 1991–92.* Chicago: American College of Surgeons, 1991.

Qvist, George. *John Hunter, 1728–1793.* London: William Heinemann Medical Books, 1981.

Rickham, P. P. *Progress in Pediatric Surgery. Vol. 20, Historical Aspects of Pediatric Surgery.* Berlin: Springer-Verlag, 1986.

Romero, Roberto, et al. *Prenatal Diagnosis of Congenital Anomalies.* Norwalk, Conn.: Appleton and Lange, 1988.

Russo, Raymond M. *Sexual Development and Disorders in Childhood and Adolescence.* New Hyde Park, N.Y.: Medical Examination Publishing Company, 1983.

Schindler, Lydia Woods. *Understanding the Immune System.* Bethesda, Md.: National Institutes of Health, 1988.

Schneider, James G. *The Navy V-12 Program: Leadership for a Lifetime.* Boston: Houghton Mifflin, 1987.

Silverstein, Alvin. *Lyme Disease, the Great Imitator: How to Prevent and Cure it.* Lebanon, N.J.: AVSTAR Publishing, 1990.

Smith, Clement A. *The Children's Hospital of Boston: Built Better Than They Knew.* Boston: Little, Brown, 1983.

Snider, Howard C., Jr. *Jury of My Peers: A Surgeon's Encounter with the Malpractice Crisis.* Montgomery, Ala.: Fountain Press, 1989.

Stephens, F. Douglas, and E. Durham Smith, eds. *Anorectal Malformations in Children: Update 1988.* New York: Liss, 1988.

Strauch, Berish, Luis O. Vasconez, and Elizabeth J. Hall-Findlay, eds. *Grabb's Encyclopedia of Flaps.* Boston: Little, Brown, 1990.

Thompson, Richard H. *Psychosocial Research on Pediatric Hospitalization and Health Care: A Review of the Literature.* Springfield, Ill.: Charles C. Thomas, 1985.

United States Pharmacopeia Convention. *Drug Information for the Consumer.* Mount Vernon, N.Y.: Consumers Union, 1988.

Van Bergen, W. S. *Obstetric Ultrasound: Applications and Principles.* Menlo Park, Calif.: Addison-Wesley, 1980.

Vogel, Morris J. *The Invention of the Modern Hospital: Boston, 1870– 1930.* Chicago: University of Chicago Press, 1980.

Walsh, Patrick C., et al., eds. *Campbell's Urology,* 6th ed. Philadelphia: W. B. Saunders, 1992.

Wangensteen, Owen H., and Sarah D. Wangensteen. *The Rise of Surgery: From Empiric Craft to Scientific Discipline.* Minneapolis: University of Minnesota Press, 1978.

Warren, John C. *Surgical Observations on Tumors, with Cases and Operations.* Boston: Ticknor, 1848.

Wertenbaker, Lael. *To Mend the Heart: The Dramatic Story of Cardiac Surgery and Its Pioneers.* New York: Viking, 1980.

Whitney, Lora Colvin. *Hail This Feisty Village!* Torrington, Conn.: Rainbow Press, 1984.

Willard, DeForest. *The Surgery of Childhood, Including Orthopaedic Surgery.* Philadelphia: J. B. Lippincott, 1910.

I also could cite an interminable list of articles from academic journals that were helpful in putting together this book, but I shall not burden the reader. I will, however, mention several that were important in the evolution of reconstructive urogenital and cloaca surgery or in Hardy Hendren's career:

Derrick, Fletcher C., Jr. "Management of the Large, Tortuous, Adynamic Ureter with Reflux." *Journal of Urology* 108 (July 1972): 153–55.

DeVries, Pieter A. "The Surgery of Anorectal Anomalies: Its Evolution, with Evaluations of Procedures." In *Current Problems in Surgery,* edited by Mark M. Ravitch. Chicago: Year Book Medical Publishers, 1984.

Gross, Robert E. "Surgical Management of the Patent Ductus Arteriosus." *Annals of Surgery* 110, no. 3 (1939): 321–56.

Hendren, W. Hardy. "Operative Repair of Megaureter in Children." *Journal of Urology* 101 (April 1969): 491–507.

——. "A New Approach to Infants with Severe Obstructive Uropathy: Early Complete Reconstruction." *Journal of Pediatric Surgery* 5 (April 1970): 184–99.

——. "Posterior Urethral Valves in Boys: A Broad Clinical Spectrum." *Journal of Urology* 106 (August 1971): 298–307.

——. "Urinary Tract Refunctionalization After Prior Diversion in Children." *Annals of Surgery* 180 (October 1974): 494–510.

———. "Surgical Management of Urogenital Sinus Abnormalities." *Journal of Pediatric Surgery* 12 (June 1977): 339–57.

———. "Urogenital Sinus and Anorectal Malformation: Experience with 22 Cases." *Journal of Pediatric Surgery* 15 (October 1980): 628–41.

———. "Megaureter." In *The Ureter,* edited by Harry Bergman. New York: Springer-Verlag, 1981.

———. "Presidential Address: Some Reflections on the Cost of Health Care." *Journal of Pediatric Surgery* 18 (December 1983): 659–69.

———. "Repair of Cloacal Anomalies: Current Techniques." *Journal of Pediatric Surgery* 21 (December 1986): 1159–76.

———. "Urinary Tract Refunctionalization After Long-Term Diversion: A 20-Year Experience with 177 Patients." *Annals of Surgery* 212 (October 1990): 478–95.

———. "Cloacal Malformations." In *Campbell's Urology,* edited by Patrick C. Walsh, et al., 6th ed. 1822–1850. Philadelphia: W. B. Saunders, 1992.

———. "Cloacal Malformations: Experience with 105 Cases." *Journal of Pediatric Surgery* 27 (July 1992): 890–901.

Johnson, Robert J., et al. "The Embryology of High Anorectal and Associated Genitourinary Anomalies in the Female." *Surgery, Gynecology and Obstetrics* 135 (November 1972): 759–62.

Khoury, Muin J., et al. "A Population Study of the VACTERL Association: Evidence for Its Etiologic Heterogeneity." *Pediatrics* 71 (May 1983): 815–20.

Ladd, William E., and Robert E. Gross. "Congenital Malformations of Anus and Rectum." *American Journal of Surgery* 23 (January 1934): 167–83.

Nesbit, Reed M., and John F. Withycombe. "The Problem of Primary Megalo-ureter." *Journal of Urology* 72 (August 1954): 162–71.

Quan, Linda, and David W. Smith. "The VATER ASSOCIATION: Vertebral Effects, Anal Atresia, T-E Fistula with Esophageal Atresia, Radial and Renal Dysplasia—A Spectrum of Associated Defects." *Journal of Pediatrics* 82 (January 1973): 104–7.

Swenson, Orvar, John Herbert Fisher, and Jean Cendron. "Megaloureter: Investigation as to the Cause and Report on the Results of Newer Forms of Treatment." *Surgery* 40 (July 1956): 223–33.

Swenson, Orvar, Harold F. Rheinlander, and Israel Diamond. "Hirschsprung's Disease: A New Concept of the Etiology, Operative Results in Thirty-four Patients." *New England Journal of Medicine* 241 (October 1949): 551–56.

Index

ABOUT THE AUTHOR

G. WAYNE MILLER is a staff writer for *The Providence Journal-Bulletin,* where he has worked since 1981, winning numerous national awards. He is a graduate of Harvard College. He has written one novel, *Thunder Rise,* and his short stories have been published in several anthologies. He lives in Pascoag, Rhode Island, with his wife, Alexis, and their two young daughters.

ABOUT THE TYPE

This book was set in a digital version of Bodoni Book, a typeface named after Giambattista Bodoni, and Italian printer and type designer of the late eighteenth and early nineteenth century. It is not actually one of Bodoni's fonts but a modern version based on his style and manner and is distinguished by a marked contrast between thick and thin elements of the letters.